世界银行贷款中国经济改革促进与能力加强技术援助项目（TCC6）

国际保险监督官协会全球保险资本标准述评

中国银行保险监督管理委员会偿付能力监管部 ◎ 编

中国金融出版社

责任编辑：肖丽敏　赵晨子
责任校对：潘　洁
责任印制：张也男

图书在版编目（CIP）数据

国际保险监督官协会全球保险资本标准述评/中国银行保险监督管理委员会偿付能力监管部编．—北京：中国金融出版社，2021.11

ISBN 978-7-5220-1376-3

Ⅰ.①国… Ⅱ.①中… Ⅲ.①保险业—国际经济组织—行业标准—评论 Ⅳ.①F841.3-65

中国版本图书馆 CIP 数据核字（2021）第 214526 号

国际保险监督官协会全球保险资本标准述评
GUOJI BAOXIAN JIANDUGUAN XIEHUI QUANQIU BAOXIAN ZIBEN BIAOZHUN SHUPING

出版	中国金融出版社
发行	
社址	北京市丰台区益泽路 2 号
市场开发部	（010）66024766，63805472，63439533（传真）
网上书店	www.cfph.cn
	（010）66024766，63372837（传真）
读者服务部	（010）66070833，62568380
邮编	100071
经销	新华书店
印刷	河北松源印刷有限公司
尺寸	185 毫米×260 毫米
印张	22.25
字数	452 千
版次	2022 年 1 月第 1 版
印次	2022 年 1 月第 1 次印刷
定价	88.00 元
ISBN 978-7-5220-1376-3	

如出现印装错误本社负责调换　联系电话（010）63263947

编委会

主　编：赵宇龙

副主编：郭　菁　魏洪涛

编委会成员：
王　浩　任　笛　张　翔　王　瀚　孙晓筱
董　扬　李　岗　崔雯昕　余贵芳　马文杰
李　鹏　朱　丽　张　佳　刘梦泽　翟　潇
于　洋　何　铮　谢继锋

目 录

一、全球保险资本标准述评 ··· 1
    《以风险为基础的全球保险资本标准》述评 ································ 3
    保险偿付能力监管标准的国际比较研究 ···································· 9
    中国人寿保险股份有限公司全球保险资本标准测试案例 ···················· 19
    中国太平保险集团有限责任公司全球保险资本标准测试案例 ················ 34

二、全球保险资本标准（ICS）2.0 版本 一级文件 ···················· 47

三、全球保险资本标准（ICS）2.0 版本 二级文件 ···················· 73

四、Level 1 Document：ICS Version 2.0 for the monitoring period ······ 179

五、Level 2 Document：ICS Version 2.0 for the monitoring period ······ 213

一、全球保险资本标准述评

《以风险为基础的全球保险资本标准》述评

一、ICS 制定背景和过程

2019 年 11 月,国际保险监督官协会(IAIS)执委会投票通过《以风险为基础的全球保险资本标准》(Risk-based Global Insurance Capital Standard,ICS),这是 IAIS 建立全球保险资本监管标准的一项重要阶段性成果。

2008 年国际金融危机后,为有效防范系统性风险,IAIS 推动了两项改革:一是评估认定全球系统重要性保险机构(G-SII)。2013 年至 2016 年,IAIS 每年评估认定 G-SII。由于各方对认定标准存在不同意见,IAIS 自 2017 年初暂停认定 G-SII,转向建立保险行业整体的系统性风险评估框架。按照这一思路,IAIS 制定了《保险业系统性风险整体框架》(Holistic Framework for the Assessment and Mitigation of Systemic Risk in the Global Insurance Sector),于 2019 年正式发布。二是针对国际活跃保险集团(Internationally Active Insurance Groups,IAIG),IAIS 制定了《国际活跃保险集团监管共同框架》(Common Framework for the Supervision of Internationally Active Insurance Groups,以下简称《共同框架》),并在此框架下制定 ICS,为 IAIG 提供全球统一的资本监管标准。

ICS 是《共同框架》的核心内容。2013 年,IAIS 成立资本工作项目组专门负责 ICS 制定工作。2014 年,发布 ICS 征求意见稿,明确了建设原则、基本框架和适用范围。2015 年起,IAIS 组织全球 50 余家保险集团开展实地测试,并多次公开征求意见。2017 年发布了 ICS 1.0 版本,2019 年发布了 ICS 2.0 版本。

二、ICS 的主要内容

ICS 2.0 版本包括一级文件和二级文件。一级文件规定监测期内 ICS 基准报告和附加报告的总体原则和基本概念。二级文件规定 ICS 具体技术细则。ICS 全面规定了 IAIG 的资产负债评估方法、实际资本评估标准和最低资本计量方法。IAIG 应按照 ICS 要求,评估集团层面偿付能力。自 2020 年起进入为期 5 年的监测期,IAIG 每年向本国(地区)监管机构报告 ICS 结果,但暂不触发监管措施。

(一)一般原则。一是实质重于形式。ICS 资产负债表不同于公认会计原则

(GAAP)下的会计报表。ICS资产负债表以审慎监管为目的，更加强调稳健性、实质性和一致性，以便更加真实地反映企业的风险状况及变化趋势。二是匹配性原则。如果考虑特定的因素或规则会导致偿付能力评估的复杂程度显著增加，而又不会明显提升计量结果或风险评估的质量，则该因素或规则可以在ICS计算中简化或不予考虑。三是穿透原则。为合理评估集合型投资基金和其他间接风险暴露，应当考虑其经济实质。保险机构应尽可能对投资资产进行穿透，评估其底层资产的风险。四是信用评级。IAIS制定了ICS信用评级和外部信用评级之间的对应关系。

（二）评估范围。ICS评估以保险公司经审计的GAAP合并资产负债表为基础，经过一系列调整得到。当保险集团没有经审计的GAAP合并资产负债表时，可以用法定财务报表（Statutory Financial Statements）简单加总作为集团层面资产负债表的基础。经审计的资产负债表的合并范围包括保险实体、与保险相关的实体，以及非保险实体。非保险实体包括金融和非金融实体。非保险金融实体应基于所在行业的资本监管要求进行评估，没有行业资本监管要求的非保险金融实体和非金融实体，应基于ICS规定的方法进行评估。对于所有的非保险实体，实际资本应按照基准ICS要求进行认定。

（三）评估方法。市场价值调整法（Market Adjusted Valuation，MAV）是ICS资产负债评估的基准方法。MAV基于经审计的GAAP合并报表或法定会计原则（SAP）的合并报表，并对保险合同负债、再保险资产和再保险负债、金融资产和金融负债、递延所得税等项目进行公允价值调整。监测期内，根据集团所在地监管机构的自主决定，IAIG可提交基于GAAP+方法或包括内部模型法在内的其他ICS方法下的结果。GAAP+和其他方法都是监测期结束时IAIS可能考虑采纳的方法之一。

（四）实际资本。实际资本基于IAIG的全部金融活动进行计量，包括合格资本工具和非资本工具项目。实际资本分为两个层级：一级资本指在持续经营和破产清算状态下均能吸收损失的资本工具和非资本工具。二级资本指仅在破产清算状态下吸收损失的资本工具和非资本工具。每级资本按照不同标准分别划分为两类：一级资本划分为一级无限制资本工具和一级有限制资本工具；二级资本划分为二级实缴资本工具和二级非实缴资本工具。

（五）最低资本。ICS最低资本是应对非预期变化、事件或其他特定风险对实际资本产生的潜在不利影响所需的资本数额。标准法下风险分为4类：保险风险、市场风险、信用风险、操作风险。计量方法主要有情景法和因子法。情景法采用的是动态方法，每项风险的资本要求由基础情景和压力情景的实际资本减少额确定。因子法由风险暴露乘以相应风险因子计算最低资本。各项风险资本要求之间考虑风险分散效应，通过相关系数矩阵聚合。

三、ICS 与中国偿二代的差异比较

ICS 主要借鉴了欧盟偿付能力 II（Solvency II）的理念、原则和方法，并结合各方意见进行完善。ICS 着眼于规范保险集团的偿付能力评估，与我国偿二代保险集团规则具有可比性。总体看，ICS 与我国偿二代保险集团监管规则第一支柱定量资本要求方面涵盖的内容基本一致，但在具体评估方法上存在差异：

（一）资产负债评估方法。资产负债评估是保险公司偿付能力评估的基础。我国偿二代采用会计调整法，即以会计账面价值为基础进行调整评估。ICS 要求 IAIG 在监测期内按照市场价值调整法报送数据，即基于市场价值对资产与负债进行评估，与欧 II 的评估方法一致。但与此同时，考虑到美国、日本和中国均提出了基于本国会计准则的调整方案，IAIS 承诺在监测期内继续完善会计调整法，监测期结束后视情况再决定是否将会计调整法纳入 ICS。

（二）保险合同负债评估。保险合同负债是保险公司最主要的负债。由于寿险业务负债期限长达数十年，折现率对寿险业务的保险合同负债评估影响重大，是国际监管规则制定中的重点问题。ICS 与偿二代的主要差异如下：

一是基础曲线。ICS 与偿二代的基础曲线均分为三段。其中，ICS 规定第一段为 0~10 年的评估日即期国债收益率曲线；第三段为 60 年以后，采用终极利率；10 年到 60 年采用插值法确定。偿二代规定第一段为 0~20 年，采用 750 日移动平均国债收益率曲线；40 年以后采用终极利率；20~40 年采用插值法确定。

二是溢价确定原则和方法。我国偿二代在 0 到 20 年根据不同保险产品的特征分别适用 30 个基点、45 个基点和 70 个基点三档溢价，40 年以后终极利率的溢价为 0。ICS 在 0 到 10 年根据保险产品的资产负债匹配程度适用三种不同的溢价确定方法，60 年以后的终极利率区分发达国家、中等发达国家和新兴国家分别适用 20 个基点、25 个基点、35 个基点的溢价。

（三）实际资本及资本分级。ICS 与我国偿二代在资本认可标准和资本分级要求方面没有明显差异，二者均根据资本的永续性、存在性、次级性、非强制性等方面特征，确定其损失吸收能力，并将资本分为四级。ICS 将资本分为一级无限制资本、一级有限制资本、二级实缴资本和二级非实缴资本；我国偿二代将资本分为核心一级资本、核心二级资本、附属一级资本和附属二级资本。偿二代二期工程对资本分级进行了完善，增加了外生性要求，并将长期寿险保单的未来盈余根据保单剩余期限，分别计入核心资本或附属资本，强化了核心资本的损失吸收能力，相较于 ICS 更为严格。

ICS 规定第三方出具的承诺，符合一定条件可以作为非实缴资本，提高保险集团的偿付能力。偿二代下的附属二级资本，既可以是实缴的，也可以是监管部门规定的其他形式，但未明确第三方出具的承诺可以作为资本。

（四）最低资本。ICS与偿二代在最低资本的计量原则上是一致的，各项目均是按照99.5%的置信区间计量未来一年可能产生的最大损失，设定相关的风险因子。但是，二者在风险覆盖、计量方法等方面还存在一些差异：

一是ICS为内部模型保留了空间。我国偿二代采用标准模型，不允许采用内部模型。ICS目前采用标准模型，同时正在研究制定内部模型法，监测期结束后再决定是否正式纳入。标准模型的优点是可比性强、实施成本低。内部模型的优点是更能体现公司个性化的风险特征，缺点是比标准模型要复杂得多，不同公司间难以直接比较，开发实施和监管成本较高。

二是对操作风险的处理不同。偿二代定量监管要求覆盖了保险风险、市场风险和信用风险。除上述风险外，ICS还覆盖了操作风险，但量化方法较为简单，主要是按照保费或保险合同负债的一定比例计提最低资本。偿二代建设时，考虑到操作风险涉及公司经营管理的各个环节以及外部环境的冲击，难以科学量化，现阶段我国保险公司还不具备量化的数据基础与模型条件。因此，我国偿二代将其作为难以资本化风险，纳入第二支柱定性监管要求中进行管理。

三是计量方法略有不同。ICS和我国偿二代均采用因子法和情景法计量最低资本，但侧重点不同。偿二代主要采用综合因子法，直接用风险暴露乘以相应的综合因子即得到最低资本。对于确实难以采用综合因子法的情形，比如寿险公司的保险风险和利率风险的最低资本，采用情景法。ICS对情景法运用范围更加广泛，市场风险和寿险业务的保险风险均采用情景法。在标准模型下，情景法的实际效果与因子法是一致的。

四、ICS面临的挑战和问题

（一）ICS面临的挑战

ICS作为资本标准，直接影响IAIG的偿付能力充足率，是各国关注的重点。从2020年起，ICS进入为期5年的监测期，IAIS将继续对其完善，并于2025年决定是否正式实施。经过多年发展，不同国家（地区）对ICS仍有不同意见，ICS能否在全球顺利落地实施，还面临不确定性。

一是尚未达成普遍共识。从国际上看，不同国家（地区）对ICS的态度存在差异。欧盟、日本、新加坡等较为支持，美国、加拿大等国家对ICS的部分理念和风险计量方法持保留意见。根据美国的意见，除现行基准方法外，IAIS将在监测期内继续推进研究美国提出的聚合方法（Aggregation Method），监测期结束后再决定是否采纳该方法。2020年11月，IAIS发布了《聚合方法与ICS等效可比的定义及判断的高层级标准（征求意见稿）》，面向全球公开征求意见。该征求意见稿主要是对等效可比的定义和标准做了原则性规定。聚合方法实际上是直接将所在国家的偿付能力充足率，换算为ICS的偿付能力充足率。监测期结束后，若IAIS采纳聚合方法，各个国家（地区）很可能倾向于采用这一相对简单的方法，从而导致基准方法失去实际约束力。

二是ICS仅适用于国际活跃保险集团（IAIG），影响力有限。目前，全球约有40家IAIG。除这些跨国经营的超大型保险集团外，各国还存在大量本地保险机构，其适用所在地的偿付能力监管标准，不受ICS约束。

三是监测期后能否正式实施存在变数。监测期内，IAIG应当每年按照ICS评估偿付能力状况，并通过当地监管机构将数据提交至IAIS。IAIG报送的数据不对外公开披露，不触发监管措施，主要供IAIG监管联席（Supervisory College）会议讨论和持续改进ICS规则使用。考虑到对ICS监管理念、计量方法等核心问题还存在一些分歧，监测期后ICS能否顺利实施存在不确定性。

四是ICS不具有法律效力，需要通过各国立法落地实施。即使ICS在5年监测期后顺利通过，仍需各国修改本国的法律法规，才能正式落地实施。预计ICS最终在各国落地实施仍需要较长时间。

（二）ICS存在的问题

一是资产负债评估采用市场一致方法（Market Consistent Method）不完全符合保险的本质特征。在理论层面，保险合同负债是长期负债，没有公开市场，也不会进行交易，采用市场价值法对保险公司的资产负债进行评估与保险的商业模式不符。在操作层面，新兴国家资本市场成熟度不高，保险公司持有的大量金融资产没有活跃的交易市场，其市场价值只能运用数学模型进行估值，客观性、可靠性难以保证，监管成本也很高。

二是折现率曲线不适用于新兴市场。ICS采用评估日即期收益率曲线评估负债是市场价值法的理念，其结果反映的是负债的市场价值或交易价值。有观点认为，保险合同负债是长期负债，没有公开市场，也不会进行交易，直接运用评估日即期收益率曲线不符合保险长期业务的商业模式，还可能导致保险公司的负债随市场利率短期大幅波动，增加不必要的公司管理成本和监管成本。与发达国家相比，发展中国家货币市场和资本市场难以达到足够的有效性，评估日即期国债利率不能反映全部市场信息，不宜作为评估负债的折现率曲线。

三是ICS规定过于具体，难以体现各国市场情况差别。各个国家由于历史文化、人口结构、经济发展程度等不同，商业保险的运营模式、产品费率差异明显，相应面临的风险也存在较大的差异。但ICS按照风险类别规定统一的风险因子，没有充分考虑到各国保险市场的差异，影响对风险评估和计量的准确性。

五、ICS在中国的测试情况

IAIG指同时满足以下两个条件的保险机构：一是保费收入至少来自3个国家（地区），境外保费占比超过10%；二是三年平均总资产不低于500亿美元或三年平均保费收入不低于100亿美元。2020年起，国寿股份、太平保险集团作为志愿者参与了为期5年的ICS2.0监测期项目，2021年起，中国再保险集团和平安保险集团也加入了志愿者行列。

我国参与监测的保险集团主要编报的数据包括MAV（Market Adjusted Valuation）方法和GAAP+方法下的资产、负债、实际资本和最低资本，以及中国会计准则下的资产、负债、净资产等数据。从ICS测试结果看，国寿股份、太平保险集团的偿付能力充足率均在200%以上。国寿股份、太平保险集团2020年底中国偿二代下偿付能力充足率分别为269%、215%，按照ICS的MAV方法测算的偿付能力充足率分别为254%、284%，较中国偿二代下分别下降15个百分点、上升69个百分点；按照ICS的GAAP+方法测算的偿付能力充足率分别为222%、226%，较中国偿二代下分别下降47个百分点、上升11个百分点。

六、对ICS的建议

ICS的发布和实施是国际保险监管领域的重要阶段性成果，对于加强IAIG的监管、增进国际保险监管合作交流、防范全球保险市场风险都具有重要意义。在ICS制定过程中，中国结合偿二代的实施经验和数据，积极参与ICS制定工作，贡献中国智慧和中国方案。

（一）建议采用原则导向。不同国家的保险市场发展程度、产品类型、风险特征等差别很大，ICS应当立足于建立相对一致的计量原则；具体规则以及各项假设、参数和风险因子等宜由各国根据自身实际情况确定。

（二）建议允许新兴市场采用移动平均国债收益率曲线。折现率曲线对保险合同负债影响重大。新兴市场的国债市场的有效性不强，评估日即期国债收益率曲线难以完全、及时地反映当前市场信息，采用移动平均国债收益率曲线进行保险合同负债评估是一个更为稳妥的选择。

（三）建议保留资产负债评估的会计调整法或类似方法。不同的资产负债评估方法体现了对保险商业模式认识的差异，进而影响到监管理念，至关重要。目前ICS按照欧盟偿付能力Ⅱ（Solvency Ⅱ）的理念，将市场价值法作为主要方法，同时承诺在监测期内继续推进研究会计调整法。市场价值法未能体现保险产品的长期性特点和保险业商业模式，且会导致保险公司资产负债的价值大幅波动，难以客观反映保险公司的长期状态和趋势。建议保留会计调整法或类似方法作为资产负债评估的可选方法。

（四）等效评估可能是建立全球资本标准的一种更好方式。不同国家（地区）保险市场存在较大差异，统一的风险因子、参数和假设难以适用于所有国家（地区）。因此，在不同国家（地区）之间进行偿付能力监管等效评估可能是建立全球资本标准的一种更好方式。目前，欧盟、中国都已在偿付能力监管等效评估上进行了实践，效果良好，可有效降低相关国家（地区）之间跨境交易成本，防范了风险的跨市场、跨领域传递。

保险偿付能力监管标准的国际比较研究

本文对国际保险监督官协会（International Association of Insurance Supervisors，IAIS）以及中国、欧盟、美国、新加坡等国家（地区）的偿付能力监管体系第一支柱（定量监管要求）进行了研究，分析比较了不同体系的异同点。

一、国际主要保险偿付能力监管标准概述

（一）全球保险资本标准 ICS

2019 年 11 月，IAIS 正式发布《以风险为基础的全球保险资本标准》（*Risk - based Global Insurance Capital Standard*，ICS），适用于国际活跃保险集团（Internationally Active Insurance Groups，IAIG）。自 2020 年起，ICS 进入为期 5 年的监测期。监测期内，IAIG 每年按照 ICS 评估偿付能力情况，通过所在地监管机构将数据报送至 IAIS。ICS 报告包括基准报告和附加报告，其中，基准报告是对所有 IAIG 的强制要求，仅向监管报送，不对外公开；附加报告由所在地的监管机构自主决定是否要求 IAIG 报送。

（二）中国偿二代

2015 年 2 月，原中国保监会发布中国风险导向的偿付能力体系（C‑ROSS，以下简称偿二代）17 项监管规则。经过一年试运行后，偿二代于 2016 年正式实施。2017 年 9 月，偿二代二期工程建设工作启动，计划用三年左右时间对偿二代监管规则进行全面修订和升级。2021 年 12 月，《保险公司偿付能力监管规则 II》正式发布，于 2022 年起正式实施。

（三）欧盟 Solvency II

2014 年 3 月，欧盟通过了由欧洲保险与职业养老金监管局（European Insurance and Occupational Pension Authority，EIOPA）研究制定的欧盟 Solvency II（以下简称欧 II）。2016 年 1 月，欧 II 正式实施。欧 II 由监管资本要求、公司治理和信息披露三个支柱组成，要求保险公司满足最低资本要求（Minimum Capital Requirement，MCR）及偿付能力资本要求（Solvency Capital Requirement，SCR）。欧 II 代表了欧盟整体层面的监管要求，欧盟各国可根据自身情况在实施中对具体规则进行必要的调整。

（四）美国 RBC

20 世纪 90 年代初，美国保险监督官协会（National Association of Insurance Commis-

sioners，NAIC）实施了风险资本标准（Risk – Based Capital，RBC）。2008 年国际金融危机后，NAIC 启动了偿付能力现代化计划（Solvency Modernization Initiative，SMI），在风险管理自评估、集团监管等方面对原有制度进行完善。2015 年，NAIC 实施了保险公司自我风险与偿付能力评估（Own Risk and Solvency Assessment，ORSA），要求保险公司自我评估所有合理的可预见的相关重大风险。2019 年，NAIC 发布了保险集团资本评估标准（Group Capital Calculation），计划于 2022 年正式实施。

（五）新加坡 RBC2

从 2012 年起，新加坡金融监管局（Monetary Authority of Singapore，MAS）开始制定新一代风险资本框架（RBC2），经过 2014 年、2016 年和 2018 年三轮定量测试（Quantitative Impact Study，QIS），RBC2 最新技术标准于 2020 年 2 月发布，并于 2020 年 3 月 31 日起正式实施。新加坡 RBC2 由偿付能力监管干预水平（Supervisory Solvency Intervention Levels）、资产和负债评估标准（Valuation of Assets and Liabilities）、总体风险资本要求（Total Risk Requirement）、实际资本评估标准（Financial Resources）四部分组成。

二、实际资本评估

（一）认可资产

ICS 采用的认可资产计量方法包括基于市场价值调整的评估方法（Market Adjusted Valuation，MAV）和会计准则调整方法（GAAP +）。MAV 即以市场价值为基础对资产进行评估。GAAP + 即以会计账面价值为基础进行调整评估。目前中国、美国等均提出了基于本国会计准则的 GAAP + 方法。ICS 下的中国 GAAP + 方法以中国会计准则下的财务报告为起点，对责任准备金负债、长期股权投资、递延所得税等进行调整。

各国家（地区）偿付能力监管体系的认可资产评估方法存在差异。在中国偿二代下，除了以物权方式或通过项目公司方式持有的投资性房地产、长期股权投资、寿险业务的应收分保准备金等项目外，均以会计账面价值作为认可价值。欧Ⅱ、新加坡 RBC2 对认可资产的计量主要采用市场价值，美国 RBC 建立了一套完整的法定会计原则（Statutory Accounting Principles，SAP），主要使用法定账面价值对认可资产进行计量。

（二）认可负债

1. 现金流现值

ICS 的准备金负债由当前估计与风险边际相加得到。中国偿二代、欧Ⅱ、新加坡 RBC2 也均由当前估计（或最优估计）、风险边际组成。在计量当前估计时，须考虑保单内嵌的选择权和保证利益相关的预期现金流。现金流现值由未来现金流按照每项负债的货币种类和分档所对应的收益率曲线折现得到。现金流包括赔付支出、保费收入、费用支出等。美国 RBC 的保险合同负债为净保费准备金（Net Premium Reserve）、确定性准备金（Deterministic Reserve）、随机性准备金（Stochastic Reserve）三者取大。其中，确定性准备金的计算思路与ICS类似。

在涉及包含选择权及保证利益的业务（如分红险、万能险）时，ICS、中国偿二代、欧Ⅱ均要求考虑选择权及保证利益的时间价值（TVOG），新加坡 RBC2 不要求考虑 TVOG。其中，对于 TVOG 的计算，ICS 采用因子法与随机性方法相结合的方法。

2. 风险边际

为了审慎评估未来现金流的不确定性，ICS、中国偿二代、欧Ⅱ、新加坡 RBC2 均要求计量风险边际，但具体计算方法有所差异。ICS、新加坡 RBC2 采用分位点法计算风险边际，中国偿二代对寿险业务采用分位点法，对非寿险业务按照最优估计准备金的一定比例进行计算。在分位点选取上，ICS 下寿险业务使用 85% 分位点，非寿险业务使用 65% 分位点；偿二代对寿险业务使用 85% 分位点；新加坡 RBC2 采用 75% 分位点。欧Ⅱ基于市场一致原则，采用以市场价格为基础的资本成本法计算风险边际。美国 RBC 体系没有显性地考虑风险边际，因为准备金的精算假设已经隐含了对未来现金流不确定性的考虑。

3. 折现率曲线

（1）折现率基础曲线

ICS、中国偿二代、欧Ⅱ、新加坡 RBC2 的折现率曲线均由三段组成：期望无风险收益率曲线、插值过渡曲线、终极利率水平。期望无风险收益率曲线通常基于政府债券或利率互换确定，其终点的选择主要依据金融市场所能观察到的最长流动性期限（Last Liquidity Point，LLP）。终极利率曲线主要考虑了预期的实际利率与通货膨胀率，其起点的设定多采用 LLP + 固定年限的方法。插值过渡曲线方面，中国偿二代目前采用二次差值方法，其他监管体系采用史密斯—威尔逊方法，二者实际差异不大。各偿付能力监管体系的折现率基础曲线具体情况如表 1 所示。

表1 不同偿付能力监管体系的折现率曲线

准则	第一段曲线终点（LLP）	期望无风险收益率基准	第三段曲线起点	终极利率曲线
ICS	人民币：10 年 美元：30 年	政府债券或利率互换	（LLP + 30）年与 60 年取大	人民币、欧元、美元：3.8%
中国偿二代	20 年	政府债券	40 年	4.5%
欧Ⅱ	欧元：20 年 美元：50 年	政府债券或利率互换	（LLP + 20）年与 60 年取大	欧元和美元：3.45% 人民币：4.5%
新加坡 RBC2	新加坡元：20 年 美元：30 年	政府债券	新加坡元：50 年 美元：70 年	新加坡元和美元：3.8% 人民币：6.0%

此外，美国 RBC 针对不同准备金负债计算采用的折现率不同，较为复杂。比如，确定性准备金负债的折现率主要使用净资产收益率（Net Asset Earned Rate，NAER），其设

定取决于 4 个因素：起始资产的收益率预测、再投资资产的收益率预测、负债净现金流的特征、起始资产与再投资资产现金流的特征。

(2) 溢价确定方法

大多数偿付能力监管体系在确定折现率时考虑溢价调整。ICS 的溢价调整使用三档法（Three-Bucket Approach），根据资产和负债的匹配程度，将负债分为低档、中档和高档，对每一档负债使用不同的溢价调整。中国偿二代在 0~20 年根据不同保险产品的特征分别适用 30 个基点、45 个基点和 70 个基点三档溢价，40 年以后终极利率的溢价为零。欧Ⅱ的溢价调整包括匹配调整（Matching Adjustment，MA）和波动调整（Volatility Adjustment，VA）。MA 基于保险公司资产负债的现金流匹配程度以及基本利差确定，VA 基于参考投资组合（Reference Portfolio）中资产的利率与相应的无风险利率之间的利差确定。新加坡 RBC2 的溢价调整可采用欧Ⅱ的 MA 方法或流动性溢价（Illiquidity Premium）调整法。

三、最低资本计量

(一) 最低资本计量原则

1. 风险分类

不同偿付能力监管体系所涵盖的风险覆盖范围基本一致，但具体分类存在差异。ICS 将风险分为四类：保险风险、市场风险、信用风险和操作风险。中国偿二代将风险分为可资本化风险和难以资本化风险。其中，可资本化风险（第一支柱风险）包括保险风险、市场风险和信用风险，难以资本化风险（第二支柱风险）包括操作风险、战略风险、声誉风险和流动性风险。新加坡 RBC2 将市场风险和信用风险合并为资产风险。美国 RBC 的风险分类标准根据公司类型有所差异，寿险公司风险分类包括关联企业风险、资产风险、保险风险、利率风险和经营管理风险；非寿险公司风险分类包括资产风险、信用风险、承保风险和表外风险，其中，表外风险和经营管理风险包括操作风险的内容。不同偿付能力监管体系的风险分类如表 2 所示。

表 2 不同偿付能力监管体系可资本化风险分类

准则	保险风险	市场风险	信用风险	操作风险
ICS	√	√	√	√
中国偿二代	√	√	√	—
欧Ⅱ	√	√	√	√
新加坡 RBC2	√	合并为资产风险		√
美国 RBC	√	√（资产风险）	√	√

2. 风险计量

风险计量方法主要采用情景法和因子法。不同国家（地区）偿付能力监管体系下各类风险所采用的计量方法如表3所示。情景法是一种动态方法，通过计量压力情景和基础情景下的资产负债的净变化来确定最低资本。因子法即以风险暴露与相应的风险因子的乘积作为最低资本。

表3 不同偿付能力监管体系最低资本风险计量方法对比

准则	保险风险		市场风险	信用风险	备注
	寿险保险风险	非寿险保险风险			
ICS	情景法	因子法	情景法（资产集中度风险采用因子法）	因子法	巨灾风险以情景法为主，其中自然灾害风险使用模型法
中国偿二代	情景法	综合因子法	综合因子法（利率风险为情景法）	综合因子法	—
欧Ⅱ	情景法	因子法	情景法	因子法	巨灾风险可使用模型法
新加坡RBC2	情景法	因子法	情景法	因子法	—
美国RBC	因子法	因子法	因子法（利率风险为情景法）	因子法	—

3. 校准目标（置信水平）

ICS的校准目标是指在一年内、99.5%的置信水平下的在险价值（VaR）。ICS、中国偿二代、欧Ⅱ、新加坡RBC2校准目标相同。

4. 资产穿透原则

ICS要求保险机构应尽可能地对投资资产进行穿透，评估底层资产的风险。ICS穿透法适用于无杠杆共同基金、其他集合型投资工具等间接投资，从而识别包括虚增实际资本在内的所有潜在风险。欧Ⅱ与ICS穿透法的适用范围类似。其中，欧Ⅱ的资产穿透适用于非直接投资风险暴露，能够获取底层资产的集合投资品种与其他投资基金均需要穿透。中国偿二代（二期）按照"全面穿透、穿透到底"的原则，识别保险资金的最终投向，基于实际投资的底层资产计量最低资本。新加坡RBC2的穿透法仅用于集合投资计划、结构化产品和衍生品。美国RBC没有要求考虑资产穿透。

ICS允许保险机构在无法进行全部穿透时，使用部分穿透。对于无法穿透的情况，ICS允许保险公司将整个投资视为未上市股权来计量最低资本。中国偿二代（二期）规定了部分穿透时计量资本要求的规则，对于无法穿透的，要求适用较高的惩罚性风险因子。欧Ⅱ规定无法穿透的资产需要根据投资指引计算，如果投资指引中的指标可在一定范围内变化，则以最低资本最大的情况为准。新加坡RBC2对无法穿透的资产也规定使用更高的风险因子。

（二）寿险保险风险

ICS的寿险保险风险包括死亡发生率风险、长寿风险、疾病发生率/失能风险、退保风险和费用风险。中国偿二代、欧Ⅱ、新加坡 RBC2 均覆盖了 ICS 的 5 种寿险保险子风险。中国偿二代、欧Ⅱ、新加坡 RBC2 的寿险保险风险还包含死亡巨灾风险。此外，中国偿二代考虑了医疗及健康赔付损失率风险，欧Ⅱ考虑了年金修正风险，新加坡 RBC2 考虑了其他保险事故（意外、健康）风险、选择权转换风险。各偿付能力监管体系的寿险保险风险计量方法均采用情景法，并采用相关系数矩阵进行风险聚合。

（三）非寿险保险风险

在 ICS、中国偿二代、欧Ⅱ、新加坡 RBC2 中，非寿险保险风险均涵盖了保费风险与准备金风险。中国偿二代、欧Ⅱ、新加坡 RBC2 的非寿险保险风险考虑了巨灾风险。欧Ⅱ的非寿险保险风险还考虑了退保风险。

各偿付能力监管体系的非寿险保险风险的计量方法以因子法为主，多采用相关系数矩阵进行聚合。ICS 分地区和业务类型计量非寿险风险最低资本，中国偿二代、欧Ⅱ、新加坡 RBC2 仅分业务类型进行计量。ICS、中国偿二代、欧Ⅱ先聚合保费风险和准备金风险，然后聚合各业务类型的保费和准备金风险最低资本。新加坡 RBC2 先聚合业务类型，分别得到涵盖所有业务的保费风险与准备金风险的最低资本，最后再对两个子风险进行聚合。

（四）巨灾风险

在 ICS 下，巨灾风险作为一级风险单独计量。在中国偿二代、欧Ⅱ、新加坡 RBC2 下，巨灾风险合并在寿险风险和非寿险风险中进行计量。

各偿付能力监管体系均考虑了自然巨灾风险，计量方法多采用因子法。中国偿二代下的非寿险巨灾风险与自然巨灾风险含义类似，计量方法采用在险价值法；ICS、欧Ⅱ考虑了人为巨灾风险，计量方法多采用情景法；中国偿二代、欧Ⅱ、新加坡 RBC2 考虑了寿险巨灾风险，计量方法采用情景法。

（五）市场风险

不同偿付能力监管体系所涵盖的市场风险基本一致。ICS 市场风险包括利率风险、非违约利差风险、权益风险、不动产风险、汇率风险、资产集中度风险 6 个子风险。中国偿二代、欧Ⅱ、新加坡 RBC2 均考虑了利率风险、权益风险、不动产风险和汇率风险。中国偿二代的非违约利差风险在信用风险中考虑。新加坡 RBC2 没有考虑集中度风险。此外，境外资产价格风险为中国偿二代独有的市场风险子风险（见表4）。

表 4 市场风险分类比较

准则	利率风险	非违约利差风险	权益风险	不动产风险	汇率风险	集中度风险	其他市场风险子风险
ICS	√	√	√	√	√	√	—
中国偿二代	√	在信用风险中考虑	√	√	√	√	境外资产价格风险
欧Ⅱ	√	√	√	√	√	√	
新加坡 RBC2	√	√	√	√	√	—	

1. 利率风险

利率风险的计量方法以情景法为主。根据到期期限（Term To Maturity）与结算货币的不同，各压力情景下的压力因子有所不同。ICS 利率风险压力情景有 5 种：均值回归情景、水平向上情景、水平向下情景、扭转上下情景、扭转下上情景，最后使用公式聚合计算压力情景前后净资产的变化。中国偿二代、欧Ⅱ、新加坡 RBC2 要求考虑利率上浮或下降两种压力情景，取最不利结果。美国 RBC 下，寿险公司使用因子法计量利率风险最低资本，根据资产的特性选择不同的风险因子。另外，中国偿二代下财产保险公司的利率风险使用综合因子法。

2. 权益风险

ICS 权益风险覆盖所有对权益价格水平变化或波动率变化敏感的资产，分为以下 4 类：发达市场上市权益资产、新兴市场上市权益资产、混合资本债/优先股、其他权益资产。欧Ⅱ、新加坡 RBC2 权益风险覆盖的资产范围与 ICS 类似。中国偿二代的权益风险仅包括境内资产权益风险，境外资产在境外价格风险下单独计量。ICS、欧Ⅱ、新加坡 RBC2 使用情景法计量权益风险，中国偿二代使用综合因子法计量权益风险。

3. 汇率风险

ICS、欧Ⅱ使用情景法计量汇率风险。中国偿二代和新加坡 RBC2 使用因子法计量汇率风险。美国 RBC 则不考虑汇率风险。各偿付能力监管体系汇率风险涉及的资产范围大多是以外币计价的各类资产。

4. 利差风险

ICS 的利差风险指非违约利差风险，即利差的水平或波动性的非预期变化（不包含违约利差部分）所带来的风险。欧Ⅱ的利差风险定义与 ICS 相似。新加坡 RBC2 的利差风险指信用利差风险，即由于资产的信用评级恶化、信用利差扩大、信用利差波动性变化和违约风险而导致的投资损失。美国 RBC 不单独考虑利差风险。ICS、欧Ⅱ使用情景法计量非违约利差风险，中国偿二代采用综合因子法，新加坡 RBC2 采用因子法。ICS 考虑利差对资产端和负债端的双向压力，中国偿二代、欧Ⅱ、新加坡 RBC2 主要在资产端考虑利差风险。

（六）信用风险

ICS、欧Ⅱ、新加坡 RBC2 中的信用风险仅指交易对手违约风险。中国偿二代的信用风险包括交易对手违约风险、利差风险和集中度风险。ICS、中国偿二代、欧Ⅱ、新加坡 RBC2 均采用因子法计量信用风险。

（七）集中度风险

ICS、中国偿二代、欧Ⅱ和美国 RBC 考虑了集中度风险，新加坡 RBC2 暂未考虑集中度风险。各偿付能力监管体系的集中度风险多考虑按地域或行业的集中，但欧Ⅱ的集中度风险则主要考虑对单一实体的集中。ICS 的集中度风险考虑了交易对手集中度风险、房地产集中度风险。欧Ⅱ、美国 RBC 的集中度风险考虑了资产集中度风险。中国偿二代集中度风险考虑了交易对手集中度风险、房地产集中度风险和资产集中度风险。ICS、中国偿二代、美国 RBC 使用因子法计量集中度风险，欧Ⅱ使用情景法。

（八）风险聚合

1. 公司整体最低资本聚合方法

考虑到各类风险的分散效应，各偿付能力监管体系均对各类风险的最低资本进行聚合，聚合方法均采用相关系数矩阵法，但在具体规定上存在差异。ICS 与中国偿二代的最低资本聚合方法基本相同，按照保险风险、市场风险和信用风险等进行聚合。欧Ⅱ先分别聚合各业务线的最低资本，再使用总体的相关系数矩阵聚合最低资本。新加坡 RBC2 则将最低资本分成保险风险要求与资产风险要求两部分，分别计算各部分资本要求，再计算总体资本要求。美国 RBC 寿险、财产与意外险、健康险三者的最低资本聚合方法计算公式区别较大。

2. 一级风险聚合

ICS、欧Ⅱ的一级风险大致相同，仅有部分差异：一是 ICS 将巨灾风险归为一级风险，与其他一级风险聚合，而欧Ⅱ将巨灾风险归为二级风险，分别在寿险保险风险和非寿险保险风险中计算；二是欧Ⅱ的非寿险保险风险和信用风险之间的相关系数是 0.5，ICS 是 0.25。

中国偿二代下的非寿险保险风险、市场风险、信用风险三类风险的相关系数取值和 ICS 存在一定差别，而且人身险公司和财险公司采用了不同的相关系数矩阵。不同监管规则的一级风险相关系数矩阵对比如表 5 所示。

表 5 不同偿付能力监管体系一级风险相关系数矩阵对比

风险		ICS	欧Ⅱ	中国偿二代二期	新加坡 RBC2
市场	寿险	25%	25%	30%（人身险公司）	0%
	非寿险	25%	25%	10%（人身险公司与财险公司）	0%
	信用	25%	25%	35%（人身险公司） 27%（财险公司）	50%
	巨灾	25%	NA	NA	NA
寿险	非寿险	0%	0%	20%（人身险公司）	0%
	信用	25%	25%	15%（人身险公司）	0%
	巨灾	25%	NA	NA	NA
非寿险	信用	25%	50%	10%（人身险公司） 15%（财险公司）	0%
	巨灾	25%	NA	NA	NA
信用	巨灾	25%	NA	NA	NA

四、偿付能力充足率要求

不同国家（地区）偿付能力监管体系的偿付能力充足率要求有所差异。ICS目前正处于5年监测期，IAIG只需要报送偿付能力报告，不触发任何监管机制。中国偿二代要求保险公司和保险集团的核心偿付能力充足率不低于50%，综合偿付能力充足率不低于100%。欧Ⅱ、新加坡RBC2要求偿付能力充足率不低于100%，偿付能力充足率不达标将触发监管机构的强制性监管措施。美国RBC偿付能力充足率要求分为多档，具体的监管干预水平与措施如表6所示。

表6 美国RBC偿付能力充足率要求水平

偿付能力充足率	监管干预水平	监管措施
≤200%	公司行动水平 CAL	保险公司需要向所在州的保险监管部门提交一份整改计划，并且该计划需经监管部门批准
≤150%	监管控制水平 RCL	保险公司必须提交整改计划，监管部门会要求执行改进措施
≤100%	授权控制水平 ACL	监管部门被授权采取任何必要的行动，来保护保单持有人和债权人
≤70%	强制控制水平 MCL	监管部门将对保险公司进行接管重建或破产清算

五、总结

通过对国际上不同国家（地区）偿付能力监管体系的比较可以发现，以风险为导向是各个国家（地区）偿付能力监管制度的主要特征。国际主流的模式在风险覆盖、风险计量、风险管理、风险监管四个方面具有趋同性，在发展方向和改革趋势方面具有一致性。

一是更加全面的风险覆盖。银行业率先采用了巴塞尔协议的三支柱监管框架。随着金融监管改革的不断深化，欧Ⅱ、中国偿二代等偿付能力监管体系都采用了三支柱框架，较为完整地覆盖了保险业面临的风险，构建了一套全面的具有风险识别、计量和防范功能的监管体系。

二是更加准确的风险计量。为了准确识别风险，各个国家（地区）监管机构对风险因子进行了持续的校准，以确保相关风险因子符合本国（地区）的实际。同时，进一步强化的风险穿透计量的要求，以更加准确地识别、计量投资资产的相关风险。比如，ICS要求保险机构尽可能地对资产进行穿透，以评估其底层资产的风险。偿二代（二期）新增了市场风险与信用风险穿透计量的监管规则，要求按照穿透原则计量其最低资本。

三是更加重视风险管理。保险公司风险管理是偿付能力监管的重要基础。各国（地区）偿付能力体系对强化保险公司风险管理更加重视。比如，美国NAIC实施了保险公司自我风险与偿付能力评估（ORSA），要求各保险公司从内部管理开始自上而下地系统审视和洞察风险，动态地管理保险公司的风险、资本与价值。中国偿二代充分考虑我国新兴保险市场的实际，采用监管评估的方法，建立偿付能力风险管理要求与评估（SARMRA）的机制，并与资本要求挂钩，推动保险公司持续提升风险管理能力。

中国人寿保险股份有限公司
全球保险资本标准测试案例

一、基本情况

中国人寿保险股份有限公司（以下简称中国人寿）是中国领先的个人和团体人寿保险与年金产品、意外险和健康险供应商，也是中国最大的机构投资者之一。2016—2019年，中国人寿参加了国际保险监督官协会（以下简称IAIS）《以风险为基础的全球保险资本标准》（Risk-based Global Insurance Capital Standard，ICS）的实地测试工作，每年向中国银保监会和IAIS提交测试数据并反馈有关意见。2020年初，IAIS发布ICS2.0，进入为期5年的ICS2.0监测期，中国人寿参与了监测期项目。

按照中国银保监会要求，中国人寿高度重视，成立了由投资管理中心、精算部、财务部骨干人员组成的ICS测试小组，并于2020年5月至9月开展了测试工作。测试小组深入研究技术标准，结合公司实际，制订了具体技术方案。测试小组对大量的保单数据和资产数据进行分类梳理，以准确计量实际资本和最低资本。在此基础上，测试小组填报了数十张测试表格，认真回答问卷，并按期向中国银保监会提交了测试结果，及时答复了IAIS的问询，测试数据得到了IAIS的肯定和认可。本文对中国人寿2020年ICS测试的整体结果以及资产端、负债端的主要测试数据进行了分析，总结了测试经验，提出了相关建议。

二、整体测试情况

（一）2020年测试结果

2020年是ICS2.0监测期的第一年，评估时点为2019年12月31日，评估范围为中国人寿及其子公司。ICS2.0有市场调整法（Market Adjusted Valuation，MAV）和会计报表调整法（GAAP+）两种方法，中国人寿需要填报两种方法下的资产、负债、实际资本和最低资本等数据，以及中国企业会计准则下的资产、负债等数据。

根据测试结果，2019年12月31日，中国人寿在MAV方法下的实际资本为9 941亿元，最低资本为3 807亿元，综合偿付能力充足率为261.2%，较中国偿二代下的综合偿付能力充足率下降15个百分点；在GAAP+方法下，实际资本为8 767亿元，最低资本为3 870亿元，综合偿付能力充足率为226.5%，较中国偿二代的综合偿付能力充足率下降50个百分点。具体情况如表1所示。

表1 整体测试结果　　　　　　　　　　　　单位：亿元

项目	MAV	GAAP+	偿二代
实际资本	9 941	8 767	9 871
最低资本	3 807	3 870	3 570
综合偿付能力充足率（%）	261.2	226.5	276.5

（二）2016年以来的测试结果

2016—2019年为ICS实地测试期，每年的技术标准均有所变动调整，与最终发布的ICS 2.0的标准也不完全相同，不同年度的测试结果不宜直接简单对比。中国人寿2016—2020年MAV方法下的测试结果（每年测试的评估时点均为上一年度末）如表2所示。

表2 2016—2020年测试结果　　　　　　　　　单位：亿元

项目＼年份	2016	2017	2018	2019	2020
实际资本	5 036	5 576	6 953	8 170	9 941
最低资本	2 744	2 907	2 716	3 154	3 807
偿付能力充足率（%）	184	192	256	259	261

三、具体测试结果

（一）实际资本

2019年12月31日，中国人寿在MAV方法和GAAP+方法下的实际资本情况如表3所示。在MAV方法下，资产和保险合同负债的计量方法与企业会计准则不同，因此，中国人寿的投资资产、应收分保准备金、保险合同负债、递延所得税资产或负债等均发生变动，主要变动项目有：投资资产增加541亿元，应收分保准备金增加234亿元，递延所得税资产增加166亿元，保险合同负债减少7 076亿元，递延所得税负债增加1 963亿元，合计导致MAV方法下的净资产较企业会计准则下净资产增加6 054亿元。MAV方法考虑资本补充工具、非认可资产的影响以及二级资本限额规定，对净资产进行调整得到实际资本，主要调整项目包括：资本补充债券增加实际资本350亿元，无形资产扣除减少实际资本61亿元，二级资本限额减少实际资本495亿元，合计导致MAV方法下的实际资本较净资产减少206亿元。

GAAP+方法与MAV方法类似，投资资产、应收分保准备金、保险合同负债、递延所得税资产或负债较财务报表数据有所变动，主要变动项目有：投资资产增加22亿元，应收分保准备金增加250亿元，递延所得税资产增加149亿元，保险合同负债减少5 886

亿元，递延所得税负债增加 1 540 亿元，合计导致 GAAP+ 方法下的净资产较企业会计准则下净资产增加 4 767 亿元。对 GAAP+ 方法下的净资产进行调整得到实际资本，主要调整项目包括：资本补充债券增加实际资本 350 亿元，无形资产扣除减少实际资本 61 亿元，二级资本限额减少实际资本 382 亿元，合计导致 GAAP+ 方法下的实际资本较净资产减少 93 亿元。

表 3　实际资本情况　　　　　　　　　　　　　单位：亿元

项目	MAV	GAAP+
企业会计准则下的净资产	4 093	4 093
ICS 对净资产的调整项目	6 054	4 767
实际资本的调整项目	−206	−93
合计（实际资本）	9 941	8 767

1. 投资资产

MAV 方法要求资产以公允价值计量，因此，需要对企业会计准则下非公允价值计量的固定收益类投资资产以及可获取公允价值的投资性房地产等进行估值调整（见表 4）。GAAP+ 方法下的资产价值与偿二代保持一致。主要受固定收益类投资资产公允价值调整影响，MAV 方法下的投资资产较企业会计准则下的数值上升约 541 亿元，上升幅度约 1.5%。

表 4　投资资产价值调整　　　　　　　　　　　单位：亿元

项目	企业会计准则	MAV	GAAP+
总投资资产	36 167	36 707	36 189
政府债券	4 046	4 203	4 046
公司债券/企业债券	15 710	16 025	15 710
基础设施投资计划	1 606	1 617	1 606
其他债权类资产	4 669	4 758	4 669
股权类资产（含股票、基金、未上市股权、长期股权投资）	7 938	7 895	7 961
投资性房地产	121	132	121
其他投资资产	2 077	2 077	2 077

2. 寿险业务保险负债

MAV 方法下寿险业务保险负债为当前估计与风险边际（MOCE）之和。当前估计为保险负债未来现金流现值的概率加权平均值，其中未来现金流的计算采用最优估计假设，现金流现值由未来现金流按照每项负债的货币种类和分档所对应的收益率曲线折现得到。当前估计须考虑保单内嵌的选择权和保证利益相关的预期现金流，所有选择权与保证利益的估计应基于无套利定价方法计算。MOCE 使用正态分布给定的分位点计算，寿险业务风险边际使用85%分位点。

GAAP+方法下寿险业务保险负债为最优估计准备金与风险边际之和。最优估计准备金与偿二代下的最优估计准备金计算方法一致,包括现金流现值、选择权及保证利益的时间价值(TVOG),其中,TVOG按照偿二代的因子法计算,风险边际按照分位点法计算。

MAV方法与GAAP+方法对保险负债计量的差异主要是收益率曲线的确定方法不同。GAAP+方法下最优估计准备金评估利率曲线与偿二代的收益率曲线一致。收益率曲线构造均由无风险利率曲线和溢价调整组成,具体方法及结果如表5、表6和图1所示。

表5 收益率曲线方法对比

项目	MAV	GAAP+	偿二代
无风险利率曲线	基于市场信息调整的无风险收益曲线,采用Smith-Wilson方法进行外推,设定终极利率。终极远期利率为6%。长期信用利差采用35个基点	基于市场信息的无风险收益曲线、过渡曲线、终极利率三段组成,采用线性插值法连接各段曲线。终极远期利率为4.5%	基于市场信息的无风险收益曲线、过渡曲线、终极利率三段组成,采用线性插值法连接各段曲线。终极远期利率为4.5%
溢价调整	使用三档法确定。根据负债和支持该负债的资产的性质,三档法将负债分为低档、中档和高档。对每一档负债使用不同的溢价调整	中国银保监会统一规定的数额。高、中、低三档,分别为70个基点、45个基点、30个基点	中国银保监会统一规定的数额。高、中、低三档,分别为70个基点、45个基点、30个基点

表6 MAV方法下溢价调整分档标准及结果

分档标准	传统	分红	万能
账户单独管理	否	是	是
无退保选择权,或退保价值不超过评估日时支持该保险负债组合对应的资产价值	是	是	是
退保风险最低资本不超过该保险负债组合使用无风险利率折现的当前估计的5%	NA	是	是
该资产组合在报告日的市值大于该保险负债组合使用无风险利率折现的当前估计	是	是	是
保险合同负债不包含未来保费,或者仅包含合同约定的固定的保费	是	是	是
组别划分	低档	中档	中档

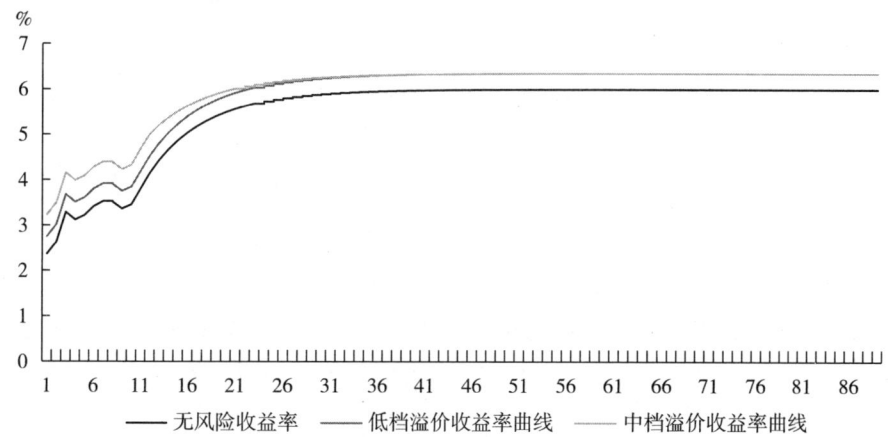

图 1　MAV 方法下收益率曲线

与 MAV 方法相比，GAAP+方法下寿险业务保险负债的变动主要由以下原因导致（见图 2）：

(1) 折现率变动：GAAP+方法的利率曲线低于 MAV 方法的利率曲线，使 GAAP+方法的现金流现值上升 1 051 亿元。

(2) 现金流变动：假设上下限、生存金和红利累计生息假设，以及分红现金流和万能结算利率的不同，使 GAAP+方法的现金流现值上升 102 亿元。

(3) TVOG 变动：MAV 方法下采用无套利定价方法，GAAP+方法下采用因子法，使 GAAP+方法的 TVOG 增加 374 亿元。

(4) 分红账户价值（UPPEA）变动：MAV 方法下所有资产都按公允价值计量，分红账户价值上升，使 GAAP+方法下 UPPEA 比 MAV 法下 UPPEA 小 265 亿元。

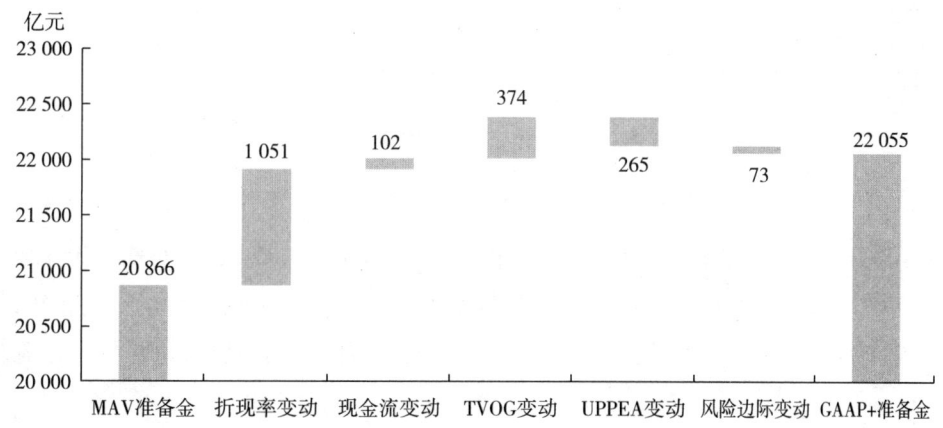

图 2　GAAP+准备金和 MAV 准备金的变动原因

(5) 风险边际变动（MOCE 变动）：MOCE 基于寿险和非寿险业务风险最低资本计

算,MAV 方法和 GAAP+方法的保险风险最低资本的差异影响 MOCE 下降 73 亿元。

3. 递延所得税资产或负债

与偿二代计提所得税准备不同,ICS 技术标准需要针对资产负债在 MAV 或 GAAP+方法下的价值与财务报表价值的差异计提递延所得税资产或递延所得税负债,同时考虑最低资本的税收调整,具体情况为：一是计提风险边际（MOCE）产生的递延所得税资产。在 MAV 方法下,MOCE 产生的递延所得税资产为 166 亿元；在 GAAP+方法下,MOCE 产生的递延所得税资产为 148 亿元。二是由于投资资产和保险负债的估值差异,在 MAV 方法下,除 MOCE 外,其他项目产生的递延所得税负债为 1 963 亿元；在 GAAP+方法下,除 MOCE 外,其他项目产生的递延所得税负债为 1 540 亿元。

（二）最低资本

ICS2.0 将保险公司面临的风险分为四大类：保险风险、市场风险、信用风险、操作风险。风险大类及下设的子类风险如图 3 所示。

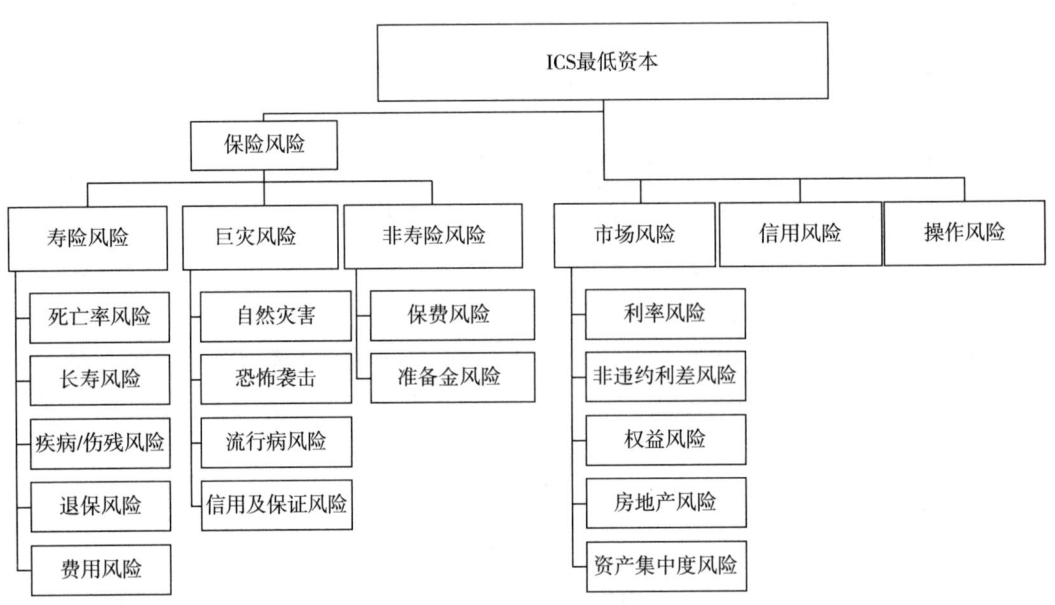

图 3　ICS 风险分类

ICS 最低资本计量方法为 99.5% 置信水平下的在险价值（VaR）,与偿二代计量方法相同。MAV 方法和 GAAP+方法对各类最低资本的计量方法一致。与偿二代相比,ICS 增加了操作风险,并将巨灾风险单独作为一类。对于寿险公司,巨灾风险仅考虑流行病风险。

2019 年 12 月 31 日,中国人寿在 MAV、GAAP+和偿二代方法下的各项风险最低资本及占比情况如表 7 所示。

表7 最低资本情况 单位：亿元

项目	MAV	占比	GAAP+	占比	偿二代	占比
寿险风险	1 623	43	1 443	37	765	21
非寿险风险	66	2	66	2	67	2
巨灾风险	33	1	36	1	—	0
市场风险	2 745	72	2 961	76	3 577	100
信用风险	335	9	328	8	603	17
操作风险	236	6	236	6	—	0
量化风险分散效应	−1 138	−30	−1 091	−28	−780	−22
损失吸收效应	—	0	—	0	−572	−16
控制风险最低资本	—	0	—	0	−90	−3
最低资本税收调整	−780	−20	−796	−21	—	0
非保险业务	686	18	686	18	—	0
最低资本合计	3 807	100	3 870	100	3 570	100

与偿二代结果相比，由于评估方法的差异，MAV方法和GAAP+方法下的市场风险、信用风险最低资本有所下降，寿险风险最低资本显著上升。

1. 保险风险

（1）ICS及偿二代下评估方法比较

ICS与偿二代的寿险保险风险最低资本及巨灾风险最低资本的评估方法对比如表8所示。

表8 ICS偿二代评估方法对比

一级风险	二级风险	ICS	偿二代
寿险风险	死亡风险	死亡发生率水平压力：12.5%	死亡发生率压力水平为10%~20%，其中压力水平根据主险保单件数确定
	长寿风险	仅考虑对死亡发生率水平的压力：死亡发生率发生水平压力下降17.5%	对未来20年分段采用3%~1%的死亡趋势改善
	疾病/失能风险	基于"Similar to life"的原则判断是否计量该风险（原则上只包括长期健康险），根据保险责任类型及产品期限设定压力因子 • 保险责任类型 责任类型1：医疗费用 责任类型2：发生特定健康问题时的一次性赔付 责任类型3：短期多次赔付 责任类型4：长期多次赔付 • 合同期限 短期合同：包括原始期限不超过（含）五年的合同 长期合同：包括原始期限超过五年的合同	长期健康险计量寿险业务保险风险：疾病发生率风险和医疗及健康赔付损失率风险的压力水平均为上升20%

续表

一级风险	二级风险	ICS	偿二代
寿险风险	退保风险	• 水平和趋势：退保率上升/下降40%取大，与100%取小 • 大规模退保：对于零售保单，退保率为30%；对于非零售保单，退保率为50%	• 水平和趋势：退保率上升/下降30%~40%取大 • 大规模退保：未来12个月退保率上升150%，上浮后区间为[25%，100%]，以所有退保时给付现价的保单为计量单元
	费用风险	• 费用风险作用于寿险和"Similar to life"的健康险 • 单位费用上浮8% • 通胀风险为阶梯式压力因子（1~10年：3%；11~20年：2%；21年以上：1%）	不对通胀率做压力，仅考虑费用水平上升的压力为10%
非寿险风险	保费风险	Max（净已赚保费，净未赚保费）	过去最近12个月自留保费
	准备金风险	准备金当前估计净值	再保后未决赔款准备金
巨灾风险		流行病巨灾压力情景为未来12个月年度死亡发生率假设+0.1%	死亡发生率巨灾为未来12个月年度死亡发生率+0.18%

MAV方法、GAAP+方法和偿二代方法下的保险风险最低资本如图4所示。从结果来看，保险风险主要来源于寿险风险，非寿险风险和巨灾风险占比较小。偿二代下巨灾风险属于寿险业务保险风险下的三级子风险，因此没有单独列示。

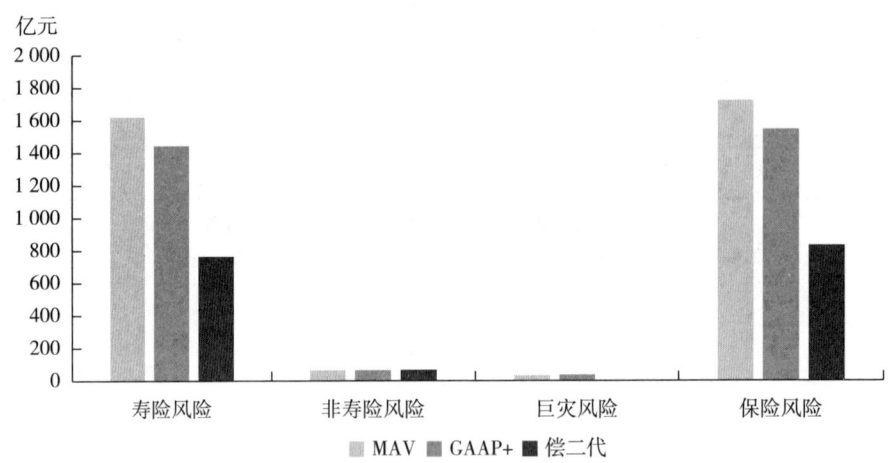

图4 保险风险最低资本

ICS下寿险风险和巨灾风险采用情景法计算，非寿险保险风险采用因子法计算，与偿二代方法相同。ICS下死亡风险、长寿风险、费用风险、巨灾风险与偿二代方法较为接近，下面主要讨论疾病/失能风险和退保风险。

（2）疾病/失能风险最低资本

根据ICS技术标准，疾病/失能风险最低资本评估方法按照业务类型分为两大类：按照类似寿险业务技术标准评估的业务和按照非寿险业务技术评估的业务。其中，按照类似寿险业务技术标准评估的业务是指计算保险合同负债时需要明确使用按照年龄划分的死亡发生率、发病率及康复率等生物统计变量。疾病/失能发生率风险的保险责任范围和偿二代保险风险中的疾病发生率风险、医疗及健康赔付损失率风险的保险责任范围基本一致。疾病/失能发生率风险的压力情景按照不同的责任类型和合同期限设定。责任类型分为以下4种独立的类型：

第1类：医疗费用。提供住院或非住院的医疗费用补偿（固定费用或基于实际费用）的产品。赔偿金取决于保单持有人花费的治疗费用，而非取决于特定健康状况的持续时间。

第2类：发生特定健康问题时的一次性赔付。在出现特定健康问题，或发生意外事故导致一定程度失能时提供一次性赔付的产品。

第3类：短期多次赔付。根据特定的临时健康状况（如无法工作或住院）的持续时间，在一段时间内提供多次给付的产品。

第4类：长期多次赔付。在健康状况长期或永久恶化的情况下提供固定年金给付的产品。

每种保险责任类型均根据原始合同条款分为短期和长期两类，分别对应原始期限不超过（含）5年的合同和原始期限超过5年的合同。

不同责任类型、合同期限下疾病/失能发生率风险压力情景因子如表9和图5所示。

表9 不同责任类型风险因子

责任类型	短期合同	长期合同
1	20%	8%
2	25%	20%
3	20%	12%
4	发病率风险压力情景因子为25%，治愈率风险压力情景因子为20%	发病率风险压力情景因子为20%，治愈率风险压力情景因子为20%

中国人寿大部分产品属于责任类型2且为长期合同，该类别压力因子为20%，与偿二代压力因子相同，故ICS健康风险最低资本与偿二代结果比较接近。

（3）退保风险最低资本

根据ICS技术标准，退保风险最低资本为水平与趋势退保风险最低资本和大规模退保风险最低资本取大。偿二代、MAV方法与GAAP+方法下退保风险最低资本如图6所示。

ICS退保风险的计算范围为长期险，与偿二代一致。ICS下水平与趋势退保率风险压力情景为退保率上浮或下浮40%，取最不利情景下的结果。偿二代下的退保率风险为退

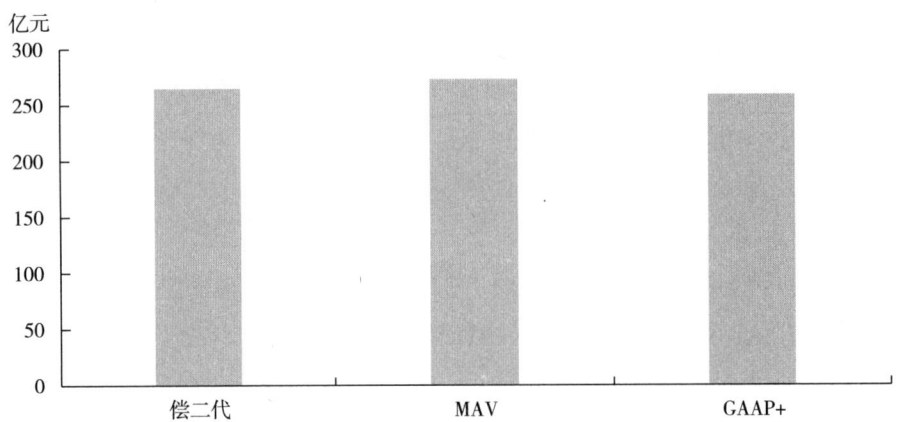

注：偿二代结果包含疾病发生率风险和医疗及健康赔付损失率风险。

图5 疾病/失能风险最低资本

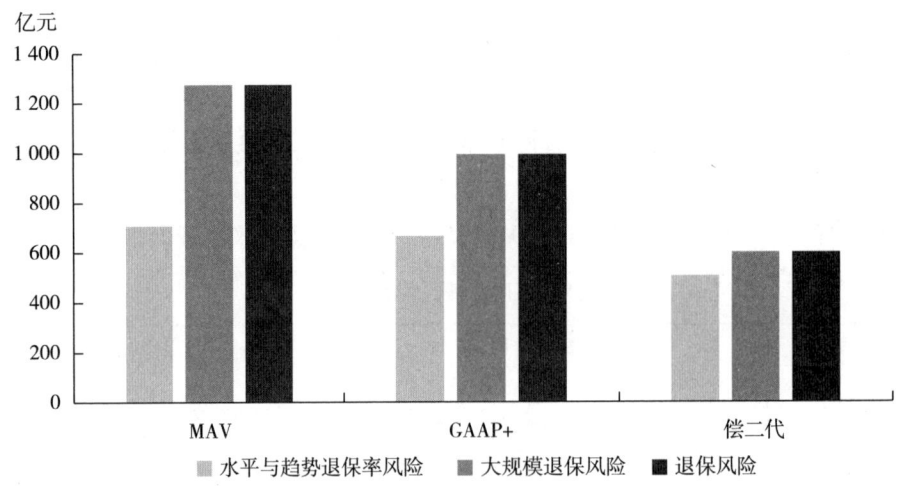

注：偿二代下水平与趋势退保率风险的值为偿二代下的退保率风险结果。

图6 退保风险最低资本

保率上浮或下浮，取最不利情景下的结果；压力情景因子为30%或40%，按照归属产品类型确定。

ICS的大规模退保风险压力情景为在评估时点30%的个险保单及50%的团险保单瞬时退保。偿二代下大规模退保风险压力情景为未来12个月退保率上升150%，且保证上浮后退保率区间为［25%，100%］。

MAV方法和GAAP+方法各子风险最低资本的差异主要来源于保险合同准备金的差异。GAAP+方法下相比偿二代方法下退保风险最低资本显著增加，主要原因是压力幅度不同以及最低资本汇总层级不同。

2. 市场风险

ICS 下的市场风险包括利率风险、非违约利差风险、权益风险、房地产风险、汇率风险和集中度风险。中国偿二代的市场风险包括利率风险、权益风险、房地产风险和汇率风险以及境外资产价格风险，但不包括非违约利差风险。

2019 年 12 月 31 日，中国人寿在 MAV 方法和 GAAP + 方法下的市场风险最低资本如图 7 所示。

（1）利率风险

ICS 利率风险最低资本基于各币种无风险收益率曲线压力情景的组合进行计量，适用于所有利率敏感的资产和负债（保险公司发行的资本工具除外），风险暴露较小的多个币种可以合并为一组进行计算。压力情景共有 5 种，分别是均值回归情景、水平向上情景、水平向下情景、扭转上下情景、扭转下上情景。

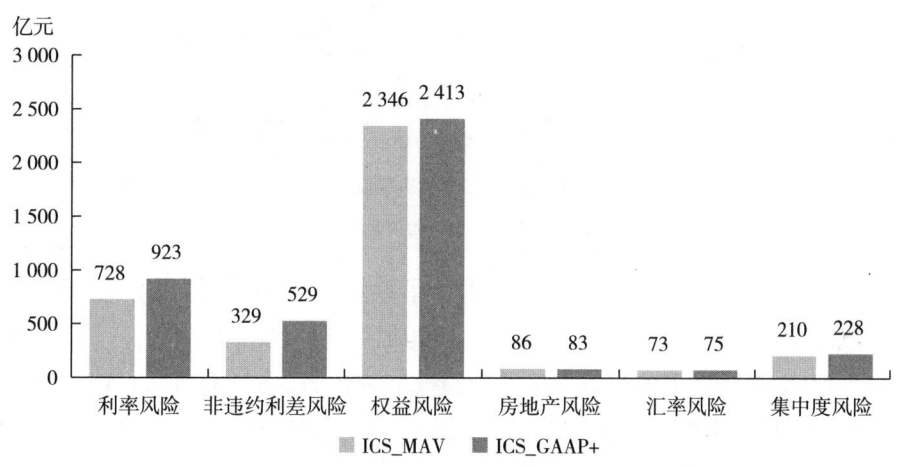

图 7 市场风险最低资本

中国人寿在 MAV 方法下的利率风险最低资本约为 728 亿元，GAAP + 方法下的利率风险最低资本约为 923 亿元。两种方法下利率风险最低资本存在差异，主要原因为中国人寿持有较多的摊余成本计量的固定收益类资产，在 MAV 方法下该类资产可以对冲负债端的利率风险（见表 10）。

表 10 MAV 和 GAAP + 方法下对冲利率风险的资产范围

MAV	GAAP +
全部利率敏感性资产，主要为固定收益类资产（含次级债和优先股，但不包含其他保险公司发行的计入实际资本的资本工具），均以公允价值计量	对于以公允价值计量的固定收益类资产，采用和 MAV 一致的方法； 对于以摊余成本计量的固定收益类资产，不适用于利率风险的计算

(2) 非违约利差风险

非违约利差风险同时考虑利差对资产端和负债端的双向压力,所有对利差变化敏感的负债和在评估中对计算利差调整有贡献的资产需计算非违约利差风险最低资本,但资产端不包括政府债券等主权类资产。

中国人寿 MAV 方法下的非违约利差风险最低资本约为 329 亿元,GAAP+ 方法下的非违约利差风险最低资本约为 529 亿元,MAV 方法下的非违约利差风险最低资本显著低于 GAAP+ 方法,主要原因为中国人寿持有较多的摊余成本计量的固定收益类资产,在 MAV 方法下该类资产可以对冲负债端的非违约利差风险。

(3) 权益风险

ICS 计算权益风险最低资本的资产分为 4 类,分别是发达市场上市权益、新兴市场上市权益、混合资本债/优先股和其他权益(见表11)。

表11 权益风险资产分类

资产分类	资产描述
发达市场上市权益	在 FTSE 发展指数中的证券交易所上市的权益
新兴市场上市权益	不包括在 FTSE 发展指数的股票市场的上市权益
混合资本债/优先股	混合资本债/优先股,包含次级债
其他权益	不包含在上述三个分类中的权益资产

计算 ICS 下的权益风险最低资本时,先计算 4 类资产权益价格水平压力结果并通过相关性系数矩阵进行聚合,再与波动压力结果相加得到最终结果。

中国人寿 MAV 方法下的权益价格风险最低资本约为 2 346 亿元,GAAP+ 方法下的权益价格风险最低资本约为 2 413 亿元,最低资本差异原因来自 MAV 和 GAAP+ 两种方法下的风险暴露口径存在差异。

在市场风险各子类风险最低资本中,权益价格风险最低资本占比最高,主要原因为:①中国人寿持有权益类资产规模较大;②持有其他权益类资产占比较高,适用的压力情景为市场价格瞬时下降49%;③持有的上市权益主要为境内 A 股,在 ICS 下划分为新兴市场上市权益,适用的压力情景为市场价格瞬时下降48%。

(4) 房地产风险

ICS 下房地产风险压力情景为房地产价格下降25%,适用于所有直接和间接面临房地产价格风险的资产,不区分商业房地产、住宅房地产和自用房地产。

中国人寿 MAV 方法下的房地产风险最低资本约为 86 亿元,GAAP+ 方法下的房地产风险最低资本约为 83 亿元,最低资本差异原因为 MAV 和 GAAP+ 两种方法下的风险暴露存在一定差异。

在市场风险各子类风险最低资本中,房地产风险最低资本占比较低,主要原因为中国人寿持有的房地产占总投资资产比重较小。

（5）汇率风险

汇率风险最低资本是指保险公司持有的外币资产和外币负债在两种压力情景下损失的较大值。

中国人寿MAV方法下的汇率风险最低资本约为73亿元，GAAP+方法下的汇率风险最低资本约为75亿元，差异原因为MAV和GAAP+两种方法下的风险暴露存在一定差异。

在市场风险各子类风险最低资本中，汇率风险最低资本占比较低，原因为中国人寿持有的投资资产主要配置在中国境内，汇率风险敞口相对较小。

（6）集中度风险

集中度风险最低资本是在市场风险和信用风险最低资本之上需额外计提的一项增量资本，需分别计量交易对手集中度风险和房地产集中度风险。

中国人寿MAV方法下的交易对手集中度风险最低资本约为210亿元，GAAP+方法下的交易对手集中度风险最低资本约为228亿元，中国人寿持有投资资产的主要交易对手为地方政府机构和国有大型股份制银行。

中国人寿持有的房地产风险暴露未超过与保险业务相关的净投资资产的3%，因此不计提房地产集中度风险最低资本。

3. 信用风险

ICS下的信用风险最低资本采用因子法，仅指交易对手违约风险。优先股和混合债务（包括次级债）不纳入信用风险最低资本计算。

信用风险的风险因子是根据ICS评级和有效期限以及风险暴露类别确定的，中国人寿的信用风险暴露集中在RC3评级，占比约94%；80%的敞口有效期限在7年以内（见图8、图9）。

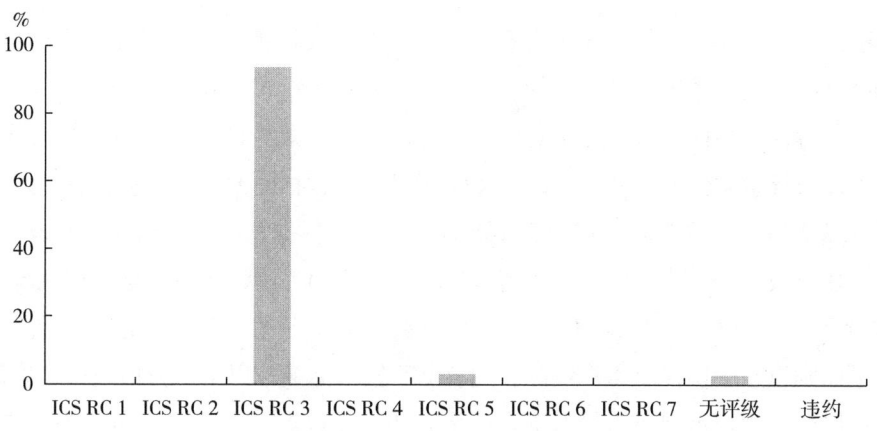

图8　信用风险敞口评级结构

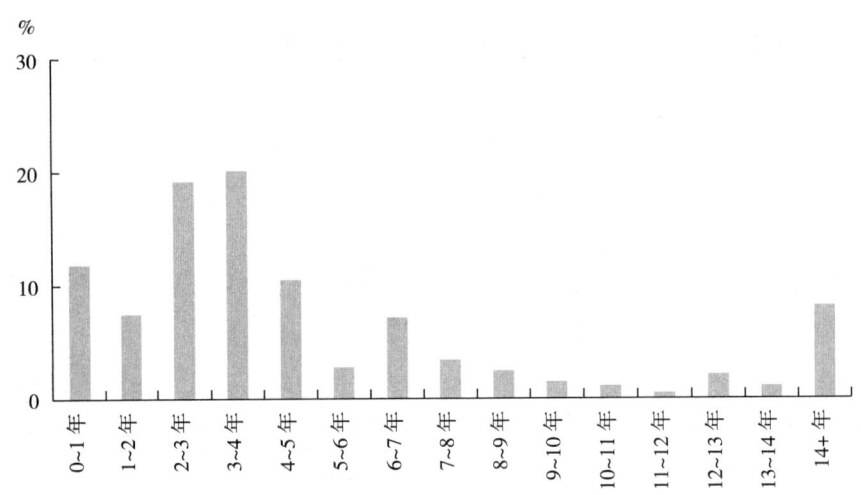

图9 信用风险敞口期限结构分布

中国人寿MAV方法下的信用风险最低资本约为335亿元,GAAP+方法下的信用风险最低资本约为328亿元。MAV方法下的信用风险最低资本略高,主要受信用风险暴露估值调整增加的影响。

4. 其他风险最低资本

ICS的操作风险最低资本,基于保险公司的保费和准备金规模使用因子法计算。在MAV和GAAP+方法下,中国人寿的操作风险最低资本均为236亿元。ICS的非保险业务风险最低资本,主要是对金融机构持有的长期股权投资计提的资本要求。在MAV和GAAP+方法下,中国人寿的非保险业务最低资本均为686亿元。

四、体会和建议

中国人寿连续5年参与ICS数据测试工作,投入大量精力深入研究技术标准,结合自身的测试结果以及中国保险市场的实际情况,对技术标准提出若干修改建议。在这个过程中,一方面,中国人寿加深了对国际偿付能力监管规则的了解,对保险公司面临的风险类别以及计量方法有了更深入的认识,提升了偿付能力风险管理水平;另一方面,中国人寿提交的测试结果是IAIS完善ICS标准的重要数据基础,中国人寿对技术标准所提的一些建议被IAIS采纳,为国际保险监管规则的制定贡献了中国智慧和力量。

2020年,中国人寿完成了ICS2.0监测期数据测算,考虑到中国偿二代监管体系的风险计量原则以及中国保险市场实际,建议ICS技术标准在以下四方面进一步修改完善。一是建议修改大规模退保风险最低资本计量方法,允许产品层面的正负抵消。二是建议对费用风险最低资本中的通货膨胀率压力因子设定上限,并评估压力因子水平的适当性。目前针对中国市场设定的费用通货膨胀率压力因子太高,对于期限较长的业务,由于几何级数的增长,会使得费用增长水平超过合理范围。而且保险公司费用水平的增长还需要综合考虑业务增长以后效率提升对费用管控的影响。因此,建议对费用通货膨胀率压力因子设定上限,并评估压力因子的水平。三是建议分国家或地区设定流行病压力因子,以反映不同国家或地区的流行病风险状况。四是建议统一 TVOG 的具体计量方法,以提升测试结果的可比性。建议结合当地监管体系要求,由中国银保监会提供 TVOG 计算方法的具体指导意见。

此外,中国人寿建议进一步深入完善 ICS 下 GAAP + 方法相关规则研究制定工作。由于 GAAP + 方法建立在报告主体对应的本地监管规则或者财务报告信息基础上,可以降低参与主体实施成本,增加参与主体不同规则下的结果可比性,便于内部管理,避免不同规则下结果差异较大或者部分项目的方向性差异。目前我国偿二代二期工程以科学有效防范保险风险、推动保险业回归本源、落实金融业全面对外开放为目标,基本完成了规则的修订和测试工作,部分规则较一期规则发生较大改变。建议中国银保监会组织行业力量搭建以偿二代二期规则为主体的 ICS – GAAP + 评估规则和标准,更多吸纳和认可中国的监管规则,形成适合中国市场特征的技术方案,以更好地对接 ICS 的监管要求。

中国太平保险集团有限责任公司全球保险资本标准测试案例

一、基本情况

中国太平保险集团有限责任公司（以下简称太平集团）于1929年在上海创立，是中国历史上持续经营最为悠久的民族保险品牌，2013年完成重组改制和整体上市。

太平集团立足香港，跨境经营，服务全球。近年来，在党中央、国务院的坚强领导下，快速发展，连续四年入榜《财富》世界500强，最新排名列第344位。2020年，太平集团总保费突破2 000亿元，经营收入2 446亿元，总资产9 837亿元，管理资产规模超过1.7万亿元，已经成为一家拥有50多万名内外勤员工、24家子公司和2 000余家各级营业机构的大型跨国金融保险集团，经营范围涉及中国内地、香港、澳门以及欧洲、大洋洲、东亚和东南亚等国家和地区，业务范围涵盖寿险、财险、养老保险、再保险、再保险经纪及保险代理、互联网保险、资产管理、证券经纪、金融租赁、不动产投资、养老医疗健康产业等领域。经过多年发展，太平集团保险业务经营体系较为完备，也是国际化特色最为鲜明的中资保险机构。

原中国保监会自2017年起提名太平集团作为中国保险集团的代表之一，连续3年参加全球保险资本标准1.0（ICS 1.0）实地测试工作，参与校准ICS技术标准。自2020年起，太平集团参与ICS 2.0为期5年的监测期数据监测及报送工作，为ICS 2.0技术标准的完善提供支持。

通过多年参与测试，太平集团深入研究国际保险业资本监管规则，对标国内现行的偿二代监管体系，对未来资本监管规则的发展趋势以及可能对中国保险业造成的影响进行分析。与此同时，积极建言献策，为国际规则制定提供中国经验。

二、太平集团测试结果分析

（一）测试结果汇总（2017—2020）

2017—2020年，太平集团参与了ICS测试，其中2017—2019年为ICS实地测试期，2020年为ICS 2.0的5年监测期的第一年。表1为太平集团过去四年的测试结果，其间的测试结果变动主要源于集团业务规模的不断提升、ICS测试标准的修改以及市场经济环境的变化等。

整体来看,太平集团2017—2020年资产规模与负债规模都在逐年大幅增加,使实际资本呈现逐年大幅上升的趋势。资产及负债规模的上升带来的风险敞口的增加,使太平集团最低资本也呈现相应的增长趋势。虽然几年间市场经济环境以及投资资产配置策略的变化导致市场风险存在一定的波动,但是整体而言,ICS充足率稳定在较高水平。

MAV口径下,2020年太平集团ICS充足率为283%,较2019年(299%)下降16个百分点。ICS充足率下降的主要原因包括:2020年ICS测试标准将寿险公司风险边际的置信度要求从75%提高到85%,导致风险边际大幅增加,减少实际资本;同时太平集团权益类资产配置比例增加,固定收益类资产占比下降,导致市场风险最低资本显著上升。

表1　太平集团2017—2020年MAV口径测试结果汇总　　单位:亿元

行次	项目	2017年	2018年	2019年	2020年
1	资产	4 618	5 554	6 690	8 425
2	负债①	-3 354	-3 975	-4 725	-5 794
3	风险边际	-140	-242	-121	-241
4	实际资本调整②	-56	-51	-47	-44
5	实际资本	1 068	1 287	1 797	2 346
6	量化风险最低资本	415	422	601	830
7	ICS充足率	257%	305%	299%	283%

根据测试要求,自2019年起太平集团新增了GAAP+口径的资本充足性测试。与MAV口径类似,虽然2019—2020年太平集团GAAP+口径下实际资本与最低资本同步上升,但是由于资产配置比例的变化以及测试标准参数假设的变化,GAAP+口径ICS充足率呈下降趋势。整体来看,2020年GAAP+口径ICS充足率略有下降,由2019年的243%下降至2020年的226%(见表2)。

表2　太平集团2019—2020年GAAP+口径测试结果汇总　　单位:亿元

行次	项目	2019年	2020年
1	资产	6 613	8 293
2	负债③	-4 937	-6 209
3	风险边际	-113	-205
4	实际资本调整④	-47	-44

---

① 负债:除风险边际外其他负债。
② 实际资本调整:由于资本分级等原因导致的其他实际资本调整。
③ 负债:除风险边际外其他负债。
④ 实际资本调整:由于资本分级等原因导致的其他实际资本调整。

续表

行次	项目	2019年	2020年
5	实际资本	1 516	1 834
6	量化风险最低资本	623	813
7	ICS充足率	243%	226%

与MAV口径相比，GAAP+口径ICS充足率较低，主要原因包括：GAAP+下保险负债折现率的基础利率曲线采用750天移动平均国债收益率曲线，投资资产采用账面价值，导致GAAP+口径实际资本显著低于MAV口径实际资本；同时，GAAP+下持有至到期债券资产不计量利率风险，使得资产端利率风险敞口显著小于负债端利率风险敞口，导致GAPP+口径利率风险最低资本高于MAV口径利率风险最低资本。随着偿二代二期工程的实施，预期两者之间的差异将会有所减小。

与GAAP+口径类似，太平集团2017—2020年偿二代口径实际资本呈现逐年上升的态势，最低资本也呈现相应的增长趋势，总体来看偿付能力充足率稳定在较高的水平（见表3）。考虑到两种方法的相似性，偿二代口径偿付能力充足率与GAAP+口径ICS充足率水平较为接近，低于MAV口径ICS充足率。

表3　太平集团2017—2020年偿二代评估结果汇总　　　　　单位：亿元

行次	项目	2017年	2018年	2019年	2020年
1	实际资本	1 173	1 420	1 662	2 110
2	最低资本	440	551	720	918
3	偿付能力充足率	266%	258%	231%	230%

（二）实际资本计量方法与结果比较分析

2017—2020年，太平集团整体业务规模逐年扩大，伴随着投资资产、保险负债规模逐年上升，递延所得税负债（资产）也在同步增加。得益于业务发展，公司MAV口径与GAAP+口径下的实际资本均取得了较大幅度的增长（见图1和图2）。

1. 认可资产

如图3所示，MAV口径下，2020年太平集团认可资产为8 425亿元，较2019年上升1 735亿元，涨幅为26%。其中，2020年投资资产为7 356亿元，较2019年上升1 640亿元，涨幅为29%。两年间认可资产规模增加主要来自太平集团投资资产的大幅增长。

2. 认可负债

MAV口径认可负债主要由保险负债及递延所得税负债构成，两项之和占比超过70%，剩余负债主要为借款及其他应付款。

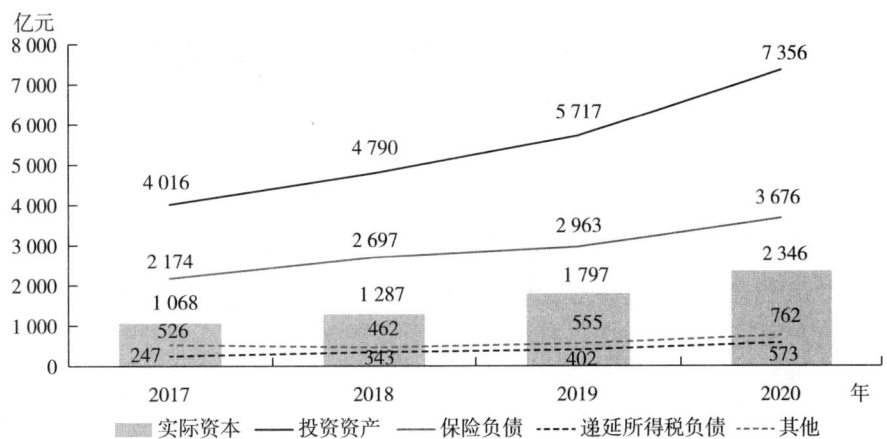

图1 太平集团2017—2020年MAV口径实际资本变动

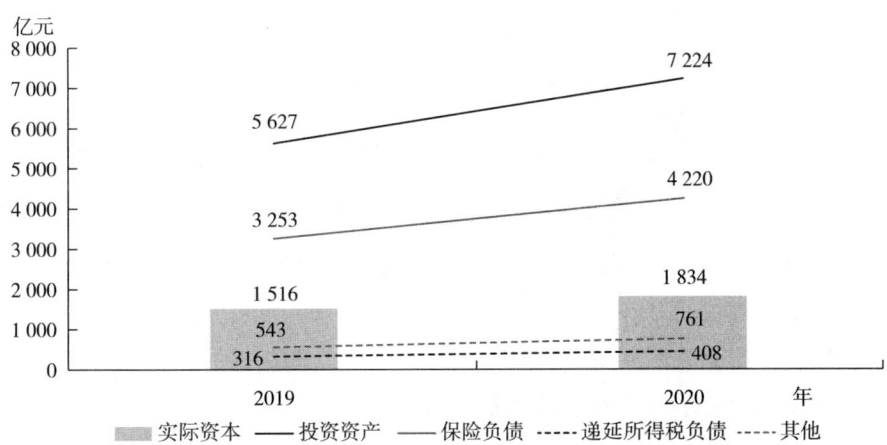

图2 太平集团2019—2020年GAAP+口径实际资本变动

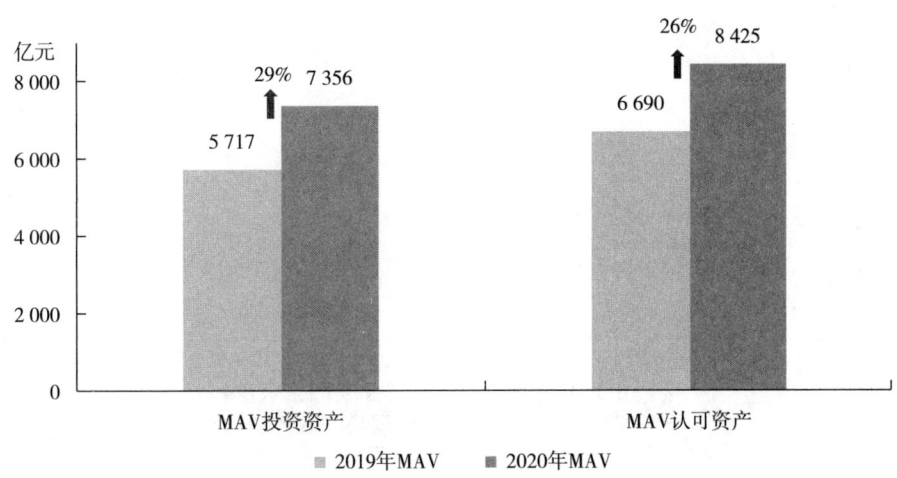

图3 太平集团2019—2020年MAV口径认可资产及投资资产变动

(1) 寿险业务保险合同负债

寿险业务保单负债包括最优估计现金流的现值和选择权及保证利益(TVOG)。

MAV 口径下计量最优估计现金流现值时采用的非金融假设（理赔发生率、退保率、费用率等）为最优估计假设。

MAV 所用的收益率曲线由无风险收益率曲线加对应溢价构成。对于溢价，ICS 规定了三档。太平集团在账户（险种大类）层面进行三档法溢价判定，2019 年及 2020 年负债判定结果如表 4 所示。相比 2019 年，太平集团 2020 年负债判定改变主要是因为 ICS 2.0 对三档法判定要求有所调整。2020 年中档与低档溢价差异为 20～30 个基点，分档变化对准备金结果影响较小。

表 4　太平集团 2019—2020 年负债分类判定结果

行次	判定结果	2019 年	2020 年
1	分红险	低档	中档
2	万能险	中档	低档
3	传统险	低档	低档
4	投连险	低档	低档

与 2019 年相比，2020 年溢价水平以及终极利率均有所升高，同时无风险利率曲线呈现先低后高的趋势，使得 2020 年折现率曲线同样呈现先低后高的趋势，并且差异逐渐增大。以低档溢价情况为例（见图 4），相比 2019 年，2020 年无风险收益率曲线前 10 年略低，10 年以后较高，折现率呈现类似趋势。

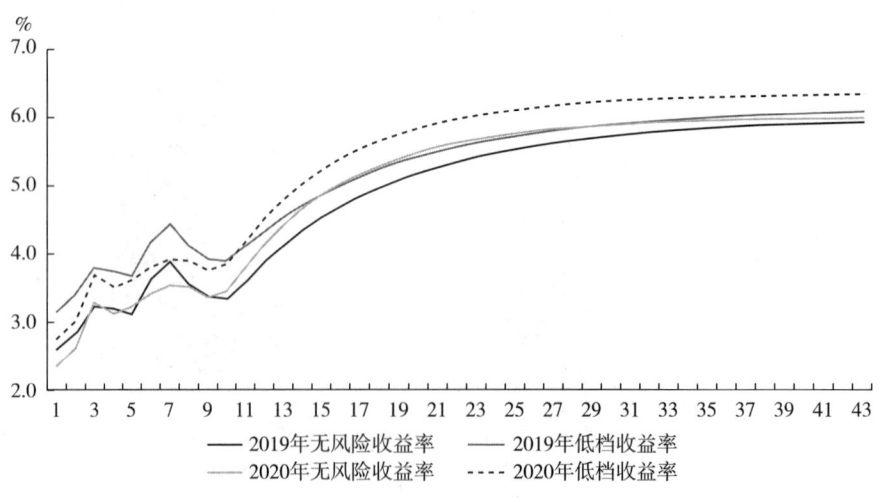

图 4　2019—2020 年折现率曲线比较

通过结果对比，折现率曲线的变化使 2020 年 MAV 口径保险合同负债减少约 2%。

太平集团 2020 年 MAV 口径下 TVOG 的计量方法与 2019 年保持一致，采用因子法。2019 年与 2020 年 TVOG 占保险合同负债下现金流现值的比例均维持在稳定的水平。

2020 年寿险业务保单负债增加约 532 亿元，主要源于太平集团寿险业务大幅增长。

（2）风险边际计量

MAV 口径下风险边际使用正态分布给定的分位点计算。如图 5 所示，2020 年太平集团风险边际较 2019 年大幅上升（增加约 99%），主要原因是相较于 2019 年，2020 年寿险业务风险边际使用的分位点从 75% 升高至 85%（乘数因子从 26% 上升至 40%），非寿险业务风险边际使用的分位点从 60% 升高至 65%（乘数因子从 10% 上升至 15%）。

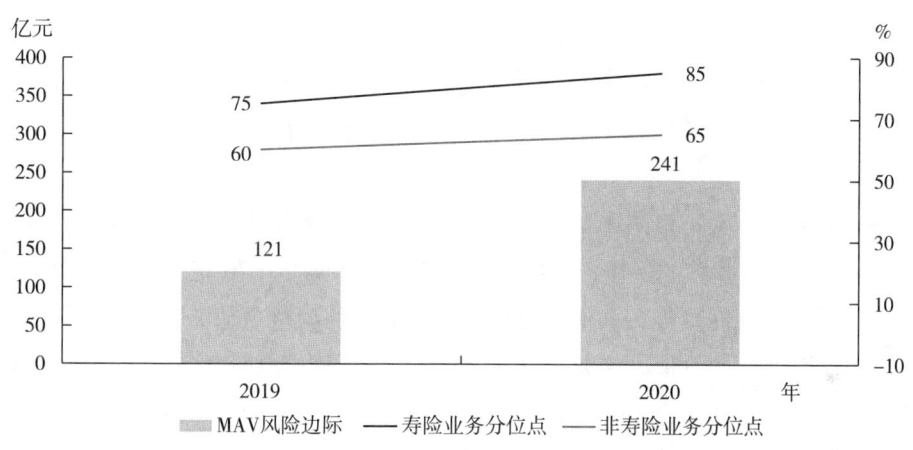

图 5　太平集团 2019—2020 年 MAV 口径风险边际比较

（3）其他认可负债

非寿险保险合同负债：2020 年 MAV 口径与 2019 年相比，非寿险保险合同负债的计量方法无变化，计量结果也无显著变化。

ICS 调整的递延所得税影响：从中国会计准则资产负债表下的投资资产和保险负债调整至 ICS 资产负债表时，将对递延所得税资产（DTA）、递延所得税负债（DTL）产生影响。2020 年太平集团对 ICS 调整的递延所得税影响的计算方法与 2019 年基本一致。ICS 口径下保险负债较资产负债表口径下降较多，从而产生较高的递延所得税负债。如图 6 所示，2020 年 DTA 及 DTL 均较 2019 年有所增加，且 DTL 增加金额更大（主要是因为 2020 年资产负债表口径调整的影响较大），使得 2020 年递延所得税调整较 2019 年增加约 139 亿元。

3. 其他实际资本调整

除了上述认可资产与认可负债的调整外，ICS 下还需要对部分资产进行扣减，并将

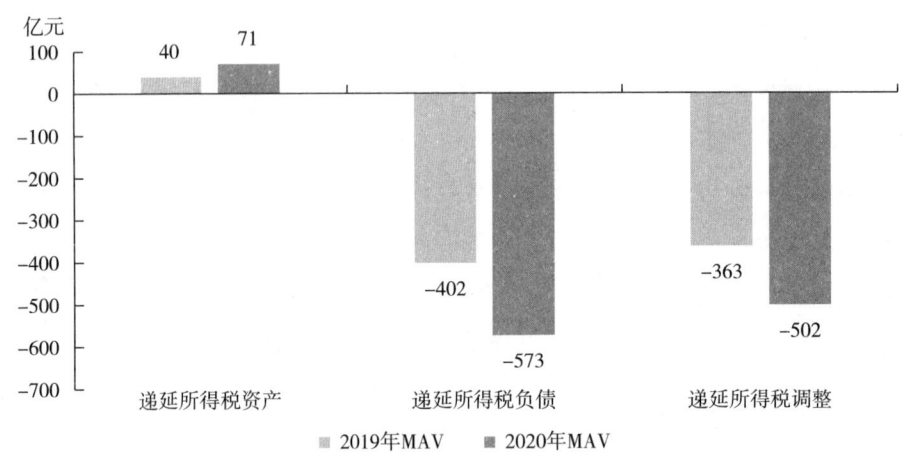

图6 太平集团2019—2020年MAV口径递延所得税调整比较

部分资本由一级资本调整为二级资本,同时将公司发行的符合ICS要求的资本工具确认为实际资本。

2019—2020年,太平集团MAV口径下一级资本扣减项以及二级资本变动较小。其中,需要从实际资本扣除的一级资本扣减项从54亿元增加至70亿元,包括商誉以及无形资产(除计算机软件)等;其他需要调入二级资本的调整项从238亿元下降至207亿元,包括处置受限资产价值、递延所得税资产以及计算机软件等无形资产的摊销净额等。另外,太平集团发行的次级债从9亿元增加至30亿元,计入二级资本。

(三)最低资本计量方法与结果比较分析

2017—2020年,随着业务规模的不断增加,太平集团MAV口径下最低资本呈上升趋势。其中,寿险保险风险与市场风险最低资本占比合计接近80%,为太平集团面临的主要风险(见图7)。伴随寿险业务负债规模以及业务结构的变化,寿险保险风险占比近年来大幅提升。同时,由于投资资产配置比例的变化以及无风险利率的变动,市场风险占比出现波动。

类似地,2019—2020年太平集团GAAP+口径下最低资本呈上升趋势,其中,寿险保险风险最低资本及市场风险最低资本占比较高(见图8)。GAAP+口径下寿险保险风险最低资本占比低于MAV口径,其原因在于两个口径下保险负债的折现率不同。GAAP+口径下市场风险最低资本占比高于MAV口径,其原因在于两个口径下利率风险最低资本计量方法存在差异。

1. 保险风险最低资本

保险风险最低资本包括寿险保险风险最低资本、非寿险保险风险最低资本及巨灾风险最低资本三部分。

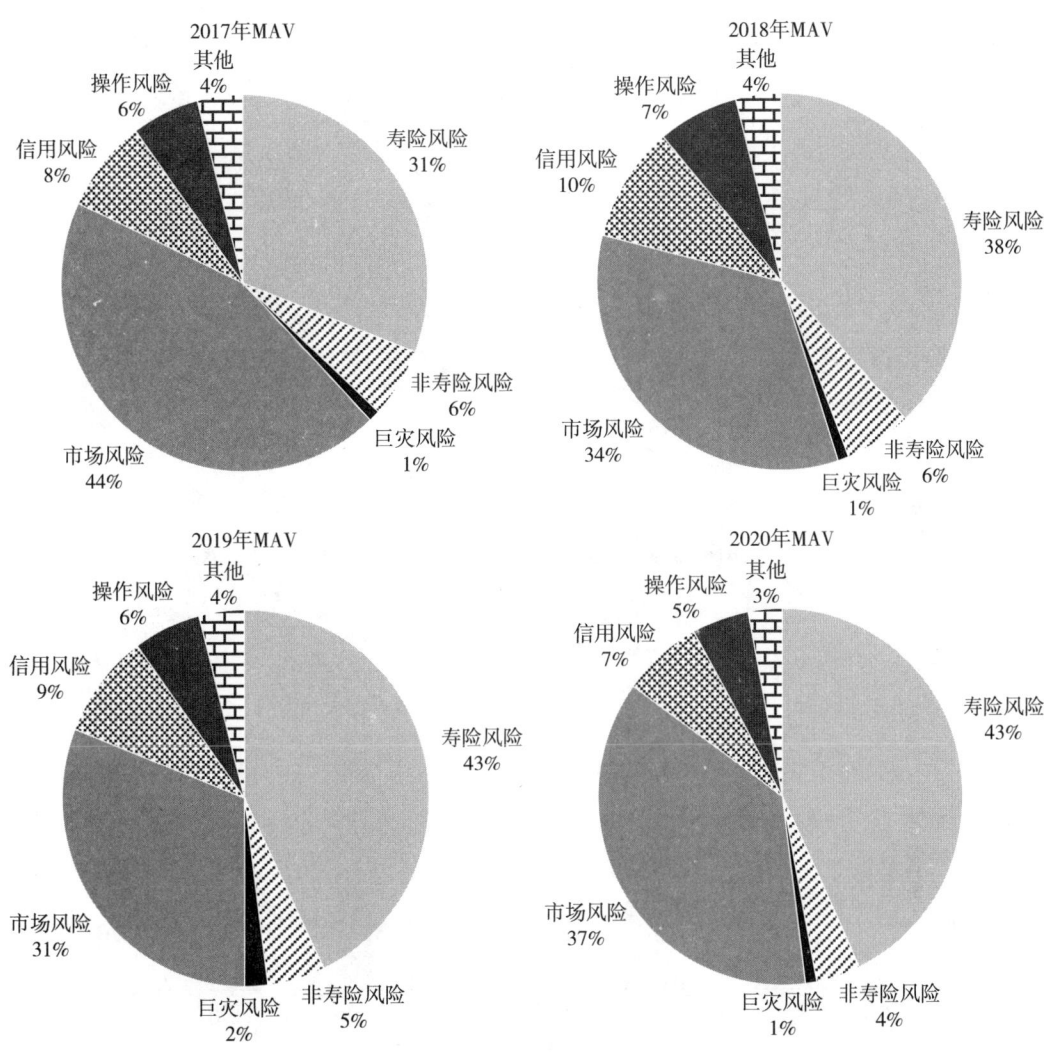

图 7　太平集团 2017—2020 年 MAV 口径下最低资本占比分布

寿险保险风险最低资本：如图 9 所示，2020 年 MAV 口径下寿险保险风险最低资本较 2019 年有所增长，其中退保风险增加较多，主要是大规模退保风险的增加。

非寿险保险风险最低资本：2020 年 MAV 口径下非寿险保险风险最低资本为 49 亿元，与 2019 年结果相近（50 亿元），差异主要源于非寿险保险业务险种分布略有变化。

巨灾风险最低资本：MAV 口径下巨灾风险同时考虑寿险和非寿险的巨灾风险，分为自然灾害和人为灾害两部分。2020 年 MAV 口径下巨灾风险最低资本为 20 亿元，高于 2019 年（16 亿元）。变化主要源于保险业务规模增长，人为灾害和自然灾害最低资本较 2019 年均有所增加。

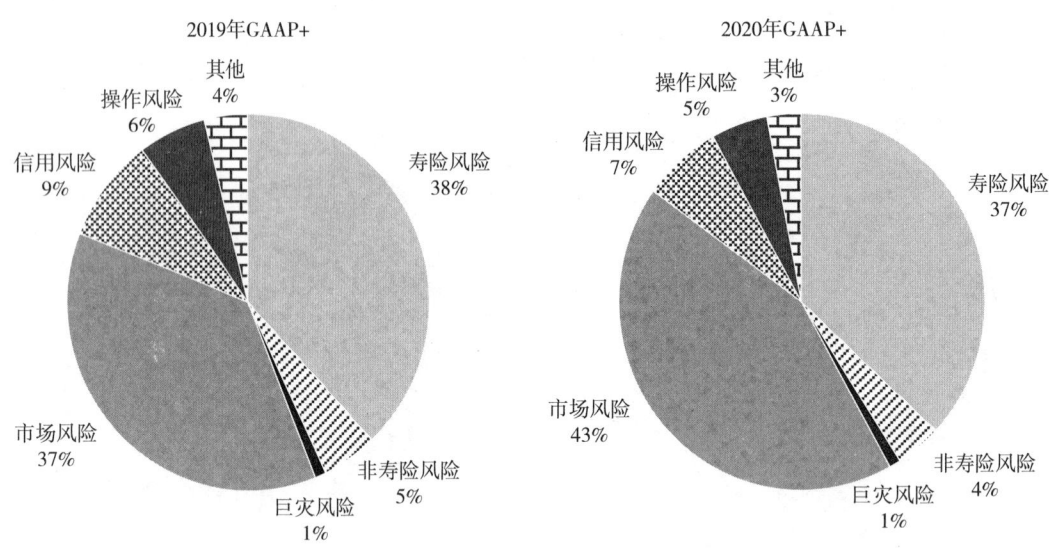

图 8　太平集团 2019—2020 年 GAAP + 口径下最低资本占比分布

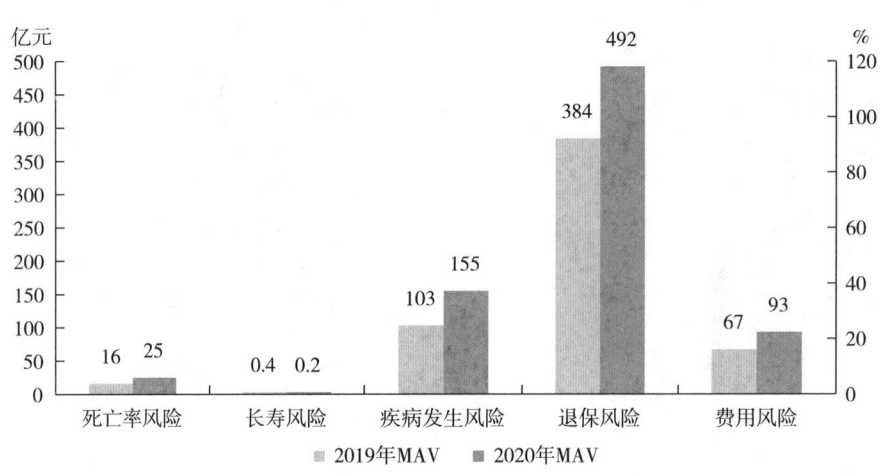

图 9　太平集团 2019—2020 年 MAV 口径下寿险保险风险最低资本比较

2. 市场风险最低资本

市场风险最低资本包括利率风险、非违约利差风险、权益风险、房地产风险、汇率风险和集中度风险等（见图10）。

利率风险：伴随资产与负债规模的增加，2020 年 MAV 口径下的利率风险最低资本较 2019 年上升约 10%，主要由于太平集团 2020 年固定收益类资产配置比例下降，资产端利率风险暴露减少。

非违约利差风险：2020 年与 2019 年非违约利差风险压力幅度相近，2020 年太平集团固定收益类资产配置比例下降，计量非违约利差风险的资产暴露比例下降，资产负债

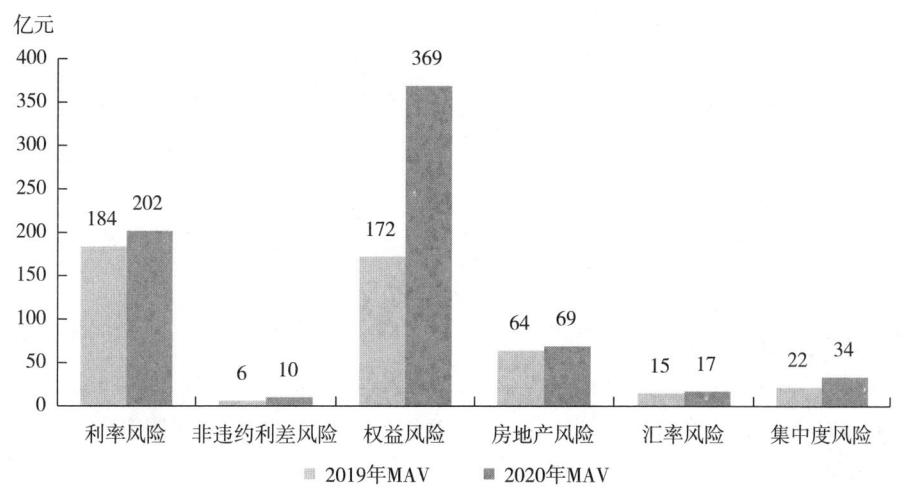

图 10　太平集团 2019—2020 年 MAV 口径市场风险最低资本变动

对冲能力下降，导致 2020 年非违约利差风险最低资本较 2019 年上升。

权益风险：2020 年 MAV 口径下权益风险最低资本较 2019 年大幅上升，主要由于太平集团 2020 年投资资产中权益类资产持仓比例大幅增加，权益风险的风险暴露增加。

房地产风险：2020 年太平集团 MAV 口径下房地产风险最低资本较 2019 年上升约 9%，主要由于 2020 年太平集团房地产资产规模的增加。

汇率风险：2020 年太平集团 MAV 口径下汇率风险最低资本较 2019 年增加了约 10%，主要由于港元由 2019 年的多头转为 2020 年的空头风险暴露，多头风险暴露中汇率风险分散效应下降，汇率风险最低资本上升。

集中度风险：2020 年 MAV 口径下集中度风险最低资本较 2019 年上升了约 55%。集中度风险基于市场风险及信用风险最低资本进行计算，2020 年集中度风险最低资本出现大幅上升，主要由于市场风险及信用风险最低资本增加。同时，IAIS 规定的 2020 年平均的集中度风险因子增加，进而导致集中度风险最低资本进一步上升。

3. 其他

信用风险：2020 年 MAV 口径下信用风险最低资本较 2019 年有所上升，主要原因是 2020 年太平集团固定收益类资产总量增加，使信用风险资产端主要风险暴露大幅增加。

操作风险：2020 年 MAV 口径下操作风险最低资本为 72 亿元，高于 2019 年的 63 亿元，变化主要源于保险业务规模增长。

最低资本计量的税收调整[①]：ICS 2.0 对税收调整增加了上下限的要求，因此 2020 年最低资本税收调整比例最终结果为 20%，较 2019 年税收调整的影响略有减小。

---

① MAV 口径最低资本要求公司需从最低资本结果中扣除税收调整的影响，与之相比，偿二代下并无此项调整。

三、风险分布的国际比较

IAIS 每年会收集汇总全球参与报送的 IAIG 的报告结果,通过与全球各个地区的比较分析,我们发现,不同地区面临的主要风险类型较为相似,细化的风险分布则存在一定的差异。

从全球来看,保险公司面临的首要风险为市场风险,其中又以利率风险和权益风险影响最大;寿险保险风险影响次之。

市场风险和寿险保险风险作为前两大风险,反映了全球保险行业以长期保障业务作为核心的经营方向,与中国银保监会提出的"保险业姓保"的要求不谋而合,即保障是保险业根本功能,投资是辅助功能,是为了更好地保障,投资必须服务和服从于保障,绝不能本末倒置。

(一) 不同地区各类风险对最低资本的贡献度

对于太平集团,寿险保险风险和市场风险分别为量化风险最低资本中占比第一大(44%)和第二大(38%)的风险。

太平集团寿险保险风险占比高于其他地区,除了因为太平集团旗下寿险业务占比较高外,人民币负债的溢价水平较高也会使得折现率较高,产生较高的退保风险。

同时,太平集团市场风险较其他地区占比较低。经过分析,主要是由于太平集团旗下寿险公司固收类资产配置比例较高,权益资产配置比例较低,且资产负债久期缺口较小,因此与其他公司相比,利率风险与权益风险相对较小。

(二) 不同地区寿险保险风险对比

相较于亚洲地区其他公司,太平集团的寿险保险风险主要集中于退保风险和疾病/失能发生率风险。形成该差异的主要原因是人民币负债的溢价水平较高,退保风险较高;另外,太平集团传统重疾和医疗保障型业务占比逐年增加,使公司面临更高的退保风险和疾病/失能发生率风险。

同时,由于太平集团定期寿险业务和年金业务占比较少,死亡发生率风险和长寿风险占比相对较低。

(三) 不同地区市场风险对比

对太平集团来说,在市场风险中,占比第一大和第二大的风险依次为权益风险(53%)和利率风险(29%)。

太平集团持有的权益类资产中,中国市场 A 股(属于新兴市场)投资占比较高,而 ICS 对于新兴市场和长期股权投资的权益风险压力参数设置较高,导致整个集团权益风险中的新兴市场上市权益最低资本占比较高,进而使权益风险在市场风险中的占比升高。

与亚洲地区其他公司相比,太平集团利率风险的分布无明显差异。

四、太平集团对 ICS 技术标准的意见及建议

在 ICS2.0 的体系下，MAV 是 IAIS 主推的 ICS 充足率测算技术标准，GAAP+是一套兼顾当地偿付能力监管规则的充足率技术标准，实际资本的计量需要基于各国偿付能力监管标准，最低资本的计量则是基于 ICS 规定。对于中国而言，GAAP+是 MAV 与中国偿二代结合的 ICS 充足率技术标准，在一定程度上反映了中国市场的实际情况与特殊性。如未来 ICS 充足率正式成为全球活跃保险集团的监管指标，太平集团建议给予 IAIG 选择权，允许 IAIG 选择更适合自身市场情况的技术标准。

在 ICS 制定过程中，太平集团积极参与并反馈意见，以反映中国的市场现状和经验，多项意见和建议得到 IAIS 的吸收采纳。

（一）认可实际资本（次级债）

根据早期 ICS 技术标准的要求，对于公司发行的资本工具，如果合同中没有规定赎回时需要获取监管机构批准的条款，则无法认定为实际资本。在中国市场，虽然保险公司在发行次级债时已通过监管机构的批准，但是由于合同条款通常没有对赎回时需要经过监管机构批准进行规定，因此无法被认定为实际资本。对此，太平集团向 IAIS 提出了反馈建议。

最新的技术标准规定，即使没有相关的赎回条款，公司也可以将次级债认定为二级实缴资本工具。

（二）风险边际方法的建议

早期 ICS 实地测试时，风险边际的计量采用资本成本法。考虑到实践中确定资本成本率的主观性较强，难以判断其合理性；同时对比来看，采用正态分布给定的分位点计算风险边际，结果更具有可比性和一致性。太平集团对此向 IAIS 提出了反馈建议。

最新的技术标准明确规定采用分位点法计算风险边际。

（三）非寿险保险风险的分类方法

ICS 下非寿险保险风险因子根据不同地区和险种区分，中国大陆地区的险种划分与偿二代险种分类一致，共 10 个险种。各险种被归类为四个 ICS 类别之一，即责任险、车险、财产险与其他险（房贷险与信用险不包含在四类中，而是纳入房地产风险与信用风险中计算），并采用各级风险层层向上聚合的方式计算非寿险保险风险。

2017 年和 2018 年测试时聚合方式依次为同一险种内保费和准备金风险进行聚合、同一地区内四大 ICS 类别间进行聚合、跨地区聚合。同一 ICS 类别里的险种假设完全正相关，不考虑风险风散效应，与偿二代差异较大。太平集团对此向 IAIS 提出了反馈建议。

2019 年测试时，IAIS 新增了同一 ICS 类别内聚合要求，在同一险种的保费与准备金风险聚合后，将属于同一 ICS 类别的各险种按照新增的风险相关系数矩阵进行聚合，考

虑了风险分散效应。

（四）其他建议

除上述已经被 IAIS 采纳的建议，太平集团建议修改保险合同负债评估的折现率曲线。

根据最新的 ICS 技术标准，人民币对应的折现率曲线的第二段曲线起点（最长流动性期限）为 10 年，第三段曲线起点（终极利率收敛点）为 60 年，考虑到中国国债市场 30 年期以上的债券交易量非常少，太平集团建议将人民币对应的终极利率收敛点由 60 年调整为 30 年，同时根据国债市场交易量变化，对第二段曲线的起点进行追踪调整。

二、全球保险资本标准(ICS)2.0版本 一级文件

目 录

1 介绍 ··· 52
   1.1 目的 ·· 52
   1.2 背景 ·· 52
   1.3 ICS 与《共同框架》的关系 ·· 53
   1.4 制定原则 ·· 54
2 ICS 2.0 监测期 ·· 55
   2.1 基准 ICS 报告 ··· 55
   2.2 附加报告 ·· 55
3 一般指导原则 ·· 55
   3.1 实质重于形式 ·· 55
   3.2 匹配性原则 ··· 55
   3.3 穿透要求 ·· 56
   3.4 信用评级 ·· 56
4 基准 ICS：评估范围 ··· 56
   4.1 ICS 资产负债表的起点 ·· 56
   4.2 MAV 方法下的资产负债表 ··· 56
5 基准 ICS：MAV 方法 ··· 56
   5.1 资产负债评估原则 ·· 56
   5.2 当前估计 ·· 57
      5.2.1 计算基础 ··· 57
      5.2.2 合同确认、合同边界和预测期限 ······························· 57
      5.2.3 数据质量和假设的设定方法 ····································· 57
      5.2.4 管理层行为 ·· 57
      5.2.5 折现方法 ··· 57
   5.3 风险边际（MOCE） ··· 58
      5.3.1 定义和基本原则 ·· 58
      5.3.2 计算方法 ··· 58
      5.3.3 MOCE 与 ICS 其他组成部分的关系 ···························· 59
   5.4 可被资产组合复制的负债 ·· 59
6 基准 ICS：实际资本 ··· 59
   6.1 一般规定 ·· 59

6.2 资本工具分级 ····· 59
6.3 非资本工具分级 ····· 60
6.3.1 一级资本项目 ····· 60
6.3.2 二级资本项目 ····· 61
6.4 资本调整和扣减 ····· 61
6.4.1 一级资本扣减项 ····· 61
6.4.2 二级资本扣减项 ····· 62
6.4.3 处置受限资产的处理 ····· 62
6.5 资本构成比例 ····· 62

7 基准ICS：最低资本—标准法 ····· 62
7.1 风险分类和基本计量方法 ····· 62
7.1.1 风险缓释 ····· 63
7.1.2 地区划分 ····· 64
7.1.3 管理层行为 ····· 64
7.2 保险风险 ····· 64
7.2.1 寿险保险风险保单分组 ····· 64
7.2.2 寿险保险风险最低资本计算 ····· 64
7.2.3 非寿险保险风险最低资本计算 ····· 65
7.2.4 巨灾风险最低资本计算 ····· 65
7.3 市场风险 ····· 66
7.3.1 市场风险最低资本计算 ····· 66
7.3.2 利率风险 ····· 66
7.3.3 非违约利差风险 ····· 67
7.3.4 权益风险 ····· 67
7.3.5 房地产风险 ····· 67
7.3.6 汇率风险 ····· 67
7.3.7 集中度风险 ····· 68
7.4 信用风险 ····· 68
7.4.1 信用风险最低资本计算 ····· 68
7.4.2 合格抵押品、担保和信用衍生工具 ····· 68
7.4.3 外部评级使用要求 ····· 68
7.4.4 监管认可评级（SOCCA）使用要求 ····· 68
7.5 操作风险 ····· 69
7.6 最低资本聚合 ····· 69

8 基准 ICS：税的计量 …………………………………………………………… 70
　8.1 一般原则 ………………………………………………………………… 70
　8.2 ICS 调整的所得税影响 ………………………………………………… 70
　8.3 最低资本的所得税影响 ………………………………………………… 70
9 附加报告 …………………………………………………………………………… 70
　9.1 GAAP+方法 ……………………………………………………………… 70
　9.2 其他方法 ………………………………………………………………… 71

1 介绍

1.1 目的

1. 全球保险资本标准（Insurance Capital Standards, ICS）即将进入为期 5 年的监测期，一级文件规定监测期内基准 ICS 年度报告（非对外公开报告），及其他附加报告的总体原则和基本概念。

2. 一级文件应结合二级文件阅读使用，二级文件规定 ICS 具体技术细则。ICS 文件共分三个层级[①]：一级文件和二级文件共同构成 ICS 2.0 版本；三级文件基于一级文件和二级文件，为开展年度非公开报告提供辅助支持信息。二级文件计划于 2020 年初公布。三级文件计划于每年第二季度年度报告启动前公布。

1.2 背景

3. 2013 年 10 月 9 日，国际保险监督官协会（International Association of Insurance Supervisors, IAIS）宣布启动以风险为基础的全球保险资本标准制定工作，回应金融稳定理事会（Financial Stability Borad, FSB）所提出的对国际活跃保险集团（Internationally Active Insurance Groups, IAIG）建立全集团综合监管框架的要求[②]。2013 年 7 月 18 日，FSB 表示建立一个健全的保险业资本及监管框架，对全球金融稳定至关重要。2014 年 11 月 6 日，FSB 进一步强调支持 ICS 制定工作[③]。

4. 自 2013 年 10 月启动以来，IAIS 一直遵循结构化、基于实证的方法研究制定 ICS，组织保险集团进行多次量化实地测试。2014—2019 年，ICS 共进行了 6 次量化实地测试，每一次测试，IAIS 都对参与机构提交的数据进行了深入分析，通过实地测试和定期讨论会等渠道收集参与机构反馈意见。除实地测试外，IAIS 还定期召开利益相关方的现场会议，广泛听取各方建议，并就 ICS 规则两次对外公开征求意见。

5. ICS 的终极目标，是通过一套 ICS 方法，实现各国和各地区的资本监管结果可比。2017 年 11 月 2 日，IAIS 在吉隆坡年会期间公布了保险集团统一资本标准的实施路径。《吉隆坡协议》规定 ICS 2.0 分两阶段实施：

- 为期 5 年的监测期：在此期间，ICS 2.0 将用于向集团主监管机构进行非公开报告，并在监管联席会议上进行讨论。监测期内，ICS 结果不会触发监管措施；

[①] 根据 ICS 监测期的定义和目标，监测期间 ICS 2.0 不用于监管决策（即 ICS 结果不会触发任何监管措施）。因此，一级文件或二级文件中提到的监管决策或监管行为在监测期尚不具效力或作用，另有规定除外。ICS 作为监管资本要求实施后，相关要求方正式生效。

[②] http://www.financialstabilityboard.org/publications/r_130718.pdf.

[③] http://www.financialstabilityboard.org/WP-content/uploads/pr_141106a.pdf.

• "ICS作为集团监管资本要求（PCR）正式实施"①。

6. 《吉隆坡协议》还声明 ICS 2.0 实施包括以下两项内容，且两项内容同等重要：

• 基准 ICS 报告：针对所有 IAIG② 的强制要求③，仅向监管报送，非对外公开；

• 附加报告：集团主监管机构可自主决定是否要求 IAIG 报送附加报告，如基于会计准则调整方法（GAAP+）④ 的 ICS，或包括内部模型法（见第9.2节）在内其他 ICS 方法。

7. 与此同时，《吉隆坡协议》同意美国研究制定聚合方法（Aggregation Method，AM）。协议声明"尽管聚合方法不是 ICS 2.0 的一部分，IAIS 认可这一方法制定的重要性，同意从相关国家和地区收集数据，支持聚合方法的开发"。

8. IAIS 的目标是，监测期结束后能够评估聚合方法是否与 ICS 等效，即结果高度相似（ICS 终极目标）。如果等效，聚合方法可作为与 ICS 结果等效的方法来计算 PCR。目前相关国家和地区正在着手制定聚合方法，已启动制定聚合方法的等效评估标准，并拟订了工作计划，以期在监测期结束前完成相关工作。

1.3　ICS 与《共同框架》的关系

9. 《国际活跃保险集团监管共同框架》（*Common Framework for the Supervision of Internationally Active Insurance Groups*，以下简称《共同框架》）是根据 IAIG 的复杂性和国际化特征量身制定的监管要求，包括定量和定性监管要求。ICS 是《共同框架》的重要组成部分。2017年6月，IAIS 同意按以下方式整合 ICS 与《共同框架》：

• ICS 2.0 将于2019年作为独立文件公布实施（监测期）；

• 暂不对《保险核心原则》第14条"资产负债评估"和《保险核心原则》第17条"资本充足性"进行修订，待 ICS 2.0 正式实施后再修订；

• 鉴于以上，2019年底公布实施的《共同框架》不含 ICS 2.0 内容；

• 待 ICS 2.0 正式实施后，ICS 2.0 将与《共同框架》进行整合。

10. ICS 将在5年监测期结束后，与《共同框架》进行整合。为了有助于监测期运行和监管联席会议的内部讨论，《共同框架》引用了包括基准 ICS 和附加报告在内的部分 ICS 内容。

---

① 根据《保险核心原则》（ICP）17.4 定义，PCR 指偿付能力控制水平线。高于该水平，监管机构不会针对资本充足情况对保险机构进行干预。ICS 是国际监管最低标准，各国监管机构可选择制定更为谨慎的、高于 ICS PCR 的本国 PCR 要求。

② 监测期内，未满足 IAIG 标准的保险机构也可自愿参与监测期基准 ICS 报告和附加报告，由集团主监管机构选择决定。

③ "强制要求"已写入《共同框架》标准，具体为集团主监管机构应要求其所管辖的 IAIG 报送 ICS 基准结果，并在监管联席会议讨论相关结果。IAIS 所有成员应致力于结合本国市场实际，推动 IAIS 各项监管规则在本国落地实施。

④ 基于国际财务报告准则（IFRS）、美国 GAAP 和中国 GAAP 的 GAAP+ 方法在监测期内继续制定并进行测试。基于日本 GAAP 的 GAAP+ 方法将从2020年起进入5年监测期，与基准 ICS 同步。

1.4 制定原则

11. IAIS 于 2014 年 9 月发布了第一版 ICS 制定原则。2014 年 ICS 公开征求意见后，IAIS 对原则 3 和原则 6 进行了修订。修订后的原则如表 1 所示，ICS 的制定遵循以下原则。

表 1　ICS 制定原则①

ICS 原则 1：ICS 是基于保险集团并表、基于风险的国际可比的资本充足性衡量标准，适用于 IAIG 和全球系统重要性保险集团（G-SII）。该标准包括资产负债一致的评估原则、实际资本定义和基于风险的最低资本要求。最低资本要求和实际资本定义基于 IAIG 的风险特征制定，与 IAIG 集团总部所属地区或国家无关
ICS 原则 2：ICS 的主要目标是保护保单持有人利益和促进金融稳定。IAIS 的使命是对保险业进行全球统一、有效的监管，从而维护保险市场公平、安全、稳定，保护消费者利益。ICS 的制定符合 IAIS 的使命
ICS 原则 3：ICS 制定的目的之一是为 G-SIIs 更高损失吸收能力（Higher Loss Absorbency，HLA）提供基础资本要求。ICS 制定完成前，HLA 基于基础资本要求（BCR）计算
ICS 原则 4：ICS 应反映 IAIG 面临的所有重大风险。ICS 应反映 IAIG 开展各类业务活动而面临的所有重大风险，包括资产、负债、非保险业务风险和表外业务风险。未在 ICS 中量化的风险，应在《共同框架》中体现
ICS 原则 5：ICS 旨在提高各国和各地区资本监管的可比性，从而增进 IAIG 主监管机构和东道国监管机构间的相互理解、提高跨境分析质量。基于全集团并表，使用统一方法计量资本充足性，有助于创造公平的国际竞争环境，减少资本套利空间
ICS 原则 6：ICS 有助于 IAIG 和 G-SII 提升风险管理水平，包括对适当的、有效的风险缓释技术的认可
ICS 原则 7：ICS 提倡监管机构和 IAIG 的审慎稳健运行，尽可能减少不当的顺周期行为。ICS 不鼓励 IAIG 在压力情形下采取加剧事件影响的行为，比如，在市场下行时仍不断销售大量具有重大风险的产品，或市场出现危机时大量抛售资产
ICS 原则 8：ICS 在风险敏感度和简单可操作之间进行适当平衡。ICS 应当具有适当的颗粒度和复杂性以反映 IAIG 各类风险。但 ICS 尽可能避免为提高有限的风险敏感度而使用过度复杂的计量方法
ICS 原则 9：ICS 应提高透明度，尤其是在最终结果披露方面
ICS 原则 10：ICS 基于特定目标校准最低资本要求。ICS 最低资本校准目标为 IAIS 认为适当的偿付能力保护水平

---

① ICS 的某些制定原则——特别是那些引用 G-SII 的原则——已经被保险业系统风险评估和缓释的整体框架所取代。IAIS 于 2019 年 11 月正式采用该整体框架。根据最终确定的整体框架，FSB 经咨询 IAIS 与各国保险监管机构后，决定从 2020 年初起暂停 G-SII 的认定。此外，针对 G-SII 的更高损失吸收能力（HLA）也未纳入整体框架。详见 IAIS 新闻稿。https：//www.iaisweb.org/page/news/press-releases/file/87183/media-release-iais-adopts-first-global-frameworks-for-supervision-of-internationally-active-insurance-groups-and-mitigation-of-systemic-risk-in-the-insurance-sector.

2　ICS 2.0 监测期

2.1　基准 ICS 报告

12. 基准 ICS 规则是针对 IAIG 全集团并表的资本标准，由以下三个部分组成：
- 基于市场价值调整的评估方法（Market Adjusted Valuation，MAV）；
- 实际资本认可标准；
- 最低资本要求的标准法。

13. 基准 ICS 偿付能力充足率计算方法如下：

$$\text{ICS 偿付能力充足率} = \text{实际资本}/\text{最低资本}$$

14. ICS 基于持续经营假设衡量资本充足性。

2.2　附加报告

15. 监测期内，根据集团主监管机构的自主决定，IAIG 可提交基于 GAAP+方法或包括内部模型法（见第 9.2 节）在内的其他 ICS 方法下的结果。GAAP+和其他方法都是监测期结束时 IAIS 可能考虑采纳的方法之一。

3　一般指导原则

3.1　实质重于形式

16. ICS 资产负债表不同于公开披露的 GAAP 下的会计报表，会计报表以向投资者提供信息为目的，而 ICS 资产负债表以审慎监管为目的。例如，GAAP 下的资产负债表中的某些资产在 ICS 下不能被确认为认可资产。

17. ICS 资产负债表应该基于交易和事件的经济实质编制，而不仅仅基于其法律形式，以便更加真实、公允地反映企业的风险状况。编制 ICS 资产负债表时需要运用专业判断。

18. 保险合同负债按照 ICS 业务类型进行分配，应遵循实质重于形式原则。保险合同负债应被分配到最能反映潜在风险性质的业务类型，而不是仅根据合同的法律形式分配。保险业务类型的定义，在二级文件中具体规定。

3.2　匹配性原则

19. ICS 计量应遵循匹配性原则。当 IAIG 能够证明在计量中考虑特定的因素或规则会导致复杂程度显著增加，而又不会明显提升计量结果或风险评估的质量，则该因素或规则在 ICS 计算中可以简化或不予考虑。

20. 使用简化方法应基于以下几个方面评估其影响：
- 简化对象的体量；
- 集团整体的体量与实际资本规模；
- 简化的风险。

3.3 穿透要求

21. 为了合理评估集合型投资基金和其他间接持有资产的风险暴露，应当考虑其经济实质。保险机构应尽可能对投资工具进行穿透，评估其底层资产的风险。二级文件提供了穿透要求的具体指引。

3.4 信用评级

22. IAIS 制定了 ICS 信用评级和外部信用评级之间的对应关系。ICS 评级分为 1 级到 8 级。二级文件中具体规定 ICS 信用评级分类指引以及和外部机构评级的对应关系。

4 基准 ICS：评估范围

4.1 ICS 资产负债表的起点

23. ICS 评估可从保险集团旗下保险控股公司或者金融集团旗下金融控股公司经审计的 GAAP 合并资产负债表作为起点，经一系列调整得到。

24. 当保险集团没有经审计的 GAAP 合并资产负债表时，可以用法定财务报表简单加总作为集团层面资产负债表的起点。

25. 经审计的 GAAP 资产负债表分为两部分：

a. 保险实体以及与保险相关的实体；

b. 非保险实体。具体定义可参考二级文件。

26. GAAP 资产负债表应拆分列示保险实体和非保险实体，二级文件另有规定的情形除外。

27. 非保险实体（金融和非金融实体）应基于其类型和所在行业是否有资本监管要求来判断是否纳入 ICS 评估。非保险金融实体应基于所在行业的资本监管要求进行评估，没有行业资本监管要求的非保险金融实体和非金融实体，应基于二级文件 ICS 规定的方法进行评估。对于所有的非保险实体，实际资本应按照基准 ICS 的要求进行认定。

4.2 MAV 方法下的资产负债表

28. MAV 资产负债表由保险实体和与保险相关的实体组成。

29. MAV 资产负债表应基于二级文件以及本文件第 5 章的要求进行调整。

5 基准 ICS：MAV 方法

5.1 资产负债评估原则

30. MAV 基于经审计的 GAAP 合并报表或法定会计准则（SAP）的合并报表，并对以下项目进行调整：

a. 保险合同负债和再保险资产；

b. 金融投资资产和负债；

c. 递延所得税。

31. MAV 保险合同负债为当前估计与风险边际（MOCE）之和。当前估计和 MOCE 的计算方法详见以下章节和二级文件，对于保险合同负债可被资产组合完全复制的情况除外（详见第 5.4 节）。

32. 对 b 和 c 的调整详见二级文件。

5.2 当前估计

5.2.1 计算基础

33. 当前估计是指保险合同负债未来现金流现值的概率加权平均值，现值由未来现金流按照每项负债的货币种类和分档（Bucket）所对应的收益率曲线折现得到。负债可以分为三档（Three Bucket），详见第 5.2.5.3 节。

34. 当前估计不应包括任何隐性或显性的边际。

35. 再保险资产计算的方法和假设应与保险合同负债当前估计保持一致。

36. 保险合同负债评估不应考虑 IAIG 自身信用状况变化的影响。

37. 关于当前估计现金流预测具体方法详见二级文件。

5.2.2 合同确认、合同边界和预测期限

38. 保险合同的确认应自 IAIG 成为合同一方起，至合同相关的保险责任全部终止。当前估计仅应包括在评估日已被确认的所有保险合同。

39. 已确认保险合同仅应考虑合同边界内的未来保费，和与之相关的赔付和费用。

40. 当前估计的预测期限应为评估日已确认的保险合同和再保险合同的所有履约现金流的整个保险期间。

41. 合同确认和合同边界的具体规定详见二级文件。

5.2.3 数据质量和假设的设定方法

42. 当前估计计算应依赖最新的可信信息和合理的假设。当前估计应客观、全面，并基于可观测的输入数据。

43. 数据质量和模型假设的具体要求详见二级文件。

5.2.4 管理层行为

44. 当前估计计算可以认可客观、合理且有依据的管理行为。被认可的管理层行为不能违反 IAIG 与保单持有人约定的义务或法律条款。

45. 当前估计计算中管理层行为确认的要求详见二级文件。

5.2.5 折现方法

5.2.5.1 确定当前估计的折现率曲线

46. 计算当前估计时，保险合同负债应使用经调整后的收益率曲线进行折现。经调整后的收益率曲线为以下两者之和：

a. 风险调整后的高流动性利率互换或政府债券（无风险收益率曲线）；

b. 溢价调整。

5.2.5.2 确定无风险收益率曲线

47. 无风险收益率曲线由以下三段组成：

a. 第一段：基于政府债券或利率互换的市场信息，包括必要的信用风险调整；

b. 第二段：第一段和第三段间的插值；

c. 第三段：基于长期稳定的终极远期利率（LTFR），在此之上增加溢价以反映再投资可能赚取的预期额外收益。

48. 对任一币种，第一段曲线的长度应为一个信息充分透明，交易活跃的金融市场所能观察到的最长流动性期限（LOT）。

49. 对任一币种，LTFR 等于预期实际利率加上目标通胀率。

50. 为了确定预期实际利率，IAIS 按照宏观经济特征对国家（地区）进行分组。分入同一组的国家和地区适用相同的预期实际利率，该利率为基于某个期限内可观测实际利率的简单平均。

51. 预期实际利率和目标通胀率需每年回顾，以反映宏观经济预期的变化。但 IAIS 对 LTFR 每年的调整幅度设定了上限，以减缓波动。

52. 对任一币种，无风险收益率曲线由使用该货币的 IAIS 成员基于 IAIS 提供的参数和指引确定。

53. 无风险收益率曲线对应的货币列表，以及 LOT 相关信息、确定 LTFR 和 LTFR 溢价的参数和假设，包括对地域差异的考虑等，详见二级文件。

5.2.5.3 确定无风险收益率曲线的溢价

54. IAIS 收益率曲线基于无风险收益率曲线进行调整。该调整使用三档法（Three - Bucket Approach）确定。

55. 根据负债和支持该负债的资产的性质，三档法将负债分为低档、中档和高档。对每一档负债使用不同的溢价调整。

56. 负债分档标准及每一档溢价设定方法详见二级文件。

5.3 风险边际（MOCE）

5.3.1 定义和基本原则

57. MOCE 是指在保险责任的当前估计上所加的边际，以获得保险合同负债经市场调整后的估值。MOCE 应覆盖与保险责任相关现金流的所有内在不确定性。

5.3.2 计算方法

58. MOCE 使用正态分布给定的分位点来计算，该正态分布参数包括：

- 均值为寿险以及非寿险业务的当前估计；
- 99.5% 分位点为寿险以及非寿险业务风险资本。

59. 寿险和非寿险业务风险边际所使用的分位点要求详见二级文件。

5.3.3 MOCE 与 ICS 其他组成部分的关系

60. 所有基于压力情景或风险因子的计量仅考虑当前估计在压力前后的变化，MOCE 在压力下保持不变。MOCE 既不从 ICS 最低资本中扣除，也不增加实际资本。

5.4 可被资产组合复制的负债

61. 如果某保险责任的未来现金流可以用具有活跃市场报价的金融工具可靠地复制，那么与这些未来现金流相关的保险合同负债的估值可以基于这些金融工具市价来确定。

62. 该方法适用的其他条件详见二级文件。

6 基准 ICS：实际资本

6.1 一般规定

63. 实际资本基于 IAIG 的全部金融活动进行计量，包括合格资本工具和非资本工具项目。

64. 合格资本需按照 6.4 相关规定进行调整，所有扣减项目都需要从 ICS 最低资本计量中扣除。

65. ICS 实际资本分为两个层级：

- 一级资本指在持续经营和破产清算状态下均能吸收损失的资本工具和非资本工具的项目；
- 二级资本指仅在破产清算状态下吸收损失的资本工具和非资本工具的项目。

66. 认定合格资本工具时，应区分相互制和非相互制 IAIG。

6.2 资本工具分级

67. 资本工具按照 5 个关键原则进行分类：

- 损失吸收能力（持续经营和破产清算状态下）；
- 次级性；
- 存在性；
- 永久性；
- 非强制性。

68. 每级资本按照不同认可标准分别划分为两类：

- 一级资本：
    - 一级无限制资本工具；
    - 一级有限制资本工具。
- 二级资本：
    - 二级实缴资本工具；
    - 二级非实缴资本工具。

69. 表 2 按照认定资本工具的 5 个关键原则，列示了一级无限制资本工具、一级有限制资本工具和二级实缴资本工具的不同属性。

表2 资本工具分类的关键原则

关键原则	一级无限制资本工具	一级有限制资本工具	二级实缴资本工具
损失吸收能力	持续经营和破产清算状态下均能吸收损失	持续经营和破产清算状态下均能吸收损失	仅在破产清算状态下能够吸收损失
次级性	受偿顺序位列最末（即最先用于吸收损失）；受偿顺序位列保单持有人、其他非次级债权人、二级资本工具持有人和一级有限制资本工具持有人之后	受偿顺序位列保单持有人、其他非次级债权人、二级资本工具持有人之后	受偿顺序位列保单持有人、其他非次级债权人之后
存在性	全额实缴	全额实缴	全额实缴
永续性	永久的	永久的。对于相互制公司，下列情形也视同满足永久性原则：经监管批准，到期赎回可以递延；或具有锁定条款，且初始到期日足够长。不允许有赎回激励。经监管批准，发行人可在规定最短期限后赎回，或在任意时刻回购	初始到期日足够长，允许有赎回激励，但有效到期日后方可行使赎回权
非强制性	IAIG对于收益分配有全权处置权（即收益分配是非累计的）；取消收益分配不被视为违约	IAIG对于收益分配有全权处置权（即收益分配是非累计的）；取消收益分配不被视为违约	不进行本息支付不被视为违约

70. 对于二级实缴资本，次级性的形式既可以是合同约定，也可以是结构化的。结构化次级性资本工具应满足特定标准。

71. 二级非实缴资本仅限于相互制IAIG。按照规定，一旦该类资本成为实缴资本，需满足成为一级或二级实缴资本的属性。

72. 各级资本的属性详见二级文件。

6.3 非资本工具分级

6.3.1 一级资本项目

73. 按6.4.1节相关规定调整后，非资本工具一级资本包含以下项目：

a. 留存收益；

b. 一级资本工具发行时产生的股本溢价，以及来自利润以外其他形式的资本公积；

c. 累计其他综合收益（AOCI）；
d. 员工股权激励计划的公允价值，相关费用应按照会计准则计入损益；
e. 其他所有者权益，包括：
　　i. 少数股东/非控制权益（NCI）；
　　ii. 经审计财务报表转换为ICS资产负债表的调整项。

6.3.2　二级资本项目

74. 按第6.4.2节相关规定调整后，非资本工具二级资本包含以下项目：

a. 发行二级实缴资本工具产生的股本溢价；

b. 处置受限资产价值超过所对应表内负债价值与增加的ICS最低资本之和部分，相应的资产和负债从一级资本扣减（参见第6.4.3节处置受限资产的处理）；

c. 其他二级资本项目，包括以下一级资本扣减项的一定比例（参见第6.4.1节）：
　　i. 在IAIG的资产负债表中作为资产项的养老金固定收益计划的资产净额，并扣除递延所得税负债；
　　ii. 递延所得税资产；
　　iii. 计算机软件等无形资产的摊销净额，并扣减递延所得税负债。

75. 二级资本项目不得超过资本要求的一定比例。

76. 以上三项及总体被认可为二级资本的比例，在二级文件文档中作详细规定。

6.4　资本调整和扣减

6.4.1　一级资本扣减项

77. 一级资本的扣减项包含：

a. 商誉；

b. 无形资产，包括计算机软件；

c. 与养老金固定收益计划相关的资产负债表项目；

d. 递延所得税资产；

e. 导致一级资本虚增的金融机构之间直接或间接的交叉持股；

f. 对自有一级资本工具的直接或间接投资；

g. 被认定为非合格再保险形成的再保险资产；

h. 处置受限资产价值超过所对应负债价值、处置受限资产对应的最低资本及对应负债的最低资本之和的部分（参见第6.4.3节处置受限资产的处理）；

i. 集团并表范围以外的实体，IAIG拥有净资产和债务的价值。

78. 从a到c的各项目均为扣除递延所得税负债后的净额，即按照评估方法，当这些项目不被认可时，也不会产生相应的所得税负债。递延所得税负债可以与d项递延所得税资产互相抵消，前提是d不包括已经与a到c各项目进行抵消的金额。

6.4.2 二级资本扣减项

79. 以下项目需要从二级资本中扣减：

a. 导致二级资本虚增的金融机构之间直接或间接的交叉持股；

b. 对自有二级资本工具的直接或间接投资。

6.4.3 处置受限资产的处理

80. IAIG持有的处置受限资产价值超过其所对应负债与所对应最低资本的部分，需要在一级资本中进行调整。

81. 调整的细节详见二级文件。

82. 从一级资本扣减的处置受限资产可以计入二级资本，但应满足二级资本的认可上限（具体参见第6.5节资本构成比例）。

6.5 资本构成比例

83. 经调整后的一级有限制资本和二级资本需满足一定比例的限制。该限制对于相互制和非相互制IAIG有所不同，具体详见二级文件。

84. 在咨询监管联席会议的意见后，集团主监管机构可以对相互制IAIG的一级有限制资本工具的比例采用临时的宽限政策，前提是该相互制IAIG已提交资本改善的计划。

85. 超过比例限制的一级有限制资本可以作为二级资本，并需满足二级资本的限制条件。

7 基准ICS：最低资本—标准法

7.1 风险分类和基本计量方法

86. 标准法的风险大类包括：保险风险、市场风险、信用风险和操作风险。表3列出了这些风险大类以及下设的子风险。

87. ICS最低资本是应对非预期变化、事件或其他特定风险对实际资本产生的潜在不利影响所需的资本数额。

88. 风险计量采用两种方法：情景法和因子法。但自然灾害风险除外，可以采用外部供应商模型。

89. 情景法采用的是动态方法，观察压力前和压力后的资产负债表：每项风险的资本要求由压力前后资产负债表的实际资本减少额来确定。为简化起见，用净资产的变动来代替实际资本的变动。

90. 因子法由风险暴露乘以相应风险因子进行计算。

91. ICS最低资本所包含的风险类别以及所适用的计算方法如表3所示。

表3　风险、定义和计量方法

风险大类	子风险	范围/定义（导致实际资本发生不利变化的风险原因）	计量方法
保险风险	死亡风险（寿险）	死亡发生率的水平、趋势或波动性的非预期变化①	情景法
	长寿风险（寿险）	死亡发生率的水平、趋势或波动性的非预期改变	情景法
	疾病/失能风险（寿险）	伤残/疾病发生率的水平、趋势或波动性的非预期变化	情景法
	退保风险（寿险）	保单失效、终止、续保、退保的水平或波动性的非预期变化	情景法
	费用风险（寿险）	费用发生非预期变化	情景法
	保费风险（非寿险）	未来保险事件发生的时间、频率、严重度的非预期变化（不含已在疾病/残疾风险覆盖的部分）	因子法
	准备金风险（非寿险）	已经发生（无论是否已向IAIG报案）和尚未结案的赔案或者事件的非预期变化（不含已在疾病/残疾风险覆盖的部分）	因子法
	巨灾风险	低频高损失事件的非预期变化	情景法（自然灾害使用模型法）
市场风险	利率风险	利率的水平或波动性的非预期变化	情景法
	非违约利差风险	利差的水平或波动性的非预期变化（不包含违约利差部分）	情景法
	权益风险	权益市场价格的水平或者波动性的非预期变化	情景法
	房地产风险	房地产市场价格水平或者波动性的非预期变化或者房地产投资现金流时间和金额的非预期变化	情景法
	汇率风险	汇率的水平、波动性的非预期变化	情景法
	资产集中度风险	资产组合缺少分散化的风险	因子法
信用风险	信用风险	实际违约以及债务人的信用状况恶化的非预期变化，包括评级迁移或实际违约带来的信用利差风险	因子法
操作风险	操作风险	由于不完善的内部操作流程、人员、系统或外部事件而导致直接或间接损失的风险。操作风险包括法律风险，但不包括战略风险和声誉风险	因子法

92. 各项风险资本要求之间考虑风险分散效应，通过相关系数矩阵聚合。

93. ICS的校准原则是在一年的时间期限内，99.5%置信水平下，IAIG实际资本不利变动的在险价值（VaR）。

7.1.1 风险缓释

94. 为促进良好的风险管理、达到适当的风险敏感度，ICS认可风险缓释技术的影

---

① 预期的变化已在资产负债评估中考虑。

响，但必须符合某些标准，以确保风险缓释技术在资本要求中得到准确和适当的反映。标准详见二级文件。

95. 认可风险缓释展期需满足特定条件，认可条件根据风险缓释安排是否应用于市场风险暴露或非寿险保费风险有所不同，详见二级文件。

7.1.2 地区划分

96. 部分风险计量考虑地域差异。地域划分详见二级文件。

7.1.3 管理层行为

97. 公司管理层行为可以对ICS各风险资本要求进行部分抵减，但受上限约束，详见二级文件。

7.2 保险风险

7.2.1 寿险保险风险保单分组

98. 寿险保险风险最低资本适用的不利情景应以具有同质风险的保险合同组合作为计量单元。详见二级文件。

7.2.2 寿险保险风险最低资本计算

99. 寿险保险风险最低资本适用于寿险业务，以及类似寿险的健康险业务（参阅第108段）。

100. 寿险保险风险最低资本使用寿险风险相关系数矩阵，对以下5类子风险最低资本进行聚合（详见二级文件）：

- 死亡发生率风险；
- 长寿风险；
- 疾病/失能发生率风险；
- 退保风险；
- 费用风险。

101. 寿险保险风险最低资本根据二级文件中指定的地区划分计算。

102. 对每一类子风险，都需计算考虑管理层行为前以及考虑管理层行为后的最低资本。

7.2.2.1 死亡发生率风险

103. 死亡发生率风险最低资本为施加死亡发生率压力前后净资产的变化值。压力情景分地区设置，详见二级文件。

104. 死亡发生率风险最低资本仅适用于因死亡发生率上升而受到不利影响的保单。

7.2.2.2 长寿风险

105. 长寿风险最低资本为施加死亡发生率压力前后净资产的变化值。压力情景分地区设置，详见二级文件。

106. 长寿风险最低资本仅适用于因死亡发生率降低而受到不利影响的保单。

7.2.2.3 疾病/失能发生率风险

107. 疾病/失能发生率风险最低资本等于对四种互不相关的赔付责任类型施加指定压力前后净资产的变化值。压力情景分地区,责任类型和合同期限设置,详见二级文件。

108. 寿险业务和非寿险业务可能具有相似的疾病/失能赔付责任,疾病/失能发生率风险最低资本仅适用于类似寿险的疾病/失能赔付责任,二级文件中提供了示例。对于类似非寿险业务的疾病/失能赔付责任,适用非寿险风险(保费风险和准备金风险)最低资本。

7.2.2.4 退保风险

109. 退保风险最低资本为退保率风险(包含水平和趋势风险)最低资本与大规模退保风险最低资本两者中的较大值。

110. 退保风险最低资本和大规模退保风险最低资本为施加指定压力前后净资产的变化值。压力情景分地区设置,详见二级文件。

111. 退保风险最低资本应考虑所有可能改变未来现金流的法律或合同约定的选择权。

7.2.2.5 费用风险

112. 费用风险最低资本等于对单位费用和通胀率假设同时施加指定压力前后净资产的变化值。压力情景分地区设置,详见二级文件。

7.2.3 非寿险保险风险最低资本计算

113. 非寿险保险风险最低资本适用于非寿险业务及类似非寿险业务的健康险业务。

114. 非寿险保险风险最低资本包括保费风险最低资本和准备金风险最低资本。非寿险保险风险最低资本使用因子法计量,风险因子分地区、分业务类型设置,详见二级文件。准备金风险最低资本包括潜在责任风险。

115. 非寿险保险风险最低资本分地区、分业务类型计量,使用相关系数矩阵进行聚合,相关系数矩阵详见二级文件。非寿险保险风险最低资本计量考虑以下风险分散效应:

- 保费风险与准备金风险的分散效应;
- ICS业务大类内各子类的分散效应;
- 地区内业务大类之间的分散效应;
- 地区间的分散效应。

116. 保费风险最低资本和准备金风险最低资本按二级文件中规定的地区分类计量。对于某些地区,各地区分类下子业务类型的划分参考当地法定报告要求设置。

7.2.4 巨灾风险最低资本计算

117. 巨灾风险应同时覆盖寿险业务和非寿险业务,指未来12个月内,发生概率低,但发生后会造成重大损失的风险。巨灾风险计量应覆盖巨灾事件发生时公司所有的有效业务。

118. 风险缓释措施（如安排再保分出）可以降低巨灾风险最低资本。

119. 巨灾风险分为自然风险（自然巨灾）和人为风险（其他巨灾）。

120. 巨灾风险带来的损失包括主要灾害损失（如飓风、地震），及与主要灾害有关的所有次生灾害损失。主要灾害和次生灾害的具体示例详见二级文件。

121. 巨灾风险类型、压力情景、风险缓释认可要求及自然巨灾计量模型的审慎性要求，详见二级文件。

7.3 市场风险

7.3.1 市场风险最低资本计算

122. 市场风险最低资本可通过聚合以下 6 类子风险最低资本得到，相关性系数矩阵见二级文件：

- 利率风险；
- 非违约利差风险；
- 权益风险；
- 不动产风险；
- 汇率风险；
- 集中度风险。

123. 计算市场风险最低资本时，应考虑以下影响：

- 指定压力情景对资产和负债价值的直接影响；
- 指定压力情景引起的保单持有人行为变化的间接影响。

124. 对每一个市场风险子风险，都需计算考虑管理层行为前以及考虑管理层行为后的最低资本。

7.3.2 利率风险

125. 利率风险最低资本基于各币种无风险收益率曲线的以下 5 种压力情景的组合进行计量：

- 均值回归情景；
- 水平向上情景；
- 水平向下情景；
- 扭转上下情景；
- 扭转下上情景。

126. 5 种压力情景的具体介绍详见二级文件。压力情景只适用于利率敏感的资产和负债，相关资产和负债的确认标准详见二级文件。因市场环境导致保单持有人行为的变化也应考虑在内，具体要求见二级文件。

127. IAIG 持有的所有币种的利率敏感资产和负债需要计算压力情景的影响，聚合得到利率风险最低资本。风险暴露较小的多个币种可以合并为一组进行计算。

128. 各币种风险暴露的重要性测试，以及 5 种压力情景、币种之间的聚合方法，详见二级文件。

7.3.3 非违约利差风险

129. 非违约利差风险同时考虑利差对资产端和负债端的双向压力，非违约利差风险最低资本为利差向上压力和利差向下压力两者的较大值（不低于零）。

130. 利差向下压力包括相对压力和绝对压力的组合，加压后利差不能为负。利差向上压力仅包括绝对压力。

131. 压力情景要求和资产负债的适用范围，详见二级文件。

7.3.4 权益风险

132. 权益风险最低资本为施加权益价格水平和波动性压力前后净资产的变化值。权益价格水平压力情景分资产类型设置，波动性压力不区分资产类型，统一设置，且允许考虑管理层行为。压力情景设置详见二级文件。

133. 所有对权益价格水平或波动性变化敏感的资产和负债（直接和间接），需计算权益风险最低资本，详见二级文件。

134. 在二级文件中，计算权益风险最低资本的资产分为以下几类：

- 发达市场上市权益；
- 新兴市场上市权益；
- 混合资本债/优先股；
- 其他权益。

7.3.5 房地产风险

135. 房地产风险最低资本为施加房地产价格压力前后净资产的变化值，且允许考虑管理层行为。压力情景设置详见二级文件。

136. 房地产压力情景适用于所有直接和间接面临房地产价格风险的资产，不区分商业房地产、住宅房地产和自用房地产。

7.3.6 汇率风险

137. 汇率风险最低资本为 IAIG 持有的外币资产和负债在两种压力情景下损失的较大值。汇率风险压力情景仅基于单一币种的净风险敞口计量。

138. 净风险敞口考虑所有直接和间接面临外汇风险的资产。如果当地监管机构对该币种交易有特定资本要求，可以从净风险敞口中扣除，但受指定上限约束。

139. 汇率风险的两种压力情景是：

- 情景 1：IAIG 持有的所有净空头的货币价值保持不变，所有净多头的货币价值下降。

- 情景2：IAIG持有的所有净多头的货币价值保持不变，所有净空头的货币价值上升。

140. 每一种压力情景下，都需要使用二级文件中的相关性系数矩阵进行聚合。

141. 每一币种的压力情景、聚合矩阵以及净风险敞口的确定，在二级文件中有进一步的说明。

7.3.7 集中度风险

142. 集中度风险最低资本是由于IAIG持有资产未充分分散，在市场风险和信用风险最低资本之上需额外计提的一项增量资本。独立账户（投资风险完全由保单持有人承担的寿险保险合同①）资产除外。

143. 对于房地产投资，超过特定阈值的资产敞口需计算集中度风险。具体要求详见二级文件。

7.4 信用风险

7.4.1 信用风险最低资本计算

144. 信用风险最低资本是将指定的风险因子作用于信用风险净敞口金额计算得到的。计算信用风险最低资本时应考虑管理层行为。

145. 风险因子根据风险暴露类别、评级类别和到期期限设置。风险暴露类别及相应的风险因子详见二级文件。

7.4.2 合格抵押品、担保和信用衍生工具

146. 确定信用风险净敞口金额时，可以考虑抵押和担保。二级文件详述了抵押品、担保和信用衍生工具的认定标准。

7.4.3 外部评级使用要求

147. 外部信用评级可被用于计算信用风险最低资本，前提是评级机构已在足够长的时间内发布信用违约和评级迁移的统计信息，并满足以下6项标准，即客观性、独立性、国际对外公开/透明度、信息披露、资源充足性和公信力。上述标准及统计信息要求的公开年限，将在二级文件中详述。

148. 根据第147段使用外部信用评级时，将关联对应至第3.4节所述的ICS评级类别，具体内容将在二级文件中详述。

149. IAIG可使用当地偿付能力计量中由本国保险监管机构认可的信用评级，但须遵守本国保险监管机构提供的该评级与ICS评级的对应关系，且得到IAIS认可。

7.4.4 监管认可评级（SOCCA）使用要求

150. SOCCA流程是一项独立、客观的信用风险评估流程，由本国监管部门制定并管理，且由本国监管机构确认适用于信用风险最低资本计量。例如，美国保险监督官协会

---

① 不考虑在投资账户之上，向投保人提供的其他保证：如变额年金产品。

（NAIC）的信用评级流程被认可为 SOCCA。ICS 认可的 SOCCA 流程标准将在二级文件中详述。

151. 在 ICS 监测期结束时，IAIS 将决定 SOCCA 流程是否可纳入由本国监管机构自主决定的 ICS 标准方法或其他方法①。在计算 ICS 充足率时，可使用 SOCCA 流程计算的 IAIG 信用风险最低资本。

152. 如果将 SOCCA 流程纳入 ICS 标准方法，在多个评级可用的情况下，IAIG 须采用 ICS 标准法②所规定的评级确认方法。如果将 SOCCA 流程纳入其他方法，无论是否有其他可用评级，IAIG 均可使用 SOCCA 评级。

7.5 操作风险

153. 操作风险最低资本由风险暴露及其对应的风险因子确定。

154. 操作风险的风险因子分地区以及以下业务线设置：

- 非寿险业务——不以人身为保险标的的保险或不类似于寿险的健康险，通常指财产险业务或者一般保险业务；
- 寿险（承担风险）——以人身为保险标的的保险或与寿险类似的健康险，保险人承担投资风险；
- 寿险（不承担风险）——投保人承担投资风险的产品，它包括独立账户和账户型累积年金。

155. 操作风险最低资本计量所需的风险因子、风险暴露和各业务分类详见二级文件。

7.6 最低资本聚合

156. ICS 最低资本采用多层级聚合：

- 第一层级为大类风险使用相关系数矩阵进行聚合，包括寿险保险风险、非寿险保险风险、巨灾风险、市场风险、信用风险和操作风险；
- 第二层级为寿险风险、巨灾风险和市场风险的子风险使用相关系数矩阵进行聚合；
- 第三层级为单项子风险使用相关系数矩阵进行聚合，如利率风险、非寿险风险等。

157. 最低资本的聚合基于风险之间的相关性，反映各风险之间的分散效应。

158. ICS 设置了寿险风险和市场风险子风险的相关系数矩阵，寿险风险、非寿险风险、巨灾风险、市场风险和信用风险的相关系数矩阵，最后加总操作风险最低资本得到

---

① 其他方法是指 ICS 最低资本要求计算的标准方法之外的其他方法。ICS 最低资本要求计算的其他方法需在监测结束前经监管审阅批准后确认方可采用。

② 在标准方法下，如果同一风险暴露有多个评级（对应不同的 ICS 评级类别），则应选用次高评级的 ICS 类别。为保证可比性，评级应基于金融工具的面值而非购买价格。对于无评级的资产，需使用 SOCCA 评级。

总的最低资本。

159. 相关系数矩阵具体设置详见二级文件，各层级风险的聚合方法在一级文件和二级文件的相应章节进行规定。

8 基准 ICS：税的计量

8.1 一般原则

160. 公认会计准则或法定准则合并资产负债表中确认的递延所得税项也可在 ICS 资产负债表中确认，确认应满足第 5 章相关要求。

161. ICS 中税的影响主要有以下两个方面：

- 公认会计准则合并资产负债表与 ICS 资产负债表之间的评估差异（ICS 调整）；以及

- 最低资本要求。

162. ICS 采用自上而下的方法，使用集团有效税率（Effective Tax Rate，ETR）计算 ICS 调整及最低资本的递延所得税影响。

163. 计算集团 ETR 的方法详见二级文件。

8.2 ICS 调整的所得税影响

164. 公认会计准则或法定准则资产负债表至 ICS 资产负债表的调整项将带来递延所得税资产、递延所得税负债变化。由于资产负债表调整产生的递延所得税资产，应进行可用性评估。相关递延所得税资产的认可条件、计算方法、可用性评估方法、是否可正负抵消等均在二级文件中进行规定。

8.3 最低资本的所得税影响

165. ICS 最低资本计量应考虑税的缓释作用。ICS 最低资本的税收缓释作用来自瞬时运营损失导致的递延所得税资产增加，等价于考虑风险分散及管理层行为后的税前最低资本。递延所得税资产增额需进行可用性评估，具体方法详见二级文件。

9 附加报告

166. ICS 2.0 包含附加报告，集团主监管机构可以自主选择是否报送 GAAP + 或其他方法下的 ICS 结果。

167. 如《吉隆坡协议》所述，"ICS 2.0 中的基准 ICS 方法和集团主监管机构可选择的附加报告是同等重要的组成部分。GAAP + 和其他计算 ICS 资本要求的方法都是可行的选择，这些都将在监测期结束时决定是否纳入 ICS"。

9.1 GAAP + 方法

168. GAAP + 最大限度地利用经审计的合并财务报告、系统和流程，包括由国际会计准则委员会（IASB）和其他准则制定机构颁布的各类公认会计准则。这些针对公认会计准则的调整是出于审慎目的,影响资产负债表上重大科目。

169. GAAP+与各国会计准则密切相关,其中一些准则目前正在修订(如国际财务报告准则和美国公认会计准则)。这些修订将促进各国评估的进一步趋同。但是,考虑到新规则的施行时间,GAAP+方法需要在2020年以后继续修改完善。此外,中国GAAP+方法由于只开展了一年实地测试,还在研究阶段。因此,适用于国际财务报告准则、美国和中国的GAAP+将在监测期内继续研究和进行实地测试。从2020年开始,日本的GAAP+将与基准ICS方法一同进入5年监测期。

170. 关于GAAP+报告的更多细节详见二级文件。

9.2 其他方法

171. 监测期内附加报告中其他方法的范围仅限于最低资本。也就是说,ICS的资产负债评估方法和资本分级不会因使用其他方法而改变,其结果与ICS标准法一致。其他方法应与标准法具有相同的风险置信水平,标准法为一年时间期限内置信区间为99.5%的VaR。此外,其他方法必须遵循《保险核心原则》和ICS各项原则。

172. 在监测期内,集团主监管机构可以在附加报告中选择采用如下其他方法:

- 内部模型法;
- 动态对冲;
- SOCCA:在监测期结束时,IAIS将决定SOCCA是否作为ICS标准法的一部分,或纳入其他方法。

173. 在监测期结束时,IAIS将决定其他方法是否可作为ICS的监管资本要求PCR实施。

三、全球保险资本标准（ICS）2.0版本 二级文件

目 录

1 介绍 ·· 78
2 ICS 2.0 监测期 ··· 78
3 一般指导原则 ·· 78
   3.1 实质重于形式 ··· 78
   3.2 匹配性原则 ·· 78
   3.3 穿透要求 ·· 78
   3.4 信用评级 ·· 78
4 基准 ICS：评估范围 ··· 79
   4.1 ICS 资产负债表的起点 ·· 79
   4.2 MAV 方法下的资产负债表 ··· 80
5 基准 ICS：MAV 方法 ··· 80
   5.1 资产负债评估原则 ·· 80
   5.2 保险合同负债的当前估计 ·· 81
      5.2.1 计算基础和现金流预测 ·· 81
      5.2.2 合同确认、合同边界和预测期限 ······································ 83
      5.2.3 数据质量和假设的设定方法 ·· 83
      5.2.4 管理层行为 ·· 83
      5.2.5 折现方法 ·· 84
   5.3 风险边际（MOCE） ··· 91
      5.3.1 定义和基本原则 ·· 91
      5.3.2 计算方法 ·· 91
      5.3.3 MOCE 与 ICS 其他组成部分的关系 ································ 91
   5.4 可被资产组合复制的负债 ·· 91
6 基准 ICS：实际资本 ··· 91
   6.1 一般规定 ·· 91
   6.2 资本工具分级 ·· 91
      6.2.1 一级无限制资本工具 ·· 91
      6.2.2 一级有限制资本工具 ·· 92
      6.2.3 二级资本工具（非结构次级性工具） ······························ 93
      6.2.4 二级资本工具（结构次级性工具） ·································· 94
      6.2.5 非实缴二级资本 ·· 95

6.3 非资本工具分级 ... 95
6.3.1 一级资本项目 ... 95
6.3.2 二级资本项目 ... 96
6.4 资本调整和扣减 ... 96
6.4.1 一级资本扣减项 ... 96
6.4.2 二级资本扣减项 ... 96
6.4.3 处置受限资产的处理 ... 96
6.5 资本构成比例 ... 96

7 基准 ICS：最低资本—标准法 ... 96
7.1 风险分类和基本计量方法 ... 96
7.1.1 风险缓释 ... 96
7.1.2 地区划分 ... 98
7.1.3 管理层行为 ... 99
7.2 保险风险 ... 99
7.2.1 寿险保险风险保单分组 ... 99
7.2.2 寿险保险风险最低资本计算 ... 100
7.2.3 非寿险保险风险最低资本计算 ... 104
7.2.4 巨灾风险最低资本计算 ... 113
7.3 市场风险 ... 116
7.3.1 市场风险最低资本计算 ... 116
7.3.2 利率风险 ... 117
7.3.3 非违约利差风险 ... 119
7.3.4 权益风险 ... 120
7.3.5 房地产风险 ... 121
7.3.6 汇率风险 ... 122
7.3.7 集中度风险 ... 126
7.4 信用风险 ... 127
7.4.1 信用风险最低资本计算 ... 127
7.4.2 合格抵押品、担保和信用衍生工具 ... 135
7.4.3 外部评级使用要求 ... 141
7.4.4 监管认可评级（SOCCA）使用要求 ... 143
7.5 操作风险 ... 143
7.6 最低资本聚合 ... 144
7.7 非保险最低资本要求 ... 145

8 基准ICS：税的计量 ··· 145
　8.1 一般原则 ·· 145
　8.2 ICS 调整的所得税影响 ·· 145
　　8.2.1 ICS 调整确认的 DTA 的可用性评估 ···································· 146
　8.3 最低资本的所得税影响 ·· 146
　　8.3.1 a：税收损失结转 ·· 146
　　8.3.2 b：压力下未来应税收入预测 ·· 147
　　8.3.3 c 和 d：递延税项 ·· 147
9 附加报告 ··· 147
　9.1 GAAP＋方法 ·· 147
　　9.1.1 概述 ·· 147
　　9.1.2 日本 GAAP＋方法 ·· 148
　9.2 其他方法 ·· 152
　　9.2.1 内部模型法 ·· 152
　　9.2.2 动态对冲 ·· 158
术语表 ·· 159
附录1：无表决权利益实体的处理（资产和保险证券化） ························ 161
附件2：ICS 非寿险业务分类 ·· 163

1 介绍

同一级文件。

2 ICS 2.0 监测期

同一级文件。

3 一般指导原则

3.1 实质重于形式

同一级文件。

3.2 匹配性原则

同一级文件。

3.3 穿透要求

1. 穿透法适用于保险安排和间接投资（包括无杠杆共同基金、其他集合型投资工具等），以识别此类安排或投资中所有潜在风险，包括可能虚增国际活跃保险集团（IAIG）实际资本的风险。

2. 当无法进行全部穿透时，可以使用部分穿透，具体可参考巴塞尔协议Ⅲ框架[①]相关指引。

3. 当完全不能穿透时，为达到计算 ICS 最低资本要求的目的，可将整个投资视为未上市股权计量最低资本。

3.4 信用评级

4. ICS 信用评级分类和外部国际评级机构的评级对应关系如表 1 所示。AM Best 的评级只能用于计算再保险风险暴露的最低资本。外部国际评级的 + 或 - 等级不影响 ICS 信用评级分类的对应关系。在表 1 一个单元格内同时列出两个评级的情况下，第一个代表长期评级，第二个代表短期评级。短期评级仅用于剩余期限为一年或更短的资本工具。

表 1　ICS 信用评级分类对应关系（不适用于已违约的金融工具）

ICS 信用评级分类	标准普尔	穆迪	惠誉	JCR	R&I	DBRS	贝氏
1	AAA	Aaa	AAA	AAA	AAA	AAA	
2	AA/A-1	Aa/P-1	AA/F1	AA/J-1	AA/a-1	AA/R-1	A+
3	A/A-2	A/P-2	A/F2	A/J-2	A/a-2	A/R-2	A

① http://www.bis.org/publ/bcbs266.htm.

续表

ICS 信用评级分类	标准普尔	穆迪	惠誉	JCR	R&I	DBRS	贝氏
4	BBB/A–3	Baa/P–3	BBB/F3	BBB/J–3	BBB/a–3	BBB/R–3	B+
5	BB	Ba	BB	BB	BB	BB	B
6	B/B	B/NP	B/B	B/NJ	B/b	B/R–4	C+
7	CCC/C 及以下	Caa 及以下	CCC/C 及以下	CCC 及以下	CCC/c 及以下	CCC/R–5 及以下	C 及以下

5. 此外，IAIG 可使用本地银行监管机构根据巴塞尔Ⅱ框架认定的外部信用评估机构（ECAI）的评级结果。此类机构评级与 ICS 信用评级分类，可根据巴塞尔Ⅱ框架下已制定的评级对应关系进行对应（评级 AAA 级或 AA 级均对应为 ICS 信用评级分类 2）。

6. 表 1 中的 ICS 信用评级分类 1 至 4 为投资级。

7. ICS 信用评级分类的使用具体要求见第 7.4.3 节。

4 基准 ICS：评估范围

4.1 ICS 资产负债表的起点

8. ICS 的评估范围为 IAIG 合并报表中所有的法人实体。

9. ICS 资产负债表的起点为 IAIG 的 GAAP 合并资产负债表，具体参见《国际保险集团监管共同框架》（ComFrame）。对于没有合并资产负债表的实体，参见第 15 段。

10. 资产负债表应分为保险实体及保险相关实体、非保险实体两个部分。保险实体及保险相关实体包括：

a. 保险人：保险公司法人实体或保险集团；

b. 保险公司法人实体：指经主管部门授权许可展业，并受其监管的法人实体，包括它的分支机构；

c. 保险相关实体：主要是支持保险人展业的法人实体。

11. 为进行某些不同于 GAAP 的会计调整，并对非保险部分设置最低资本要求，合并资产负债表中涉及的法人实体根据以下定义进行分类：

a. 保险人和保险相关实体；

b. 受监管的非保险金融实体；

c. 不受监管的非保险金融实体；

d. 非金融实体。

12. ICS 基于 GAAP 会计准则进行并表，但以下情况除外：

a. 对于根据 GAAP 确定为合营企业、联营企业①的保险人和保险相关实体，应采用

---

① 合营企业、联营企业指各方对企业有共同控制权，对企业净资产享有共同权利的一种合营安排。

比例合并法进行并表。如经集团主监管机构确认采用比例法不可行，保险人和保险相关实体可不作调整，仍按 GAAP 下的权益法进行并表。

b. 对于根据 GAAP 确定为联合经营主体①的保险人和保险相关实体，其财务报告已确认各方资产、负债和交易，各方共享部分按照各自份额确认，该实体无须调整（已按比例合并法并表）。

c. 对于根据 GAAP 确定为联合经营主体的非保险金融实体和非金融实体，其财务报告已确认各方资产、负债和交易，各方共享部分按照各自份额确认，但在 ICS 中应改为权益法并表。

d. 对于根据 GAAP 确定为合营企业、联营企业的非保险金融实体和非金融实体，采用权益法进行并表。

13. 无表决权利益实体②的调整项目如下：

a. 对 GAAP 确定为不在并表范围内的无表决权利益实体，如果 IAIG 或者集团主监管机构评估后认定，该实体或此类实体合计将对集团产生重大影响③，则应在 ICS 中进行并表。

b. 符合附录 1 "集团内部发起的资产证券化"全部条件的实体，不强制要求并表。

c. 对满足以上条件未进行并表的实体，如集团主监管机构认定该实体的风险实质、规模以及复杂程度可能带来重大影响，该实体应进行并表。

14. 其他非 GAAP 调整：如果赔付已结清，且非寿险公司的风险取决于寿险公司（含保障基金，如有）是否有足够支付能力，则与第三方机构签订的结构性结算协议可以净额认可（在准备金和应收分保准备金中扣减）。

15. 累加资产负债表：当 IAIG 无合并财务报表或集团层面财务报表时，可将对母公司及子公司财务数据累加作为 ICS 资产负债表的起点。

4.2 MAV 方法下的资产负债表

同一级文件。

5 基准 ICS：MAV 方法

5.1 资产负债评估原则

16. 在对保险合同负债、再保险资产、金融资产和金融负债、递延所得税进行调整

---

① 联合经营主体指有共同控制权的合营各方根据协议安排对合营资产、负债享有权利的一种合营安排。
② 无表决权利益实体是指在评估控制权时，表决权等类似权益不是确定控制权归属主要因素的实体。该类实体一般是轻资本或无资本，为特殊目的而存在的（如特殊目的实体，结构化实体，普通合伙/有限合伙结构，信托，合伙企业）。
③ 重大影响，在本文中指集团面临的风险。在考虑哪些关联实体会对集团产生重大影响时，可通过评估关联实体总资产或总营业收入是否超过集团总资产或总营业收入的 1%。此外，如果所有的非重要性实体合计资产、营业收入超过集团总资产或营业收入的 5% 以上时，为防止遗漏重大风险，这些实体应当被合并。

时，IAIG 应遵循以下原则：

a. 自用房地产按照 GAAP 公允价值计量指引调整为公允价值，如 IAIG 不编制 GAAP 合并资产负债表，则按照其所在国家（地区）的 GAAP 公允价值计量原则进行调整。

b. 按揭与贷款按照 GAAP 公允价值计量指引调整为公允价值，如 IAIG 不编制 GAAP 合并资产负债表，则按照其所在国家（地区）的 GAAP 公允价值计量原则进行调整。

c. 再保险资产按照与保险合同负债一致的基础进行计量。已支付和未支付的再保余额应扣除预计不可回收金额。

d. 递延所得税资产（DTA）和递延所得税负债（DTL）根据第 7.7 节处理。

e. 递延保单获取成本和其他递延费用：资产负债表中的递延保单获取成本和其他递延费用在报告日当天应调整为零。与未来保费相关的获取成本（需在合同边界内，详见第 5.2.2 节）应体现在保险合同负债中。

f. 应收保费：应收日在报告日之后的，应收保费应作为现金流入体现在保险合同负债计量中。应收日在报告日之前的，不属于保险合同负债的一部分，应在资产负债表上作为资产认可。

g. 保单贷款：单独列报，不在保险合同负债中扣除。

h. 金融负债：基于 IAIG 的 GAAP 财务报告计量，不因 IAIG 自身的信用状况变化而调整。

5.2 保险合同负债的当前估计

5.2.1 计算基础和现金流预测

5.2.1.1 总体考虑

17. 当前估计是所有可能情景下的未来现金流的概率加权现值，考虑以下不确定性：

a. 赔付事件发生的时间、频率和严重性；

b. 赔付金额和赔付通胀，如赔付金额与特定指数关联，也包括相关指数的不确定性；

c. 理赔所需时间；

d. 费用金额；

e. 保单持有人行为。

18. 现金流预测需要反映未来人口结构、法律环境、医疗科技、社会和经济发展的变化，并基于适当的通胀率假设，包括公司可能遇到的不同类型通胀。如适用，保费调整相关的条款也需考虑在内。

19. 当前估计需包括再保险和特殊目的载体（SPV）。再保险摊回和 SPV 单独计算并确认为资产。

20. 预测现金流在合同边界内至少包括以下项目：

a. 保单责任赔付；

b. 直接和间接费用；

c. 实收保费；

d. 除了再保险和 SPV 以外的代位支付和追偿；

e. 理赔产生的其他费用。

21. 所有报告日已生效合同、未生效但已确认合同的相关费用都应计入当前估计。计入未生效已确认合同费用，主要为体现 IAIG 未来将承保相关合同。未确认业务或其他未来新业务相关费用无须计入当前估计。

22. 如未来现金流预测与未来投资收益相关，IAIG 应使用 IAIS 规定的收益率曲线进行假设。

5.2.1.2 选择权与保证利益

23. 当前估计须考虑保单内嵌的选择权和保证利益相关的预期现金流。选择权与保证利益估计需考虑与承保风险相关的所有支付，包括分红。

24. 所有选择权与保证利益的估计应基于无套利定价方法①，使用调整后的收益率曲线近似无风险利率曲线。

5.2.1.3 保单持有人行为

25. 如适用，未来现金流预测应反映合同赋予保单持有人的改变保单责任金额、时间或性质的权利。

26. 未来现金流应前瞻性地考虑保单持有人行使合同权利的可能性，包括退保、失效等，特别需考虑以下因素：

a. 保单持有人行为如何随公司管理层行为变化而变化，包括过往实际经验和未来预期；

b. 给定情况下，保单持有人行使相关权利会带来什么利益；

c. 经济环境。

27. 保单持有人行为假设应基于合理的统计和经验数据，并反映对未来的合理预期。

28. 保单持有人行为假设应基于 IAIS 给定的收益率曲线设置。

5.2.1.4 非保证利益

29. 未来非保证利益（FDB）包括所有非保证的责任给付，如 IAIG 投资收益或承保利润按照法定或合同约定分配给保单持有人的利益。

30. 当前估计仅应纳入与负债评估所使用的经济情景、保单持有人的合理预期一致的 FDB。

31. 预测 FDB，应与保单评估折现率曲线和保单持有人行为模型（详见第 5.2.1.3 节）保持一致。

---

① 如适用，选择权和保证利益估计需考虑路径依赖。

5.2.2 合同确认、合同边界和预测期限

32. 自 IAIG 成为合同的缔约一方，且不可能改变或取消合同，保险合同即需要进行确认和评估。即使保险责任尚未开始，如满足以上条件，也应进行确认和评估。

33. 当合同的所有可能赔付都已完成，所有未来现金流为零时，合同不再被确认。

34. 当前估计仅应考虑报告日确认的保险合同，不包括未来新业务。

35. 当前估计现金流预测应考虑与确认合同相关的所有义务，包括确认合同的未来保费收入。以下任一日期后的保费（及与之相关的赔付和费用）不在当前估计中考虑，IAIG 证明其能够要求保单持有人持续交费的情况除外：

a. IAIG 根据合同有权单方面决定终止合同或拒收应缴保费的日期；

b. IAIG 根据合同有权单方面决定调整应缴保费或收益，以使得保费充分反映风险的日期。

36. 以上规则对团险保单同样适用。如果团险保单的整体保费可以由 IAIG 单方面调整以充分反映风险，也适用上述条件 b。

5.2.3 数据质量和假设的设定方法

37. 为计算当前估计，选择经验数据时，IAIG 应考虑：

a. 基于准确度、完整度和适当性评估数据质量；

b. 收集和处理数据时使用的方法和假设；

c. 数据更新频率，需要进行额外更新的触发条件。

38. 如果 IAIG 自身的经验数据有限且可信度不高，IAIG 应积极通过其他渠道收集数据进行补充。如果 IAIG 自身经营的业务特点与外部数据所对应的业务不同，应对外部数据做出适当调整以保证其与 IAIG 业务风险特征保持一致。

39. 当前估计所使用的假设，应为基于所有当前可用信息对未来进行的合理预测。制定假设需要对未来进行判断，特别要考虑以下情况：

a. 有证据表明历史趋势不会延续，例如，已出现经济环境、人口结构变化新趋势，将影响现有保单的未来现金流。

b. 承保和理赔流程已发生改变，导致历史数据与未来预测的相关性下降。

c. 历史数据不能体现可能影响当前估计的风险事件。

5.2.4 管理层行为

40. 当前估计可考虑的管理层行为，仅限于 IAIG 对分红产品、可调整产品的未来红利或其他非保证利益的管理层决策。

41. 管理层行为假设应与 IAIG 当前的实际操作和业务策略保持一致，除非 IAIG 能够向集团主监管机构提供充分证据表明其能够改变策略。

42. 当前估计仅应考虑在相应情况下合理可行可实施的行为。

43. 管理层行为假设也应考虑相应行为实施所需的时间以及额外产生的费用。

5.2.5 折现方法

5.2.5.1 确定当前估计折现的收益率曲线

同一级文件。

5.2.5.2 确定无风险收益率曲线

44. 对所有币种，ICS 一级文件第 47 段所述之第三段曲线的起点，应为以下时间点的较大者：

- 最长流动性期限（LOT）+ 30 年；
- 60 年。

45. 无风险收益率曲线分以下币种设置，各币种主要参数如表 2 所示。

表 2　无风险收益率曲线币种列表及相关参数

货币		观测工具	LOT（年）	终极远期利率（%）
AUD	澳元	政府债券	30	3.8
BRL	巴西雷亚尔	政府债券	10	7.0
CAD	加元	政府债券	30	3.8
CHF	瑞士法郎	政府债券	20	2.8
CLP	智利比索	利率互换	10	5.0
CNY	人民币	政府债券	10	6.0
COP	哥伦比亚比索	利率互换	10	6.0
CZK	捷克克朗	利率互换	15	3.8
DKK	丹麦克朗	利率互换	20	3.8
EUR	欧元	利率互换	20	3.8
GBP	英镑	利率互换	50	3.8
HKD	港元	利率互换	15	4.4
HUF	福林	政府债券	15	6.0
IDR	印度尼西亚卢比	利率互换	10	8.0
ILS	以色列谢克尔	利率互换	20	4.4
INR	印度卢比	利率互换	10	7.0
JPY	日元	政府债券	30	3.8
KRW	韩元	政府债券	20	4.4
MXN	墨西哥比索	政府债券	20	5.0
MYR	马来西亚林吉特	政府债券	15	5.0
NOK	挪威克朗	利率互换	10	3.8
NZD	新西兰元	利率互换	20	4.8
PEN	索尔	利率互换	10	6.0
PHP	菲律宾比索	利率互换	10	7.0
PLN	兹罗提	政府债券	10	5.0

续表

货币		观测工具	LOT（年）	终极远期利率（%）
RON	罗马尼亚列伊	政府债券	10	5.0
RUB	卢布	利率互换	10	7.0
SAR	沙特阿拉伯里亚尔	利率互换	15	6.0
SEK	瑞典克朗	利率互换	10	3.8
SGD	新加坡元	政府债券	20	3.8
THB	泰铢	政府债券	10	5.0
TRY	土耳其里拉	政府债券	10	7.0
TWD	新台币	政府债券	10	4.4
USD	美元	政府债券	30	3.8
ZAR	南非兰特	政府债券	30	7.0

46. 终极远期利率（LTFR）为以下两部分之和：

a. 预期实际利率，为实际年利率的简单算术平均。实际年利率 r 按照以下公式计算：

r =（短期名义利率 – 通胀率）/（1 + 通胀率）

预期实际利率四舍五入取整到最近的 5 个基点。

b. 目标通胀率按如下方式设置：

• 对央行发布通胀率目标的币种，基于央行发布的通胀率设置。目标通胀率为：

如央行通胀率≤1%，目标通胀率设为1%；

如1% < 央行通胀率 < 3%，目标通胀率设为2%；

如3%≤央行通胀率 < 4%，目标通胀率设为3%；

其他情况，目标通胀率设为4%。

• 对央行未发布通胀率目标的币种，目标通胀率设为2%。如果某一币种的历史通胀经验和一般通胀假设都表明，目标通胀率应显著高于或低于2%，目标通胀率将考虑相关因素设置。

47. 预期实际利率按国家（地区）分以下三组设置：

• 组别1包括：澳元、加元、瑞士法郎、捷克克朗、丹麦克朗、欧元、英镑、日元、挪威克朗、新西兰元、瑞典克朗、新加坡元、美元；

• 组别2包括：港元、以色列谢克尔、韩元、新台币；

• 组别3为其他币种。

48. 预期实际利率取值如下：

• 组别1为1.8%；

• 组别2为2.4%；

• 组别3为3.0%。

49. LTFR 每年的变动上限为 15 个基点。LTFR 按照以下公式计算：

$$LTFR_t = \begin{cases} LTFR_{t-1} + 15bps, & LTFR_t^* \geq LTFR_{t-1} + 15bps \\ LTFR_{t-1} - 15bps, & LTFR_t^* \leq LTFR_{t-1} - 15bps \\ LTFR_t^* & 其他 \end{cases}$$

其中：

- $LTFR_t$ 为第 t 年已反映变动上限约束的 LTFR；
- $LTFR_{t-1}$ 为第 $t-1$ 年已反映变动上限约束的 LFTR；
- $LTFR_t^*$ 为第 t 年未反映变动上限约束的 LTFR。

50. 按第 46 段至第 49 段计算出的 LTFR，另需增加以下溢价：

- 组别 1 为 20 个基点；
- 组别 2 为 25 个基点；
- 组别 3 为 35 个基点。

5.2.5.3 确定无风险收益率曲线的溢价

5.2.5.3.1 分档标准

51. 如果保险合同负债满足以下所有标准，可以使用高档溢价：

a. 退保无现金价值的人寿保险或失能年金，且满足以下标准。

b. 支持保险合同负债的资产组合可独立识别，与保险合同负债一起独立管理，不会用于偿付 IAIG 的其他业务。[①]

c. 在无风险收益率曲线 LOT 内，资产组合的预期现金流能够匹配同一币种保险合同负债组合的预期现金流。资产负债错配可通过前期到期的资产的累积现金弥补，但现金弥补额度不得超过不考虑贴现的负债现金流总额的 10%，且不得带来显著风险。如果保险合同负债由与负债不同的币种资产支持，且币种错配已充分对冲，对冲成本已在资产现金流中扣除，则现金流测试中可纳入此类资产，否则不予纳入。

d. 现金流测试中，负债现金流不考虑未来保费收入。

e. 保单持有人无退保选择权，或在报告日及未来所有时间点，退保现金价值都不会超过保险合同负债对应的资产价值。

52. 评估保险合同负债是否可使用高档溢价时，不得拆分保单。

53. 如果保险合同负债满足以下所有标准，可以使用中档溢价：

a. 支持保险合同负债的资产组合可独立识别，与保险合同负债一起独立管理，不会用于偿付 IAIG 的其他业务[①]。

[①] 对高档和中档溢价，资产独立管理并不要求法律意义上的完全隔离，而是指支持保险合同负债的资产能够明确辨识分离，且保单整个存续期间均可辨识分离。特殊情况下，如发生业务重组，资产组合可能与保险合同负债一同转入其他账户，不受本条约束。正常业务经营中的资产组合变化也不受此条约束。

b. 保单持有人无退保选择权,或在报告日退保现金价值不超过保险合同负债对应的资产价值。

c. ICS 退保风险最低资本未超过使用无风险收益率曲线折现的当前估计的5%。

d. 在报告日,资产组合总市场价值大于使用无风险收益率曲线折现的保险合同负债当前估计。计算资产组合总市场价值时需考虑该组合的所有资产,不受表3资产分类影响。

e. 现金流测试中,负债现金流不考虑未来保费收入,或仅考虑合同已约定需按期支付的未来保费。

54. 评估保险合同负债是否可使用中档溢价时,不得拆分保单。

55. 不满足高档或中档溢价条件的保险合同负债均使用低档溢价。

5.2.5.3.2 溢价调整

5.2.5.3.2.1 合格资产

56. 计算高档和中档溢价时,仅应考虑表3中的合格资产。

表3 合格资产

投资种类	合格性
不以投资为目的的现金和流动性资产	(从资产组合中剔除)
应收/累积投资收益	否
固定利率中央政府债券	是
固定利率企业债券	是
固定利率市政债券	是
浮动利率中央政府债券	是
浮动利率企业债券	是
浮动利率市政债券	是
可转换票据	否
住房抵押贷款	是
非住房抵押贷款	是
其他(非按揭)贷款	是
保单持有人贷款	是
住房抵押贷款证券化	是
商业抵押贷款证券化	是
其他结构化证券/产品	是
保险连结证券	否
股票	否
对冲基金	否

续表

投资种类	合格性
私募基金	否
房地产（投资目的）	否
基础设施债权	是
基础设施股权	否
其他投资资产	否

57. 使用 ICS 一级文件第 5.4 节所述的资产复制方法对保险合同负债进行估值时，不考虑投连或独立账户对应的资产。

58. 中央政府债券仅指由中央政府发行或担保的债务工具，不包括由市政和其他公共部门发行的债务工具。

59. 有赎回权的资产（发行方有赎回权）不能视为合格资产，不能用于计算溢价。IAIG 证明行使赎回权不会对 IAIG 带来损失，且资产负债现金流能够持续匹配的情况除外。

5.2.5.3.2.2 高档溢价

60. 高档溢价指合格资产在无风险收益率曲线之上的平均溢价。合格资产为支持可使用高档溢价负债的资产组合中，满足表 3 合格条件的资产。

61. 如 IAIG 识别了多个资产组合，可分组合计算高档溢价。

62. 各资产溢价不得超过溢价上限，以限制违约概率较高资产使用过高溢价。溢价上限为同一币种评级为 ICS 评级 4 的资产所对应的溢价。如 IAIG 没有此类资产，IAIS 中档溢价为溢价上限。

63. 溢价应扣除信用风险及其他风险，扣除方法见第 68 段。

64. 保险合同负债可在无风险收益率曲线上增加 100% 的溢价进行折现。

65. IAIG 应根据保险合同负债现金流的币种，使用对应币种的无风险收益率曲线和溢价。

66. 如果保险合同负债由与负债不同的币种资产支持，且币种错配已充分对冲，则 IAIG 可使用负债币种对应的溢价。对冲成本应在溢价中扣除。

67. 以上溢价对无风险收益率曲线平行上移，平行上移的期限可以超过 LOT。

5.2.5.3.2.3 中档溢价

68. IAIS 对各币种提供分评级、分期限的溢价和风险调整，用于计算中档溢价。

69. 全集团同一币种使用同一中档溢价，不分资产组合设置。中档溢价基于中档负债所对应的全部合格资产，采用多资产组合加权平均的方法（WAMP）计算得到。

70. 如果保险合同负债由外币资产支持，且币种错配已充分对冲，则加权平均溢价计算可包括这些外币资产。对冲成本应在溢价中扣除。如果汇率对冲为滚动对冲，则对冲成本在溢价中扣除,且整体溢价应额外折减 20%。

71. 中档溢价按下列段落中所述的 WAMP 方法计算。

72. 对于给定货币,WAMP 溢价按照如下方法计算:

$$Wamp_{spread} = W_{政府债券} \times spread_{风险调整后政府债券}$$
$$+ w_{ICS评级1} \times (\sum_{durations} w^{ICS评级1}_{指定期限范围} \times spread^{风险调整后ICS评级为1的债务工具}_{指定期限范围})$$
$$+ w_{ICS评级2} \times (\sum_{durations} w^{ICS评级2}_{指定期限范围} \times spread^{风险调整后ICS评级为2的债务工具}_{指定期限范围})$$
$$+ \cdots$$
$$+ w_{非合格资产} \times 0$$

其中:

- $W_{政府债券}$ 指中央政府债券权重;
- $W_{ICS评级i}$ 指 ICS 评级为 i 的债务工具的权重;
- $W_{ICS评级i指定期限范围}$ 指在指定期限范围内,ICS 评级为 i 的债务工具的权重;
- $W_{非合格资产}$ 指非合格资产在总资产组合中的权重;
- $spread_{风险调整后政府债券}$ 指中央政府债券进行风险调整后的溢价。如果中央政府债券利率为无风险收益率,该溢价为零;
- $spread_{风险调整后债务评级为i的债务工具}$ 指在指定期限范围内,ICS 评级为 i 的债务工具进行风险调整后的溢价。

73. 评级为 ICS 评级 4 类或更低的债务工具,以及无评级债务工具均按 ICS 评级 4 计算。

74. 同一货币联盟内,各国主权风险暴露(以及在 WAMP 计算中相应的权重)可分开计算。

75. 可观测匹配比例(TOM)计算方法如下:

$$TOM = \min\left(\frac{M-1}{\min(LOT, lifetime\ of\ liability)}, 100\%\right)$$

其中:负债期限(Lifetime of Liability)指超过该期限,保险合同负债预计不再产生任何现金流,M 是指按照 51 段 c 所述的现金流测试中,现金余额超过 10% 限额或变为负数的第一个时间点。计算 M 时,与负债现金流币种不同的资产现金流,如满足以下条件,可纳入现金流测试:

- 资产现金流汇率风险完全对冲;或
- 采用滚动对冲,且对冲滚动频率不少于一个月。此种情况下,资产现金流将折减 20%。

对冲成本应从预期现金流中扣除。

76. 最终确定的中档溢价如下,中档溢价应大于或等于低档溢价。

中档溢价调整 = max [90% × (TOM × WAMP 溢价 + (1 − TOM) 低档溢价), 80% × 低档溢价]

77. 以上溢价对无风险收益率曲线进行平行上移至 M 年，M 年后逐渐过渡到溢价，且溢价调整后的中档即期折现率曲线不低于低档即期折现率曲线。

5.2.5.3.2.4 低档溢价

78. 低档溢价（$Spread_{AdjGB}$）由 IAIS 提供。低档溢价基于各币种 IAIG 持有的平均资产组合设置。

79. 低档溢价反映信用风险及其他风险调整。

80. 对企业债券，上述风险调整基于假定的 10 年期债券年累计违约率通过转换矩阵计算得出。

81. 对中央政府债券，上述风险调整基于相应的无风险利率数据得出。如果无风险利率基于利率互换，除流动性风险以外的风险溢价为 10 年平均利差的 30%。如果无风险利率基于中央政府债券，则风险调整为零。

82. 根据以上方法确定的溢价乘以 80%，对无风险收益率曲线第一段进行平行上移，直至 LOT。对收益率曲线的第二段和第三段，使用与无风险收益率曲线同样的差值方法得到。

83. IAIG 根据保险合同负债现金流的币种使用相应的折现率曲线。

5.2.5.3.3 低档溢价的其他调整

84. IAIG 使用低档溢价时可额外进行以下两项调整：
- 对使用同一货币的不同国家（地区）进行特定调整；
- 对 IAIG 大量投资与负债不同币种的外币资产进行特定调整。

85. 以上两种情况下，IAIG 可替换特定货币溢价，但不同资产类别的权重保持不变。

5.2.5.3.3.1 货币联盟机制

86. 多个国家（地区）为货币联盟，使用同一货币时，IAIG 可用以下定义的溢价（Src）代替 IAIS 提供的该货币溢价（Src_{crncy}），计算方法如下：

如果

$Src_{adjusted} − Src_{crncy} \geq 50bps$

则

$Src = Src_{adjusted} − 50bps$

其中：

Src_{crncy} = IAIS 提供的币种 crncy 和风险评级 rc 的溢价

$Src_{adjusted}$ = 风险评级 rc 的调整后溢价，即基于 IAIG 业务所在国家（地区）资产组合计算的加权平均溢价。

5.2.5.3.3.2 外币资产机制

87. IAIG 可用以下定义的溢价（Src）代替 IAIS 提供的该货币溢价（Src_{crncy}），计算方法如下：

如果

套期保值的外币资产/总资产（不包括现金）≥5%

则

$Src = Src_{crncy} + 50\% \times (Src_{adjusted} - Src_{crncy})$

其中：

Src_{crncy} = IAIS 提供的币种 crncy 和风险评级 rc 的溢价

$Src_{adjusted}$ = 调整后溢价，反映超过 5% 阈值的已对冲外币资产收益。当多个资产类别风险暴露超过 5% 阈值时，阈值按比例分配给不同的资产类别。

5.3 风险边际（MOCE）

5.3.1 定义和基本原则

同一级文件。

5.3.2 计算方法

88. 寿险业务 MOCE 计算使用 85% 分位点，非寿险业务 MOCE 使用 65% 分位点。

5.3.3 MOCE 与 ICS 其他组成部分的关系

同一级文件。

5.4 可被资产组合复制的负债

89. 在任何情况下，保险合同负债现金流都能被对应资产的现金流完全匹配，则该保险合同负债认为能被可靠地复制。

90. 在下列情况下，与保险合同负债有关的现金流不认为能被可靠复制：

a. 保单持有人可以行使合同选择权，包括保单失效和退保。

b. 保险责任与死亡率、失能率和发病率相关。

c. 与保险责任有关的费用不能被可靠地复制。

91. 用于复制保险合同负债的金融资产工具必须来自信息充分透明，交易活跃的金融市场。

6 基准 ICS：实际资本

6.1 一般规定

同一级文件。

6.2 资本工具分级

6.2.1 一级无限制资本工具

92. 一级无限制资本工具需满足以下标准：

a. 全额实缴;

b. 损失发生时,最先用于吸收损失;

c. IAIG 清算时,受偿顺序位列最后。所有其他债务偿付后,对剩余资产按照所发行的股份比例清偿,没有设置上限;

d. 永续性的(即资本应当没有到期日);

e. 除法律允许的回购或清算,本金不能返还;

f. 发行时,IAIG 没有未来回购或取消该工具的预期;

g. 任何情况下,收益分配不是公司的强制义务,且取消分配收益不被视为违约;

h. 收益分配来自可分配项目,包括留存收益;

i. 不因担保而影响受偿顺序。特别要强调的是,受偿顺序不因 IAIG 或受其控制或具有重大影响的关联方,为了投资者利益而做出的担保或保证的影响;

j. IAIG 或受其控制、具有重大影响的关联方不得购买此资本工具,且 IAIG 不得直接或间接为购买该工具提供融资;

k. 实缴金额可被认可为权益(即不作为负债),负债超过资产将视为偿付能力不充足。

6.2.2 一级有限制资本工具

93. 不满足一级无限制资本工具的标准,但满足所有下列标准的资本工具被认可为一级有限制资本:

a. 全额实缴。

b. 受偿顺序在保单持有人、其他非次级债权和二级资本工具之后,但在一级无限制资本工具之前。

c. 永久性(无到期日)。对于相互制 IAIG[①],下列情形也视同满足永久性原则:经监管批准,到期赎回可以递延;或有期限不短于 10 年的锁定条款[②]。

d. 不得含有利率跳升机制及其他赎回激励。

e. 至少自发行之日起五年后,发行人方可赎回,且行使赎回权应得到监管部门的批准。但是,经监管事先批准,工具发行后的任何时候,可以进行特别赎回(指税务和监管事件赎回)。但在发行时,IAIG 不得产生该工具的任何赎回权将被行使的预期。此外,IAIG 不得在发行后的五年内行使特别赎回权。除非行使赎回权之前,IAIG 可使用同等或更高质量的资本工具替换被赎回的工具,并且只有在收入能力具备可持续性的条件下才能实施资本工具的替换。

f. 经监管部门批准,发行人可以在任何时间回购。

[①] 相互制的典型特征包括不能发行大量普通股,以及在集团母公司不能发行普通股。

[②] 锁定条款,指如 IAIG 因偿还或赎回资本工具违反资本监管要求的,可以暂停偿还或者赎回。

g. IAIG 不得通过资本工具的条款形成赎回权将被行使的预期,或者行使赎回权将得到监管部门批准的预期。

h. 任何时候,IAIG 有权取消资本工具的分红或派息(股利或者付息是非累积的),且不构成违约。

i. 收益分配来源于可分配项目,如留存收益。

j. 资本工具的收益分配与 IAIG 及其关联方信用或财务状况无关时,收益分配可能会导致加速清算。

k. 不因担保而影响受偿顺序。要特别强调的是,受偿顺序不因 IAIG 或受其控制、具有重大影响的关联方,为了投资者利益而做出的担保的影响。

l. IAIG 或受其控制或有重要影响的关联方不得购买此资本工具,且 IAIG 不得直接或间接为购买该工具提供融资。

m. 实缴的金额应被认可为权益(不作为负债),负债超过资产将视为偿付能力不充足。

n. 资本工具不应具备阻碍资本结构调整的属性,例如要求发行人在特定时间内以较低价格发行新资本工具时,则需对投资者给予补偿。

o. 如果资本工具不是由 IAIG 的经营实体或控股公司发行的(由 SPV 发行),发行获得的资金应无条件立即转移给 IAIG 的经营实体或控股公司。发行要求必须符合或超过前述一级有限制资本工具标准(SPV 仅可以持有 IAIG 或其关联方发行的公司间资本工具形成的资产,且该资产满足或超过一级有限制资本工具标准)。

6.2.3 二级资本工具(非结构次级性工具)

94. 不满足一级无限制及一级有限制资本工具的标准,但满足所有下列标准的资本工具被认可为二级资本:

a. 全额实缴。

b. 受偿顺序位列 IAIG 的保单持有人和其他非次级债权人之后。

c. 初始到期日至少为五年,有效期为以下日期中较早者:

　i. 利率跳升或其他赎回激励条款的首个赎回日;

　ii. 规定的合同到期日。

d. 随着资本工具逐渐接近到期日,损失可以用下列方式之一来估计:

　i. 在到期前最后五年,使用直线法将资本工具价值从初始金额的 100% 降低到零;

　ii. 具有锁定条款。

e. 如果自发行之日起五年内可赎回该资本工具,则:

- 任何此类赎回权仅能由发行人行使;
- 任何此类赎回须经监管部门批准;
- 赎回前或赎回时,被赎回的资本工具必须由新发行同等或更高质量资本工具全额替换。

除上述替换情况外，资本工具只能在自发行之日起至少五年后，由发行人选择是否赎回。同时，合同到期之前，任何赎回都需得到监管部门的批准[①]；

f. 经监管部门批准后，发行人可在任何时间回购资本工具；

g. IAIG 不得通过资本工具的条款形成赎回权将被行使的预期，或行使赎回权将得到监管部门批准的预期；

h. 资本工具的收益分配与 IAIG 及其关联方的信用或财务状况无关，收益分配可能会导致加速清算；

i. 资本工具持有人不具备提前偿还约定本金或利息的权利，清算时除外。

j. 担保不影响受偿顺序。特别要强调的是，受偿顺序不因 IAIG 或受其控制或具有重大影响的关联方，为了投资者利益而做出的担保或保证的影响；

k. IAIG 或受其控制、具有重大影响的关联方不得购买此资本工具，且 IAIG 不得直接或间接为购买该工具提供融资；

l. 如果资本工具不是由 IAIG 的经营实体或控股公司发行的（由 SPV 发行），发行所筹集的资金应无条件立即转移给 IAIG 的经营实体或控股公司。发行要求必须符合或超过前述一级有限制资本标准（SPV 仅可以持有 IAIG 或其关联方发行的公司间资本工具形成的资产，且该资产满足或超过一级有限制资本标准）。

6.2.4 二级资本工具（结构次级性工具）

95. 债务的结构次级性是指控股公司直接向第三方投资者发行资本工具，然后将发行收入注入保险子公司。

96. 满足二级资本工具标准，并满足 b、e、f 和新标准 n、o、p 的结构次级性资本工具，可以被认定为二级资本工具：

b. 相比 IAIG 其他非次级债权人，结构次级性资本工具的次级性与 IAIG 的控股公司向高级债权人发行的结构次级性资本工具无关；

e. 如果监管部门实施了限制、推迟或禁止发行或赎回资本工具等监督控制和监督审查，则视同满足了自发行之日起五年内赎回须经监管批准的要求；

如果保险子公司向控股公司支付股利前须经监管批准，则视同满足了自发行之日起五年后赎回须经监管批准的要求；

---

① 无须事先须经监管批准的，需满足以下条件：
- 资本工具包含锁定条款，防止当公司不满足资本监管标准（或赎回可能导致不达标的）时赎回；
- 以下条件满足其一的：
  —监管部门接到赎回的事先通知；或
  —赎回日期是固定的、已知的，监管部门能够监测到潜在的赎回行为。以及
- 监管部门有权阻止赎回。

f. 如果保险子公司向控股公司支付股利前须经监管批准①，则视同满足了回购的监管审批要求；

n. 债务工具由不经营实际业务的集团控股公司发行，即独立资产负债表中不包含保险合同负债的控股公司；

o. IAIG 及其 GWS（集团主监管机构）已经决定将资本工具发行收入注入保险子公司的，需接受一定的追踪和报告；

p. 资本工具的发行收益已经注入控股公司下属保险子公司，在保险子公司所处的监管辖区内，监管机构能够通过对收益分配进行适当的监管控制，主动强制执行结构次级性②。

6.2.4.1 国家自行裁量的加速偿还条款

97. 第 94 段中的标准 i 可由国家自行决定。当 GWS 选择使用国家自行裁量权，所有受 GWS 管辖的集团本部不需要符合标准 i。

98. 国家自行裁量的方式，提供了 IAIG 更多适用 ICS 的选择。

6.2.5 非实缴二级资本

99. 非实缴资本指 IAIG 从不相关的第三方获得资本的约定。

100. 相互制 IAIG 的各种资本项目、合同及资本安排，如果满足所有下列标准，则被认可为非实缴资本二级：

a. 已获监管批准，在特征和金额上满足如下标准 b 到 g；

b. 在相互制 IAIG 需要时即可行使约定以获得资本，同时不受任何干扰或限制；

c. 当行使约定时，即可转化为满足一级或者二级实缴资本所有条款的资本工具，满足第 6.3 节列明的所有条件；

d. 任何相关司法管辖范围内的法律均视为有效；

e. 一旦相互制 IAIG 需要，签署约定的合同方能够且愿意支付承诺的数额；

f. 不因担保而受影响；

g. 相互制 IAIG 应当告知监管部门任何可能影响监管审批的事实或环境变化。

6.3 非资本工具分级

6.3.1 一级资本项目

同一级文件。

---

① 如监管部门发现发行人当前或有可能发生财务危机，能够对其收益分配实施监管控制，包括限制、递延或取消分配支付普通股利，则视同满足了结构次级性资本工具应经监管审批的要求。

② 监管对保险子公司收益分配实施控制，指监管部门对收益分配进行监管审阅或事前批准，如果监管部门发现发行人当前或有可能发生财务危机，能够对收益分配实施监管控制，包括限制、递延或取消收益分配。作为监管审阅或事前批准的一部分，监管部门需要考虑盈余的充足性、财务灵活性、盈余质量，以及与发行人财务质量或投保人保护相关的因素。

6.3.2 二级资本项目

101. 二级资本包含以下三个项目且不超过 ICS 最低资本要求的 15%：

a. IAIG 资产负债表中确定收益型养老金资产净额的 50%，且需要扣减符合条件的递延所得税负债；

b. 一级资本中所扣除的递延所得税资产金额的 100%；

c. 一级资本中所扣除的计算机软件无形资产摊销净额的 10%，扣减符合条件的递延所得税负债。

6.4 资本调整和扣减

6.4.1 一级资本扣减项

同一级文件。

6.4.2 二级资本扣减项

同一级文件。

6.4.3 处置受限资产的处理

102. 处置受限资产价值超过所对应负债价值、处置受限资产对应的最低资本及对应负债的最低资本之和的部分，应从 ICS 一级资本中扣除。

103. 与表外证券融资交易相关的处置受限资产，如证券借贷、卖出回购和买入返售资产，由于其不产生资产负债表内负债，故无须进行一级资本扣减。

6.5 资本构成比例

104. 对于非相互制 IAIG，资本结构应当满足以下限制：

a. 一级有限制资本不得超过 ICS 最低资本的 10%。如超出 10% 的部分拥有本金吸损机制（PLAM），则上限可以放宽至 15%；

b. 二级资本不得超过 ICS 最低资本的 50%；

c. 不允许非实缴二级资本。

105. 104 段规定中提到的 PLAM 指，在合同约定的持续经营条件下，允许债务的本金或利息进行减记或转换为一级无限制资本工具（如第 6.2.1 节定义）的一种机制。

106. 对于相互制 IAIG，应当满足以下规定：

a. 一级有限制资本工具不得超过 ICS 最低资本的 30%；

b. 一级有限制资本工具和二级资本之和不得超过 ICS 最低资本的 60%；

c. 非实缴二级资本不得超过 ICS 最低资本的 10%。

7 基准 ICS：最低资本—标准法

7.1 风险分类和基本计量方法

7.1.1 风险缓释

107. 在符合以下所有要求的情况下，风险缓释技术可以在 ICS 最低资本要求计算中进行考虑。

　　a. 该风险缓释技术在所有相关地区都是有效的、可依法执行的，风险确实有效地转移给第三方；

　　b. 合同条款约定确保风险转移是定义清楚的；

　　c. 在计算 ICS 最低资本要求时，可以通过降低与风险缓释程度相同的最低资本要求来体现风险缓释技术的影响。在压力情景下，由于风险缓释假设和关系的变化导致的任何基差风险影响需要在最低资本计量中考虑。隐含在风险缓释技术（如信用风险）中的风险也需要进行适当处理。上述两种影响需要分别考虑；

　　d. 以 ICS 报告日的资产和负债为基础进行计算；

　　e. 不重复计算缓释影响；

　　f. 合约文件中有规定：当交易对手违约、无力偿债、破产或发生其他信用事件时，IAIG 可直接向其索赔；

　　g. 风险缓释创设机构应具有充足的信用水平（可通过适当的评级、资本化或担保水平来证明），以确保 IAIG 可以在合同相关方规定的情况下得到保护。信用水平按照第 7.4 节规定的信用类别定义进行评估。

108. 除以上要求外，市场风险的缓释技术应针对明确的一个特定风险暴露或一组风险暴露。

109. 如果风险缓释技术的有效期少于 12 个月，并且符合上述定性标准，则对 ICS 最低资本要求中考虑的风险缓释效果适用一个比例系数，该系数定义为以下两者之一：

　　a. 当风险暴露期限少于 12 个月，风险缓释技术覆盖期限占整个风险暴露期限的比例，最高为 100%；

　　b. 当风险暴露期限为 12 个月或以上，风险缓释技术覆盖期限占 12 个月的比例，最高为 100%。

110. 当市场风险暴露相关的风险缓释安排到期时，若 IAIG 计划用一个相似的合约替换，如果 IAIG 预计会续期，并且考虑了在时间范围内续期的所有可预见成本，则可将续期考虑在内。当符合以下所有条件时，则可视为符合预计续期的要求：

　　a. 续期与以往的业务实践和策略记录相一致。

　　b. 风险缓释工具的更换频率不超过每三个月一次，除了汇率风险或权益风险，其风险缓释工具的更换频率不超过每月一次。

　　c. 在不同的市场情况下，因市场缺乏流动性而无法更换风险缓释安排的风险并不重大，并且不存在重大的基差或操作风险。如果汇率或权益风险的缓释工具被替换的频率比每三个月一次频繁，则 IAIG 需要向其集团主监管机构提供以下证明：

　　i. 这些缓释工具的市场在相关期限内具有充足的流动性；

　　ii. 与那些大于每三个月更换一次的工具相比，这些缓释工具不会显著增加风险。

d. 替换风险缓释安排并不依赖于任何未来发生的不在 IAIG 控制范围内的事件。如果风险缓释安排的替换是以 IAIG 控制范围内的任何未来事件为条件，则条件应在 a 中所述的策略记录中明确说明。

e. 基于合约的可获得性，风险缓释工具续期是切实可行的，其成本将从该工具的价值中扣除。这一扣除需要考虑在评估日后 12 个月内其成本可能增加的风险。

f. 任何因风险缓释安排（如信用风险）而产生的额外风险都应在 ICS 最低资本要求中予以考虑。

g. IAIG 能够向它的集团主监管机构证明，在接下来的 12 个月内，在所有合理可预见的情况下，所需风险缓释工具将可从一个具有活跃度和流动性的市场中获得续期。若情况并非如此，续期风险缓释合约所确认的利益将限于报告日该合约的全部风险缓释价值的 80%。

111. 对于非寿险保费风险的风险缓释安排，如果 IAIG 预计会续期并考虑续期时间范围内的成本，则允许考虑续期。如果满足以下所有条件，则可认为符合预计续期的要求：

a. 续期与以往的业务实践和策略记录相一致；

b. 基于合约的可获得性和成本①，风险缓释工具续期是切实可行的；以及

c. 任何因风险缓释安排而产生的额外风险（如信用风险）都会在相关的 ICS 最低资本要求中予以考虑。

112. 在为自然灾害风险建模时，如果满足以下所有条件，可考虑合约续期：

a. 续期与以往的业务实践和策略记录相一致；

b. 基于合约的可获得性和成本，续期是切实可行的；以及

c. 任何因风险缓释安排而产生的额外风险（如信用风险）都会在自然灾害风险建模中予以考虑。

113. 在计算 ICS 操作风险最低资本时不得考虑风险缓释安排。

7.1.2 地区划分

114. 对于基于地域划分计算最低资本的风险，采用以下区域划分：

a. 欧盟经济区（EEA）和瑞士；

b. 美国和加拿大；

c. 中国；

d. 日本；

e. 其他发达市场；以及

f. 其他新兴市场。

---

① 成本包括但不限于再保费和手续费。

115. 表4列出了每个区域所包含的国家或地区。

表4 地域划分

区域	包括的国家或地区
欧盟经济区和瑞士	奥地利、比利时、保加利亚、克罗地亚、塞浦路斯共和国、捷克共和国、丹麦、爱沙尼亚、芬兰、法国、德国、希腊、匈牙利、爱尔兰、意大利、拉脱维亚、立陶宛、卢森堡、马耳他、荷兰、波兰、葡萄牙、罗马尼亚、斯洛伐克、斯洛文尼亚、西班牙、瑞典、英国、冰岛、列支敦士登、挪威和瑞士
美国和加拿大	美国①和加拿大
中国	中国大陆和中国澳门特别行政区
日本	日本
其他发达市场②	澳大利亚、新西兰、以色列、圣马力诺、韩国、新加坡、中国台北和中国香港特别行政区
其他新兴市场	国际货币基金组织《世界经济展望》（2016年4月）统计附录表E提供了一份新兴市场清单③。为完整起见，如果一个国家没有被列入上述区域，则归入"其他新兴市场"

7.1.3 管理层行为

116. 管理层行为对各项风险的影响均按第5.2.4节中的规定计算。管理层行为的影响以现实假设为基础，并反映IAIG对保单持有人的责任以及适用于IAIG的法律规定。

117. 管理层行为影响的上限设定为：未来红利或其他非保证利益的保险合同负债总额。这一上限应用在风险分散后的管理层行为影响聚合总额上。

7.2 保险风险

7.2.1 寿险保险风险保单分组

118. 压力情景下的现金流预测采用和基本情景下相同的颗粒度。如果基本情景下现金流已经采用了一些保单分组规则，则压力情景下的现金流预测采用相同的分组规则。

119. 从实操层面来看，可以对具有同质保险风险的产品（或保单）组合进行分组。同质风险组合应包括具有相似风险特征的一系列保单。

120. 同质风险组合应随着时间的推移保持合理稳定。在确定同质风险组合时，IAIG需考虑以下因素：

a. 核保政策；

b. 理赔结算模式；

c. 保单持有人的风险状况；

d. 产品特征，特别是保证责任；

---

① 包括美属萨摩亚、关岛、北马里亚纳岛、波多黎各和美属维尔京群岛。

② "其他发达市场"取自国际货币基金组织的发达经济体清单，但不包括其他地区中提到的国家和地区，截至2016年4月。

③ 参见 http://www.imf.org/external/pubs/ft/weo/2016/01/pdf/text.pdf（accessed on 12 May）。

e. 未来的管理措施。

7.2.2 寿险保险风险最低资本计算

121. 寿险业务保险风险最低资本汇总相关系数矩阵如表5所示。

表5　寿险业务保险风险相关系数矩阵

	死亡发生率风险	长寿风险	疾病发生率/失能风险	退保风险	费用风险
死亡发生率风险	100%	-25%	25%	0%	25%
长寿风险	-25%	100%	0%	25%	25%
疾病发生率/失能风险	25%	0%	100%	0%	50%
退保风险	0%	25%	0%	100%	50%
费用风险	25%	25%	50%	50%	100%

7.2.2.1 死亡发生率风险

122. 计算死亡发生率风险最低资本的压力情景为：所有保单所有年龄段被保险人的死亡发生率上浮一定比例（x%），并导致净资产价值（NAV）下降。

123. 死亡发生率风险的压力情景如表6所示。

表6　死亡发生率风险压力情景

地区	x%
欧洲经济区和瑞士	12.5%
美国和加拿大	12.5%
中国	12.5%
日本	10.0%
其他发达市场	12.5%
其他新兴市场	12.5%

7.2.2.2 长寿风险

124. 计算长寿风险最低资本的压力情景为：所有保单所有年龄段被保险人的死亡发生率下降一定比例（x%），并导致净资产价值（NAV）下降。

125. 长寿风险的压力情景如表7所示。

表7　长寿风险压力情景

地区	x%
欧洲经济区和瑞士	17.5%
美国和加拿大	17.5%
中国	17.5%
日本	17.5%
其他发达市场	17.5%
其他新兴市场	17.5%

7.2.2.3 疾病/失能发生率风险

7.2.2.3.1 分类

126. 疾病/失能发生率风险适用于按照类似寿险技术进行评估的赔付责任。不论保险责任的法律或合同分类如何，对寿险或非寿险业务的分类均基于计算保险赔付责任的技术基础[①]。

7.2.2.3.2 子风险

127. 计算疾病/失能发生率风险最低资本时，类似寿险业务的保险责任，划分为以下4种独立的类型：

a. 第1类：医疗费用

提供住院或非住院的医疗费用补偿（固定费用或基于实际费用）的产品。赔偿金取决于保单持有人花费的治疗费用，而非取决于特定健康状况的持续时间。

b. 第2类：发生特定健康问题时的一次性赔付

在出现特定健康问题，或发生意外事故导致一定程度失能时提供一次性赔付的产品。

c. 第3类：短期多次赔付

根据特定的临时健康状况（如无法工作或住院）的持续时间，在一段时间内提供多次给付的产品。

d. 第4类：长期多次赔付

在健康状况长期或永久恶化的情况下提供固定年金给付的产品。

128. 第3类和第4类责任类型的区别是多次赔付的暂时性和永久性。适用于所有保单持有人并且保险合同约定了给付期限的赔付责任，归类为短期多次赔付。需要终身给付，或根据个体保单持有人的情况确定给付期间，且没有事先约定短期赔付期限的责任，则归类为长期多次赔付。

129. 每种保险责任类型均根据原始合同条款分为两类：

a. 短期：包括原始期限不超过（含）5年的合同。

b. 长期：包括原始期限超过5年的合同。

130. 当一张保单包含上述几种类型的保险责任时，该保单的不同组成部分均将适用相应的压力情景。当一张保单提供医疗费用和短期多次赔付（第1类和第3类）的组合赔付责任时，可将赔付责任拆分至两类责任，也可以全部归入第3类。

7.2.2.3.3 计算

131. 计算疾病/失能发生率风险最低资本的压力情景取决于保险责任类型：

a. 当责任类型 $i=1$、2和3时，压力情景被定义为发病率瞬时相对增加，如表8、

[①] 类似寿险技术，指的是明确使用按年龄划分的死亡率、发病率和治愈率等生物统计变量。

表 9 所示。

根据不同责任类型,压力情景可以在发病率上采取不同的作用方式:

- 对于直接使用发病率或治愈率对理赔成本建模的责任类型,压力情景仅作用于发病率。若仅使用治愈率建模,则压力情景为治愈率的降低。
- 对于第 1~3 类中没有明确的发病率或治愈率的保单,压力情景直接作用于医疗赔付金额。

b. 当责任类型 $i=4$ 时,无论合同期限是短期或长期,疾病/失能发生率风险最低资本均采用发病率风险最低资本和治愈率风险最低资本中的最大值,其中:

- 发病率风险最低资本是随表 8 和表 9 中指定的发病率上升而导致的净资产价值变化;
- 治愈率风险最低资本是治愈率下降 20%(短期和长期合同的压力情景相同)导致的净资产价值的变化。

表 8 疾病/失能发生率风险压力情景—日本

责任类型	短期合同	长期合同
1	20%	8%
2	25%	8%
3	20%	10%
4	发病率风险压力情景为 25%,治愈率风险压力情景为 20%	发病率风险压力情景为 20%,治愈率风险压力情景为 20%

表 9 疾病/失能发生率风险压力情景—其他地区

责任类型	短期合同	长期合同
1	20%	8%
2	25%	20%
3	20%	12%
4	发病率风险压力情景为 25%,治愈率风险压力情景为 20%	发病率风险压力情景为 20%,治愈率风险压力情景为 20%

7.2.2.4 退保风险

132. 按照一级文件第 109 段要求,退保率风险最低资本(包含水平和趋势风险)和大规模退保风险最低资本两者取大,按照本文件第 7.1.2 节列示的地区维度进行计算。

133. IAIG 的退保风险最低资本是所有地区退保风险最低资本之和。

7.2.2.4.1 退保率风险(水平和趋势风险)

134. 对于第 7.1.2 节所列的每个地区,退保率风险最低资本取上浮和下浮压力中最不利情景下的结果。

135. 上浮压力情景是:对于所有受此风险不利影响的同质风险组合在未来所有年

份,退保率上浮 x%,上浮后结果最高不超过 100%。

136. 下浮压力情景是:对于所有受此风险不利影响的同质风险组合在未来所有年份,退保率下浮 x%。

137. 压力情景如表 10 所示。

表10 退保率风险压力情景

地区	x%
欧洲经济区和瑞士	40%
美国和加拿大	40%
中国	40%
日本	20%
其他发达市场	40%
其他新兴市场	40%

138. 所有可能影响保险责任金额的选择权,包括部分或全部终止,或增加保险责任,均受退保率风险压力情景的影响。

139. 对于第 7.1.2 节所列的每个地区,计算退保率风险最低资本时应先确定每个同质风险组的退保率风险最低资本,再对所有同质风险组的退保率风险最低资本进行加总。

140. 当退保现金流的计算涉及使用动态退保模型①时,退保率风险压力情景将作用于动态退保模型的基础假设。

7.2.2.4.2 大规模退保风险

141. 对于第 7.1.2 节所列的每个地区,用于计算大规模退保风险最低资本的压力情景包括:

- 30%的个险保单瞬时退保;
- 50%的团险保单瞬时退保。

142. 每个同质风险组的大规模退保风险最低资本最低为零。

143. 对于第 7.1.2 节所列的每个地区,计算大规模退保风险最低资本时应先确定每个同质风险组的大规模退保风险最低资本,再对所有同质风险组的大规模退保风险最低资本进行加总。

7.2.2.5 费用风险

144. 计算费用风险最低资本的压力情景为,单位费用相对上浮 x%,以及通货膨胀每年绝对增长 y%,x 和 y 的设定参如表 11 所示。

---

① 动态退保模型,是指根据保险公司在其保单上提供的利益与竞争对手提供的利益之间的差异,调整计算保险合同负债时使用的退保率假设。

表 11 费用风险压力情景

地区	x%（单位费用）	y%（通胀）
欧洲经济区和瑞士	6%	1%
美国和加拿大	6%	1%
中国	8%	第1—10年：3%；第11—20年：2%；第21年及以后：1%
日本	6%	1%
其他发达市场	8%	第1—10年：2%；第11年及以后：1%
其他新兴市场	8%	第1—10年：3%；第11—20年：2%；第21年及以后：1%

145. 对单位费用和通胀假设的压力情景是同时应用的。

7.2.3 非寿险保险风险最低资本计算

7.2.3.1 业务类型/业务线

146. 每个保费风险和准备金风险的风险暴露都基于该风险所在地区对应到一个业务线。每个业务线都对应一个ICS业务类型，详见表13。没有明确列示在表13中的地区将被归入到其他发达市场或其他新兴市场，详见表4。

7.2.3.2 ICS业务类型及最低资本的定义

147. 每个ICS业务类型指定：

a. 其所对应的ICS业务大类：更高层级的业务分类，如财产险类、责任险类、车险类、其他险类、抵押贷款类及信用险类；

b. 计量最低资本所需的风险因子。

148. 在ICS中，巨灾风险是单独的风险，因此，保费风险因子不包括巨灾事件的影响。

149. 部分准备金风险因子考虑了潜在责任风险。潜在责任风险最低资本的目的是覆盖历史理赔经验中无法充足反映的准备金计提不充足的风险。

150. 表13列示了ICS业务类型，相关的ICS业务大类以及保费及准备金风险因子。ICS业务类型的定义见附件2。

7.2.3.3 风险聚合

151. 每个ICS业务类型的非寿险风险最低资本的计量均考虑了风险分散效应。

152. 风险聚合的第一步是合并各ICS业务类型内的保费风险和准备金风险最低资本，所有业务类型内的保费风险和准备金风险最低资本的相关系数均为25%（下述所列的抵押贷款和信用保险除外）。

153. 所有地区的抵押贷款和信用保险业务的保费风险和准备金最低资本直接加总，分别与房地产风险和信用风险聚合。

154. 风险聚合的第二步是在各 ICS 业务大类内的聚合，对每个业务大类中的各业务类型均使用下列相关系数矩阵聚合。具体相关系数如表 12 所示。

表 12　业务大类内部相关系数

ICS 业务大类	该大类内各业务类型之间的相关系数
责任险	50%
车险	75%
财产险	50%
其他	25%

155. 风险聚合的第三步是在第 7.1.2 节中列示的各地区内，在四个 ICS 业务大类之间使用 50% 的相关系数聚合。

156. 风险聚合的第四步是各地区间的聚合，在各地区的总最低资本之间采用 25% 的相关系数进行聚合。

157. 图 1 展示了非寿险风险暴露如何归类到地区、国家、ICS 业务大类和 ICS 业务类型。

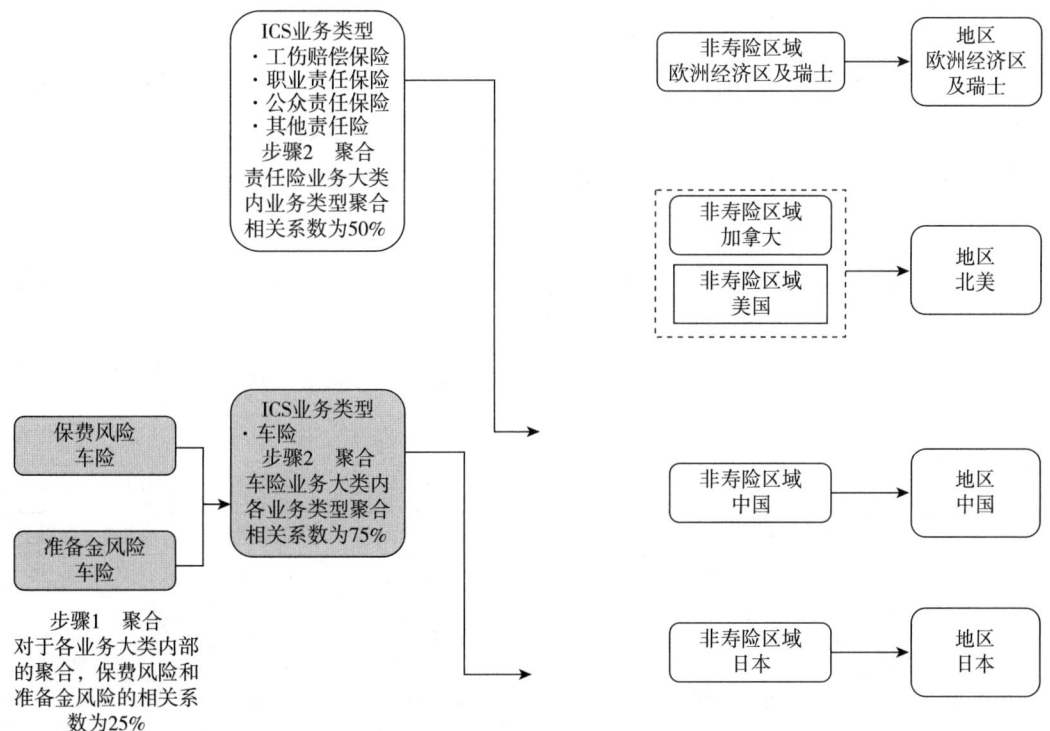

图 1　非寿险风险暴露分类，以新加坡为例的 ICS 类车险业务大类的聚合方法

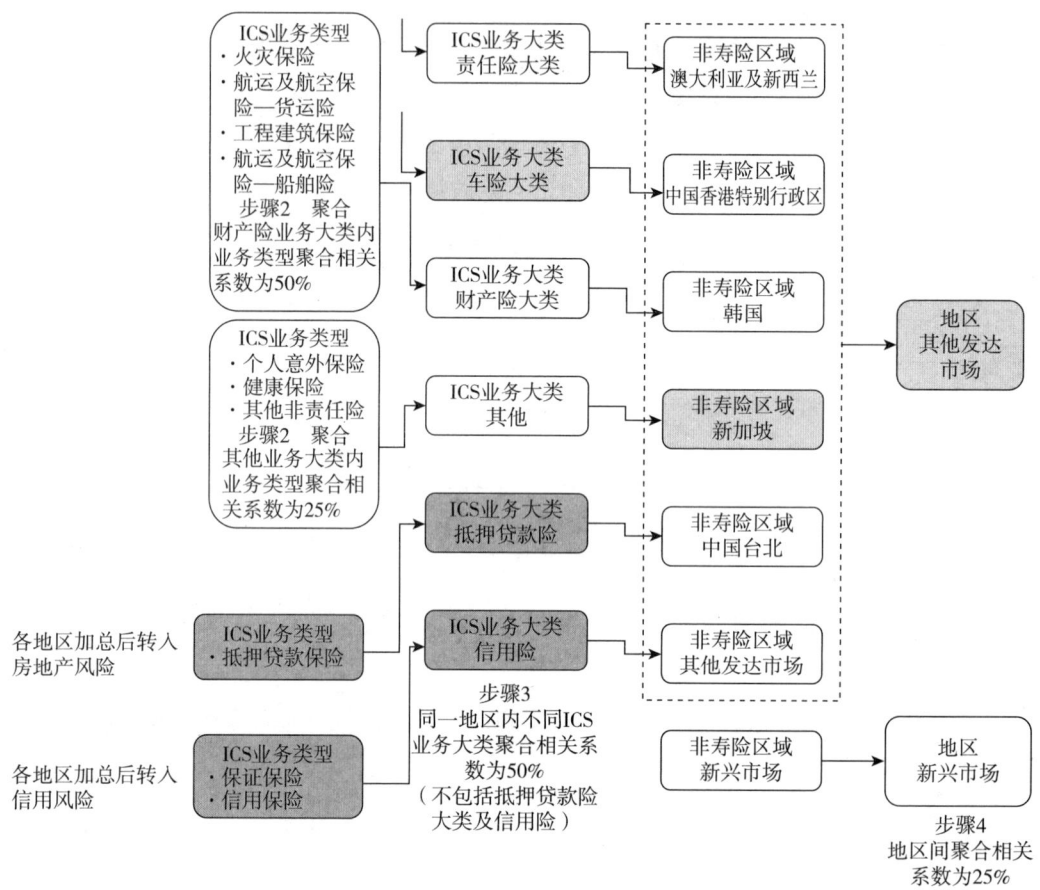

图 1　非寿险风险暴露分类，以新加坡为例的 ICS 类车险业务大类的聚合方法（续）

7.2.3.4　输入数据要求

158. 对每个 ICS 业务类型，其保费风险最低资本等于相应的风险因子乘以净已赚保费和净未赚保费两者中的较大者。

159. 对每个 ICS 业务类型，其准备金风险最低资本等于相应的风险因子乘以再保后的保险合同负债当前估计。

表 13　ICS 非寿险业务分类

	ICS 业务类型	ICS 业务大类	保费风险因子	准备金风险因子
欧洲经济区及瑞士	医疗费用保险	其他	15%	10%
	收入保障保险	其他	25%	35%
	工伤保险	责任险	25%	27%
	机动车责任—机动车第三者责任险	车险	20%	15%
	机动车—其他险	车险	20%	15%
	海上、航空及运输保险	财产险	35%	25%

续表

	ICS业务类型	ICS业务大类	保费风险因子	准备金风险因子
欧洲经济区及瑞士	火灾及其他损失保险	财产险	17.5%	17.5%
	一般责任险—第三者责任险	责任险	35%	27%
	信用和保证保险	信用险	35%	50%
	法律诉讼费用保险	其他	15%	40%
	救援保险	其他	15%	50%
	其他经济损失保险	其他	30%	35%
	非比例健康再保险	其他	50%	45%
	非比例意外伤害再保险	责任险	55%	45%
	非比例海上、航空及运输再保险	财产险	55%	40%
	非比例财产再保险	财产险	45%	40%
加拿大	财产险—个人	财产险	35%	25%
	房屋保修保险	财产险	30%	25%
	产品质量保证保险	财产险	30%	25%
	财产险—商业	财产险	30%	30%
	航空保险	财产险	45%	35%
	车险—责任险/人身意外险	车险	35%	20%
	车险—其他	车险	35%	20%
	锅炉及机器保险	财产险	30%	25%
	设备质量保证保险	财产险	30%	25%
	信用保险	信用险	45%	30%
	信用保障险	信用险	45%	30%
	忠诚保险	其他	45%	30%
	冰雹保险	财产险	35%	30%
	法律诉讼费用保险	其他	45%	40%
	责任险	责任险	50%	38%
	抵押贷款保险	抵押贷款险	45%	30%
	保证保险	信用险	45%	30%
	产权保险	责任险	35%	30%
	海上保险	财产险	45%	35%
	意外和疾病保险	其他	45%	30%
	其他认可保险产品	其他	45%	35%
美国	机动车辆损失保险	车险	12.5%	10%
	业主/农场主保险	财产险	30%	15%
	特殊财产保险	财产险	25%	17.5%
	私家车责任/医疗保险	车险	15%	15%

续表

	ICS 业务类型	ICS 业务大类	保费风险因子	准备金风险因子
美国	商用车/卡车责任/医疗保险	车险	15%	15%
	工伤保险	责任险	15%	16%
	商业综合保险	责任险	30%	26%
	医疗职业责任保险—损失发生制	责任险	40%	45%
	医疗职业责任保险—索赔发生制	责任险	30%	35%
	其他责任险—损失发生制	责任险	17.5%	28%
	其他责任险—索赔发生制	责任险	15%	20%
	产品责任保险	责任险	45%	47%
	再保险—非比例分入财产险	财产险	35%	25%
	再保险—非比例分入责任险	责任险	45%	39%
	特殊责任险	责任险	30%	25%
	抵押贷款保险	抵押贷款险	45%	30%
	忠诚保险/保证保险	信用险	35%	40%
	金融保证保险	信用险	45%	25%
	其他险	其他	25%	35%
	再保险—非比例分入经济损失险	其他	45%	20%
中国	车险	车险	10%	20%
	财产险,包括企业财产保险、家庭财产保险和工程保险	财产险	30%	45%
	船货特险	财产险	25%	45%
	责任险	责任险	10%	36%
	农业险	财产险	25%	35%
	信用保证险	信用险	45%	35%
	短期意外险	其他	10%	10%
	短期健康险	其他	10%	10%
	短期寿险	其他	10%	20%
	其他险	其他	35%	20%
日本	火灾保险	财产险	20%	35%
	船舶保险	财产险	40%	35%
	货物保险	财产险	35%	40%
	运输保险	财产险	40%	35%
	人身意外保险	其他	10%	15%
	机动车保险	车险	7.5%	10%
	航空保险	财产险	50%	45%
	保证保险	信用险	35%	40%

续表

	ICS 业务类型	ICS 业务大类	保费风险因子	准备金风险因子
日本	机器保险	财产险	35%	40%
	一般责任险	责任险	17.5%	27%
	建筑工程一切险	财产险	35%	40%
	动产一切险	财产险	17.5%	25%
	工伤保险	责任险	35%	22%
	其他经济损失保险	其他	35%	45%
	护理保险	其他	35%	45%
	其他险	其他	35%	40%
澳大利亚及新西兰	家庭财产保险	财产险	30%	20%
	商用车保险	车险	25%	20%
	私家车保险	车险	25%	20%
	其他 A 类保险	其他	25%	20%
	旅游保险	其他	35%	25%
	火灾及工业特殊风险保险	财产险	30%	25%
	海运及航空保险	财产险	35%	25%
	消费信用保险	信用险	35%	15%
	其他意外险	其他	35%	25%
	其他 B 类保险	其他	35%	35%
	抵押贷款保险	抵押贷款险	45%	30%
	强制第三者责任保险	车险	45%	35%
	公众责任及产品责任保险	责任险	45%	31%
	职业责任保险	责任险	45%	35%
	雇主责任保险	责任险	45%	36%
	短尾医疗费用保险	其他	15%	25%
	其他 C 类保险	其他	45%	35%
	家庭财产保险—非比例再保险	财产险	45%	30%
	商用车保险—非比例再保险	车险	45%	30%
	私家车保险—非比例再保险	车险	45%	30%
	其他 A 类非比例再保险	其他	45%	30%
	旅游保险—非比例再保险	其他	45%	35%
	火灾及工业特殊风险保险—非比例再保险	财产险	55%	40%
	海运及航空保险—非比例再保险	财产险	55%	40%
	消费信用保险—非比例再保险	信用险	55%	40%
	其他意外伤害保险—非比例再保险	其他	55%	40%
	其他 B 类非比例再保险	其他	55%	35%

续表

	ICS 业务类型	ICS 业务大类	保费风险因子	准备金风险因子
澳大利亚及新西兰	抵押贷款保险—非比例再保险	抵押贷款险	50%	35%
	强制第三者责任险—非比例再保险	车险	55%	40%
	公众责任及产品责任保险—非比例再保险	责任险	55%	43%
	职业责任保险—非比例再保险	责任险	55%	40%
	雇主责任保险—非比例再保险	责任险	55%	43%
	其他 C 类非比例再保险	其他	55%	40%
中国香港特别行政区	意外健康保险	其他	30%	25%
	机动车辆保险，包括车辆损失保险及责任保险	车险	25%	15%
	航空保险，包括航空设备损失保险及责任保险	财产险	45%	40%
	船舶保险，包括损失保险及责任保险	财产险	45%	40%
	货物运输保险	财产险	45%	50%
	火灾及财物损失保险	财产险	35%	20%
	一般责任保险	责任险	45%	26%
	经济损失保险	其他	45%	35%
	非比例合约再保险	财产险	45%	25%
	比例合约再保险	财产险	35%	35%
韩国	火灾、技术及海外保险	财产险	25%	30%
	一揽子保险	财产险	35%	50%
	海事保险	财产险	45%	45%
	人身伤害保险	其他	35%	50%
	劳工意外和责任险	责任险	12.5%	31%
	非本国居民保险	其他	15%	10%
	预付款退还保证保险	信用险	50%	50%
	其他非寿险	其他	45%	50%
	私家车保险（人身伤害）	车险	15%	30%
	私家车保险（财产及车辆损失）	车险	25%	35%
	商用车保险（人身伤害）	车险	25%	20%
	商用车保险（财产及车辆损失）	车险	25%	20%
	其他车险	车险	15%	20%
新加坡	人身意外保险	其他	30%	25%
	新加坡/健康保险	其他	25%	20%
	新加坡/火灾保险	财产险	30%	25%
	海运及航空保险—货运险	财产险	35%	30%
	车险	车险	30%	25%
	工伤保险	责任险	35%	31%

续表

	ICS业务类型	ICS业务大类	保费风险因子	准备金风险因子
新加坡	履约保证保险	信用险	35%	30%
	建筑工程保险	财产险	35%	30%
	信用保险	信用险	35%	30%
	抵押贷款保险	抵押贷款险	35%	30%
	其他险—非责任险	其他	35%	30%
	海运及航空保险—船舶险	财产险	45%	35%
	职业责任保险	责任险	35%	35%
	公众责任保险	责任险	35%	31%
	其他险—责任险	责任险	35%	31%
中国台北	火灾保险—居民楼	财产险	25%	40%
	火灾保险—商业建筑	财产险	55%	45%
	海运—内陆运输	财产险	30%	25%
	海运—海外运输	财产险	30%	25%
	海运—船体保险	财产险	55%	45%
	海运—渔船	财产险	45%	45%
	海运—航空器	财产险	55%	45%
	车险—私家车	车险	25%	25%
	车险—商用车	车险	25%	25%
	车险—私家车责任险	车险	25%	25%
	车险—商用车责任险	车险	25%	25%
	责任保险—包括公众责任、雇主责任、产品责任等	责任险	35%	36%
	责任保险—职业责任	责任险	35%	35%
	工程保险	财产险	55%	45%
	核电站保险	财产险	55%	45%
	保证保险—信用保证和忠诚保证	信用险	55%	45%
	信用保险	信用险	55%	45%
	其他财产损失保险	财产险	35%	40%
	意外伤害保险	其他	15%	10%
	财产损失保险—商业财产地震损失	财产险	45%	35%
	综合险—个人财产及责任保险	财产险	45%	45%
	综合险—商业财产及责任保险	财产险	45%	45%
	财产损失保险—台风及洪水损失	财产险	55%	45%
	财产损失保险—强制地震损失保险	财产险	55%	45%
	健康险	其他	15%	10%

续表

	ICS业务类型	ICS业务大类	保费风险因子	准备金风险因子
其他发达市场	车险	车险	30%	20%
	财产损失保险	财产险	30%	25%
	意健险（Accident, Protection and Health, APH）	其他	35%	30%
	短尾医疗费用险	其他	35%	25%
	其他短尾保险	其他	35%	30%
	海运，航空及运输保险（MAT）	财产险	35%	35%
	工伤保险	责任险	35%	36%
	公众责任保险	责任险	35%	31%
	产品责任保险	责任险	35%	43%
	职业责任保险	责任险	35%	35%
	其他责任保险及其他长尾保险	责任险	35%	36%
	非比例车险，财产损失保险，意健险及运输保险	财产险	50%	40%
	巨灾再保险	财产险	50%	40%
	非比例责任险	责任险	50%	44%
	非比例职业责任保险	责任险	50%	40%
	抵押贷款保险	抵押贷款险	45%	35%
	商业信用保险	信用险	45%	35%
	其他中期保险	其他	50%	40%
其他新兴市场	车险	车险	35%	25%
	财产损失保险	财产险	35%	30%
	意健险（APH）	其他	35%	30%
	短尾医疗费用险	其他	35%	25%
	其他短尾保险	其他	35%	30%
	海运，航空及运输保险（MAT）	财产险	35%	35%
	工伤保险	责任险	45%	36%
	公众责任保险	责任险	45%	36%
	产品责任保险	责任险	45%	47%
	职业责任保险	责任险	45%	35%
	其他责任保险及其他长尾保险	责任险	45%	36%
	非比例车险，财产损失保险，意健险及运输保险	财产险	50%	45%
	巨灾再保险	财产险	50%	45%
	非比例责任险	责任险	50%	48%
	非比例职业责任保险	责任险	50%	45%
	抵押贷款保险	抵押贷款险	50%	40%
	商业信用保险	信用险	50%	40%
	其他中期保险	其他	55%	40%

7.2.4 巨灾风险最低资本计算

7.2.4.1 计量范围

160. 计算巨灾风险最低资本时，所有暴露于巨灾风险的业务线都应涵盖在内。为避免与其他的 ICS 最低资本重复计算，应遵循下列原则：

a. 寿险和类寿险健康业务线，只有在流行病和恐怖袭击情景下才会被纳入；

b. 金融市场和整体经济（市场风险和信用风险）的影响不纳入巨灾风险的计量。

7.2.4.2 巨灾风险涵盖的风险

161. 巨灾风险包含的风险如下：

a. 自然巨灾：

i. 热带气旋，飓风，台风；

ii. 特大热带风暴/暴风雪；

iii. 地震；

iv. 其他重大自然灾害，比如：

- 洪水
- 龙卷风，冰雹，对流风暴
- 其他风险

b. 其他巨灾（人为灾因）；

i. 恐怖袭击；

ii. 流行病；

iii. 信用和担保。

162. 巨灾理赔事件的影响包括主要灾害和与主要灾害有关的所有次生灾害。

7.2.4.3 自然巨灾

163. 随机巨灾模型可用来计算自然巨灾事件导致的损失总额。

164. 损失总额的计算应考虑：

a. 自然巨灾对所有相关业务线的影响；

b. 未建模的风险暴露，包括在未来一年内可预期的，会被上文所列灾害影响的新业务线；

c. 未建模的风险和地区，应在报告中列为其他自然巨灾损失的一部分。这可能包括没有独立或具体建模的风险或地区，但通过其他方式评估了其潜在的巨灾损失。

165. 自然巨灾最低资本等于年度累计净损失总额分布的 99.5 分位点和均值之差。年度累计净损失是所有地区和所有巨灾灾因的净损失总和。

7.2.4.4 其他巨灾情景

166. 下列灾因的损失总额取决于下面所描述的情景。

167. 巨灾情景的影响需要包括所有受相关情景影响的业务线，除非在计算范围中被明确排除。

7.2.4.4.1 恐怖袭击

168. 恐怖袭击的最低资本是下面两部分损失的总和：

a. 保险合同所承保的财产（包括建筑物、财物和机动车）总损失，以及财产损失直接导致的其他保险合同的损失；

b. 寿险、健康险以及工伤保险的损失。

169. 对寿险和非寿险业务而言，该情景为风险敞口最集中的区域部分或全部位于发生5吨炸药爆炸500米半径范围内产生的所有损失。计算该损失时，地理区域内的所有建筑（包括自用财产）都应考虑在内。风险敞口最集中的区域应对寿险和非寿险业务分别计算。

170. 关于财产损失计算，包括已投保财产和相关保险，采用下列假设：

a. 200米半径的圆形区域内，100%破坏率；

b. 200米半径和400米半径之间的环形区域内，25%破坏率；

c. 400米半径和500米半径之间的环形区域内，10%破坏率。

171. 关于致死率，采用下列假设：

a. 200米半径内的致死率为15%；

b. 200米半径与500米半径之间的环形区域内的致死率为1.5%。

172. 关于致残率，采用下列假设：

a. 200米半径内的致残率为20%；

b. 200米半径与500米半径之间的环形区域内的致残率为10%。

7.2.4.4.2 流行病

173. 该情景指全球流行病导致死亡人数上升。流行病风险最低资本是由死亡发生率绝对值增加千分之一带来的IAIG各地区所有个人和团体保险的损失总额。

7.2.4.4.3 信用和担保

174. 信用和担保的最低资本是下列三部分的损失总额：

a. 抵押贷款保险；

b. 贸易信用；

c. 担保。

7.2.4.4.3.1 抵押贷款保险

175. 该情景是因房屋价格按指定幅度下降引起的出险频率和严重程度上升而导致的保险损失总额的增加。房屋价格下降25%的假设情形将持续一整年时间。总损失包括因犯罪率和违约率上升，以及因房价下降导致贷款损失增加的影响。

7.2.4.4.3.2 贸易信用

176. 贸易信用的信用压力情景是保单持有人的客户无力支付已发货物或已提供服务

而导致的损失总额。贸易信用涵盖对保单持有人因客户无力支付而造成的坏账损失的赔偿。保单持有人的客户是否无力支付,可根据客户违约概率的上升以及违约损失的增多来判断。总损失额度需根据已有的减损条款进行调整,包括保单持有人的补偿和自担损失等。

表 14 贸易信用的信用风险因子

评级分类	风险因子
投资级别	80%
非投资级别	200%

7.2.4.4.3.3 担保

177. 担保的信用风险压力情景基于履约保证违约金的净潜在损失总金额。履约保证保险因合同一方无力履行其合同义务而需赔偿保单持有人。违约赔偿总额是指 IAIG 被要求支付给受益人的最大金额。IAIG 应当用下列方法计算其担保合同的前十大交易对手的最大净潜在损失。假设前两大净损失已经发生,净潜在损失总额等于前两大净损失之和。

7.2.4.5 巨灾风险的聚合

178. 在计算巨灾风险最低资本时,需假设其他巨灾(人为灾因)情景都相互独立并均与自然巨灾风险独立。因此,ICS 巨灾风险最低资本总额为:

$$\text{ICS}_{\text{巨灾风险}} = \sqrt{\text{ICS}^2_{\text{自然巨灾风险}} + \text{ICS}^2_{\text{恐怖袭击风险}} + \text{ICS}^2_{\text{流行病风险}} + \text{ICS}^2_{\text{信用和担保风险}}}$$

7.2.4.6 用于计算或有信用风险的可摊回金额的计量方法

179. 可摊回金额等于下述两项最低资本之差,一是假设没有风险缓释措施的巨灾风险最低资本,二是考虑了有效风险缓释措施的巨灾风险最低资本。

180. 可摊回金额基于信用评级分摊,采用下列步骤:

a. 对于自然巨灾风险和每个其他巨灾(人为灾因)情景的聚合,按信用评级、摊回前和摊回后损失计算对应的可摊回金额。

b. 按前述方法对所有摊回前损失和摊回后损失进行聚合。总可摊回金额是聚合摊回前损失和聚合摊回后损失之差。

c. 各信用评级的可摊回金额,等于总可摊回金额乘以该信用评级分类下所有情景的可摊回金额总和与所有信用评级分类所有情景的可摊回金额总和之比。

7.2.4.7 自然巨灾模型的保障措施

181. 为评估随机自然巨灾模型的适用性,IAIG 应提供下列保障措施的信息:

● 保障措施 1——应用范围的描述:IAIG 描述了自然巨灾模型计算的边界;

● 保障措施 2——验证:IAIG 证明其建立了科学严格的程序,能够评估其自然巨灾模型的框架是否合理,以及是否需要修订完善;

- 保障措施 3——由高级管理层批准：IAIG 的高级管理层对自然巨灾模型负责，该模型遵从自然巨灾模型管理流程所规定的验证过程；
- 保障措施 4——统计检验测试：该测试解决了自然灾害模型以下技术方面相关的问题：
  - 方法论和假设
  - 重大风险保险责任
  - 数据（包括外部数据）和专家判断
  - 风险分散效应
  - 与技术性准备金计量方法的一致性
  - 风险缓释技术及管理层行为的相关情况
  - 合同约定的选择权
- 保障措施 5——管理流程：使用测试（Use Test）反映了 IAIG 的风险观并用来协助决策；
- 保障措施 6——文档记录标准：自然巨灾模型的文档包括其使用方法和其他相关细节：
  - 便于对模型的监督审查
  - 帮助高级管理层理解该模型
  - 识别模型缺陷
- 保障措施 7——未建模的巨灾风险来源的清单：IAIG 认识到其自然巨灾模型范围的局限性。如果 IAIG 未对 ICS 列出的自然巨灾风险进行建模，应解释原因。

7.3 市场风险

7.3.1 市场风险最低资本计算

182. 市场风险最低资本聚合的相关系数矩阵。

表 15 市场风险最低资本聚合的相关系数矩阵

	利率风险	非违约利差风险上升	非违约利差风险下降	权益风险	不动产风险	汇率风险	集中度风险
利率风险	100%	25%	25%	25%	25%	25%	0%
非违约利差风险上升	25%	100%	100%	75%	50%	25%	0%
非违约利差风险下降	25%	100%	100%	0%	0%	25%	0%
权益风险	25%	75%	0%	100%	50%	25%	0%
不动产风险	25%	50%	0%	50%	100%	25%	0%
汇率风险	25%	25%	25%	25%	25%	100%	0%
集中度风险	0%	0%	0%	0%	0%	0%	100%

7.3.2 利率风险

183. 所有利率敏感的资产和负债应计算利率风险最低资本，IAIG 发行的资本工具除外。

184. 计算保险合同负债当前估计时使用利率为输入变量的动态退保模型，在利率压力情景下，退保率相应进行变化。

185. 利率风险最低资本计算公式为：

$$\max(0, \sum_i MR_i + \text{VaR}_{BBS}(\sum_i LT_i))$$

其中：

- i 为 IAIG 所有暴露于利率风险的货币种类；
- MR_i 为货币 i 的均值回归情景的结果，计算方法详见第 188 段；
- LT_i 为随机变量，包括货币 i 的水平向上、水平向下、扭转上下、扭转下上情景的结果，计算方法详见第 186 段。

186. 对货币 i，LT_i 计算如下：

$$\frac{1}{N^{-1}(0.995)} \times (LU_i \max(X_i, 0) - LD_i \max(X_i, 0) + TU_i \max(Y_i, 0) - TD_i \min(Y_i, 0))$$

其中：

- $N^{-1}(0.995)$ 是标准正态分布的 99.5% 分位点；
- LU_i 和 LD_i 分别为水平向上和水平向下情景的结果，计算方法详见第 188 段；
- TU_i 和 TD_i 分别为扭转上下、扭转下上情景的结果，计算方法详见第 188 段；
- X_i 和 Y_i 为标准正态分布的独立随机变量。

187. 此外，X_i 和 Y_i 还应满足：

- 对于任意 $i \neq j$，$corr(X_i, X_j) = corr(Y_i, Y_j) = 0.75$
- 对于任意 i 和 j，$corr(X_i, Y_j) = 0$

188. 对于货币 i，MR_i、LU_i、LD_i、TU_i 和 TD_i 为 IAIG 分别在均值回归、水平向上、水平向下、扭转上下、扭转下上的压力情景前后净资产的变化，计算方法详见第 189 段至第 197 段。

189. 对每种货币，最长流动性期限之前的均值回归压力曲线，通过将以下收益曲线和原始收益曲线相加得到：

$$\Delta L. \text{ Level curve} + \Delta S. \text{ Slope curve} + \Delta C. \text{ Curvatrue curve}$$

其中：

- *Level curve* 在所有期限上均为 1；
- 对任意期限 τ，*Slope curve* 等于 $\frac{1 - e^{-\lambda \tau}}{\lambda \tau}$；

- 对任意期限 π，Curvature curve 等于 $\frac{1-e^{-\lambda\tau}}{\lambda\tau} - e^{-\lambda\tau}$；

- λ 是无风险收益率曲线的 Nelson Siegel 模型[①]的指数衰减率；

- 向量 $\begin{pmatrix} \Delta L \\ \Delta S \\ \Delta C \end{pmatrix}$ 定义为 $(I - e^{-K})(\mu - V_0)$；

- I 是 3×3 单位矩阵；

- 其中参数 K 和 μ 分别为：

$$K = \begin{pmatrix} K_1 & & 0 \\ & K_2 & \\ 0 & & K_3 \end{pmatrix}, \mu = \begin{pmatrix} \mu_1 \\ \mu_2 \\ \mu_3 \end{pmatrix};$$

K 和 μ 是通过矩阵 V_t 获得，V_t 可用如下公式表示：

$$dV_t = K(\mu - V_t)dt + \sum dW_t$$

- $V_t = \begin{pmatrix} \beta_{1t} \\ \beta_{2t} \\ \beta_{3t} \end{pmatrix}$，$\beta_{1t}$、$\beta_{2t}$、$\beta_{3t}$ 为无风险收益率曲线在 t 时刻的 Nelson Siegel 模型参数；

- W_t 是一个三维维纳过程，$\sum$ 表示非负的下三角形矩阵。

190. 在均值回归情景中，LTFR 保持不变。

191. 对每种货币，最长流动性期限之前的水平向上压力曲线，通过将以下收益曲线和原始收益曲线相加得到：

$$s. N^{-1}(0.995). [sl_1. Level\ cruve + sl_2. Slope\ curve + sl_3. Curvatrue\ curve]$$

其中：

- $\begin{pmatrix} sl_1 \\ sl_2 \\ sl_3 \end{pmatrix} = \cos(\theta)Me_1 + \sin(\theta)Me_2$；

- $M = \sqrt{\left(\sum \sum^T\right) \odot \left(\frac{1-e^{-(k_i+k_j)}}{k_i+k_j}\right)_{ij}}$ $\sum$ 和 K_i 与第 189 段参数意义相同，$\odot$ 是 Hadamard 乘积运算符号；

- e_1 和 e_2 分别是 $N^T N$ 矩阵的最高和次高特征向量；

[①] 详见 Diebold, F. X. and Li, C (2006) Forecasting the Term Structure of Government Bond Yields in Journal of Econometrics, 130, 337–364。

- $N = \begin{pmatrix} LOT & 0 \\ & a \\ 0 & b \end{pmatrix} M$;

- $\theta = Arctan \dfrac{\sum_{T=1}^{LOT} h_2(\tau)}{\sum_{T=1}^{LOT} h_1(\tau)}$;

- $h_i(\tau) = \left(1, \dfrac{1-e^{-\lambda\tau}}{\lambda\tau}, \dfrac{1-e^{-\lambda\tau}}{\lambda\tau} - e^{-\lambda\tau}\right) Me_i$, $I = 1, 2$; and

- $s = \begin{cases} 1 \ if \ (sl_1. \ Level \ curve_{LOT} + sl_2. \ Slope \ curve_{LOT} + sl_3. \ Curvature \ curve_{LOT}) \geq 0 \\ -1 \ otherwise \end{cases}$

192. 在水平向上情景中，LTFR 增长 10%。

193. 对每种货币，最长流动性期限之前的水平向下压力曲线，通过将以下收益曲线和原始收益曲线相加得到：

$-s. \ N^{-1}(0.995). \ [sl_1. \ Level \ curve + sl_2. \ Slope \ curve + sl_3. \ Curvatrue \ curve]$

194. 在水平向下情景中，LTFR 降低 10%。

195. 对每种货币，最长流动性期限之前的扭转上下压力曲线，通过将以下收益曲线和原始收益曲线相加得到：

$N^{-1}(0.995). \ [sl_1. \ Level \ curve + sl_2. \ Slope \ curve + sl_3. \ Curvatrue \ curve]$

其中：

$\begin{pmatrix} s_{t_1} \\ s_{t_2} \\ s_{t_3} \end{pmatrix} = \cos(\theta) Me_1 - \sin(\theta) Me_2$

196. 对每种货币，最长流动性期限之前的扭转下上压力曲线，通过将以下收益曲线和原始收益曲线相加得到：

$-N^{-1}(0.995). \ [sl_1. \ Level \ curve + sl_2. \ Slope \ curve + sl_3. \ Curvatrue \ curve]$

197. 在扭转情景中，LTFR 保持不变。

7.3.3 非违约利差风险

198. 所有对利差变化敏感的负债，需计算非违约利差风险最低资本，IAIG 发行的资本工具除外。

199. 在评估中对计算利差调整有贡献的资产（详见第 5.2.5.3.2.1 节的表 3），需计算非违约利差风险最低资本，主权债券等主权类资产除外。

200. 压力适用于风险修正后的利差。对于保险合同负债，利差根据评估中适用的利差调整风险类型（详见第 5.2.5 节）在压力下直接平移。

201. 计算非违约利差风险最低资本的向上和向下压力如表16所示。

表16 非违约利差风险最低资本的向上和向下风险因子

ICS 评级	向上（bp）	向下（bp）
1	+50	−50
2	+50	−50
3	+70	−70
4—7	+100	−100
同时受到如下比例限制，该比例基于超出无风险收益率曲线的绝对利差值计算		
比例限制	无比例限制	50%

7.3.4 权益风险

202. ICS 一级文件中所列示的权益资产类别的定义如下：

203. 发达市场上市权益是指在 FTSE 发展指数中的证券交易所上市的权益：包括澳大利亚、奥地利、比利时、卢森堡、加拿大、丹麦、芬兰、法国、德国、中国香港特别行政区、爱尔兰、以色列、意大利、日本、荷兰、新西兰、挪威、波兰、葡萄牙、新加坡、韩国、西班牙、瑞典、瑞士、英国和美国。

204. 新兴市场上市权益是指不包括在 FTSE 发展指数的股票市场的上市权益。

205. 混合资本债/优先股包含次级债。

206. 其他权益是指不包含在上述三个分类中的权益资产。

207. 权益价格水平和波动性的四种压力情景如下：

a. 所有发达市场上市权益的市场价格瞬时下降 35%。

b. 所有新兴市场上市权益的市场价格瞬时下降 48%。

c. 所有混合资本债/优先股的市场价格瞬时下降 x%，x 根据资产的信用评级确定，如表 17 所示。

表17 混合资本债/优先股的风险因子

ICS 评级	x%
1—2	4%
3	6%
4	11%
5	21%
6—7	35%

d. 所有其他权益资产的市场价格瞬时下降 49%。

e. 所有资产的隐含波动性瞬时增加绝对数额 x%，x 的值如表 18 所示。其他期限可根据线性差值计算。

表18 隐含波动率风险因子的绝对数额

到期期限（月）	x%
0—1	42%
3	28%
6	23%
12	20%
24	17%
36	16%
48	15%
60	14%
84	14%
120	12%
144	11%
180	10%
240	7%
300	4%
360（及以上）	0%

208. 以上压力结果分两步进行聚合；

表19 权益风险相关系数矩阵

权益风险类别	发达市场	新兴市场	混合资本债/优先股市场	其他市场
发达市场	100%	75%	100%	75%
新兴市场	75%	100%	75%	100%
混合资本债/优先股市场	100%	75%	100%	75%
其他市场	75%	100%	75%	100%

- 第一步：权益价格水平压力结果通过以下相关性系数矩阵进行聚合：
- 第二步：第一步权益价格水平压力和波动性压力聚合结果相加得到权益风险最低资本。

7.3.5 房地产风险

209. 房地产风险压力情景指房地产价格下降25%，适用于以下资产和负债：

a. 商业投资性房地产；

b. 住宅投资性房地产；

c. 自用房地产；

d. 其他价值受房地产价格变化影响的资产；

e. 其他价值受房地产价格变化影响的保险合同负债和其他负债。

7.3.6 汇率风险

210. IAIG 需确定除报表币种外其他货币的净敞口。每种货币的净敞口为下列几项之和：

a. 净即期敞口，即资产减负债，包括应记利息和应记费用；

b. 净远期敞口，即外汇远期的净值，包括外汇远期、外汇互换的利息和本金；

c. 外汇期权的 Δ 等价金额；

d. 确定在将来会执行并不可撤销的担保及其他类似金融工具；

e. 根据 IAIG 的判断，已完全套期保值却尚未在账面确认的未来收入和费用的净值；

f. 任何其他代表外汇收益或损失的项目；

g. 减去用于支持在当地外汇交易所需的资本（不超过该货币保险负债净额的 10%）。

211. 第 210 段第 g 点减值仅适用于多头，且扣减后多头不得转变为空头。减值仅适用于 IAIG 在外汇所在国家或地区有业务经营的情况。

212. 净外汇敞口不包括从资本中已经剔除的资产，以及已经包含在并表资本中的负债。

213. 报表上的每种货币的净保险合同负债，为保险合同负债减去再保险资产，加上与当前估计和再保险资产相关的递延所得税资产和其他负债。

214. 远期外汇敞口根据报表日即期市场汇率进行计算。

215. 汇率风险最低资本为以下两种情景导致损失中的较大值：

- 情景 1：IAIG 持有的所有净空头的货币价值保持不变，所有净多头的货币价值下降，下降幅度如表 20 所示。

- 情景 2：IAIG 持有的所有净多头的货币价值保持不变，所有净空头的货币价值上升，上升幅度如表 20 所示。

216. 以上每种情景，聚合所有币种汇率损失时，设定每两种外币之间的相关性系数为 50%。

表 20 汇率风险压力情景

币种	AUD	BRL	CAD	CHF	CLP	CNY	COP	CZK	DKK	EUR	GBP	HKD
AUD	0%	50%	25%	40%	35%	40%	40%	35%	35%	35%	35%	40%
BRL	50%	0%	50%	65%	50%	55%	55%	60%	60%	60%	55%	55%
CAD	25%	50%	0%	35%	30%	25%	35%	35%	30%	30%	30%	25%
CHF	40%	60%	35%	0%	45%	35%	45%	25%	20%	20%	30%	35%
CLP	35%	50%	30%	45%	0%	30%	40%	40%	40%	40%	35%	30%
CNY	35%	55%	25%	35%	30%	0%	35%	35%	30%	30%	25%	5%

三、全球保险资本标准（ICS）2.0版本 二级文件

续表

币种	AUD	BRL	CAD	CHF	CLP	CNY	COP	CZK	DKK	EUR	GBP	HKD
COP	40%	55%	35%	50%	40%	35%	0%	45%	45%	45%	40%	35%
CZK	35%	55%	35%	30%	40%	35%	45%	0%	15%	15%	30%	35%
DKK	35%	55%	30%	20%	35%	30%	40%	15%	0%	5%	25%	30%
EUR	35%	55%	30%	20%	35%	30%	40%	15%	5%	0%	25%	30%
GBP	35%	55%	30%	30%	35%	25%	40%	30%	25%	25%	0%	25%
HKD	35%	55%	25%	35%	30%	5%	35%	35%	30%	30%	25%	0%
HUF	40%	60%	40%	35%	45%	45%	50%	25%	25%	25%	35%	45%
IDR	45%	60%	40%	50%	45%	35%	45%	50%	45%	45%	45%	35%
ILS	35%	55%	30%	35%	35%	25%	35%	35%	30%	30%	30%	25
INR	35%	50%	25%	35%	30%	20%	35%	35%	30%	30%	30%	15%
JPY	50%	65%	40%	35%	45%	30%	50%	45%	35%	35%	40%	30%
KRW	30%	50%	25%	40%	30%	25%	35%	35%	35%	35%	30%	25%
MXN	35%	50%	30%	45%	35%	30%	35%	40%	40%	40%	40%	30%
MYR	35%	50%	25%	35%	30%	15%	30%	35%	30%	30%	25%	15%
NOK	35%	55%	30%	30%	40%	35%	40%	25%	20%	20%	30%	35%
NZD	20%	55%	30%	40%	40%	40%	45%	40%	35%	35%	35%	40%
PEN	35%	50%	25%	35%	30%	15%	30%	35%	30%	30%	30%	15%
PHP	35%	50%	25%	35%	30%	15%	35%	35%	30%	30%	30%	15%
PLN	35%	55%	35%	40%	40%	40%	45%	25%	25%	25%	35%	40%
RON	35%	50%	35%	30%	40%	30%	45%	25%	20%	20%	30%	30%
RUB	45%	60%	40%	50%	40%	35%	45%	45%	40%	40%	45%	35%
SAR	40%	55%	25%	35%	30%	5%	35%	35%	30%	30%	25%	5%
SEK	35%	55%	30%	30%	40%	35%	45%	25%	20%	20%	30%	35%
SGD	30%	50%	20%	30%	30%	15%	30%	30%	25%	25%	25%	15%
THB	35%	55%	30%	35%	30%	20%	35%	35%	30%	30%	30%	20%
TRY	70%	75%	70%	75%	70%	70%	75%	70%	70%	70%	70%	70%
TWD	35%	50%	25%	30%	30%	10%	35%	35%	25%	25%	25%	10%
USD	40%	55%	25%	35%	30%	5%	35%	35%	30%	30%	25%	5%
ZAR	45%	60%	45%	55%	50%	55%	55%	50%	50%	50%	50%	55%

币种	HUF	IDR	ILS	INR	JPY	KRW	MXN	MYR	NOK	NZD	PEN	PHP
AUD	40%	45%	35%	35%	50%	30%	35%	35%	35%	20%	0%	35%
BRL	60%	60%	55%	55%	70%	50%	50%	50%	55%	55%	55%	55%
CAD	40%	40%	30%	25%	40%	25%	30%	25%	30%	30%	25%	25%
CHF	35%	50%	35%	35%	35%	40%	45%	35%	25%	40%	35%	35%

续表

币种	HUF	IDR	ILS	INR	JPY	KRW	MXN	MYR	NOK	NZD	PEN	PHP
CLP	45%	45%	35%	30%	45%	30%	35%	30%	40%	40%	30%	30%
CNY	45%	35%	25%	15%	30%	25%	30%	15%	35%	40%	15%	15%
COP	50%	45%	35%	35%	50%	35%	35%	30%	40%	45%	35%	35%
CZK	25%	50%	35%	35%	45%	35%	40%	35%	25%	40%	35%	35%
DKK	25%	45%	30%	30%	35%	30%	40%	30%	20%	35%	30%	30%
EUR	25%	45%	30%	30%	35%	35%	40%	30%	20%	35%	30%	30%
GBP	35%	45%	30%	30%	40%	30%	35%	25%	30%	35%	30%	30%
HKD	45%	35%	25%	15%	30%	25%	30%	15%	35%	40%	15%	15%
HUF	0%	55%	40%	40%	55%	40%	45%	40%	30%	40%	45%	45%
IDR	55%	0%	40%	35%	50%	40%	45%	35%	45%	50%	35%	35%
ILS	40%	40%	0%	25%	40%	30%	30%	25%	35%	40%	25%	25%
INR	40%	35%	25%	0%	35%	25%	30%	20%	35%	35%	20%	20%
JPY	50%	50%	40%	35%	0%	40%	50%	35%	40%	50%	35%	35%
KRW	40%	40%	30%	25%	40%	0%	30%	25%	35%	35%	25%	25%
MXN	45%	45%	35%	30%	50%	30%	0%	25%	40%	40%	30%	30%
MYR	40%	35%	25%	20%	35%	25%	25%	0%	30%	35%	20%	20%
NOK	30%	45%	35%	35%	40%	35%	40%	30%	0%	35%	35%	35%
NZD	40%	50%	40%	35%	50%	35%	40%	35%	35%	0%	40%	40%
PEN	45%	35%	25%	20%	35%	25%	30%	20%	35%	40%	0%	20%
PHP	40%	35%	25%	20%	35%	25%	30%	20%	35%	35%	20%	0%
PLN	25%	50%	40%	40%	55%	35%	40%	40%	30%	40%	40%	40%
RON	30%	45%	30%	30%	40%	35%	40%	30%	30%	40%	35%	35%
RUB	50%	50%	40%	35%	50%	40%	40%	35%	40%	50%	35%	40%
SAR	45%	35%	25%	15%	30%	25%	30%	15%	35%	40%	15%	15%
SEK	25%	45%	35%	35%	45%	35%	40%	30%	20%	35%	35%	35%
SGD	35%	35%	20%	15%	30%	20%	30%	15%	25%	30%	15%	15%
THB	40%	35%	25%	20%	35%	25%	35%	20%	35%	35%	20%	20%
TRY	70%	75%	70%	70%	75%	70%	70%	70%	70%	70%	70%	70%
TWD	40%	35%	25%	15%	30%	20%	30%	15%	30%	35%	15%	15%
USD	45%	35%	25%	15%	30%	25%	30%	15%	35%	40%	15%	15%
ZAR	50%	60%	50%	50%	65%	45%	50%	45%	45%	50%	50%	50%

三、全球保险资本标准（ICS）2.0 版本　二级文件

币种	PLN	RON	RUB	SAR	SEK	GD	THB	TRY	TWD	USD	ZAR
AUD	35%	40%	45%	40%	35%	30%	35%	55%	35%	40%	45%
BRL	55%	50%	60%	55%	55%	50%	55%	70%	55%	55%	65%
CAD	35%	30%	40%	25%	30%	20%	30%	55%	25%	25%	45%
CHF	35%	30%	45%	35%	30%	25%	35%	65%	30%	35%	55%
CLP	40%	40%	40%	30%	40%	30%	35%	60%	30%	30%	50%
CNY	40%	30%	35%	5%	35%	15%	20%	60%	10%	5%	50%
COP	45%	45%	45%	35%	45%	35%	35%	60%	35%	35%	55%
CZK	25%	25%	45%	35%	25%	30%	35%	60%	35%	35%	50%
DKK	25%	20%	40%	30%	20%	25%	30%	60%	25%	30%	50%
EUR	25%	20%	40%	30%	20%	25%	30%	60%	25%	30%	50%
GBP	35%	30%	40%	25%	30%	25%	30%	60%	25%	25%	50%
HKD	40%	30%	35%	5%	35%	15%	20%	60%	10%	5%	55%
HUF	25%	30%	50%	45%	25%	35%	40%	60%	40%	45%	50%
IDR	50%	45%	50%	35%	45%	35%	35%	70%	35%	35%	60%
ILS	35%	30%	40%	25%	35%	20%	25%	55%	25%	25%	50%
INR	40%	30%	35%	15%	35%	15%	20%	55%	15%	15%	50%
JPY	50%	40%	50%	30%	40%	30%	35%	70%	30%	30%	65%
KRW	35%	35%	40%	25%	35%	20%	25%	55%	20%	25%	45%
MXN	40%	40%	40%	30%	40%	30%	35%	60%	30%	30%	50%
MYR	35%	30%	35%	15%	30%	15%	20%	55%	15%	15%	45%
NOK	30%	30%	40%	35%	20%	25%	35%	60%	30%	35%	45%
NZD	40%	40%	50%	40%	35%	30%	35%	60%	35%	40%	50%
PEN	40%	30%	35%	15%	35%	15%	20%	60%	15%	15%	50%
PHP	40%	30%	40%	15%	35%	15%	20%	55%	15%	15%	50%
PLN	0%	30%	45%	40%	30%	35%	40%	55%	40%	40%	50%
RON	30%	0%	40%	630%	25%	25%	35%	60%	30%	30%	50%
RUB	45%	40%	0%	35%	45%	35%	40%	65%	35%	40%	55%
SAR	40%	35%	35%	0%	35%	15%	20%	60%	10%	5%	55%
SEK	30%	25%	45%	25%	0%	30%	35%	60%	30%	30%	50%
SGD	35%	25%	35%	15%	20%	0%	15%	55%	10%	15%	45%
THB	40%	30%	40%	20%	35%	15%	0%	55%	20%	20%	50%
TRY	70%	70%	75%	70%	70%	65%	70%	0%	70%	70%	75%
TWD	35%	30%	35%	10%	30%	10%	20%	55%	0%	10%	50%
USD	40%	30%	35%	5%	35%	15%	20%	60%	10%	0%	55%
ZAR	50%	50%	55%	55%	50%	45%	50%	60%	50%	55%	0%

7.3.7 集中度风险

7.3.7.1 除房地产外资产的集中度风险

217. 除房地产外资产的集中度风险最低资本计量如下：

$$f \times \left(\frac{\sum_{E_i > T}(E_i - T)(d.T_i^{eq} + K_i^{cr})}{(d.K^{eq} + K^{cr})} + T \right)$$

其中：

- $f = 0.71656$；
- $d = 0.95$；
- E_i 为第 i 个关联交易对手组的净风险暴露；
- T 为 IAIG 确定的风险暴露阈值，使得公司计算集中度风险的交易对手多于 10 个，少于 100 个；
- K_i^{eq} 为第 i 个交易对手的权益风险最低资本（考虑风险分散和公司管理行为之前）；
- K_i^{cr} 为第 i 个交易对手的信用风险最低资本（考虑风险分散和管理层行为之前）；
- K^{eq} 为 IAIG 权益风险最低资本总和（考虑风险分散和管理层行为之前）；
- K^{cr} 为 IAIG 信用风险最低资本总和（考虑风险分散和管理层行为之前）。

218. 关联交易对手组按照巴塞尔银行监管委员会（BCBS）相关定义[①]确定。如果两个及以上自然人或法人至少满足以下一个条件，则认为是一个关联交易对手组：

a. 控制关系，其中一个交易对手直接或间接控制其他几个；

b. 经济依赖，如果其中一个交易对手遭遇财务问题，另外几个也可能会遇到财务问题。

219. 对中央政府的风险暴露免除计量集中度风险最低资本。公共部门的风险暴露，如果没有中央政府的担保或保证，例如，省、州或市政债务，需要根据相应的权益风险最低资本和信用风险最低资本计算集中度风险最低资本。

220. 总的交易对手风险暴露包括表内和表外业务，应考虑以下因素：

a. 再保险交易对手风险暴露以压力前的基础情景确定[②]；

b. OTC 衍生品风险暴露以适当的信用等价基础确定，不计算中央交易对手的风险暴露；

c. 投资基金和结构性产品根据穿透方法计算风险暴露；

d. 非关联（外部）担保、承诺、银行存款、收据和其他由于交易对手违约导致可

[①] 详见 BCBS 出版物《计量和控制大规模风险敞口的监管框架》（2014 年 4 月），该框架还概述了评估是否存在"控制"或"经济依赖"的标准。

[②] 与巨灾情景相关的或有风险不计算在风险暴露里。

能的金融损失，应包括在内；

e. 除有特别说明外，总风险暴露以第 5 节所描述的 MAV 方法计算。

221. 净交易对手风险暴露根据以下情况来确定：

a. 独立账户（或投资风险完全由保单持有人承担的寿险保险合同）资产除外，任何用于支持对保单持有人提供的保证条款的资产计算在内；

b. 如果某些负债有法律强制性权利可以用于抵消资产，则可抵消资产的风险暴露；

c. 抵押或者无条件不可逆担保的风险暴露，可以采用第 7.4.2.1.1 节和第 7.4.2.2.3 节所述的替代法计算抵押或担保的覆盖比例。对初始交易对手的风险暴露由提供抵押或担保方的风险暴露代替。如果对公司的风险暴露，由中央政府代替，则该部分风险暴露不计算交易对手集中度风险最低资本，与第 219 段保持一致；

d. 对于有担保的非寿险再保险的风险暴露，采用第 7.4.2.1.2 节所述的折减法。

7.3.7.2 房地产

222. 房地产风险暴露是指公司直接持有和间接持有的，单一房地产，或者一个在 250 米直径范围内的房地产群。

223. 上述房地产风险暴露超过 IAIG 与保险业务相关的净投资资产的 3%，按超过部分的 25% 计量集中度风险最低资本。净房地产风险暴露根据第 220 段和第 221 段计算。

7.4 信用风险

7.4.1 信用风险最低资本计算

7.4.1.1 风险类别

224. 信用风险最低资本适用于借款人特定敞口类别的所有高级债务。优先股和混合债务，包括次级债，不纳入信用风险最低资本计算，应参照第 7.3.3 节中规定计提权益风险最低资本。

225. 中央政府、多边开发银行和跨国家组织发行的债务敞口不计算信用风险最低资本。非中央政府发行或担保的地方政府、市政机构以及其他政府实体敞口划归为"公共部门实体"类。对政府或市政部门拥有但不予担保的商业机构敞口划归为"公司"类。

226. "公司"类敞口包括银行和证券公司发行的债务，但不包括再保险公司发行的债务。有评级的商业抵押贷款应归入"公司"类敞口。

227. "证券化"类涵盖所持全部抵押支持证券和其他资产支持证券，同时也涵盖底层资产现金流通过 SPV 用于偿还债券持有人款项的其他资产。如果底层的资产池本身包括"证券化"资产，则对上述资产的敞口属于"再证券化"类。

228. "受监管银行短期债务"类包括活期存款、初始期限少于 3 个月的债务。受监管银行指的是受《巴塞尔框架》偿付能力监管的银行。所有其他的银行敞口均属于"公司"类。

229. 投连险业务资产，或由保单持有人承担资产全部信用风险的独立账户，均不计提信用风险最低资本。然而，因上述资产信用风险损失产生的相关负债增加（如由于未来费用收入减少），IAIG 按本节所述，计提信用风险最低资本。

230. 可计入实际资本的非实缴金融工具，也需计提信用风险最低资本。视同对或有资本提供人的直接信用风险暴露。

231. 表外敞口的信用风险最低资本基于第 7.4.1.4 节中规定的信用等额计算。

7.4.1.2 敞口期限分布

232. 计算信用风险最低资本时，对于每个信用敞口的有效期限计算方法如下：

$$\text{有效期限} = \sum_t t_t \times CF_t / \sum_t CF_t$$

其中，CF_t 表示借款人在 t 期间合同约定应付的现金流（本金、利息和费用）。

233. 如果无法按照上述方法计算合同付款的有效期限，则可采用保守法计算，例如使用借款人在合同约定中被允许充分履行义务（本金、利息和费用）的最长剩余时间（以年为单位）。

234. 对于净额结算的场外交易衍生工具总合约，期限为净额结算交易期限的加权平均值，权重与交易名义本金成正比。

235. 计算有效期限前，应将对一个集团的所有敞口汇总并按评级类别分组。

236. 当存在合格的担保或抵押，使风险敞口评级类别发生改变时，应根据底层敞口的期限，而非担保或抵押的期限来计算有效期限。

7.4.1.3 再保险敞口

237. 贝氏评级（AM Best）的信用评级结果仅限于计算再保险敞口信用风险最低资本。保险公司财务实力评级贝氏评级（AM Best）与 ICS 评级类别的对应关系详见第 3.4 节。

238. 再保险敞口包括资产负债表上所有再保险正资产和应收款。负敞口不包括在内。

239. 再保险敞口应考虑由政府实体或保险市场共同支持的强制保险池分保后的净额。对该部分强制保险池的分保需单独计算。

240. 再保险敞口应包括所有因再保险业务产生且被 ICS 风险计量要求所认可的信用风险。

241. 巨灾压力情景和寿险业务压力情景的影响（在考虑管理层行为前）应基于再保前总额和再保后净额计算。根据再保险公司的情况，再保险前总额与再保后净额之差划归为相应的信用风险类别。该计算在巨灾风险最低资本和寿险风险最低资本层面进行（上述风险最低资本分散后）。

242. 即使资产负债表内无再保险资产或已被应付款全额抵消，修正共保和资金预扣仍需计提最低资本。

243. 对于资金预扣及类似措施，如满足以下所有条件，IAIG 可按照处理抵押品的方式处理再保险公司的应付款及其他负债：

a. IAIG 已与再保险公司书面签订双边净额结算合同或协议，约定资产到期产生单一法律义务。根据此类协议，如果再保险公司由于违约、破产、清算或类似情况未能履约，IAIG 仅有一项付款义务或索赔要求，金额为负债与应付款的净额之和。

b. IAIG 拥有合理的书面法律意见并在其中明确，如遇任何法律挑战，相关法院或行政机关可认定，净额结算协议下所欠金额为所有相关司法辖区法律规定的净额。得此结论前，法律意见须在其条款中解决全部净额结算协议的有效性和可执行性问题。

i. 所有相关司法辖区的法律包括：

● 再保险公司成立所处司法辖区的法律；此外，如果涉及再保险公司的国外分支机构，则还需包括该分支机构所在司法辖区的法律；

● 管辖保险交易的法律；以及

● 管辖实施净额结算所需合同或协议的法律。

ii. 法律意见在 IAIG 所在国司法辖区的法律界，或在以合理方式解决所有相关问题的法律备忘录中获得认可。

c. IAIG 已制定流程，旨在根据相关法律可能发生的变化，在必要时更新法律意见，以确保净额结算持续有效。

7.4.1.4　表外信用风险敞口

7.4.1.4.1　场外交易衍生工具的信用等额

244. 场外交易衍生工具的信用等额根据《巴塞尔框架》[①] 附件 4、第 VII 节中的当期风险暴露法计算。依此方法，IAIG 根据以下要素相加计算当前重置成本：

a. 以公允价值计算且合约价值为正的总体重置成本；

b. 基于票面名义本金计算的潜在信用风险暴露，系数按照剩余期限划分，参照表 21。

表 21　潜在信用风险暴露的计算

剩余期限	利率	汇率和黄金	权益	贵金属（除黄金外）	其他大宗商品
小于等于 1 年	0.00%	1.00%	6.00%	7.00%	10.00%
大于 1 年且小于等于 5 年	0.50%	5.00%	8.00%	7.00%	12.00%
大于 5 年	1.50%	7.50%	10.00%	8.00%	15.00%

245. 信用衍生工具不使用当期风险暴露法。信用保护买方按照担保和信用衍生工具处理（参阅第 7.4.2.2 节），信用保护卖方则视为表外直接信用替代，使用 100% 的信用

---

① 详见 http://www.bis.org/publ/bcbs128.pdf。

转换因子(详见第 7.4.1.4.2 节)。

246. 对于涉及本金多次交换的合约,因子应乘以合约中的剩余付款次数。

247. 对在指定付款日期后清算未偿敞口的合约,且该合约通过重置条款在特定日期使其合约价值为零,则剩余期限是距下一重置日期的时间。对于剩余期限超过一年且满足上述条件的利率合约,附加因子下限为 0.5%。

248. 表 21 中未涵盖的合约类别按其他大宗商品处理。

249. 单一货币浮动利率互换不计算潜在信用风险暴露,仅基于市场价值计算信用风险暴露。

250. 附加金额根据有效金额而非名义金额计算。如果通过交易结构对于名义金额加杠杆或进行增强,IAIG 应在确定潜在未来敞口时,使用实际或有效的名义金额。

251. 无论重置成本为正或为负,所有场外交易合约需计算潜在信用敞口(单一货币浮动利率互换除外)。

252. 如满足以下条件,IAIG 可对合约更替[①]或其他任何法定允许的合约进行净额结算。

a. IAIG 已与每个交易对手书面签订双边净额结算合同或协议,从而形成单一法律义务,涵盖所有净额结算的双边交易。如果交易对手由于违约、破产、清算或类似情况未能履约,IAIG 则仅有一项付款义务或索赔要求,金额为该交易对手交易正负市场价值的净额之和。

b. IAIG 拥有合理的书面法律意见,并在其中明确,如遇任何法律挑战,相关法院或行政机关将认定,净额结算协议下的风险敞口为所有相关司法辖区法律规定的净额。应确保法律意见在其条款中解决全部净额结算协议的有效性和可执行性问题。

i. 所有相关司法辖区的法律包括:

● 交易对手注册成立所处司法辖区的法律;此外,如果涉及交易对手的国外分支机构,还需该分支机构所在司法辖区的法律;

● 管辖保险交易的法律;以及

● 管辖实施净额结算所需合同或协议的法律。

ii. 法律意见在 IAIG 所在国司法界,或在以合理方式解决所有相关问题的法律备忘录中获得认可。

c. IAIG 已制定内部流程核准,在计量资本时能够认可该净额结算交易,针对该交易的法律意见显示其符合上述标准。

d. IAIG 已制定流程,旨在根据相关法律可能发生的变化,在必要时更新法律意见,

[①] 合约更替指两个交易对手根据书面的双边合同约定,对对方在指定日期有给付指定货币的义务,自动与其他相同币种相同日期的支付义务合并,法律上认可其以单一结算金额替代之前的各项支付义务。

确保净额结算持续有效。

e. IAIG 须在其档案中保留所有必要文件。

253. 任何包含免责条款①的合约均不能基于净额结算计算信用风险最低资本。

254. 双边净额远期、互换、已购期权及类似衍生工具交易的信用敞口，为净市值重置成本（如为正）与各基础合约名义本金附加额的总和。而对于合法有效且名义本金等于现金流的合约，计算其潜在信用风险暴露时，名义本金则定义为各货币在各评估日到期的净收入。

255. 总附加额是所有货币的法定债务现金流，在每个评估日，通过相同货币，以净额结算所有应收和应付金额来计算。净债务现金流通过每个评估日的当前远期汇率转换为报告货币。转换后，将评估日应收额相加，并乘以适当的附加因子，即计算出总附加额。

256. 净额交易潜在信用风险暴露为以下要素之和：

a. 根据第 255 段计算得出的附加额的 40%；以及

b. 当前净重置成本与当前正重置成本比率（NGR）乘以附加额的 60%，其中：
NGR = 净重置成本水平/法定净额结算的正重置成本水平

7.4.1.4.2 其他表外敞口的信用等额

257. 非场外衍生工具产生的表外敞口通过其名义金额乘以信用转换因子（CCF）转换为信用敞口等额：

a. 对于原始期限不超过 1 年和 1 年以上的承付款项，CCF 分别为 20% 和 50%。对于无须事先通知可被 IAIG 随时无条件取消，或由于借款人信用恶化而自动取消的承付款项，CCF 为 0%；

b. 直接信用替代对应的 CCF 为 100%。如果 IAIG 已担保，或出售信用衍生工具，或以其他方式承担债务证券的信用风险，其最低资本与 IAIG 直接持有基础证券的最低资本相同；

c. 对于回购协议及进行有追索权的资产出售（信用风险仍处于 IAIG 一方），CCF 为 100%；

d. 对于远期资产购买、远期存款及部分缴足的股票和证券（代表已部分提款的承付款项），CCF 为 100%；

e. 对于交易相关的或有项目，CCF 为 50%；

f. 对于票据发行便利（NIF）和循环包销便利（RUF），CCF 为 50%；

g. 对于 IAIG 签发或确认的、因货物运输产生的短期自偿贸易信用证，CCF 为 20%；

h. 如有机构对表外项目提供承付款项，IAIG 则采用两个适用 CCF 中的较低一个；

---

① 免责条款允许不违约的交易对手只向违约方有限付款或不付款。

i. 表外证券化 CCF 为 100%。

7.4.1.5 证券融资交易

258. 证券融资交易的评级类别，以交易对手方或出借证券评级类别较低的为准。证券融资交易中收到的抵押品认定标准与普通贷款交易相同（详见第 7.4.2.1 节）。

7.4.1.6 信用风险因子

259. 表 22 ~ 表 25 按 ICS 评级和期限列出了不同敞口类别对应的 ICS 信用风险因子。

表 22　公共部门实体信用风险因子

ICS RC	期限													
	0—1	1—2	2—3	3—4	4—5	5—6	6—7	7—8	8—9	9—10	10—11	11—12	12—13	13—14	14 +
1 或 2	0.1%	0.4%	0.5%	0.6%	0.7%	0.8%	0.9%	1.0%	1.0%	1.1%	1.1%	1.2%	1.2%	1.2%	1.3%
3	0.4%	1.0%	1.3%	1.5%	1.8%	2.0%	2.2%	2.4%	2.5%	2.7%	2.8%	2.9%	3.0%	3.0%	3.1%
4	1.0%	2.2%	2.6%	3.0%	3.3%	3.6%	3.9%	4.1%	4.2%	4.4%	4.5%	4.6%	4.7%	4.8%	4.9%
5	2.5%	5.1%	6.0%	6.6%	7.0%	7.3%	7.5%	7.6%	7.6%	7.7%	7.8%	7.8%	7.9%	7.9%	7.9%
6	6.3%	10.8%	11.8%	12.3%	12.5%	12.7%	12.7%	12.7%	12.7%	12.7%	12.7%	12.7%	12.7%	12.7%	12.7%
7	22.0%	24.7%	25.2%	25.3%	25.3%	25.3%	25.3%	25.3%	25.3%	25.3%	25.3%	25.3%	25.3%	25.3%	25.3%
未评级	2.5%	5.1%	6.0%	6.6%	7.0%	7.3%	7.5%	7.6%	7.6%	7.7%	7.8%	7.8%	7.9%	7.9%	7.9%
违约	35.0%	35.0%	35.0%	35.0%	35.0%	35.0%	35.0%	35.0%	35.0%	35.0%	35.0%	35.0%	35.0%	35.0%	35.0%

表 23　公司和再保险机构信用风险因子

ICS RC	期限													
	0—1	1—2	2—3	3—4	4—5	5—6	6—7	7—8	8—9	9—10	10—11	11—12	12—13	13—14	14 +
1 或 2	0.2%	0.7%	0.9%	1.2%	1.4%	1.6%	1.7%	1.9%	2.0%	2.1%	2.2%	2.3%	2.4%	2.4%	2.5%
3	0.6%	1.3%	1.6%	1.8%	2.1%	2.3%	2.6%	2.8%	3.0%	3.2%	3.3%	3.4%	3.5%	3.6%	3.7%
4	1.4%	3.0%	3.6%	4.1%	4.5%	4.9%	5.1%	5.3%	5.4%	5.6%	5.7%	5.8%	5.9%	6.0%	6.0%
5	3.6%	7.1%	8.3%	9.0%	9.4%	9.7%	9.8%	9.8%	9.8%	9.8%	9.8%	9.8%	9.8%	9.8%	9.8%
6	8.9%	14.4%	15.3%	15.6%	15.6%	15.6%	15.6%	15.6%	15.6%	15.6%	15.6%	15.6%	15.6%	15.6%	15.6%
7	35.0%	35.0%	35.0%	35.0%	35.0%	35.0%	35.0%	35.0%	35.0%	35.0%	35.0%	35.0%	35.0%	35.0%	35.0%
未评级	6.3%	10.7%	11.8%	12.3%	12.5%	12.6%	12.7%	12.7%	12.7%	12.7%	12.7%	12.7%	12.7%	12.7%	12.7%
违约	35.0%	35.0%	35.0%	35.0%	35.0%	35.0%	35.0%	35.0%	35.0%	35.0%	35.0%	35.0%	35.0%	35.0%	35.0%

表 24　证券化信用风险因子

ICS RC	期限													
	0—1	1—2	2—3	3—4	4—5	5—6	6—7	7—8	8—9	9—10	10—11	11—12	12—13	13—14	14 +
1 或 2	0.2%	0.7%	0.9%	1.2%	1.4%	1.6%	1.7%	1.9%	2.0%	2.1%	2.2%	2.3%	2.4%	2.4%	2.5%
3	0.6%	1.3%	1.6%	1.8%	2.1%	2.3%	2.6%	2.8%	3.0%	3.2%	3.3%	3.4%	3.5%	3.6%	3.7%

续表

ICS RC	期限														
	0—1	1—2	2—3	3—4	4—5	5—6	6—7	7—8	8—9	9—10	10—11	11—12	12—13	13—14	14+
4	1.4%	3.0%	3.6%	4.1%	4.5%	4.9%	5.1%	5.3%	5.4%	5.6%	5.7%	5.8%	5.9%	6.0%	6.0%
5	10.8%	21.3%	24.9%	27.0%	28.2%	29.1%	29.4%	29.4%	29.4%	29.4%	29.4%	29.4%	29.4%	29.4%	29.4%
6	100.0%	100.0%	100.0%	100.0%	100.0%	100.0%	100.0%	100.0%	100.0%	100.0%	100.0%	100.0%	100.0%	100.0%	100.0%
7	100.0%	100.0%	100.0%	100.0%	100.0%	100.0%	100.0%	100.0%	100.0%	100.0%	100.0%	100.0%	100.0%	100.0%	100.0%
未评级	100.0%	100.0%	100.0%	100.0%	100.0%	100.0%	100.0%	100.0%	100.0%	100.0%	100.0%	100.0%	100.0%	100.0%	100.0%
违约	100.0%	100.0%	100.0%	100.0%	100.0%	100.0%	100.0%	100.0%	100.0%	100.0%	100.0%	100.0%	100.0%	100.0%	100.0%

表25 再证券化信用风险因子

ICS RC	期限														
	0—1	1—2	2—3	3—4	4—5	5—6	6—7	7—8	8—9	9—10	10—11	11—12	12—13	13—14	14+
1或2	0.4%	1.4%	1.8%	2.4%	2.8%	3.2%	3.4%	3.8%	4.0%	4.2%	4.4%	4.6%	4.8%	4.8%	5.0%
3	1.2%	2.6%	3.2%	3.6%	4.2%	4.6%	5.2%	5.6%	6.0%	6.4%	6.6%	6.8%	7.0%	7.2%	7.4%
4	2.8%	6.0%	7.2%	8.2%	9.0%	9.8%	10.2%	10.6%	10.8%	11.2%	11.4%	11.6%	11.8%	12.0%	12.0%
5	21.6%	42.6%	49.8%	54.0%	56.4%	58.2%	58.8%	58.8%	58.8%	58.8%	58.8%	58.8%	58.8%	58.8%	58.8%
6	100.0%	100.0%	100.0%	100.0%	100.0%	100.0%	100.0%	100.0%	100.0%	100.0%	100.0%	100.0%	100.0%	100.0%	100.0%
7	100.0%	100.0%	100.0%	100.0%	100.0%	100.0%	100.0%	100.0%	100.0%	100.0%	100.0%	100.0%	100.0%	100.0%	100.0%
未评级	100.0%	100.0%	100.0%	100.0%	100.0%	100.0%	100.0%	100.0%	100.0%	100.0%	100.0%	100.0%	100.0%	100.0%	100.0%
违约	100.0%	100.0%	100.0%	100.0%	100.0%	100.0%	100.0%	100.0%	100.0%	100.0%	100.0%	100.0%	100.0%	100.0%	100.0%

260. 保单贷款的信用风险因子为零。第228段定义的受监管银行短期债务的风险因子为0.4%。代理机构和经纪公司应收账款的风险因子为6.3%。其他所有资产的风险因子均为8%。如果保险合同负债中包含与应收保费相关的责任，且保险合同因投保人违约而失效时，核销应收保费且减少保险合同负债，则IAIG可将应收保费排除在风险敞口之外。

7.4.1.7 抵押贷款

7.4.1.7.1 还款依赖财产收入的商业和农业抵押贷款

261. 根据数据的可得性，最低资本可通过以下三种方法之一（优先级依次递减）计算：

- 方法1：基于贷款价值比（LTV）和偿债备付率（DSCR）确定ICS商业抵押贷款（CM）类别的最低资本；
- 方法2：仅基于贷款价值比（LTV）确定ICS商业抵押贷款（CM）类别的最低资本；或
- 方法3：不使用信用质量区分工具。

262. 对于农业和商业抵押贷款方法1，表26列示ICS CM1至CM5与LTV和DSCR

的对应关系。CM6 和 CM7 分别用于逾期贷款和丧失抵押品赎回权贷款。

表 26 ICS CM 类别关联表，方法 1

		LTV					
	CM	<60%	60%~69.9%	70%~79.9%	80%~89.9%	90%~99.9%	≥100%
DSCR	<0.6	CM3	CM3	CM3	CM4	CM4	CM5
	0.6~0.79	CM3	CM3	CM3	CM4	CM4	CM5
	0.8~0.99	CM3	CM3	CM3	CM4	CM4	CM5
	1~1.19	CM2	CM2	CM3	CM3	CM4	CM4
	1.2~1.39	CM2	CM2	CM3	CM3	CM3	CM3
	1.4~1.59	CM1	CM2	CM3	CM2	CM3	CM3
	1.6~1.79	CM1	CM1	CM1	CM2	CM3	CM3
	1.8~1.99	CM1	CM1	CM1	CM2	CM2	CM2
	≥2	CM1	CM1	CM1	CM2	CM2	CM2

263. 对于农业和商业抵押贷款方法 1，应用以下风险因子：

表 27 农业和商业抵押贷款风险因子，方法 1

ICS CM 类型	压力因子
CM1	4.80%
CM2	6.00%
CM3	7.80%
CM4	15.80%
CM5	23.50%
CM6	35%
CM7	35%

264. 对于方法 2 下仅有 LTV 数据的农业和商业抵押贷款，ICS CM1 至 CM4 与 LTV 及相关风险因子的对应关系详见表 28。与方法 1 相同，CM6 和 CM7 分别适用于逾期贷款和丧失抵押品赎回权贷款。

表 28 农业和商业抵押贷款风险因子，方法 2

ICS CM 类别	压力因子	LTV 最小值	LTV 最大值
CM1	4.80%	0%	59%
CM2	6.00%	60%	79%
CM3	7.80%	80%	99%
CM4	15.80%	100%	不适用
CM5	不适用	—	—
CM6	35%	—	—
CM7	35%	—	—

265. 对于无法获得 LTV 和 DSCR 数据的农业和商业抵押贷款方法 3，均统一使用 8% 的风险因子。

7.4.1.7.2 还款不依赖财产收入的商业和农业抵押贷款

266. 当抵押贷款的 LTV 比率高于 60% 时，风险因子为对借款人常规信用敞口的风险因子。当抵押贷款的 LTV 比率为 60% 或更低时，风险因子为 3.6% 或对借款人常规信用敞口的风险因子二者中较低的一项。

7.4.1.7.3 住房抵押贷款

267. 对于正常履约①、其还款依赖基础资产产生收入的住房抵押贷款，抵押贷款 LTV 比率对应的适用因子如表 29 所示。

表 29　住房抵押贷款（还款依赖基础资产产生收入）风险因子

LTV	压力因子
LTV≤60%	4.20%
60% < LTV≤80%	5.40%
LTV > 80%	7.20%

268. 对于正常履约、其还款不依赖基础资产产生收入的住房抵押贷款，抵押贷款 LTV 比率对应的适用因子如表 30 所示。

表 30　住房抵押贷款（还款不依赖基础资产产生收入）风险因子

LTV	压力因子
LTV≤40%	1.50%
40% < LTV≤60%	1.80%
60% < LTV≤80%	2.10%
80% < LTV≤90%	2.70%
90% < LTV≤100%	3.30%
LTV > 100%	4.50%

269. 对于不良抵押贷款，适用因子为 35%。

7.4.2　合格抵押品、担保和信用衍生工具

7.4.2.1　抵押品的认定

270. 抵押交易指：

a. IAIG 有信用风险敞口或潜在信用风险敞口；且

b. 信用风险敞口或潜在信用风险敞口全部或部分由交易对手或代表交易对手的第三

---

① 正常履约和不良贷款的定义与巴塞尔委员会一致，该定义以拖欠状况（逾期 90 天）和违约可能性为中心为贷款和债务证券建立了分类标准。不良敞口包括：①巴塞尔框架下定义的所有已违约敞口；或者②所有受损风险敞口（即因其信用恶化而对其估值进行下调的风险敞口）；或者③逾期超过 90 天的重大风险敞口，或者有证据表明，无论逾期天数如何，都不太可能在不变现抵押品的情况下全额偿还本息。

方提供的抵押品对冲。

271. 仅以下抵押品类别可被认定：

a. 由主权实体发行或具有 ICS 评级 4 或更高级别的证券；

b. 黄金；

c. 满足以下条件的共同基金：

- 每日公开报价；且

- 该共同基金仅限于投资上述合格抵押品。

d. 信用证。

272. 如满足以下所有条件，计算信用风险最低资本时应考虑抵押品：

a. 抵押品的影响不能重复计算。特别是对已在特定债项评级中反映的抵押品，不予认定。关于评级使用的所有标准均适用于抵押品。

b. 用于抵押交易的所有文件对各方均有约束力，并在所有相关司法辖区具有法律效力。IAIG 已通过充分的法律审查对上述文件进行验证，并拥有充分的法律依据得出结论，且在必要时通过进一步审查以确保法律的持续效力。

c. 涉及抵押品质押或转移的法律机制，在发生违约、无力清偿债务或破产（或其他交易文件中规定的一项或多项信用事件）时，确保 IAIG 有权及时清算或合法拥有交易对手（如适用，以及持有抵押品的托管人）的抵押品。此外，IAIG 已采取所有必要措施，满足适用 IAIG 从抵押品中获取和维持有效担保权益的相关法律要求，例如，在注册服务商注册，或行使与抵押品所有权转让相关的净值权或抵消权。

d. 交易对手信用状况和抵押品价值不存在实质性正相关。例如，交易对手（或任何相关集团）发行的证券就不符合要求。

e. IAIG 拥有清晰稳健的及时清算抵押品流程，确保宣布交易对手违约和清算抵押品的法定条件可被遵守，且抵押品可被迅速清算。

f. 如托管人持有抵押品，IAIG 应采取合理步骤，确保托管人将抵押品与自身资产分割。

g. 抵押品抵押应至少覆盖全部敞口期。

273. 如果抵押品币种与敞口币种不同，按当前汇率换算，受保敞口金额应为抵押品金额的 80%。

7.4.2.1.1 抵押品认定的默认方法：替代法

274. 风险敞口中，以市值计价合格抵押品担保的部分，应划为适用于抵押品工具的评级类别，其余部分应划为适用于交易对手的评级类别。

7.4.2.1.2 有抵押的非寿险再保险敞口的替代方法：折减法

275. 依据折减法，抵押品如满足第 272 段 a 至 f 的要求，且质押至少满一年，则符合认定条件。

276. 折减法降低了分出保险人持有的有抵押品的敞口金额。调整后的再保险敞口定义为：

调整后的再保险敞口 = 再保险资产和应收款 + 资本要求 − 抵押品

其中，资本要求包括再保险业务和/或其支持抵押品的非寿险风险、巨灾风险、市场风险和信用风险最低资本，运用第 7.6 节的相关规定进行风险聚合计算。

277. 非寿险风险和巨灾风险最低资本等于再保险合约引起的 ICS 最低资本的降低金额。该金额可通过 25% 的相关性，与市场风险最低资本和信用风险最低资本聚合计算。

278. 信用和市场风险最低资本特定情形如下：

a. 作为抵押品的所有资产都应计提信用风险最低资本。

b. 作为抵押品的所有资产应基于颗粒度调整法计提资产集中度风险最低资本，且单独计算（与分出保险人自身资产组合相隔离）。

c. 已分保负债和作为抵押品的资产应合并单独计算汇率风险最低资本，按已分保负债的基础货币计价，且不适用于第 210 段 g 中所述的扣除。

d. 已分保负债和作为抵押品的资产应合并单独计算利率和非违约利差风险最低资本。

e. 作为抵押品的所有资产都应计提权益风险最低资本和房地产风险最低资本。

f. 运用第 7.3.1 节的相关系数矩阵，聚合资产集中度、汇率、利率、非违约价差、权益和房地产各子类风险最低资本，计算得到市场风险最低资本。

279. 有抵押的非寿险再保险的信用风险最低资本等于调整后的再保险暴露乘以适用于再保险人的信用风险因子。

7.4.2.2　担保和信用衍生工具的认定

280. 为确定交易对手的 ICS 评级，如满足以下所有条件，IAIG 可考虑担保和信用衍生工具提供的信用保护：

a. 担保或信用衍生工具是直接、明确、不可撤销和无条件的。

b. 担保人或保护提供人比被担保或被保护的交易对手具备更高的评级。

c. IAIG 符合第 7.4.2.2.1 节中有关风险管理的最低特定条件。

281. 资本的计算基于替代法，交易对手敞口的受保部分使用担保人或保护提供人的评级类别，而未受保部分使用交易对手的评级类别。

7.4.2.2.1　风险管理要求

282. 第 280 段中提到的适用于担保和信用衍生工具的最低条件如下：

• 信用保护的影响未重复计算。特别是如果该敞口的抵押品已在其债项评级中反映，则不予认定。关于评级使用的所有标准仍适用于抵押品和信用衍生工具。

• 除第 296 段中规定的主权国家提供的信用保护外，担保、反担保或信用衍生工具必须代表对保护提供人的直接索偿，且必须明确提及特定敞口或敞口池，使保护范围定义明确且无可争议。

- 信用保护合同不可撤销，除非保护购买人未付清与信用保护合同有关的款项。
- 合同中无任何条款可允许保护提供人单方面取消信用担保，或因对冲敞口的信用质量恶化而增加担保有效费用。
- 合同为无条件合同，即在IAIG的直接控制之外，合同中无任何条款可在原始交易对手未支付到期款项的情况下阻止保护提供人履行及时付款义务。
- 用于记录担保和信用衍生工具的所有文件，对各方均具有约束力，并在所有相关司法辖区具有法律效力。IAIG已对此进行了充分的法律审查，并拥有充分的法律依据得此结论，同时还将在必要时采取进一步审查确保其持续有效。

283. 除第282段中规定的要求外，担保认定还须满足以下所有条件：

a. 对于交易对手的违约/未付款，IAIG需及时要求担保人根据交易文件，针对逾期款项采取措施。担保人将根据该文件向IAIG一次性支付所有款项，或由担保人承担被担保交易对手未来的付款义务。IAIG无须事先采取法律措施推动付款。

b. 担保是担保人承担的、明确的书面义务。

c. 除另行说明，否则担保已涵盖基础债务人根据交易文件规定的所有付款类型，例如名义金额、保证金支付等。如担保不涵盖某些付款类型，相应金额则按无抵押处理。

284. 除第282段的相关规定外，信用衍生合约的认定还须满足以下所有条件：

a. 协议各方商定的信用事件至少涵盖：

i. 未能支付违约时有效基础债务条款中的应付款项（宽限期与基础义务的宽限期一致）；

ii. 债务人破产、资不抵债或无力偿还债务，或债务人未能偿还到期债务，或以书面形式承认其无力偿还到期债务及类似事件；和

iii. 涉及因免除或延迟本金、利息、费用导致信用损失事件（冲销、专项计提或损益账户中其他类似借记）的基础债务重组。

b. 如果信用衍生工具涵盖的义务超出基础债务，应参考g项中规定的允许资产错配的条件。

c. 在因未能支付而发生标的债务违约的任何宽限期到期前，信用衍生工具不会终止。

d. 只要根据可靠的估值程序严谨地估算损失，允许现金结算的信用衍生工具即可按照资本计量目的予以认定。要设置一段明确的时间来获取基础债务的信用事件期后评估。如果用于现金结算的信用衍生工具规定的参考债务与基础债务不同，应参考g项中规定的允许资产错配的条件。

e. 如果信用保护买方转让基础债务至保护卖方的权利/能力对于结算是必需的，则基础债务条款需规定，任何涉及此类转让的、必要的许可不得被无理拒绝。

f. 负责确定是否发生信用事件的各方，其身份应予以明确。确定是否发生信用事件并非保护卖方的专有责任。保护购买人也有权利/能力将风险事件的发生通知保护提供人。

g. 以下情况，允许基础债务与信用衍生工具的参考义务（用于确定现金结算价值的义务或可交付义务）发生错配：

i. 参考债务与基础债务同等优先，或次于基础债务；且

ii. 基础债务和参考债务具有相同的债务人（同一法人实体），且具有合法有效的交叉违约或交叉加速条款。

h. 以下情况，允许基础债务与用于确定是否发生信用事件的债务发生错配：

i. 用于确定是否发生信用事件的债务与基础债务同等优先，或次于基础债务；且

ii. 基础债务和参考债务具有相同的债务人（同一法人实体），且具有合法有效的交叉违约或交叉加速条款。

i. 只有等同于担保的信用违约掉期和总收益掉期才可被认定为信用保护。如果 IAIG 通过总回报掉期来购买信用保护，并将掉期中收到的净付款记为净收入，但未记录受保资产价值的抵消性恶化（通过减低公允价值或增加准备金），则其无法认定为信用保护。

285. 基础债务重组产生的无信用保护部分，若满足上述其他要求，可被部分认定为信用衍生工具，上限为以下金额较低者的 60%：

a. 信用衍生工具的金额；

b. 基础债务的金额。

7.4.2.2.2 合格担保人

286. 仅以下交易对手提供的信用保护才符合认可条件：

a. 主权实体；

b. 经外部评级的公共领域实体、银行和证券公司，其评级高于交易对手；和

c. 其他实体，包括债务人的母公司、子公司和关联公司，须具备比债务人更高的评级。

IAIG 的关联方（母公司、子公司或关联公司）提供的担保或信用保护不符合认可条件。

7.4.2.2.3 资本计量

287. 交易对手的受保部分使用信用保护卖方的评级，未受保部分使用基础交易对手的评级。

288. 如果担保或信用保护覆盖的金额小于敞口金额，且担保与未担保部分的优先级相同（IAIG 和担保人按比例分担损失），敞口的受保部分可视为担保和信用衍生工具，其余部分则被视为无担保。

289. 如果 IAIG 将一份或多份特定比例的风险转至保护卖方，并保留一定风险，且转移风险与留存风险具有不同优先级，则根据担保人评级，各份敞口均视为证券化敞口。如其中一份敞口未经评级，即使基础风险敞口经过评级，也视为未评级的证券化敞口。如果此类处理导致信用风险最低资本高于考虑担保前的最低资本，IAIG 则可忽略担保。

290. 应付款的实质阈值（损失发生时，金额低于该阈值则不予支付）视为未评级的证券化敞口。

7.4.2.2.4 汇率错配

291. 如果信用保护计价货币与敞口计价货币不同，则按当前汇率换算，受保敞口金额为信用保护名义金额的 80%。

7.4.2.2.5 期限错配

292. 如果信用保护的剩余期限小于基础敞口的剩余期限（期限错配），且信用保护的原始期限小于 1 年或剩余期限小于 3 个月，则该保护不予认定。

293. 如出现除第 292 段描述的期限错配，将运用以下方法调整：

$$Pa = P \times (t - 0.25)/(T - 0.25)$$

其中：

- Pa 是基于期限错配调整后的信用保护价值；
- P 是信用保护名义金额，如适用，则根据货币错配情况进行调整；
- T 为 5 年和敞口剩余期限（以年为单位）之间的较低值；
- t 取 T 与信用保护剩余期限（以年为单位）之间的较低值。

294. 基础敞口的剩余期限为交易对手履行债务前的最长剩余时间，且需考虑所适用的宽限期。

295. 对于信用保护，应考虑可能缩短保护期限的嵌入式期权，因此应采用最短的有效期限。特别是：

a. 如果保护卖方可以行权，剩余期限为到第一个行权日的剩余时间。

b. 如果购买保护的 IAIG 可以自主行权，但发起时的条款安排会激励 IAIG 在合约到期前进行交易，则剩余期限为到第一个行权日的剩余时间。

7.4.2.2.6 主权反担保

296. 主权间接反担保覆盖的具有担保的索赔，可按主权担保覆盖的索赔处理，但前提是：

a. 主权反担保覆盖索赔的所有信用风险要素；

b. 原始担保和反担保均满足担保的所有操作要求，但反担保不必直接、明确地对应原始索赔；且

c. 担保应是稳健的，且没有历史证据显示反担保与直接主权担保二者的担保范围不

可有效等同。

7.4.2.2.7 其他项目

297. 如果 IAIG 对单一暴露拥有多种类型的风险缓释安排，则这一暴露需依据每种风险缓释所覆盖的部分进行细分，并分别确定每一部分的评级类别。

298. 当单一保护提供人提供的信用保护期限不同时，应将其细分为单独的保护。

7.4.3 外部评级使用要求

7.4.3.1 合格的外部信用评级

299. 如果同时满足以下两项要求，IAIG 可使用 ICS 一级文件的第 149 段以外的其他任何评级机构评级：

a. 在所有 IAIG 选择使用评级的司法辖区内，评级机构都应受该辖区相应监管机构的监管或认可。

b. 评级机构至少每年公开发布一次违约和迁移的统计数据（至少追溯 7 年），并满足以下所有六项标准：

i. 客观性：评级机构的信用评级方法应是严格、系统且可经历史经验验证的。评级还须经受持续审查，并对财务状况变化及时响应。该机构对每个细分市场都有评级方法，包括严格的回溯测试（至少已应用一年、三年为佳）。

ii. 独立性：评级机构应是独立的，不受任何可作用于评级结果的政治或经济压力影响。董事会组成或评级机构股东结构造成利益冲突时，评级过程不受该利益冲突可能引发的任何限制。

iii. 国际开放/透明度：每项评级、评级的关键要素以及发行人是否参与评级过程，均应无差别地公开提供。此外，评级机构用于得出评估结果的一般程序、方法和假设也须予以公开。

iv. 信息披露：评级机构应披露以下信息：行为准则；针对受评估实体收费的一般原则；评估方法，包括违约的定义、时间范围以及每项评级的含义；每个评级类别中的实际违约率；以及评级的迁移，例如，AA 级可能随时间推移转变为 A 级。

v. 资源：评级机构应有充分资源高质量开展信用评级。这些资源确保评级机构能够与被评级实体的管理层和运营层进行持续的实质性接触，从而提升信用评级的质量。评级方法应为定性法与定量法相结合。

vi. 公信力：评级机构的外部信用评级应被独立机构（投资机构、保险机构、贸易伙伴）广泛使用。此外，评级机构还应设有相关内部流程，防止机密信息滥用。

7.4.3.2 评级类别的定义

300. 信评机构评级与 ICS 评级的关联对应基于与其评级相关的 3 年累计违约率（CDR）均值，如表 31 所示。

表31 其他信评机构评级关联表

ICS RC	3年CDR均值基于20年以上的公开数据	3年CDR均值基于7年至20年的公开数据
1	—	—
2	0≤CDR≤0.15%	—
3	0.15%＜CDR≤0.35%	0≤CDR≤0.15%
4	0.35%＜CDR≤1.20%	0.15%＜CDR≤0.35%
5	1.20%＜CDR≤10.00%	0.35%＜CDR≤1.20%
6	10.00%＜CDR≤25.00%	1.20＜CDR≤10%
7	CDR＞25%	CDR＞10%

7.4.3.3 评级的使用

301. IAIG应选择可靠的评级机构，对每种类型的信用敞口，均持续使用该机构的评级。

302. 用于确定ICS评级的任何评级均应为公开信息，即该评级应公开发布，并纳入评级机构的迁移矩阵。

303. 如果一家IAIG使用多个评级机构，但对某一证券只有一个评级，那么该评级将用于确定ICS评级。如果一家IAIG使用的评级机构对某一证券有两个评级，且这两个评级对应不同的ICS评级，则IAIG应使用两个评级中较低一个所对应的ICS评级。如果IAIG选择的评级机构对某一证券有三个或三个以上评级，则需排除对应最高ICS评级的一个评级，并选择对应次高ICS评级的评级。

304. 如果某一证券具有一个或多个特定债项评级，则该证券的ICS评级应基于这些评级确定。否则，应适用以下原则：

a. 如借款人某一特定债券有评级，但IAIG所投资债券没有评级，只有全面高于或等于评级债券的优先级时，IAIG的未评级投资才可适用ICS评级4或更高的债券评级。若非上述情况，该信用评级则不予使用，IAIG的投资将被视为未评级债务。

b. 如果借款人有信用主体评级，则只有该发行人发行的高等级债券才可获得投资级（ICS评级4或以上）评级；该发行人发行的其他未经评估的债券视为未评级。如果债券发行人或其发行人之一为ICS评级5或更低，则该评级将用于确定发行人未评级索赔的ICS评级。

c. 针对特定债券或机构的短期评估只能用于评定该债券或该机构发行的债券。这类评估既不能扩展至其他短期债券，也不能用于确定未评级长期债券的评级类别。

d. 如果未评级敞口的评级类别要基于借款人对等敞口的评级确定，则外币评级只可用于以该外币计价的风险敞口，本币评级只可用于确定以本币计价债券的评级类别。

305. 以下附加条件适用于评级的使用：

a. 集团内一个实体的外部评级不应用于确定同一集团内其他实体的评级类别。

b. 对于未评级实体，不应依据该实体拥有的资产推断其评级，不允许使用内部评级。

c. 如果增信措施已在特定债项评级中反映，则 IAIG 不应在计算信用风险最低资本时将其认定为抵押品或担保。

d. 如果评级是部分或全部基于 IAIG 或其附属机构提供的非资金支持（比如保证、增信或流动性工具）确定的，则不应使用该评级。

e. IAIG 使用的任何评估均应考虑其所有应收欠款的全部信用敞口金额。特别是，如果 IAIG 同时被拖欠本金和利息，评估应充分考虑偿还本金和利息的信用风险。

7.4.3.4 违约敞口

306. 对及时收取全部本金或利息存有合理怀疑的资产，包括未履行合同约定逾期90天以上的资产，计算信用风险最低资本时应视为违约敞口。

307. 违约资产的敞口金额应扣除所有资产负债表减记项和已记为该资产特定拨备的净额。

7.4.4 监管认可评级（SOCCA）使用要求

308. 如满足以下所有条件，则可在 ICS 中认定为 SOCCA 流程：

a. 客观性：SOCCA 进行信用评级的方法是严格、系统且可经验证的。评级还须经受监管的持续审查，并对财务状况变化及时响应。

b. 独立性：SOCCA 流程与监管部门的监管目标相一致，即信用评估流程得到监管部门的批准。信评外包应符合与内部信评流程相同的胜任性和独立性标准。

c. 国际开放/透明度：在 SOCCA 流程适用地区外运营的 IAIG 可要求对其拥有的证券分配标识/进行评级。评级结果可通过第三方平台公开访问。

d. 信息披露：须对每个标识/评级进行违约统计，以便根据公开数据计算三年累计违约率（CDRs）。

e. 资源：相关人员应具备与开展信评工作相匹配的能力和经验。SOCCA 流程须拥有充分资源，以便开展符合监管部门要求的信用评估。

f. 公信力：SOCCA 流程须拥有内部程序防止机密信息滥用。在评估证券信用风险方面，SOCCA 流程具有至少 10 年以上扎实的业务历史，具有较充分的绩效统计数据。所有标识/评级至少每年更新一次；此外，一旦发生可能影响标识评级的重大事件，会立即开展复查。

g. 与审慎监管的利益一致性：实体机构开展信用评估完全经监管部门认可并把控。监管部门批准了信用评估流程的相关政策。

7.5 操作风险

309. 操作风险最低资本要求计算如下所示：

操作风险最低资本要求 = max［非寿险保费风险暴露×因子，非寿险负债暴露×因子］+非寿险增速暴露×因子 + max［寿险（承担风险的）保费风险暴露×因子，寿险

（承担风险的）负债暴露×因子]＋寿险（承担风险的）增速暴露×因子＋寿险（不承担风险的）负债暴露×因子

310. 操作风险组成部分的计算方式是因子乘以风险暴露。第 7.1.2 节中划分的地域类别可使用相同的系数。

311. 操作风险的风险暴露和风险因子如表 32 所示。

表 32 操作风险的风险暴露和风险因子

	保费	增速	负债
非寿险操作风险			
风险暴露	最近财务年度的整体签单保费收入	相比于上一财务年度的签单保费收入，最近一个财务年度整体签单保费收入超过增长阈值（20%）部分	当前估计总额
风险因子	2.75%	2.75%	2.75%
寿险操作风险			
风险暴露	寿险（承担风险的）：最近财务年度的整体签单保费收入	寿险（承担风险的）：相比于上一财务年度的签单保费收入，最近一个财务年度整体签单保费收入超过增长阈值（20%）部分	寿险（承担风险的）：当前估计总额 寿险（不承担风险的）：当前估计总额
风险因子	寿险（承担风险的）：4%	寿险（承担风险的）：4%	寿险（承担风险的）：0.45% 寿险（不承担风险的）：0.40%

312. 整体签单保费收入包括指定财务年度内签单的所有业务（新业务和续期业务），但不包括扣减再保险或者类似可收回科目的金额。对于趸交保险保单，当期保费就是全部保费，对于其他保单，整体签单保费包括指定期间（财务年度）内所有 IAIG 有效业务的应收保费之和。

313. 当前估计总额不扣减再保险业务或者类似可收回科目的金额。

314. 为了计算操作风险增速子风险，应使用最近两年非寿险和寿险（承担风险的）的整体签单保费。这些数字是在合并报表口径下并且不考虑再保险分出。

7.6 最低资本聚合

315. 风险大类之间使用的相关系数矩阵见表 33。

表 33 风险之间相关系数矩阵

	寿险	非寿险	巨灾	市场	信用
寿险	100%	0%	25%	25%	25%
非寿险	0%	100%	25%	25%	25%
巨灾	25%	25%	100%	25%	25%
市场	25%	25%	25%	100%	25%
信用	25%	25%	25%	25%	100%

7.7 非保险最低资本要求

316. 对于保险或保险相关机构,最低资本按照第7.1~7.6节描述进行计算。

317. 对于所在行业有资本监管要求的非保险金融机构,资本要求按如下计算:

a. 对于合并报表下的银行机构,取巴塞尔协议III下风险加权资产或杠杆率两者的较大值;

b. 对于合并报表下的非银行机构,取行业资本监管要求和最近三年平均总收入的15%两者的最大值;

c. 对于采用权益法计量的银行和非银行机构,按比例计算行业监管资本要求;

d. 对于采用市场价值计量的银行和非银行机构,按照第7.3.4节描述的权益风险最低资本计算。

318. 对于所在行业没有资本监管要求的非保险金融机构,资本要求如下:

a. 对于合并报表下的银行机构,等于由杠杆率决定的风险暴露的4%;

b. 对于合并报表下的非银行机构,等于最近三年平均总收入的15%;

c. 对于采用权益法计量的银行机构,按行业资本要求的比例计算;

d. 对于采用权益法计量的非银行机构,等于三年平均总收入的15%;

e. 对于采用市场价值计量的银行和非银行机构,按照第7.3.4节描述的权益风险最低资本方法计算。

319. 对于非金融机构,按照第207段中a到d所描述的权益法或市值投资计算的权益风险最低资本来计算资本要求。

8 基准ICS:税的计量

8.1 一般原则

320. 集团有效税率(ETR)为过去三年法定有效税率的加权平均数,使用集团内各实体GAAP税前收益加权。加权平均税率计算仅覆盖与保险相关的业务,GAAP税前收益不得为负。

321. 计算ETR的法定有效税率,指截至报告日已执行或已宣布即将执行[①]的税率要求。

8.2 ICS调整的所得税影响

322. 如果同时满足以下两个标准,在进行第323段所规定的可用性评估之前,由ICS调整产生的DTA和DTL可被抵消:

a. 该实体在法律上有合法权利,可以用税收资产抵减税收负债。

---

① 例如,税务当局已宣布但尚未实施的税率变化,将对未来产生重大影响。在这种情况下,应使用新宣布的法定税率计算ETR。

b. 与收入所得税相关的递延税项是由同一税务机关征收，且满足以下任一条件：

● 征税对象为同一应税实体；或者

● 征税对象为不同应税实体，但各实体对税收资产和税收负债进行净额结算，或税收资产与税收负债在未来有大量税项结算的时刻均同时存在或灭失。

8.2.1 ICS 调整确认的 DTA 的可用性评估

323. 因 ICS 调整确认的 DTA，不得超过 GAAP DTL 净额与因 ICS 调整产生的 DTL 之和，具体计算方法如下：

增加项：

a. 经审计的当地 GAAP DTL 总额。

b. 因 ICS 调整产生的 DTL 总额。

扣减项：

c. 经审计的当地 GAAP DTA 总额；

d. 因一级资本扣除项产生的 DTL（见一级文件第 6.4.1 节）。

324. 如以上计算结果为负，因 ICS 调整产生的 DTA 应为零。

325. 第 323 段中提及的经审计的当地 GAAP DTL 和 DTA 仅限于与保险相关业务的 DTL 和 DTA。

8.3 最低资本的所得税影响

326. ICS 最低资本应体现可用的税收效应。

327. ICS 最低资本的可用税收效应按如下公式计算：

Max [0, Min (ICS 最低资本的名义税收效应，20% × ICS 最低资本，a + b + c − d)]

其中：

● 最低资本的名义税收效应 = 最低资本 × 集团 ETR；

● $a = 85\% \times \sum_{成员公司} \times$ Min（税收损失结转额度，最低资本的名义税收效应）

● b = 压力下未来应税收入 × 集团 ETR；

● c = Max (0, ICS 资产负债表内保险相关业务的 DTL − ICS 资产负债表内保险相关业务的 DTA)；和

● d = Max [0, Min (15% × ICS 最低资本, ICS 资产负债表内保险相关业务的 DTA − ICS 资产负债表内保险相关业务的 DTL)]。

8.3.1 a：税收损失结转

328. 税收损失结转是指集团内各成员公司可使用当期运营损失抵减往年税收义务的机制，各国家（地区）允许抵减的过往年数有所不同。

329. 可用税收效应中的 a 按如下计算：

● 保险相关业务的税收损失结转能力应在法人或成员公司层面计算，包括截至 ICS 报告日的所有应税的财务实体。

- ICS 最低资本的名义税收效应按 GAAP/SAP 准则下的保险合同负债规模比例分配到集团内各成员公司。

8.3.2 b：压力下未来应税收入预测

330. 可用税收效应中的 b 按以下计算：

- 当 IAIG 预计未来五年的累积利润为负时，b 应为零。
- 其他情况下，b 为合并财务报表中过去五年 GAAP 税前利润的 50%，体现兼并收购处置的影响。

8.3.3 c 和 d：递延税项

331. c、d 中的 DTA 和 DTL 应扣除一级资本扣减项产生的递延税项（见一级文件第 6.4.1 节）。

9 附加报告

9.1 GAAP+方法

9.1.1 概述

332. GAAP+方法以第 4 部分中描述的集团资产负债表为起点。以下 GAAP+方法为 IAIG 适用的各地区公认会计准则进行调整提供了指导方针和具体示例，以便在应用这些调整后，每种会计准则都可以得出合并的 GAAP+资产负债表。与 ICS 基准的市场价值调整法（MAV）一样，GAAP+调整仅针对资产负债表上最重要或重大的项目，特别是与保险相关的负债和投资资产。

333. GAAP+包含 4 种主要方法：美国公认会计准则/法定会计准则、日本公认会计准则、国际财务报告准则和中国偿二代。日本 GAAP+（J GAAP+）受本文件规定的监测期的约束。美国公认会计准则/法定会计准则、国际财务报告准则和中国偿二代方法不包括在本文件中，因为它们仍在研究阶段，需要进行实地测试。

334. 对于日本 GAAP+，适用以下注意事项：

a. 根据 IAIG 适用的各地区公认会计准则确认和终止确认负债。

b. 合同边界的定义符合 IAIG 适用的各地区公认会计准则。

c. GAAP+保险合同负债（和相关的再保险摊回）的评估应使用各地区公认会计准则规定的或者特定 GAAP+方法规定的折现率曲线。

d. GAAP+调整的计算基于最新信息和可信的假设。

e. 保单质押贷款单独列报，不与保险合同负债抵消。

f. 非保险合同负债（如发行的债务）根据各地区公认会计准则列报。按成本法计量的账面价值不需要调整为公允价值。

g. 如果保险合同负债不是作为一个整体计量，那么风险边际、审慎假设和不利偏差需要从保险合同负债评估中剔除。

h. 根据基准方法定义的风险边际（MOCE），应作为资产负债表中的一项负债。

i. 对递延税款的调整应遵循第 7.7 节中描述的基准方法。

335. 如果保险合同负债需要根据一套以上的公认会计准则计算，IAIG 对合并资产负债表中保险合同负债的每个组成部分都要使用最适当的所在地 GAAP＋方法，以将余额调整为当前估计负债。

336. 累计其他综合收益（AOCI）调整纳入实际资本，以剔除满足第 9.1.2.1 节设定标准的可供出售债务证券的未实现损益。

337. 除了累计其他综合收益（AOCI）调整，第 6 节中详述的 ICS 基准方法所有调整同样适用于日本 GAAP＋方法。

338. 日本 GAAP＋为某些最低资本要求提供了特定的方法。除非另有规定，资本要求的计算与第 7 节一致。这些计算方法在第 9.1.2.2 节到第 9.1.2.5 节中详述。

9.1.2 日本 GAAP＋方法

339. 以下内容是基于 IAIG 经审计的日本公认会计准则合并财务报告。

340. 投资资产：不需要调整。投资资产的处理与日本公认会计准则一致。一些支持寿险合同负债的资产需要进行 AOCI 调整，该调整转回了累计其他综合收益（AOCI）中报告的未实现损益，实质上是将资产价值从公允价值调至成本计量。具体参见第 9.1.2.1 节中 GAAP＋的 AOCI 调整。

341. 寿险合同负债（不包括团体保单）：寿险合同负债需要调整为当前估计，基于日本公认会计准则法定现金流测试（假设全保险期间）的结果计算。

a. 根据全保险期间现金流分析，寿险公司必须评估由流动性资产产生的未来现金流是否覆盖保险合同负债的未来现金流（现金流入和现金流出净额）。

b. 在有效业务终止时，保险合同负债的缺口或盈余的净额需要折现，折现值相应增加（或减少）保险合同负债。

c. 贴现率是当前投资组合的收益率（账面收益率）加上再投资假设，该假设与第 341 段 d 中定义的资产产生现金流的假设一致。

d. 为了预测现金流，再投资的投资回报和新钱的假设为，IAIG 投资日本政府债券的平均期限等于 IAIG 上一个会计年度投资的日本政府债券的平均期限。

e. 在计算保险合同负债的未来现金流时，需要利用实际经验数据，如死亡率、退保率、费用率和利率等。

f. 不考虑新业务。

g. 当前投资组合收益率（账面收益率）用于计算当前资产组合产生的未来现金流。

h. 未来现金流预测是税前基础。

342. 团体寿险合同负债：团体寿险合同不受日本公认会计准则法定现金流测试的限制。团体寿险合同的日本 GAAP＋评估方法与日本公认会计准则规定相同，因此无须进行调整。

343. 非寿险合同负债：非寿险负债调整为日本公认会计准则法定现金流测试的结果（假设全保险期间）。

a. 根据全保险期间现金流分析，非寿险公司需要评估保险合同负债（公认会计准则下的未到期责任准备金）是否充足以覆盖所有预期的未来现金流。

b. 保险合同负债的缺口或盈余的净额需要折现，折现值相应增加（或减少）保险合同负债。

c. 计算保险合同负债的未来现金流时，需要利用实际经验数据，如赔付频率、退保率、费用率和利率。不考虑新业务。

d. 折现需使用《日本保险法》第121条未来现金流量分析中指定的政府债券收益率曲线。

344. 选择权和保证负债：日本 GAAP + 方法下的选择权和保证负债使用 MAV 中的方法。

9.1.2.1　实际资本：累计其他综合收益（AOCI）调整

345. 当寿险合同负债采用资产账面收益率折现，而支持这些负债的可供出售债券以公允价值计量时，日本 GAAP + 下适用 AOCI 调整。AOCI 调整不适用于使用市场利率或曲线贴现的负债。为了解决会计处理的不对称性和由此导致的实际资本波动，在日本 GAAP + 中定义了 AOCI 调整，使得在满足以下所有标准的情况下，将可供出售债券相关的未实现损益从一级资本中扣除：

a. IAIG 必须满足以下所有操作标准，才能够使用 AOCI 调整：

i. IAIG 应建立界定资产/负债组合和久期匹配策略的资产/负债管理政策。

ii. IAIG 应建立评估久期匹配有效性的体系和流程，包括独立验证、定期测试和向董事会报告。

iii. 久期匹配有效性评估满足以下测试标准，相关资产才能纳入 AOCI 调整的范围：

iv. $0.8 \leq \dfrac{D(L)}{D(A)} \leq 1.25$，其中 D 为久期。

b. 要扣除的未实现损益净额必须与归类为可供出售且支持长期负债的债券有关。

c. 投资组合应根据资产/负债匹配的目的进行拆分。

d. 未实现损益有很大可能性不会被实现。

346. 在计算信用风险最低资本要求（第7.4节）时，相关资产余额要按照摊余成本法重述，但不需在日本 GAAP + 资产负债表上调整。AOCI 调整作为实际资本的直接调整项列报。

347. AOCI 调整是从日本 GAAP + 资产负债表其他综合收益（OCI）中的可供出售债券的累计未实现收益（损失）开始计算的。以下情况的未实现损益需要扣除：

a. 支持短期保险合同负债的债券。短期合同的定义是合同期限为一年或一年以下。

b. 支持以市场利率/曲线折现的负债的债券。

c. 被指定为公允价值套期会计计量的债券。

d. 不符合操作标准的债券（例如，未在单独的资产组合中明确资产/负债匹配策略或未满足操作标准有效性测试的债券）。

e. 根据管理层的判断，很可能会通过出售、转换、提前偿还等方式实现未实现损益的债券。例如，这可能包括某些赎回价格低于市场价格的可赎回债券，或可能已提前偿还的住宅抵押支持证券（RMBS）、学生贷款、消费或其他资产支持证券（ABS）。本文定义的"很有可能"是指基于管理层在报告日已知的事实和情况，大于50%的发生概率。

f. 经过重大信用减值的债券。

348. AOCI调整是扣除税项后计算的，与AOCI中处理未实现损益的方式一致。

9.1.2.2 最低资本要求：利率风险

9.1.2.2.1 背景

349. 在日本GAAP+方法下，寿险合同负债当前估计采用的贴现率为当前资产账面收益率加上相当于政府债券利率的再投资假设。支持这些负债的可供出售债券实质上是通过对实际资本的调整（称为AOCI调整）以摊余成本计量的（参阅第9.1.2.1节）。其他资产，如贷款、分类为持有至到期的或储备证券也按成本法计量。对于日本GAAP+下的非寿险产品，保险合同负债使用政府债券收益率曲线折现，可供出售债券通常按公允价值计量。

350. 市场利率曲线的变动并不会对按成本计量的资产（包括使用AOCI调整的资产）的价值造成影响。此外，它不会影响用于衡量某些寿险合同负债现金流折现值的账面收益率。这种变动只会对贴现率的再投资假设部分产生影响。因此，IAIG采用以下方法计算其日本GAAP+下的利率风险最低资本。

9.1.2.2.2 负债

351. 对于日本GAAP+资产负债表上的保险合同负债，使用基于当前市场信息的收益率曲线/利率进行评估的部分，利率风险最低资本使用ICS基准方法计算。因此，标准方法的利率风险计量方法适用于日本GAAP+下的所有非寿险产品以及任何选择权和保证负债的评估。

352. 对于日本GAAP+资产负债表上的寿险合同负债中使用账面收益率和再投资收益率假设折现的部分，IAIS收益率曲线压力情景仅适用于反映各期限和各货币的再投资假设的部分。

9.1.2.2.3 资产

353. 对于在日本GAAP+资产负债表上以市场价值计量的资产，压力情景与ICS基准方法一致。

354. 对于在日本 GAAP+资产负债表上以摊余成本计量的资产（如贷款、分类为持有至到期的或储备债券），不适用利率风险压力情景。

355. 如果未实现损益通过 AOCI 调整（见第 9.1.2.1 节）加回到实际资本中，资产本质上是按摊余成本计量。通过资产价值变化体现的利率风险压力被 AOCI 调整的变化所抵消。因此，压力的净影响为零，或者说与按成本法计量的资产相同。

9.1.2.3　资本要求：非违约利差风险（NDSR）

9.1.2.3.1　背景

356. 在日本 GAAP+方法下，寿险当前估计采用的贴现率为当前资产账面收益率加上相当于政府债券利率的再投资假设。支持这些负债的资产本质上通过对实际资本的调整，即 AOCI 调整，按摊余成本计量（见第 9.1.2.1 节）。其他资产，如贷款、持有至到期的或储备债券，也可以按成本法计量。对于日本 GAAP+下的非寿险产品，保险合同负债使用政府债券收益率曲线进行估值，可供出售的证券通常按公允价值计量。

357. 非违约利差风险（NDSR）压力不会对按成本法计量的资产价值造成影响（通过 AOCI 调整或对于日本 GAAP+资产负债表上按成本计量的资产）。此外，它不影响用于评估寿险合同负债的贴现率，也不影响用于贴现非寿险合同负债的政府债券收益率曲线。因此，IAIG 根据保险合同负债和资产的估值方式，采用不同的方法计算其 GAAP+非违约利差风险（NDSR）资本要求。

9.1.2.3.2　负债

358. 对于使用政府债券收益率曲线计量的日本 GAAP+资产负债表上的非寿险合同负债，不适用 NDSR 压力。

359. 对于日本 GAAP+资产负债表上使用账面收益率及基于政府债券收益率的再投资利率进行折现的寿险合同负债（如日本寿险合同负债），不适用 NDSR 压力。

9.1.2.3.3　资产

360. 对于在日本 GAAP+资产负债表上使用当前收益率曲线信息的以公允价值计量的资产，NDSR 压力的影响采用 ICS 基准方法计算。

361. 对于日本 GAAP+资产负债表上按成本法计量的资产，不适用非违约利差风险（NDSR）压力。

362. 如果未实现损益通过 AOCI 调整（见第 9.1.2.1 节）加回到实际资本中，资产本质上按摊余成本计量。通过资产价值变化体现的非违约利差风险（NDSR）压力被 AOCI 调整的变化所抵消。因此，压力的净影响为零，或者说与按成本计量的资产相同。

9.1.2.4　资本要求：信用风险

363. 在日本 GAAP+方法下计算信用风险最低资本时，AOCI 调整中的可供出售债券按照摊余成本计量。信用风险因子应用于摊余成本余额，以保持与实际资本中的评估方法一致。

9.1.2.5 资本要求：房地产风险

364. 在日本 GAAP+方法下，自用房地产的房地产风险最低资本，按照日本 GAAP+报告日的资产负债表价值减去该房地产在报告日公允价值的75%的差额（如果该差额是正数）计算。如果无法获得该房地产的公允价值，则最低资本为该房地产账面价值的25%。最低资本按逐项房地产计算。

9.2 其他方法

9.2.1 内部模型法

365. 内部模型的主要目标是计算更适合 IAIG 承担风险的最低资本要求（在单项风险层级或在聚合层级）。IAIG 标准方法无法覆盖的特性（如特定的风险缓释安排）可以通过内部模型反映出来。内部模型还可以覆盖标准方法中未包含的对某些 IAIG 特别重要的风险。内部模型对在多个国家地区运营的大型、复杂的保险集团尤其相关。

366. 基于保险核心原则 17，确定了在监测期内提交 ICS 最低资本时使用内部模型法的 10 个前提条件。

367. 为在监测期间将内部模型法作为附加报告的一部分，IAIG 需要填报后续章节中列明的 1~10 项前提条件的自我评估模板，模板中 IAIG 必须：

a. 简要描述内部模型的应用范围（如部分或全部使用内部模型）。

b. 提供证据，证明计算集团最低资本要求的内部模型已经过独立验证（前提条件2）（内部或外部），并得到 IAIG 董事会的批准（前提条件3）。

c. 说明内部模型符合前提条件 4 至 7 的程度：

- 统计检验测试；
- 校准测试；
- 使用测试和管理流程；以及
- 文档记录标准。

d. 在部分使用内部模型的情况下，IAIG 还必须完成关于前提条件 8 至 10 的自我评估模板，即需要：

- 证明内部模型范围有限的原因（没有进行有目的的选择）；
- 提供证据，证明由此计算的 ICS 最低资本更恰当地反映了 IAIG 的风险状况；和
- 解释如何整合部分内部模型和标准方法的结果。

368. 如果前提条件没有完全满足，但是 IAIG 希望在监测期间提交内部模型结果，那么 IAIG 应该与 GWS 讨论这个问题。此外，IAIG 应在其自我评估模板中说明不符合所有前提条件但仍提交内部模型结果的原因，以及内部模型没有满足所有前提条件的细节。

369. 在监测期内，提交内部模型结果不需要监管事前批准。此外，不必为满足在监

测期使用内部模型的前提条件专门设计最低资本模型,而提交内部模型结果。

370. 作为附加报告的一部分提交的内部模型结果见三级文件详述。

9.2.1.1　前提条件1:内部模型应用范围的描述

371. IAIG必须描述其内部模型的应用范围(内部模型计算的界限)。对于监测期间内部模型结果的附加报告,有两种可采用的方法:

a. 部分内部模型——替换标准方法中的某些部分。例如:

　i. ICS标准方法中的一项或多项风险最低资本(如市场风险)。

　ii. ICS标准方法中的一项或多项子风险最低资本(如权益风险)。

　iii. ICS标准方法的最低资本中未覆盖的一项或多项风险或子风险最低资本。

　iv. IAIG的全部业务,或仅适用于一个或多个主要业务单元或法人实体。

b. 完全内部模型——替换整个标准方法计算。

9.2.1.2　前提条件2:验证

372. 内部模型验证要求IAIG证明其建立了一个严格的程序,通过这个程序可以确定内部模型框架是否合理或者是否需要改进。内部模型验证应使其能够更好地理解内部模型的功能和局限,并确认内部模型和支持程序是充分和适当的。验证应该是一个迭代的过程,通过这个过程,IAIG使用内部模型周期性地改进验证工具,以响应不断变化的市场和操作条件。没有通用的验证方法,验证方法的结构取决于内部模型的技术规格、目的和预期用途。

373. 保险核心原则17.13.6规定,"……保险公司应审查自己的内部模型并对其进行验证,以确定该模型是否适合作为其风险和资本管理流程的一部分"。除了内部审查,保险公司可以考虑由适当的专家对其内部模型进行定期、独立的外部审查。

374. 保险核心原则17.18规定,当保险公司使用内部模型来确定监管资本要求时,应该:

- "……监控其内部模型的性能,并定期审查和验证模型技术规格的持续适用性";
- "……根据统计检验测试、校准测试和使用测试的标准,证明该模型在不断变化的环境中仍然适用于资本监管目的";
- "……向监管机构报告其对内部模型所做的重大更改……";
- "……合理记录内部模型更改";
- "……报告监管审查所需的信息……"。

375. 验证应包括定量和定性两个要素。虽然可以将验证视为一种纯粹的技术/数学过程,在此过程中,使用统计技术将结果与预测值进行比较,但仅关注预测值与结果的比较是不够的。在评估内部模型的整体性能时,评估模型整体及其关于结构、治理、数据和流程的每个模块都非常重要。

376. 最后,为了实现有效的验证,客观地评判质询至关重要。独立的模型验证有助于 IAIG 评估和验证其内部模型的整体性能。因此，验证职能的适当独立性非常重要，无论验证是内部还是外部的，执行验证的个人必须具备必要的技能、知识、专业素养和经验。

9.2.1.3　前提条件 3：IAIG 董事会签字

377. 这一前提条件旨在确保董事会对于内部模型负责，并且该模型符合内部模型管理流程规定的验证流程。

378. 此外，保险核心原则 17 建议董事会就内部模型进行一定程度的参与，作为使用测试的一部分，这将在前提条件 6 部分中进一步详细说明。

9.2.1.4　前提条件 4：统计检验测试

379. 基于保险核心原则 17.14，IAIG 需要：

- "……进行统计检验测试，评估内部模型的基本定量方法，以证明该方法的适当性，包括模型输入和参数的选择，并证明模型所依据的假设的合理性"，并提供证据。
- "……使用内部模型确定监管最低资本要求时考虑了保险公司的总体风险状况，并且模型中使用的基础数据是准确和完整的"。

380. 统计检验测试解决了与内部模型相关的技术方面的问题，即

- 方法和假设；
- 重大风险的覆盖范围；
- 数据（包括外部数据）和专家判断；
- 风险分散效应；
- 与准备金计算方法的一致性；
- 考虑风险缓释技术和管理层行为的影响；
- 财务担保和合同约定的选择权。

381. 统计检验测试集中在内部模型的每个模块上。组成内部模型的不同要素和输入值必须通过这个测试。

382. 保险核心原则 17 中规定的统计检验测试为保险公司提供了相当大的建模自由。例如，保险核心原则 17.14.1 规定，"构建用于风险和资本管理的有效内部模型可以使用一系列方法，监管者应鼓励使用一系列适合不同保险公司性质、规模和复杂程度以及不同风险敞口的方法。有几种不同的技术来量化风险，保险公司可以使用这些技术来构建其内部模型。广义而言，这些方法可以包括从基本的确定性情景到复杂的随机模型。确定性情景方法通常包括使用反映事件或条件变化的压力和情景测试，以设定的概率模拟特定事件（如股票价格下跌）对保险公司资本状况的影响，其中基本假设是固定的。相反，随机模型方法通常包括模拟大量的情景，以反映保险公司所需资本的可能分布和不同的风险暴露"。IAIG 应了解其所承担风险的性质、规模和复杂性以及业务模式和结构，建模方法应该与此类风险和业务状况相称。

383. 统计检验测试还设定了界限，IAIG 应在该界限内设计其评估和汇总风险的方法。结合内部模型验证要求，统计检验测试能够促进形成一个结构良好、记录完备且受控的模型开发和完善过程，该过程应在 IAIG 内不同的建模领域间保持一致。例如，保险核心原则 17.14.3 指出，"IAIS 认为，通常要求保险公司决定如何最好地汇总和考虑其整个业务的风险。通过内部模型确定总体监管最低资本要求时，应考虑风险类别之内和之间的相关性。如果内部模型考虑到了分散效应，保险公司应能够证明其分散效应影响的合理性，并证明其已考虑到在压力情景下相关性如何增加"。

384. 用于构建内部模型的数据是影响模型性能的主要因素之一。保险核心原则 17.14.4 指出，"内部模型需要高质量的数据，以产生足够可靠的结果。用于内部模型的数据应该是最新的，并且足够可信、准确、完整和适当。因此，'统计检验测试'应审查在构建内部模型时使用的基础数据是否适当"。保险核心原则 17.14.6 提到外部数据的使用时，规定"……任何非该保险公司的特定数据都需要经过仔细考虑，然后再决定是否将其用作保险公司统计检验测试的基础。即使在认为适当的情况下，仍有必要对数据进行调整，以反映数据源和保险公司之间的特征差异"。

385. 为内部模型选择数据时，总会涉及一定程度的专家判断。为此，保险核心原则 17.14.7 规定，"在评估数据和其他输入项（如假设）对内部模型的适用性时，应运用专家判断，并以适当的理由、文件和验证作为依据"。

386. 保险核心原则 17.14.8 强调了"方法论也应与用于计算准备金的方法相一致"的重要性。

387. 此外，保险核心原则 17.14.9 规定，"统计检验测试还应包括对内部模型的审查，以确定模型中所代表的资产和产品是否真正反映了保险公司的实际资产和产品。这包括分析所有合理可预见和相关的重大风险是否已覆盖，包括任何财务担保和嵌入式选择权。保险公司还应考虑使用的算法是否已反映对管理层行为和投保人行为的合理预期。测试应包括模型内的未来预测，并在可行的范围内进行'反向测试'（将模型预测与实际经验进行比较的过程）"。

9.2.1.5 前提条件 5：校准测试

388. 保险核心原则 17.15 规定 IAIG 应"……进行校准测试，以证明内部模型确定的监管最低资本要求满足规定的建模标准"。

389. 保险核心原则对校准的定义不同于统计学和精算学中使用的校准一般定义。例如，模型校准通常在统计学中被定义为调整模型参数的过程，以获得满足预先约定的标准（如拟合优度），保险核心原则 17.15.2 规定，"IAIG 应使用校准测试来证明内部模型已正确校准，以便针对监管者规定的特定风险度量、置信度和时间范围进行合理、无偏的估计"。ICS 标准法下，校准目标是一年时间期限内置信区间为 99.5% 的 VaR。

390. 如果 IAIG 使用了与 ICS 标准法最低资本计算不同的置信区间（如 99.7%，以保持一定的投资等级评级)、风险度量(如针对巨灾风险使用 TVaR)或时间范围(如至无限期),则可能需要根据 ICS 最低资本要求目标标准(一年时间期限内置信区间为 99.5% 的 VaR)重新校准其模型。或者,IAIG 可以提供定量证据,说明该结果与 ICS 目标标准有何差异。

9.2.1.6 前提条件6:使用测试和管理流程

391. 根据保险核心原则 17.16,IAIG 需要:

- "……将内部模型的方法和结果完全嵌入保险公司的风险战略和运营流程(使用测试)";
- 他们的"……董事会和高级管理层对构建和使用用于风险管理目的的内部模型具有全面的控制和责任,并确保在保险公司组织架构的适当级别对模型构建有充分的理解。"特别是,保险公司需要提供证据,证明他们的董事会和高级管理层了解内部模型输出的结果及其对于风险和资本管理决策的局限性;和
- "……对内部模型进行充分的管理流程和内部控制"。

392. 使用测试是支持监管者和被监管者之间建立信任关系的证据。监管者需要这种信任,以确保内部模型反映了 IAIG 对其风险的看法,并将其用于决策,而不是为了减少最低资本。

393. 根据保险核心原则 17.16.1,IAIG 应证明其内部模型被广泛使用,并在不同管理层级的风险管理和决策制定中,以及评估经济资本和偿付能力方面发挥重要作用。

394. 此外,保险核心原则 17.16.5 指出,使用测试是一种关键方法,保险公司可以通过这种方法证明其内部模型已嵌入其风险和资本管理以及公司治理的流程和系统。换言之,IAIG 必须提供证据,证明内部模型完全嵌入其运营和组织架构中,并证明该模型一直得到运用且保持有效。

395. 此外,IAIG"应向监管者证明,用于计算最低资本目的的内部模型一直得到运用且保持有效,而且董事会和高级管理层应全力支持并对其负责"。

396. 使用测试的另一个关键方面是,根据保险核心原则 17.16.6,IAIG 高级管理层对内部模型的设计和实施负责,并确保模型的持续适当性。

397. 保险核心原则 17.16.7 还指出,"模型如果要通过使用测试,保险公司应该建立一个跨业务部门使用模型的框架机制。这一框架机制应明确生产和使用模型所产生信息的责任"。

398. 保险核心原则 17.16.8 强调模型的治理、沟通、质询和理解的重要性。"内部模型应接受适当的审查和质询,以便在保险公司使用时具有相关性和可靠性。内部模型的关键要素和结果应被保险公司内部的关键人员(包括董事会)所理解,而不仅仅是构建模型的人员。这种理解应该确保内部模型仍然是一个有用的决策工具。如果内部模型没有被广泛理解,它将无法实现其目的并为业务增加价值。'使用测试'是确保内部模

型与保险公司业务相关性的关键。"

9.2.1.7 前提条件7：文档记录标准

399. 在保险核心原则17.17的基础上，IAIG应"……记录内部模型的设计、构建和治理情况，包括支持其方法的原理和假设的概要"。保险核心原则17.17进一步规定，"监管者要求，文档应当足以证明内部模型符合监管验证要求，包括统计检验测试、校准测试和使用测试"。

400. 文档的主要目的：

- 降低关键人员风险；
- 有助于模型的监管审查和批准；
- 有助于高级管理层的理解；和
- 认识到模型的弱点。

401. 如保险核心原则17.17.1所述，文档应充分、详细和完整，足以"……使该领域有足够知识的专业人员能够理解其设计和结构"。该文档应包括对基本方法、假设、量化和财务基础的论述和详细信息，以及用于评估所需资本水平的建模标准的信息。

402. 此外，保险核心原则17.17.2规定，"保险公司还应持续记录模型的发展和重大变化，以及模型未能有效运行的情况。如果依赖外部供应商，则应将其记录在案，并说明使用外部供应商的适当性"。

9.2.1.8 前提条件8：不得根据结果进行有目的的选择

403. 根据保险核心原则17.12.4规定，IAIS支持在适当的情况下使用内部模型，因为它可能是一种更现实的、反映风险的最低资本要求计算方法。但不鼓励保险公司采取任何"有目的的选择"。

404. 从监管者的角度来看，对某些风险和业务使用内部模型，而对其余风险或业务使用标准方法，这可能引起对"有目的的选择"的担忧。为了减轻这些顾虑，根据保险核心原则17.12.14，IAIG应"……证明其为什么选择只对某些风险或业务线使用内部模型"。为此，IAIG应在其自我评估中提供内部模型范围受限的理由。

9.2.1.9 前提条件9：ICS最低资本结果能够更恰当地反映保险公司的风险状况

405. 根据保险核心原则17.12.15规定，"……应要求保险公司证明模型使用范围受限的合理性，以及为什么认为部分使用内部模型来计算监管最低资本要求比标准法更符合业务的风险状况，或者为什么它完全符合监管最低资本要求"。

9.2.1.10 前提条件10：解释如何整合部分使用内部模型、部分使用标准方法的结果

406. 对部分使用内部模型、部分使用标准方法的结果进行整合必须审慎、一致，以便得出ICS的总体最低资本要求。为此，IAIG应提供证据，证明部分使用内部模型、部分使用标准方法的结果可以整合。这个前提条件特别针对于内部模型架构和标准方法的

设计完全不同（例如，风险没有按照标准方法中的类似思路定义或划分，目标标准不同等）的 IAIG。

9.2.2 动态对冲

407. 基准 ICS 不考虑针对报告日之后新增资产和负债的市场风险缓释技术对最低资本要求的影响。ICS 标准方法的原则是，只认可针对 IAIG 在报告日承担风险的风险缓释措施。

408. 因与标准法的原则相抵触，动态对冲安排不被认可，这是因为标准方法中的最低资本要求是使用瞬时冲击来计算的，瞬时冲击因其构造方法无法覆盖后续风险对冲调整的缓释影响。

409. 但是，IAIG 可以提供动态对冲计划的相关信息，以支持未来是否将其纳入 ICS 的决策。IAIS 正在研究是否有其他方法来评估这些风险缓释措施，以更好地反映 IAIG 的风险暴露，并将其纳入 ICS，而不是对特定产品和风险使用标准方法。

术语表

术语	首字母缩写	定义/参考
累计其他综合收益	AOCI	参见第9.1节
巴塞尔银行监管委员会	BCBS	https://www.bis.org/bcbs/
共同框架	ComFrame	https://www.iaisweb.org/page/supervision-material/insurance-core-principles-and-comframe
递延所得税资产	DTAs	参见第6.3节"资本工具"和第8节"税的计量"
递延所得税负债	DTL	参见第6.3节"资本工具"和第8节"税的计量"
金融稳定理事会	FSB	http://www.fsb.org/
未来非保证利益	FDB	参见第5.2.1.4节
会计准则调整法	GAAP+	参见第9.1节
通用会计准则	GAAP	http://en.Wikipedia.org/wiki/Generally_accounting_principles
全球保险资本标准	ICS	http://www.iaisweb.org/page/supervision-material/insurance-capital-standard
ICS信用评级	ICS评级	参见第3.4节
保险核心原则	ICP	https://www.iaisweb.org/page/supervision-material/insurance-core-principles-and-comframe
国际保险监管官协会	IAIS	http://www.iaisweb.org/home
国际财务报告准则	IFRS	http://www.IFRS.org/About-us/IASB/Pages/home.aspx
国际货币基金组织	IMF	http://www.imf.org/external/index.htm
国际活跃保险集团	IAIG	见2019年11月通过的国际比较方案和共同框架（ComFrame） https://www.iaisweb.org/page/supervision-material/insurance-core-principles-and-comframe
最长流动性期限	LOT	参见第5.2.5节"折现"
终极远期利率	LTFR	参见第5.2.5节"折现"
管理层行为	Management Actions	参见第7.1.3节"管理层措施"
风险边际	MOCE	超出当前估计技术条款估价的差额，以涵盖这些义务的内在不确定性。 http://www.iaisweb.org/page/supervision-material/glossary 另见国际比较方案14.7

续表

术语	首字母缩写	定义/参考
市场价值调整法	MAV	参见第5节"市价调整估值(市价调整估值(MAV))法"
美国保险监督官协会	NAIC	http://www.naic.org/
净资产价值	NAV	资产价值减去负债价值
非违约利差风险	NDSR	参见第7.3.3节
监管认可评级	SOCCA	参见第7.4.4节
在险价值	VaR	在给定的置信水平下,对某段时间内最坏的预期损失的估计 http://www.iaisweb.org/page/supervision-material/glossary
多资产组合加权平均法	WAMP	参见第5.2.5.3.2节"收益率曲线的调整"

附录1：无表决权利益实体的处理（资产和保险证券化）

资产证券化

保险公司满足以下所有情形，可以对集团内部发起的证券化产品进行并表（摘自《巴塞尔协议Ⅲ》）：

a. 底层资产重大信用风险已转移给第三方。

b. 出让方对转让后的资产不再拥有实际或间接控制。资产以真实销售或从属参与的形式从法律上与出让方进行风险隔离，即使出现破产或接管的情形，底层资产与出让方和债权人无关。银行应获取法律意见来支持真实销售。

c. 以下情况，出让方将被视为对转让后的资产仍有实际控制：（i）能够从受让方手中回购资产并实现收益；或（ii）有义务继续承担转移后的风险。出让方继续履行风险资产贷后管理工作不一定代表是对风险资产的间接控制。

d. 发行的证券不是出让方的一种义务。因此，购买证券的投资者仅可对所购资产要求权利。

e. 受让方是特殊目的实体，并且该实体的受益人拥有不受限制地质押或交换的权利。

f. 结清选择权必须满足以下条件：（i）结清选择权不论是在形式上还是实质上，均不能是强制性的，而是由发起行决定；（ii）结清选择权不得通过结构化设计来规避增信方、投资者持有头寸应承担的损失，也不得通过其他结构化设计提高增信；（iii）只有当剩余的原始基础投资组合或已发行证券占初始额的10%或以下时，才能执行结清选择权；对于合成型资产证券化，比例限制为原始参考投资组合价值的10%或以下。

g. 证券化产品不包含以下条款：（i）要求发起银行变更底层资产，以改善资产池的信用质量，除非这种信用提升是通过向独立且无关联的第三方按照市价出售资产来实现的；（ii）交易起始日后，允许增加发起行第一损失责任或进行增信；或（iii）提高给发起行之外的其他相关方的收益率，如投资者、提供增信措施的第三方，以应对基础资产池信用质量恶化。

h. 除符合条件的结清选择权，以及因税收和法规的特定变更、提前清偿条款导致的终止外，不得有其他任何终止条款或触发机制。

保险证券化

保险公司满足以下所有情形，可以不对集团内部发起的证券化产品进行并表（摘自欧盟偿付能力 Ⅱ）：

a. 特殊目的实体不同于保险或再保险公司，它是通过发行债务或其他任何融资安排来募集资金以吸收（再）保险人通过再保险合同或类似安排所转移出风险的实体，在这些融资安排中，融资方的求偿权位于（再）保险人履行完再保险合同有关义务之后。

b. 当特殊目的实体吸收来自多家（再）保险人的风险时，其偿付能力不会因任何一家的停业整顿而受到不利影响。

c. 特殊目的实体应始终满足以下条件：

　　i. 特殊目的实体始终拥有市场价值等于或超过其最大付款额（包含费用支出）的资产，并且该特殊目的实体应能够在债务到期时及时付清。

　　ii. 债务发行或其他融资机制的款项全额缴纳。

d. 有关将风险从保险（再保险）公司转移到特殊目的实体，并从特殊目的实体到出资人的合同安排，应当符合以下条件：

　　i. 风险转移在所有情况下均有效；

　　ii. 风险转移程度清晰无异议；

　　iii. 出资人的求偿权应始终位于 SPV 对 IAIG 的再保险义务之后；

　　iv. 如果支付资金会导致特殊目的实体的资金不足，出资人不会得到该笔资金给付；

　　v. 出资人对保险（再保险）公司没有资产追索的权利；

　　vi. 出资人无权申请特殊目的实体清盘整顿。

附录2：ICS 非寿险业务分类

ICS 分类	定义
欧洲经济区和瑞士 医疗费用保险	保险责任包括对疾病、意外事故、残疾或体弱的预防性或治疗性医疗和护理提供费用报销或者经济补偿
欧洲经济区和瑞士 收入保障险	保险责任包括对疾病、意外事故、残疾或体弱提供经济补偿（不包括医疗费用保险责任）
欧洲经济区和瑞士 工伤保险	与工作意外事故、工伤和职业病有关的健康保险责任，其业务实质与寿险业务不同
欧洲经济区和瑞士 机动车责任—机动车第三者责任险	保险责任包括在陆地上使用机动车而产生的所有责任（包括承运人的责任）
欧洲经济区和瑞士 机动车—其他险	保险责任包括陆地车辆（包括铁路机车车辆）的所有损坏或损失
欧洲经济区和瑞士 海上、航空及运输保险	保险责任包括因在海上、湖泊、河流或运河上使用飞机、船舶，而产生的飞机、船舶的损坏或损失，以及在途货物或行李的损坏或损失，不受运输方式影响（包括承运人的责任）
欧洲经济区和瑞士 火灾及其他损失险	保险责任包括因火灾、爆炸、自然灾害（包括风暴、冰雹或霜冻）、核能、地面沉降和其他事件（如盗窃）造成的所有财产损坏或损失（机动车—其他责任和海运/航空/运输保险中的保险责任除外）
欧洲经济区和瑞士 一般责任险—第三者责任险	保险责任包括除机动车责任险和海洋、航空及运输保险以外的所有责任
欧洲经济区和瑞士 信用和保证保险	保险责任包括破产、出口信贷、分期付款信贷、抵押贷款、农业信贷以及直接或间接担保
欧洲经济区和瑞士 法律诉讼费用保险	保险责任包括法律费用和诉讼费用
欧洲经济区和瑞士 救援保险	保险责任包括对在旅行、离家或离开常住地时遇到困难的人提供援助
欧洲经济区和瑞士 其他经济损失保险	保险责任包括就业风险、收入不足、恶劣天气、福利损失、持续性一般费用、不可预见的交易费用、市场价值损失、租金或收入损失、上述以外的间接交易损失，其他经济损失（非交易）以及上述业务范围未涵盖的任何其他非寿险风险

续表

ICS 分类	定义
欧洲经济区和瑞士 非比例健康再保险	健康保险的非比例再保险
欧洲经济区和瑞士 非比例意外伤害再保险	意外伤害保险（机动车责任险和一般责任险）的非比例再保险
欧洲经济区和瑞士非比例海上、航空及运输再保险	海洋、航空及运输保险的非比例再保险
欧洲经济区和瑞士非比例财产再保险	财产险（机动车—其他险、火灾保险、信用保证保险、法律诉讼费用险和救援保险）的非比例再保险
加拿大 财产险—个人	承保财产损失或损坏，包括由于伪造引起损失的保险。保险包括居住财产保单和多重风险保单等，包含公寓、旅馆、制造业与商业建筑在内的住宅相关责任，以及不可分割保费的个人一揽子保单责任。保险范围包括火灾、住户物品和业主个人风险、住宅盗窃以及特殊住宅玻璃的风险。意外伤害保险，例如人身伤害，不包括在这一类别中
加拿大 房屋保修保险	指由保修供应商签发的保险合同，承保新房屋建造过程中的缺陷以及业主由此产生的间接损失或费用
加拿大 产品质量保证保险	承保除机动车以外的个人财产的损失或损坏，保险人承诺支付修理或更换个人财产的费用，但不附带任何其他类别保险
加拿大 财产险—商业	承保财产损失或损坏，包括由于伪造引起损失的保险，以及所有商业财产和多重风险保单，但不包括监管机构定义的所有单独类别的保险
加拿大 航空保险	承保范围： 1. 因飞机或飞机的使用造成的人身伤害或死亡、财产损失或损坏而产生的责任； 2. 飞机的损失、无法使用或损坏
加拿大 车险—责任险/人身意外险	承保范围： 1. 因汽车或使用和操作汽车而造成的人身伤害或死亡、财产损失或损坏而产生的责任； 2. 因汽车或使用和操作汽车引起的意外事故，其责任属于意外和疾病保险定义第（i）或（ii）条范围内的保险，保单承保因汽车或使用和操作汽车造成的人身伤害或死亡而产生的责任
加拿大 车险—其他险	承保汽车损失、无法使用或损坏的保险
加拿大 锅炉及机器保险	承保范围： 1. 因任何种类的压力容器或与该压力容器相连或由该压力容器操作的管道、发动机和机器发生爆炸、破裂或意外事故而导致的人身伤害或死亡、财产损失或损坏的责任； 2. 因机械故障而导致的人身伤害或死亡、财产损失或损坏的责任

附录2：ICS非寿险业务分类

续表

ICS分类	定义
加拿大 设备质量保证保险	锅炉和机器保险的一个子类别，包括机动车或设备因机械故障造成的损失或损坏，但不包括汽车保险或汽车保险附带的保险
加拿大 信用保险	承保已授信者由于被授信者破产或违约而造成损失的保险
加拿大 信用保障险	保险公司承诺在个人收入或收入能力受损，或潜在受损的情况下，偿还个人全部或部分信贷余额或债务的保险
加拿大 忠诚保险	承保身居要职因盗窃、滥用信用或失信造成损失的风险，以及保证雇员正常履行职责的保险
加拿大 冰雹保险	承保由冰雹造成的田间作物损失或损坏的保险
加拿大 法律诉讼费用保险	承保由一人或多人提供保单中规定的法律服务而产生费用的保险，包括为提供服务而产生的任何聘请费用，以及与提供服务有关的其他费用
加拿大 责任险	承保范围（不包括属于其他类别保险的责任）： 1. 因人身伤害、伤残或死亡（包括雇员）而产生的责任； 2. 因财产损失或损坏而产生的责任； 3. 如果保单包含子条款（i）所述的保险，则承保范围包括除被保险人及被保险人家庭成员以外的人身伤害而产生的费用，无论责任是否存在。还包括一般责任、网络责任、董事责任、超额责任、职业责任、伞式责任和污染责任
加拿大 抵押贷款保险	承保由不动产抵押或押记，或其他担保权益担保的贷款项下借款人违约造成损失的保险
加拿大 保证保险	保险人承诺对合同或承诺的适当履行，或对任何违约行为支付罚款或赔偿的保险
加拿大 产权保险	承保因下列原因造成的损失或损坏的保险： 1. 不动产存在抵押、押记、留置权、产权负担、地役权或任何其他限制； 2. 个人财产存在抵押、押记、留置权、质押、产权负担或任何其他限制； 3. 证明有子条款（i）或（ii）中所述限制的任何文件中的缺陷； 4. 财产所有权上的缺陷； 5. 任何影响财产所有权或者财产使用权、享有权的其他事项
加拿大 海上保险	承保下列原因产生的责任： 1. 人身伤害或死亡；或者 2. 财产的损失或损坏；或者 3. 发生在海上或内河航线或海上冒险的财产损失或损坏，或由于海上或内河航线或海上冒险所附带发生的延迟或非水路运输过程中发生的财产损失或损坏
加拿大 意外和疾病保险	—

续表

ICS 分类	定义
加拿大 其他认可保险产品	承保其他风险的保险
美国 机动车辆损失保险	承保被保险人车辆损失（包括碰撞、故意破坏、火灾和盗窃）的机动车保险
美国 业主/农场主保险	业主保险：承保个人财产或具有广泛个人责任的建筑物，包括住宅、附属建筑物、计划外个人财产和额外生活费用的保险 农场主保险：承保农业和牧场风险；包括个人和商业损失的财产和责任险、农场住所和物品（如移动设备和牲畜）、谷仓、马厩、其他农场建筑物和农场内陆海洋
美国 特殊财产保险	保险种类繁多，包括：火灾保险，联合保险，内河航运保险，地震保险，盗窃保险等。火灾保险承保因火灾或雷电危险造成的不动产或个人财产损失，包括营业中断、租金损失等。联合保险通常与财产保险一起签订，承保范围包括玻璃、龙卷风、风暴和冰雹、洒水器和水灾、爆炸、暴乱和内乱、农作物种植、洪水、雨水、飞机和车辆损坏等。内河航运保险承保由受托人持有的，在运输中或在固定地点的财产，或位于不同地点的可移动货物（如越野施工设备），或指定财产（如房主个人可移动财产），包括活体动物和具有收藏品价值的财产。这类业务还承保运输和通信工具，如桥梁、隧道、桥墩、码头、管道、电力和电话线以及广播和电视塔
美国 私人车责任/医疗保险	承保因与机动车有关的伤害（包括人身伤害和医疗赔偿）而负法律责任所造成的经济损失，或因拥有、维修及使用机动车而导致对他人造成的财产损坏。不包括商用车的保险范围
美国 商用车/卡车责任/医疗保险	类似于私家车责任/医疗保险，但承保车辆为商用车
美国 工伤保险	根据州或联邦劳工赔偿法和其他法规的规定，承保雇主对其雇员的伤害、残疾或死亡应负的责任，不考虑雇主是否存在过错。保险责任包括雇员伤害的判例法责任（区别于劳工赔偿法规定的责任）。不包括超额工伤保险
美国 商业综合保险	同一保单中包括的两个或多个商业企业保险，包括各种财产和责任风险，但不包括农场主保险、业主保险和汽车保险的责任
美国 医疗职业责任保险—损失发生制	承保因被保险人在提供专业服务时的不当行为、疏忽或不称职而导致他人死亡或受伤的持牌医疗机构或医疗保健机构的法律责任。保险范围包括在保险期内发生的事件
美国 医疗职业责任保险—索赔发生制	承保因被保险人在提供专业服务时的不当行为、疏忽或不称职而导致他人死亡或受伤的持牌医疗机构或医疗保健机构的法律责任。保险范围包括在保险期内提出的索赔

续表

ICS 分类	定义
美国 其他责任险—损失发生制	承保因疏忽大意或不作为而导致他人财产损失或人身伤害的法律责任保险。保险范围通常包括以下责任：施工和改建；或有责任；承包商责任；电梯和自动扶梯；错误和遗漏；环境污染；超额止损、超额保险或自保金额及伞式责任；酒类；人身伤害；经营场所和运营；完工运营；非医学专业人员等。保险范围还包括在超额损失基础上向自保雇主提供的赔偿（超额工伤赔偿）。保险范围包括在保险期内发生的事件
美国 其他责任险—索赔发生制	与上述其他责任险—损失发生制的类型相同，但保险范围包括在保险期内提出的索赔，其保险事故不需要在保险期内发生
美国 产品责任保险	产品责任险—损失发生制：承保在保险期内发生的事件。产品责任险—索赔发生制：承保在保险期内提出的索赔。本保险承保产品制造商、分销商、销售商或出租人因产品缺陷而对任何个人或实体造成人身伤害或损害所承担的法律责任
美国 再保险—非比例分入财产险	非比例财产分入再保险，包括火灾保险、海上保险、内陆航运保险、地震保险、团体意外和健康险、信用意外和健康险、其他意外和健康险、汽车损坏保险、锅炉和机器保险、玻璃保险、盗窃保险和国际保险（上述各项）
美国 再保险—非比例分入责任险	非比例责任分入再保险，包括农场主综合险、业主综合险、商业综合险、医疗职业责任险、工伤保险、其他责任险、产品责任险、汽车责任险、飞机（一切险）和国际保险（上述各项）
美国 特殊责任险	包括海上保险、飞机（一切险）、锅炉和机器保险等各种保险。海上保险承保海洋和内陆水上运输风险；如商品或货物，船舶或船体，收入与责任。飞机保险承保航空器机身及其内容物；飞机所有人和飞机制造商对乘客、机场和其他第三方责任。锅炉和机器保险承保锅炉、机器及电气设备故障，保险范围包括被保险人因意外事故直接受损的财产、临时修理费用和加急费用以及对他人财产损害的责任
美国 抵押贷款保险	抵押贷款保险是对贷款人因借款人未能支付所需的抵押付款而遭受的损失进行赔偿
美国 忠诚保险/保证保险	忠诚保险承保雇主因雇员的不忠诚行为而遭受的损失（如现金、证券或贵重物品的损失）。保证保险是一种三方协议，保险人同意向第二方支付或履行义务，以应对第三方的违约、作为或不作为
美国 金融保证保险	金融保证保险是指保险人出具的保证书、保险单、赔偿合同及类似于上述类型的任何担保，根据这些担保，被保险人、债权人或受偿人因未履行财务义务而发生经济损失的，应当予以赔偿
美国 其他险	其他险种不包含的保险范围，包括信用保险、保证保险，以及财产/人身伤害险、意外/健康险的一部分。附表"国际保险"应分配给风险所在的地区；如不可能，可以将其纳入该部分

续表

ICS 分类	定义
美国 再保险—非比例分入经济损失险	非比例分入经济损失险包含以下分类：抵押保证保险、金融保证保险、忠诚保险、保证保险、信用保险和国际保险（上述各项）
日本/火灾保险	承保因火灾、风暴、冰雹、水灾、地震等给商业或者个人家庭带来的财产损失
日本/船舶保险	承保船体的损坏
日本/货物保险	承保轮船运输中货物和财产的损坏
日本/运输保险	该保险被称为内陆海运保险，承保除轮船和飞机外的工具运输的财产
日本/人身意外保险	承保人身意外伤害造成的损失。根据该保险，保单持有人将根据实际发生的损失获得赔偿，或者因某种意外事件而获得定额赔偿
日本/机动车保险	承保被保险人遭受的人身伤害或汽车损坏，以及被保险人对第三方造成损失的责任。请注意，此处应包括车队汽车保险
日本/航空保险	承保由飞机运输和发射到太空的飞机、货物及财产，以及因运输途中货物或财产的损失或损坏，或对第三方造成人身伤害或财产损失或损坏而产生的责任
日本/保证保险	承保因已获得信贷的客户破产或拖欠付款而造成的经济损失
日本/机器保险	承保被保险人因机器故障而遭受的损失
日本/一般责任险	承保对第三方造成人身伤害、财产损失或损害而需要支付赔偿和费用的法律责任
日本/建筑工程一切险	承包商购买该保险是为了赔偿在建财产的损失
日本/动产一切险	承保除汽车、飞机和船舶以外的其他财产损失或损坏
日本/工伤保险	该保险为在受雇期间遭受人身伤害或职业病的雇员提供无过错补偿金，并为雇主提供保护，防止其雇员人身伤害或职业病而提出的侵害索赔
日本/其他经济损失保险	该保险为被保险人提供量身定制的保险，以弥补其他任何业务所不包括的间接损失
日本/护理保险	该保险提供福利以满足被保险人得到护理。根据该保险，保单持有人将根据实际发生的护理费用获得赔偿或获得定额赔偿
日本/其他险	包括上述未列出的其他非寿险
中国/车险	车辆保险的保险对象是车辆本身及其相关的赔偿责任
中国/财产险，包括企业财产保险、家庭财产保险和工程保险	保险对象为财产及其相关利益
中国/船货特险	保险对象为船舶及其相关的赔偿责任
中国/责任险	保险对象为被保险人对第三方的赔偿责任
中国/农业险	保险对象为农业灾害造成的财产损失
中国/信用保证险	保险对象为因债务人无行为能力或拒绝偿付债务而给债权人造成的经济损失
中国/短期意外险	短期意外伤害保险以被保险人因意外事故而死亡或伤残为给付条件，保险期限通常不超过一年
中国/短期健康险	短期健康保险期限不超过一年，且没有可持续续保的保证

附录2：ICS非寿险业务分类

续表

ICS 分类	定义
中国/短期寿险	保险对象为被保险人的生命。其保险期限通常不超过一年
中国/其他险	其他保险
澳大利亚和新西兰/家庭财产保险	承保一般的家庭财产保险，包括以下类别/风险：室内设施、个人财产、纵火和入室盗窃。通常附属于这些保险的公共责任是分开的。这类保险还包括相应的比例再保险
澳大利亚和新西兰/商用车保险	保险范围在以下家用车车险定义之外的机动车保险（包括第三方财产损失），包括中长途运输卡车、起重机和特种车辆，以及商用车车队包括相应的比例再保险
澳大利亚和新西兰/私家车保险	机动车保险（包括第三方财产损失）承保私家使用的机动车辆，包括公用货车、摩托车、私人大篷车、厢式和船式拖车，以及通常不属于商用或商业保单承保范围内的其他车辆。该类别还包括私家车保险的比例再保险
澳大利亚和新西兰/其他 A 类保险	与家财和车险类似的其他业务类别。该类别还包括其他 A 类保险的比例再保险
澳大利亚和新西兰/旅游保险	承保与旅行相关的损失，包括行李和个人物品损失，航班取消损失及海外医疗费用。该类别还包括旅游保险的比例再保险
澳大利亚和新西兰/火灾及工业特殊风险保险	包括所有通常归类为火灾（包括喷头泄漏、下沉、风暴、冰雹、作物、纵火和利润损失）和工业特殊风险的所有保单。该类别还包括火灾及工业特殊风险保险的比例再保险
澳大利亚和新西兰/海上及航空保险	包括船体和海运责任（含游艇）及海运货物（包括海上和内陆运输保险）。还包括航空（包括飞机机身和飞机责任）。该类别还包括海上及航空保险的比例再保险
澳大利亚和新西兰/消费信用保险	保障消费者在因人身伤害、疾病或失业而死亡或收入损失的情况下偿还个人贷款和信用卡金融贷款的能力。该类别还包括消费信用保险的比例再保险
澳大利亚和新西兰/其他意外险	包括各种意外事故、一切险（行李、运动装备、枪支）、不属于火灾保险和工业特殊风险保险的工程险、不带包装的平板玻璃、牲畜、暴风雨以及疾病和意外。该类别还包括其他意外险的比例再保险
澳大利亚和新西兰/其他 B 类保险	与火灾保险和工业特殊风险保险、海上保险、航空保险、消费者信贷保险和其他意外伤害保险具有类似特征的其他 B 类业务。该类别还包括其他 B 类保险的比例再保险
澳大利亚和新西兰/抵押贷款保险	承保借款人在以住宅或其他财产抵押担保的贷款发生贷款违约时对贷方造成的损失。该类别还包括抵押贷款保险的比例再保险
澳大利亚和新西兰/强制第三者责任保险	强制第三方责任业务。该类别还包括强制第三者责任险的比例再保险

续表

ICS 分类	定义
澳大利亚和新西兰/ 公众责任及产品责任保险	公共责任保险承保因被保险人经营业务而造成公众人身伤害或财产损失所需承担的法律责任。产品责任包括因使用产品造成的损失和伤害,以及由于污染泄漏而造成的环境清理费用(火灾保险和工业特殊风险保险未涵盖的情况)。包括家庭财产保单附带的建筑商保障和公共责任部分。该类别还包括公众及产品责任的比例再保险
澳大利亚和新西兰/ 职业责任保险	职业责任保险承保专业人员在履行专业服务时因错误或疏忽而导致第三方遭受的经济损失。包括董事和高级职员责任险及法律费用保险。该类型的保单通常包括法律费用保险。该类别还包括职业责任的比例再保险
澳大利亚和新西兰/ 雇主责任保险	包括工伤赔偿、海员赔偿和家政工人赔偿。该类别还包括雇主责任的比例再保险
澳大利亚和新西兰/ 短尾医疗费用保险	保险责任包括为医疗费用或护理相关费用提供补偿,包括在保单有效期内或保险期满后不久(通常为一年),因疾病、事故、伤残或虚弱而进行的预防性或治疗性的医疗或护理
澳大利亚和新西兰/ 其他C类保险	与抵押贷款保险,强制第三者责任保险和其他责任险具有类似特征的其他业务类别,包括其他C类比例再保险
澳大利亚和新西兰/ 家庭财产保险—非比例再保险	家庭财产业务的非比例再保险(具体见定义)
澳大利亚和新西兰/ 商用车保险—非比例再保险	商用车业务的非比例再保险(具体见定义)
澳大利亚和新西兰/ 私家车保险—非比例再保险	家用车业务的非比例再保险(具体见定义)
澳大利亚和新西兰/ 其他A类非比例再保险	其他A类业务的非比例再保险(具体见定义)
澳大利亚和新西兰/ 旅游保险—非比例再保险	旅游业务的非比例再保险(具体见定义)
澳大利亚和新西兰/ 火灾及工业特殊风险保险—非比例再保险	火灾及工业特殊风险业务的非比例再保险(具体见定义)
澳大利亚和新西兰/ 海上及航空保险—非比例再保险	海上及航空业务的非比例再保险(具体见定义)
澳大利亚和新西兰/ 消费信用保险—非比例再保险	消费信贷业务的非比例再保险(具体见定义)
澳大利亚和新西兰/ 其他意外伤害保险—非比例再保险	其他意外事故业务的非比例再保险(具体见定义)
澳大利亚和新西兰/ 其他B类非比例再保险	其他B类业务的非比例再保险(具体见定义)

附录2：ICS非寿险业务分类

续表

ICS 分类	定义
澳大利亚和新西兰/ 抵押贷款保险—非比例再保险	抵押贷款业务的非比例再保险（具体见定义）
澳大利亚和新西兰/ 强制第三者责任险— 非比例再保险	强制第三者责任险的非比例再保险（具体见定义）
澳大利亚和新西兰/ 公众责任及产品责任保险— 非比例再保险	公共责任和产品责任业务的非比例再保险（具体见定义）
澳大利亚和新西兰/ 职业责任保险—非比例再保险	职业责任业务的非比例再保险（具体见定义）
澳大利亚和新西兰/ 雇主责任保险—非比例再保险	雇主责任业务的非比例再保险（具体见定义）
澳大利亚和新西兰/ 其他C类非比例再保险	其他C类业务的非比例再保险（具体见定义）
中国香港/意外健康保险	在被保险人发生下列风险时，提供固定给付或按照实际经济损失报销： 1. 由于意外事故导致受伤或死亡； 2. 疾病导致的失能； 3. 疾病
中国香港/机动车辆保险， 包括车辆损失保险及责任保险	包括：1. 乘坐机动车时意外受伤或意外死亡的风险保障；2. 在陆路上使用机动车的过程中意外受伤，但不包括铁路上行驶的轨道类车；3. 在陆路上使用机动车的过程中对第三方或者乘客带来意外伤害
中国香港/航空保险，包括 航空设备损失保险及责任保险	包括：1. 乘坐航空设备时意外受伤或意外死亡的风险保障；2. 航空设备及其的机器设备、组件、内饰和其他等遭受的损坏；3. 使用航空设备对第三方或者乘客带来意外伤害
中国香港/船舶保险， 包括损失保险及责任保险	包括：1. 乘坐船只时意外受伤或意外死亡的风险保障；2. 海上或内河航线上使用的船只及其机器设备、组件、内饰和其他等遭受的损坏；3. 海上或内河航线上使用船只对第三方或者乘客带来意外伤害
中国香港/货物运输保险	对水陆空运输过程中的商品、货物等其他物品的损坏的保险
中国香港/火灾及财物损失保险	由于下列原因导致的财产损失的保险： 1. 火灾、爆炸、风暴、其他自然灾害、核灾害或陆地沉降；2. 冰雹、霜冻或原因1以外的灾害类事故
中国香港/一般责任保险	被保险人对第三方责任的保险，但不包括车、船和飞机等相关的第三方责任险
中国香港/经济损失保险	包括：1. 被保险人因债务人破产或违约所遭受的经济性损失的保险；2. 保证保险；3. 因下列原因造成的损失的保险：被保险人经营的业务中断或减少经营范围；4. 被保险人因法律费用（包括诉讼费用）而遭受损失的保险

续表

ICS 分类	定义
中国香港/非比例合约再保险	如果无法将合约再保险归类到以上八类业务中,可归为以下两大类:非比例合约再保险和比例合约再保险
中国香港/比例合约再保险	如果无法将合约再保险归类到以上八类业务中,可归为以下两大类:非比例合约再保险和比例合约再保险
韩国/火灾、技术及海外保险	包括火灾保险,技术保险,海外直接保险,海外分入再保险。 火灾保险:住宅火灾、工厂火灾、一般火灾(任何普通建筑物和移动式建筑物的火灾保险,不包括住宅和工厂)以及其他火灾的保险。 技术保险:工程、装配保险,机械、电子设备及其他保险,定义如下所示: 1. 工程:对在建大楼损害的保护; 2. 装配:防止装配过程中的构件的损坏; 3. 机器:机器损坏的保险; 4. 电子设备:电子设备损坏保险以及恢复数据的成本和费用的保险; 海外直接保险:位于外国的财产损失保险,涵盖人身伤害或与任何货物有关的损害赔偿责任; 海外分入再保险:作为再保险人对其他海外保险公司的风险的再保险
韩国/一揽子保险	包括为家庭和企业设计的一揽子保险: 1. 家庭保险:为以下两种或两种以上的损失提供保险,个人财产损失、人身伤害保险,以及损失责任险; 2. 商业保险:对下列两种或两种以上损害的保险,企业财产损失、企业损害赔偿责任和企业雇员人身伤害保险
韩国/海事保险	包括海运、陆运和航空。具体地说,包括以下责任: 1. 货物:海上货物运输风险的保险; 2. 船舶:船舶损坏的保险; 3. 一般海事保险:为海上活动中的风险投保,如海上施工的风险; 4. 海洋责任:承保海上损害赔偿责任,如海洋污染责任保险等(不包括船舶和一般海事人员); 5. 运输:内陆货物运输的保险; 6. 航空:飞机操作和航行造成的飞机损坏的保险,飞行事故有关的损害责任赔偿; 7. 航空空间:发射和执行人造卫星任务(财产)失败的风险和与人造卫星事故有关的损害赔偿责任保险; 8. 其他海事保险:除上述以外的海上保险产品

附录2：ICS非寿险业务分类

续表

ICS分类	定义
韩国/人身伤害保险	包括意外伤害、旅行和其他责任（被保人不包括非本国居民）。 1. 因突发意外事故造成被保险人身体伤害的保险； 2. 旅行：韩国国内旅行过程中的人身伤害保险，海外旅行的人身伤害保险，长期留在国外（如留学生和驻外人员）的人身伤害保险； 3. 其他：以上未列出的人身伤害保险
韩国/劳工意外和责任险	给劳动者提供工伤事故赔偿保险以及责任保险。 工伤事故赔偿保险包括： 1. 国内：意外事故赔偿和雇主责任赔偿； 2. 海外：意外事故赔偿和雇主责任赔偿； 3. 海员：意外事故赔偿和雇主责任赔偿； 4. 实习生：意外事故赔偿和雇主责任赔偿。 责任保险包括：1. 一般责任：个人责任、商业责任、船主责任、远足及渡轮业务、道路交通运输业务中的责任、煤气事故、体育设施责任、地方政府责任和其他方面； 2. 产品责任：产品责任、产品召回和产品质量保证责任； 3. 职业责任：渎职、玩忽职守（E&O）
韩国/非本国居民保险	为非本国居民提供意外受伤、旅行和其他类别责任的保险
韩国/预付款退还保证保险	买方购买的保险，主要针对建造者不退还与建造船舶或建造海洋设施有关的买方支付的预付款而导致买方可能遭受的损害的风险
韩国/其他非寿保险	除以上以外的其他一般的保险产品
韩国/私家车保险（人身伤害）	被保险人使用机动车辆的期间中，发生导致他人死亡或受伤的意外事故，从而使投保人免予承担对受害者造成的损害的赔偿责任的保险，由私人机动车的机动车保险提供保障，应包括《汽车事故赔偿保证法》第5条第1部分规定的责任保险范畴
韩国/私家车保险（财产及车辆损失）	因投保人使用机动车辆期间所造成本车或其他车辆损失，从而对保险所有人进行赔偿的风险保险，由机动车保险单提供保障
韩国/商业车保险（人身伤害）	在投保人拥有或管理机动车辆的过程中，由于投保人拥有或管理机动车辆，而发生的意外事故而导致他人死亡或受伤，从而使投保人免予承担对受害者造成的损害的赔偿责任的保险，由商用机动车的机动车保险条款提供保障，应包括《汽车事故赔偿保证法》第5条第1款规定的责任保险
韩国/商业车保险（财产及车辆损失）	由于投保人拥有或管理机动车辆，而发生的意外事故而导致对投保人所有车及其他车辆损失，从而进行赔偿的风险，其由商用机动车保险条款提供保障
韩国/其他车险	除上述保险产品外的汽车保险
新加坡/人身意外保险	指人身意外保险业务
新加坡/健康保险	指健康保险业务

续表

ICS 分类	定义
新加坡/火灾保险	此保险保障因火灾、风暴、冰雹、水灾和地震等对商业或家庭财产造成的损失
新加坡/海运及航空保险—货运险	包括针对任何船舶或飞机运输中的货物遗失或损坏等此类运输中的责任风险的保险
新加坡/车险	包括针对使用机动车所造成的财产损失以及人身伤害的风险以及其他使用机动车的第三方责任风险的保险
新加坡/工伤保险	包括针对在工作期间因工作导致身体伤害和工作相关疾病的雇员的赔偿金
新加坡/履约保证保险	包括佣人保险和保险人承诺担保（不包括与"信贷/信用有关"的担保有关的）合同或承诺的正当履约，或因违约而支付的罚款或赔偿的保险
新加坡/建筑工程险	包括针对建设，架设或工程风险（例如，建设项目涉及的损失或损坏以及已建成的建筑工程项目的安装和架设）的保险。它还包括锅炉和压力容器保险，建筑一切险保险，工程一切险保险，安装一切险保险，机械一切险保险以及不属于标准财产保险的任何其他专用设备或机械的保险
新加坡/信用保险	针对购买者、进口商不支付服务费和货款风险的保险
新加坡/抵押贷款险	防止借款人违约导致抵押贷款损失的保险
新加坡/其他非责任保险	除提及以外的其他非责任保险
新加坡/海运及航空保险—船舶险	包括针对在海上或内陆水域或飞机上使用的船只或船舶的物理损失或损坏风险，此类船只或船舶或飞机所引起的任何责任以及在建造中船只或船舶或飞机的损坏的保险。它还包括海上码头运营人保险和机场运营人保险以及航空航天风险保险
新加坡/职业责任险	包括针对专业人士的保险，以防止因疏忽或错误导致其对委托人，客户或任何第三方无法正常履行职责的风险。它还包括董事和高层干部责任保险，以及失误担责保险
新加坡/公众责任保险	包括针对被保险人因疏忽而造成的第三方人身伤害，财产损失的风险的保险（除"货物""船只""航空飞机"和"机动车"等类别相关的保险以外）
新加坡/其他险—责任险	以上除外的其他责任保险
中国台北/火灾保险—居民楼	个人住宅火灾保险
中国台北/火灾保险—商业建筑	商业建筑火灾保险
中国台北/海运—内陆运输	内陆货物的海运保险
中国台北/海运—海外运输	海外货物的海运保险
中国台北/船体保险	船舶海运保险
中国台北/海运—渔船	渔船海运保险
中国台北/海事—飞机	航空保险
中国台北/车险—私家车	个人车辆的机动车辆保险
中国台北/车险—商用车	商业车辆的机动车辆保险
中国台北/车险—私家车责任险	个人责任的机动车辆保险

附录2：ICS非寿险业务分类

续表

ICS 分类	定义
中国台北/车险—商用车责任险	商业责任的机动车辆保险
中国台北/责任险—公共责任、雇主责任、产品责任等	公共责任保险、雇主责任保险、产品责任保险等
中国台北/责任险—职业责任	职业责任保险
中国台北/工程保险	工程保险
中国台北/核电站保险	核电厂保险
中国台北/信用保证和忠诚保证	保证保险、雇员忠诚保险、抵押贷款保险等
中国台北/信用保险	商业信用保险、信用卡保险、小额贷款信用保险等
中国台北/其他财产损失保险	不包括在其他贷款中的财产损失保险，如现金保险、偷盗保险、玻璃保险等
中国台北/意外伤害保险	人身伤亡意外保险
中国台北/财产损失保险—商业财产地震损失	地震保险（强制性地震保险除外）
中国台北/综合险—个人财产及责任保险	个人财产及责任综合保险
中国台北/综合险—商业财产及责任保险	商业财产及责任综合保险
中国台北/财产损失保险—台风及洪水损失	台风及洪水带来的财产损失保险
中国台北/财产损失—强制地震损失保险	强制性地震保险（个人住宅的强制保险）
中国台北/健康险	健康保险
其他/车险	包括：机动车财产损失：由于意外事故、盗窃、火灾和天气事件对自有和第三方机动车造成的损害（以及相关财产损失），不包括人身伤害责任；机动车辆人身保险：与第三方因机动车辆或涉及机动车辆的事故而受伤或死亡有关的保险。这也可能扩展到包括涉及的驾驶员
其他/财产损失保险	包括但不限于：1. 财产保险：房屋或其他财产（包括房屋内物品）因火灾、暴风雨等造成的损失，房屋内物品因盗窃、火灾、风暴、地震、撞击、破坏、水灾和其他自然及人为危险造成损失的保险。房屋内物品保险可能延伸到房屋或房屋外的财产损失或损坏； 2. 火灾和工业损失：由于火灾、暴风雨和其他危险而导致的商业建筑物和其他实物损失或损坏而产生的损失； 3. 间接损失：这个细分市场主要涵盖间接损失的产品（如"利润损失"或"业务中断"）； 4. 施工：包括"施工险和安装一切险"（CAR/EAR）或与施工项目有关的类似的风险。包括基础设施项目和建筑物的建造和安装

续表

ICS 分类	定义
其他/意健险（APH）	包括但不限于： 1. 事故和疾病：如果意外导致人身伤害或死亡，那么意外保险提供理赔金，理赔金是一次性或周期性的（通常最多为 2 年）。疾病保险通常是意外保险的延伸； 2. 其他消费者事故：除住户或机动车外的财产损害。例如，旅游保险； 3. 其他商业事故：商业财产保险（不包含火灾、工业风险、MAT 和商业长期负债）； 4. 消费信贷：因非自愿丧失就业机会而偿还消费信贷合同的保证； 5. 消费者责任：指个体通过个人行为或财产造成人身伤害的责任
其他/短尾医疗费用险	保险责任涵盖了因疾病、事故、伤残或体弱而对被保险人而进行的预防性或治疗性医疗或护理的经济补偿，通常在保单有效期内或保险期结束后不久（通常为 1 年）
其他短尾保险	任何不符合上述细分市场、不符合非寿险中期业务定义的非寿险产品，以及通常在保单有效期内或保险期结束后不久（通常长达 1 年）提出索赔的非寿险产品
其他/海上、航空及运输保险（MAT）	包括： 1. 在河、渠、湖、海内使用运输工具（渔船、货轮）或者使用飞机等过程中存在的对货物或者运输工具的责任； 2. 运输过程中的财产损失，间接地对他人的财产造成的损失、间接地对其他人（如乘客）的人身带来伤害
其他/工伤保险	该保险包括对在受雇期间遭受人身伤害或职业病的雇员的赔偿金
其他/公众责任保险	包括人身伤害或财产损害责任的公共责任保险
其他/产品责任保险	产品责任保险包括因产品的使用导致人身伤害或财产损害的责任
其他/职业责任保险	承保专业人士或组织在履行专业服务时因错误或疏忽而导致损失的索赔。例如，医疗事故、董事及高级职员的责任类保险产品
其他/其他责任保险及其他长尾保险	任何不符合上述定义的细分市场的非寿险产品，不符合非寿险中等期业务的定义，索赔可能需要多年（通常在保险的承保期已满后一年或更长时间）。所有其他未涵盖的责任类别
其他/非比例车险，财产损失保险，意健险及运输保险	非比例分保的再保险类：机动车责任险、财产险、事故/保护/健康业务、海上、航空和运输类险种（具体见定义）
其他/巨灾再保险	巨灾再保险是一种内部再保险业务，针对单个或多个事件所造成的总损失提供超额损失保险或比例保险。通常，这类业务涵盖财产损失，出售时附带额外条款，并针对风暴、地震等自然灾害和恐怖主义行为等人为灾难提供保护
其他/非比例责任险	非比例再保险的公共责任、产品责任和其他责任（具体见定义）
其他/非比例职业责任保险	专业赔偿责任险的非比例再保险（具体见定义）

附录2：ICS非寿险业务分类

续表

ICS 分类	定义
其他/抵押贷款保险	因借款人未能偿还以财产抵押担保的贷款而给信贷提供者造成损失的赔偿
其他/商业信用保险	赔偿由于商业实体未能偿还剩余贷款或无法交付服务或合同产品带来的经济损失，其中短期贸易信贷和保证保险除外
其他/其他中期保险	无法归入以上类别的其他非寿险中期保险产品。包括但不限于：用于融资或货币化的保险连结证券（如巨灾债券）。例如，将未来利润现值或内含价值证券化，以财务风险为主要触发条件

四、Level 1 Document: ICS Version 2.0 for the monitoring period

四、Level 1 Document: ICS Version 2.0 for the monitoring period

Table of Contents

1 Introduction ········ 184
  1.1 Purpose ········ 184
  1.2 History/background ········ 184
  1.3 ICS as Part of ComFrame ········ 186
  1.4 Principles for ICS Development ········ 186
2 Components of ICS Version 2.0 for the monitoring period ········ 188
  2.1 Reference ICS ········ 188
  2.2 Additional reporting ········ 188
3 General Guiding Principles ········ 188
  3.1 Substance over Form ········ 188
  3.2 Proportionality ········ 188
  3.3 Look – Through ········ 189
  3.4 ICS Rating Categories ········ 189
4 Reference ICS: Perimeter of the ICS Calculation ········ 189
  4.1 Scope for Starting ICS Balance Sheet ········ 189
  4.2 Development of Starting MAV Balance Sheet ········ 190
5 Reference ICS: Market – Adjusted Valuation ········ 190
  5.1 Valuation Principles ········ 190
  5.2 Current Estimate ········ 190
    5.2.1 Basis for calculation ········ 190
    5.2.2 Contract recognition, contract boundaries and time horizon ········ 191
    5.2.3 Data quality and setting of assumptions ········ 191
    5.2.4 Management actions ········ 191
    5.2.5 Discounting ········ 191
  5.3 Margin over Current Estimate (MOCE) ········ 193
    5.3.1 Definition and underlying principles ········ 193
    5.3.2 Calculation of the MOCE ········ 193
    5.3.3 Interaction of MOCE with other components ········ 193
  5.4 Obligations replicable by a portfolio of assets ········ 193
6 Reference ICS: Qualifying Capital Resources ········ 193
  6.1 General considerations ········ 193

6.2	Classification of financial instruments	194
6.3	Capital elements other than financial instruments	196
6.3.1	Tier 1 capital elements	196
6.3.2	Tier 2 capital elements	196
6.4	Capital adjustments and deductions	197
6.4.1	Deductions from Tier 1 capital resources	197
6.4.2	Deductions from Tier 2 capital resources	197
6.4.3	Treatment of encumbered assets	197
6.5	Capital composition limits	198
7	Reference ICS: Capital Requirement – The Standard Method	198
7.1	ICS Risks and Calculation Methods	198
7.1.1	Risk mitigation techniques	200
7.1.2	Geographic segmentation	201
7.1.3	Management actions	201
7.2	Insurance risks	201
7.2.1	Grouping of policies for life insurance risks	201
7.2.2	Calculation of life insurance risk charge	201
7.2.3	Calculation of Non – Life Risk Charge	202
7.2.4	Calculation of Catastrophe Risk Charge	203
7.3	Market Risks	203
7.3.1	Calculation of the market risk charge	203
7.3.2	Interest rate risk	204
7.3.3	Non – Default Spread Risk	205
7.3.4	Equity risk	205
7.3.5	Real estate risk	205
7.3.6	Currency risk	206
7.3.7	Asset concentration risk	206
7.4	Credit Risk	206
7.4.1	Calculation of Credit risk charge	206
7.4.2	Recognition of collateral, guarantees and credit derivatives	207
7.4.3	Use of external credit ratings	207
7.4.4	Supervisor – owned and controlled credit assessment (SOCCA) processes	207
7.5	Operational risk	208

四、Level 1 Document: ICS Version 2.0 for the monitoring period

  7.6 Aggregation/Diversification of ICS Risk Charges ……………………………… 208
8 Reference ICS: Tax ………………………………………………………………………… 209
  8.1 General principles ……………………………………………………………………… 209
  8.2 Deferred tax from the ICS Adjustment ……………………………………………… 209
  8.3 Tax effect on the ICS insurance capital requirement ……………………………… 209
9 Additional Reporting ……………………………………………………………………… 210
  9.1 GAAP Plus ……………………………………………………………………………… 210
  9.2 Other methods of calculation of the ICS capital requirement (other methods) … 210

1 Introduction

1.1 Purpose

1. The purpose of this Level 1 document is to set out the overarching principles and concepts (ie ICS architecture) for the annual confidential reporting of the reference ICS and, at the option of group-wide supervisors (GWS), additional reporting during the five-year monitoring period.

2. This Level 1 document should be read in conjunction with the more detailed specifications contained in the Level 2 document for ICS Version 2.0 for the monitoring period (Level 2 document). The documentation framework for ICS Version 2.0 for the monitoring period consists of three document levels:① Levels 1 and 2 together form ICS Version 2.0 for the monitoring period; Level 3 builds on the information in Levels 1 and 2, with additional information to enable the annual confidential reporting. The Level 2 document will be issued in early 2020. Level 3 documents will be issued annually in the second quarter to launch confidential reporting.

1.2 History/background

3. On 9 October 2013, the IAIS announced its plan to develop a risk-based global insurance capital standard (ICS). This was in response to the request by the Financial Stability Board (FSB) that the IAIS produce a work plan to create "a comprehensive group-wide supervisory and regulatory framework for Internationally Active Insurance Groups (IAIGs)."② In its statement of 18 July 2013 the FSB stated that "a sound capital and supervisory framework for the insurance sector more broadly is essential for supporting financial stability." The FSB further reinforced its support for the development of the ICS in its statement of 6 November 2014.③

4. Since this announcement in October 2013, the IAIS has followed a structured and evidence-based approach to the development of the ICS by undertaking a multi-year quantitative Field Testing process with Volunteer Insurance Groups (Volunteer Groups). The IAIS has conducted six quantitative Field Testing exercises throughout the development stage of the ICS – from 2014 to 2019. Each quantitative ICS Field Testing exercise has been informed by IAIS

---

① Consistent with the objectives and definition of the monitoring period, ICS Version 2.0 for the monitoring period is not for decision making by supervisors (ie ICS results will not be used as a basis to trigger supervisory action). As such, any mention either in the Level 1 or Level 2 documents of a supervisory decision or action does not have any force or effect during the monitoring period, unless explicitly indicated otherwise. Such references, provided they are maintained in the agreed specifications of ICS as a PCR, will come into effect only once the ICS is implemented as a PCR.

② http://www.financialstabilityboard.org/publications/r_130718.pdf.

③ http://www.financialstabilityboard.org/wp-content/uploads/pr_141106a.pdf.

四、Level 1 Document: ICS Version 2.0 for the monitoring period

analysis of submitted data, as well as additional feedback and comments provided by Volunteer Groups as part of their submissions or through dedicated Field Testing workshops. In addition to the Field Testing process, the IAIS has reached out to the broader group of stakeholders during dedicated, in-person stakeholder meetings and by engaging in two public consultations on ICS matters.

5. On 2 November 2017, at its Annual Conference in Kuala Lumpur, the IAIS announced a unified path to convergence of group capital standards, in furtherance of its ultimate goal of a single ICS that includes a common methodology by which one ICS achieves comparable (ie substantially the same) outcomes across jurisdictions. The Kuala Lumpur Agreement (KL Agreement) sets out that implementation of ICS Version 2.0 will be conducted in two phases:

• A five-year "monitoring period", during which ICS Version 2.0 will be used for confidential reporting to the GWS and discussion in supervisory colleges. During the monitoring period, ICS results will not be used as a basis for triggering supervisory action; and

• The "implementation of the ICS as a group-wide Prescribed Capital Requirement (PCR)"[1].

6. The KL Agreement also stated that implementation of ICS Version 2.0 will have two equally important components:

• Mandatory confidential reporting by all IAIGs[2] of a reference ICS[3]; and

• Additional reporting, at the option of the GWS, of ICS based on Generally Accepted Accounting Principles (GAAP) with Adjustments (GAAP Plus)[4] valuation and/or other methods of calculation of the ICS capital requirement, including internal models (see section 9.2).

7. At the same time, the KL Agreement acknowledged the development of the Aggregation Method (AM) within the United States. The KL Agreement states that "The IAIS has agreed to collect data from interested jurisdictions relevant to the development of the aggregation method. Although this is not part of ICS Version 2.0, the IAIS appreciates the significance of this

---

[1] Insurance Core Principle (ICP) 17.4 defines a PCR as a solvency control level above which the supervisor does not intervene on capital adequacy grounds. As the ICS is designed as a minimum standard, national supervisory authorities may elect to take a more prudent approach and set a PCR that is higher than the ICS PCR.

[2] During the monitoring period, other interested Volunteer Groups that do not meet the definition of an IAIG may choose to participate in the mandatory confidential reporting and additional reporting, at the option of the GWS.

[3] Mandatory confidential reporting has been reflected in ComFrame in terms of a standard that requires GWSs to require IAIGs to report their reference ICS and to discuss the results in supervisory colleges. IAIS Members commit to implement IAIS supervisory material taking into account specific market circumstances.

[4] GAAP Plus will continue development and field testing (for IFRS, U.S. GAAP and Chinese GAAP) into the monitoring period. Japanese GAAP will enter the five-year monitoring period, along with the reference ICS, beginning in 2020.

development, and so it will collect data from interested jurisdictions that will aid in the development of the aggregation method."

8. The IAIS aims to be in a position, by the end of the monitoring period, to assess whether the AM provides comparable, ie substantially the same (in the sense of the ultimate goal), outcomes to the ICS. If so, it will be considered an outcome-equivalent approach for implementation of ICS as a PCR. Development of the AM by interested jurisdictions is underway. Work has begun on developing criteria to assess whether the AM provides comparable outcomes to the ICS, starting with a project plan focused on delivery by the end of the monitoring period.

1.3 ICS as Part of ComFrame

9. The Common Framework for the Supervision of IAIGs (ComFrame) consists of both quantitative and qualitative supervisory requirements tailored to the complexity and international scope of IAIGs. The ICS is one of the components of ComFrame. In June 2017, the IAIS agreed to take the following steps regarding the integration of the ICS into ComFrame:

- ICS Version 2.0 will be adopted in 2019 as a stand-alone document;
- ICP 14 (Valuation) and ICP 17 (Capital Adequacy) will not be reviewed until after ICS Version 2.0 is adopted;
- ComFrame text will be adopted, minus ICS Version 2.0, by end-2019 taking the above into account; and
- Integration of ICS Version 2.0 text into ComFrame text will occur after the adoption of ICS Version 2.0.

10. Subsequently, the five-year monitoring period for ICS Version 2.0 was agreed. As such, the integration of ICS text into ComFrame will occur by the end of the monitoring period. In order to facilitate the monitoring period and discussion within supervisory colleges, ComFrame includes references to the ICS, covering both the reference ICS and additional reporting.

1.4 Principles for ICS Development

11. The IAIS published a first version of the principles, set forth in Table 1 below, in September 2014. Principles 3 and 6 were subsequently amended following the 2014 ICS consultation. The amended principles are listed in Table 1 and have been followed in the ICS development.

四、Level 1 Document: ICS Version 2.0 for the monitoring period

Table 1 The ICS Principles[①]

ICS Principle 1: The ICS is a consolidated group – wide standard with a globally comparable risk – based measure of capital adequacy for IAIGs and G-SIIs. The standard incorporates consistent valuation principles for assets and liabilities, a definition of qualifying capital resources and a risk-based capital requirement. The amount of capital required to be held and the definition of capital resources are based on the characteristics of risks held by the IAIG irrespective of the location of its headquarters.
ICS Principle 2: The main objectives of the ICS are protection of policyholders and to contribute to financial stability. The ICS is being developed in the context of the IAIS Mission, which is to promote effective and globally consistent supervision of the insurance industry in order to develop and maintain fair, safe and stable insurance markets for the benefit and protection of policyholders and to contribute to global financial stability.
ICS Principle 3: One of the purposes of the ICS is the foundation for Higher Loss Absorbency (HLA) for G-SIIs. Initially, the Basic Capital Requirements (BCR) is the foundation for HLA for G-SIIs.
ICS Principle 4: The ICS reflects all material risks to which an IAIG is exposed. The ICS reflects all material risks of IAIGs' portfolios of activities taking into account assets, liabilities, non-insurance risks and off-balance sheet activities. To the extent that risks are not quantified in the ICS they are addressed in ComFrame.
ICS Principle 5: The ICS aims at comparability of outcomes across jurisdictions and therefore provides increased mutual understanding and greater confidence in cross-border analysis of IAIGs among group-wide and host supervisors. Applying a common means to measure capital adequacy on a group-wide consolidated basis can contribute to a level playing field and reduce the possibility of capital arbitrage.
ICS Principle 6: The ICS promotes sound risk management by IAIGs and G-SIIs. This includes an explicit recognition of appropriate and effective risk mitigation techniques.
ICS Principle 7: The ICS promotes prudentially sound behaviour while minimising inappropriate pro-cyclical behaviour by supervisors and IAIGs. The ICS does not encourage IAIGs to take actions in a stress event that exacerbate the impact of that event. Examples of pro-cyclical behaviour are building up high sales of products that expose the IAIG to significant risks in a downturn or fire sales of assets during a crisis.
ICS Principle 8: The ICS strikes an appropriate balance between risk sensitivity and simplicity. Underlying granularity and complexity are sufficient to reflect the wide variety of risks held by IAIGs. However, additional complexity that results in limited incremental benefit in risk sensitivity is avoided.
ICS Principle 9: The ICS is transparent, particularly with regard to the disclosure of final results.
ICS Principle 10: The capital requirement in the ICS is based on appropriate target criteria which underlie the calibration. The level at which regulatory capital requirements are set reflects the level of solvency protection deemed appropriate by the IAIS.

[①] Note that certain of these principles – specifically those that reference Global Systemically Important Insurers (G-SIIs) – have been superseded by the development of the holistic framework for the assessment and mitigation of systemic risk in the insurance sector. The holistic framework was adopted by the IAIS in November 2019. In light of the finalised holistic framework, the FSB, in consultation with the IAIS and national authorities, decided to suspend G-SII identification as from the beginning of 2020. Furthermore, a standardised form of a Higher Loss Absorbency (HLA) standard does not form part of the holistic framework. See also IAIS Press Release.

2 Components of ICS Version 2.0 for the monitoring period

2.1 Reference ICS

12. The reference ICS constitutes a consolidated group-wide standard for IAIGs that consists of three components:

- Market-adjusted valuation (MAV);
- Criteria for qualifying capital resources; and
- Standard method for the ICS capital requirements.

13. The reference ICS coverage ratio is calculated as

$$\text{ICS Ratio} = \text{Qualifying capital resources} / \text{ICS capital requirement}$$

14. The ICS is intended to be a going-concern measure of capital adequacy.

2.2 Additional reporting

15. During the monitoring period, IAIGs will be able to submit additional reporting, at the option of the GWS, of ICS based on GAAP Plus valuation and/or other methods of calculation of the ICS capital requirement, including internal models (see section 9.2). Both GAAP Plus and other methods of calculation of the ICS capital requirement are viable options that will be considered for inclusion in the ICS by the end of the monitoring period.

3 General Guiding Principles

3.1 Substance over Form

16. The ICS balance sheet differs from publicly reported GAAP financial statements, as it reflects a different objective (prudential supervision as opposed to investor information). For example, certain assets in a GAAP balance sheet do not qualify as assets for the ICS.

17. The economic substance of transactions and events are recorded in the balance sheet rather than just their legal form, in order to present a true and fair view of the risk profile of the entity. This may require the use of judgment when preparing the balance sheet.

18. The allocation of insurance liabilities to the ICS line of business segments follows the principle of substance over form. This means that insurance liabilities are allocated to the segment that best reflects the nature of the underlying risks rather than the legal form of the contract. The definitions for the insurance line of business segmentation are specified in the Level 2 document.

3.2 Proportionality

19. Calculations and valuation are subject to the proportionality principle. When the IAIG

can demonstrate that taking into account a specific factor/rule in their calculation or valuation would lead to a significant increase in complexity, without material improvement to the quality of the figure produced or to the assessment of risk linked to this figure, then this factor or rule can be ignored or simplified.

20. The materiality of the impact of using a simplification is assessed with regard to:
- The volume of the item valued;
- The overall volume of the group's business and capital resources; and
- The assessment of risk.

3.3 Look-Through

21. In order to assess properly the risk inherent in collective investment funds and other indirect exposures, their economic substance needs to be taken into account. This should be achieved, to the extent possible, by applying a look-through approach in order to assess the risks of the assets underlying the investment vehicle. Additional guidance on the use of look-through is provided in the Level 2 document.

3.4 ICS Rating Categories

22. The IAIS has developed a mapping between ICS Rating Categories (ICS RC) and credit rating agency ratings. ICS Rating Categories range from 1 to 8. Additional guidance on ICS Rating Categories, including the mapping to agency ratings, is included in the Level 2 document.

4 Reference ICS: Perimeter of the ICS Calculation

4.1 Scope for Starting ICS Balance Sheet

23. The starting point of the ICS is the audited consolidated GAAP balance sheet of the insurance holding company of an insurance group or financial holding company of a financial conglomerate.

24. Where an insurer does not prepare audited consolidated GAAP financials, statutory financial statements are aggregated to reflect the group level starting balance sheet.

25. The audited GAAP balance sheet is split into two components: (1) entities that are insurers, and entities whose purpose is insurance related; and (2) non-insurance entities. A further description of which entities are considered insurance related and non-insurance can be found in the Level 2 document.

26. The non-insurance entities are reported separately from insurance entities, on a GAAP basis, with the exceptions described in the Level 2 document.

27. Non-insurance entities (financial and non-financial) are incorporated into the reference

ICS, based on the entity type and whether or not the entity is subject to a sectoral capital requirement. The capital requirement for financial non-insurance entities is based on the entity's sectoral capital rules, when available. For financial non-insurance entities without sectoral capital rules and for non-financial entities, the capital requirement included in the reference ICS is described in the Level 2 document. For all non-insurance entities, capital resources follow the capital resources framework set out for the reference ICS.

4.2 Development of Starting MAV Balance Sheet

28. The starting MAV balance sheet is comprised of the insurance and insurance-related entities.

29. The beginning MAV balance sheet is subject to adjustments as described in the Level 2 document and Section 5.

5 Reference ICS: Market-Adjusted Valuation

5.1 Valuation Principles

30. The MAV approach is based on the amounts as reported on audited, consolidated, general-purpose GAAP or Statutory Accounting Principles (SAP) accounts, and includes adjustments to the following items:

a) Insurance liabilities and reinsurance balances;

b) Financial investments (assets) and instruments (liabilities); and

c) Deferred taxes.

31. Unless they are replicable by a portfolio of assets (reference Section 5.4), MAV insurance liabilities are the sum of a current estimate and a margin over current estimate (MOCE). The details underpinning the calculation of the current estimate and the MOCE are developed in the following sub-sections as well as in the Level 2 document.

32. The adjustments to items b) and c) are described in the Level 2 document.

5.2 Current Estimate

5.2.1 Basis for calculation

33. The current estimate corresponds to the probability-weighted average of the present values of the future cash-flows associated with insurance liabilities, discounted using the yield curve relevant for the currency and bucket of each liability. The three buckets to which liabilities can be allocated are described in Section 5.2.5.3.

34. The current estimate does not include any implicit or explicit margins.

35. Reinsurance recoverables are calculated in a way that is consistent with the current estimates of insurance liabilities, based on the same assumptions and inputs.

36. When valuing insurance liabilities, no adjustment is made to take into account the IAIG's own credit standing.

37. More details on how to project cash-flows for the current estimate calculation can be found in the Level 2 document.

5.2.2　Contract recognition, contract boundaries and time horizon

38. A contract is recognised when the IAIG becomes a party to that contact, until all obligations related to that contract are extinguished. All contracts that are recognised at the valuation date, and only those, are taken into account for the current estimate calculation.

39. The future premiums and associated claims and expenses linked to those recognised contracts are taken into account up to each contract boundary.

40. The projection horizon used in the calculation of the current estimate should cover the full lifetime of all the cash in- and out-flows required to settle the obligations (within contract boundaries) related to recognised insurance and reinsurance contracts at the valuation date.

41. The details for contract recognition and contract boundaries are specified in the Level 2 document.

5.2.3　Data quality and setting of assumptions

42. The calculation of the current estimate is based on up-to-date and credible information and realistic assumptions. The determination of the current estimate is objective, comprehensive, and uses observable input data.

43. The requirements relating to data quality and modelling assumptions are specified in the Level 2 document.

5.2.4　Management actions

44. The current estimate calculation may recognise management actions when such actions are objective, realistic and verifiable. Management actions recognised in the calculation cannot be contrary to the IAIG's obligations to policyholders or to legal provisions applicable to the IAIG.

45. Further details regarding the recognition of management actions in the current estimate calculation are provided in the Level 2 document.

5.2.5　Discounting

5.2.5.1　Determination of yield curves for current estimate discounting

46. In order to calculate a current estimate, insurance liabilities are discounted using an adjusted yield curve. The adjusted yield curve is based on:

a) Risk adjusted liquid interest rate swaps or government bonds (risk-free yield curve); and

b) An adjustment.

5.2.5.2 Determination of the risk-free yield curve

47. The risk-free yield curve is determined based on a three-segment approach:

a) Segment 1: based on market information from government bonds or swaps, including a credit risk correction, where necessary;

b) Segment 2: extrapolation between the first and third segments; and

c) Segment 3: based on a stable currency specific long-term forward rate (LTFR), to which a spread is added in order to represent the expected spread that may be earned from reinvestments in the long-term.

48. For each currency, the transition from the first to the second segment occurs at the last maturity for which market information can be observed in deep, liquid and transparent financial markets (the last observed term or LOT).

49. For each currency, the LTFR is the sum of an expected real interest rate and an inflation target.

50. For the purpose of determining the expected real interest rate, jurisdictions are allocated according to areas that share common macroeconomic characteristics. The same expected real interest rate is used for all currencies within a given area. For each area, the expected real interest rate is based on a simple average of observed real interest rates over a certain period of time.

51. The two components of the LTFR are reviewed annually, in order to reflect potential changes in macroeconomic expectations. However, the magnitude of annual changes to the LTFR is capped in order to mitigate its potential volatility.

52. For each currency, the risk-free curve is determined by the relevant IAIS Member for that currency, based on the quantitative parameters and guidance provided by the IAIS.

53. The list of currencies for which risk-free yield curves are determined, as well as relevant information regarding the LOT, the parameters and assumptions to determine the LTFR and the spread over the LTFR, including considerations on geographical differentiation, are provided in the Level 2 document.

5.2.5.3 Determination of the adjustment to the risk-free yield curve

54. The IAIS yield curves include an adjustment to the risk-free curves. This adjustment is determined using the Three-Bucket Approach.

55. The Three-Bucket Approach classifies liabilities into the General Bucket, the Middle Bucket and the Top Bucket, depending on the nature of the liabilities and the assets backing these liabilities. A different yield curve adjustment is determined for each bucket.

56. The criteria used for the classification of liabilities and the adjustment relevant for each bucket are specified in the Level 2 document.

5.3 Margin over Current Estimate (MOCE)

5.3.1 Definition and underlying principles

57. The MOCE is a margin added to the current estimate of insurance obligations in order to achieve a market adjusted value of insurance liabilities. The MOCE covers the inherent uncertainty in the cash flows related to insurance obligations. As such, MOCE considers all uncertainties attached to these obligations.

5.3.2 Calculation of the MOCE

58. The MOCE is calculated as a given percentile of the normal distribution characterised by:
- A mean equal to the current estimate of life (and non-life) obligations; and
- A 99.5% percentile equal to the life (and non-life) risk charge.

59. The percentiles for life and non-life insurance normal distributions are specified in the Level 2 document.

5.3.3 Interaction of MOCE with other components

60. All stress-based calculations include only current estimates for determining the pre- and post-stress Net Asset Value (NAV), ie the MOCE remains constant during the stress. Factors applied to insurance liabilities should only be applied to current estimates. MOCE is neither deducted from the ICS capital requirement, nor added to qualifying capital resources.

5.4 Obligations replicable by a portfolio of assets

61. Where future cash flows associated with insurance obligations can be replicated reliably, using financial instruments for which a market value is observable, the value of insurance liabilities associated with those future cash flows is determined on the basis of the market value of those financial instruments.

62. Additional conditions under which such an approach is applicable are specified in the Level 2 document.

6 Reference ICS: Qualifying Capital Resources

6.1 General considerations

63. Qualifying capital resources are determined on a consolidated basis for all financial activities and comprise qualifying financial instruments and capital elements other than financial instruments.

64. Qualifying capital resources are subject to adjustments, exclusions and deductions, as

defined in Section 6.4. Any item deducted from capital resources should be excluded from the calculation of the ICS capital requirement.

65. The ICS identifies two tiers of capital:

- Tier 1 capital resources comprise financial instruments and capital elements, other than financial instruments, that absorb losses on a going-concern basis and in winding-up; and

- Tier 2 capital resources comprise financial instruments and capital elements, other than financial instruments, that absorb losses only in winding-up.

66. In determining qualifying capital resources, the ICS differentiates between mutual and non-mutual IAIGs.

6.2 Classification of financial instruments

67. Financial instruments are classified into those two tiers based on consideration of a number of criteria, focused on five key principles:

- loss absorbing capacity (on a going-concern basis and/or in winding-up);
- subordination;
- availability to absorb losses;
- permanence; and
- absence of both encumbrances and mandatory servicing costs.

68. Within each tier, financial instruments are allocated into two categories with differing qualifying criteria:

- Tier 1:
  ○ Tier 1 financial instruments for which there is no limit (Tier 1 Unlimited); and
  ○ Tier 1 financial instruments for which there is a limit (Tier 1 Limited).
- Tier 2:
  ○ Tier 2 Paid-Up financial instruments (Tier 2 Paid-Up); and
  ○ Tier 2 Non-Paid-Up financial instruments (Tier 2 Non-Paid-Up).

69. Table 2 presents the features of Tier 1 Unlimited, Tier 1 Limited and Tier 2 Paid-Up capital with respect to the classification of financial instruments against the five key principles:

Table 2　Key Principles for tiering in capital resources

Key Principles	Tier 1 Unlimited	Tier 1 Limited	Tier 2 Paid-Up
Loss absorbing capacity	Absorbs losses on both a going-concern basis and in winding-up.	Absorbs losses on both a going-concern basis and in winding-up.	Absorbs losses in winding-up.

四、Level 1 Document: ICS Version 2.0 for the monitoring period

续表

Key Principles	Tier 1 Unlimited	Tier 1 Limited	Tier 2 Paid-Up
Level of subordination	Most subordinated (ie is the first to absorb losses); subordinated to policyholders, other non-subordinated creditors, holders of Tier 2 capital instruments, and holders of Tier 1 Limited capital instruments.	Subordinated to policyholders, other non-subordinated creditors and holders of Tier 2 capital instruments.	Subordinated to policyholders and other non-subordinated creditors.
Availability to absorb losses	Fully paid-up	Fully paid-up	Fully paid-up
Permanence	Perpetual	Perpetual For mutuals, this requirement is considered to be met if redemption at maturity (for a dated instrument) can be deferred, subject to supervisory approval or a lock-in feature, subject to a sufficiently long initial maturity. No incentives to redeem permitted. Issuer may redeem after a minimum specified period after issuance or repurchase at any time, subject to prior supervisory approval.	Sufficiently long initial maturity - may have incentives to redeem but first occurrence deemed to be "effective maturity date".
Absence of both encumbrances and mandatory servicing costs	IAIG has full discretion to cancel distributions (ie distributions are non-cumulative); the instrument is neither undermined nor rendered ineffective by encumbrances.	IAIG has full discretion to cancel distributions (ie distributions are non-cumulative); the instrument is neither undermined nor rendered ineffective by encumbrances.	The instrument is neither undermined nor rendered ineffective by encumbrances.

70. With regard to Tier 2 Paid-Up capital, the form of subordination can be either contractual or structural. Structurally subordinated instruments are subject to certain conditions that capture the specificities of structural subordination.

71. The recognition of Tier 2 Non-Paid Up capital is restricted to mutual IAIGs. It is also required that once these items become paid-up, the resulting capital element will possess the features required of Tier 1 or Tier 2 Paid-Up capital resources.

72. The list of criteria and conditions associated with each tier of capital is specified in the Level 2 document.

6.3 Capital elements other than financial instruments

6.3.1 Tier 1 capital elements

73. Subject to any exclusion, adjustment or deduction as specified in Section 6.4.1, Tier 1 capital elements, other than financial instruments, include the following items:

a) Retained earnings;

b) Share premium, resulting from the issuance of instruments included in Tier 1, and other forms of contributed surplus earned from sources other than profits;

c) Accumulated Other Comprehensive Income (AOCI);

d) The fair market value of equity-settled employee stock options, provided that a corresponding expense is recorded in the profit and loss account of the IAIG, under applicable accounting standards; and

e) Other allocated to equity, which includes:

i. Minority/Non-controlling interests (NCI); and

ii. Adjustments applied to the IAIG's consolidated balance sheet (as per audited financial statements) to produce the ICS balance sheet.

6.3.2 Tier 2 capital elements

74. Subject to any exclusion, adjustment or deduction as specified in Section 6.4.2, Tier 2 capital elements, other than financial instruments, include the following:

a) Share premium resulting from the issuance of instruments included in Tier 2 Paid-Up capital resources;

b) The value of encumbered assets in excess of the on-balance sheet liabilities secured by the encumbered assets and incremental ICS capital requirement, in respect of those assets and liabilities excluded from Tier 1 (see Section 6.4.3 for details on the treatment of encumbered assets); and

c) The Tier 2 basket, comprised of proportions of the following three items which relate to deductions from Tier 1 (see Section 6.4.1):

i. the value of each net defined benefit pension fund that is an asset on the IAIG's balance sheet, net of any eligible Deferred Tax Liability (DTL);

ii. Deferred Tax Asset (DTA) deducted from Tier 1 capital resources; and

iii. the value of computer software intangibles (net of amortisation) deducted from Tier 1 capital resources, net of any eligible DTL.

75. The Tier 2 basket is subject to a limit, expressed as a percentage of the ICS capital requirement.

76. The proportions of the three items included in the Tier 2 basket, as well as the overall

limit applicable to the basket, are specified in the Level 2 document.

6.4 Capital adjustments and deductions

6.4.1 Deductions from Tier 1 capital resources

77. To the extent that they have not already been excluded through valuation in the ICS balance sheet, the following items are deducted from Tier 1 capital resources:

a) Goodwill;

b) Intangible assets, including computer software intangibles;

c) Each asset recognised on the IAIG's balance sheet that relates to a defined benefit pension fund;

d) DTAs on the ICS balance sheet;

e) Reciprocal cross holdings, arranged either directly or indirectly between financial institutions and that artificially inflate the Tier 1 capital position of the IAIG;

f) Direct and indirect investments in own Tier 1 capital instruments, not otherwise eliminated;

g) Reinsurance assets arising from arrangements deemed to constitute non-qualifying reinsurance;

h) Encumbered assets in excess of the on-balance sheet liabilities secured by the encumbered assets and incremental ICS capital requirement in respect of those assets and liabilities (see Section 6.4.3 for details on the treatment of encumbered assets); and

i) The value of equity and debt owned by the IAIG in entities that are excluded from the scope of the group.

78. Items a) to c) are net of any associated DTL that would be extinguished if the item becomes impaired or derecognised under the valuation approach. DTLs are permitted to be netted against DTAs (item d) above provided that they exclude amounts that have already been netted against items a) to c).

6.4.2 Deductions from Tier 2 capital resources

79. To the extent that they have not already been excluded through valuation in the ICS balance sheet, the following items are deducted from Tier 2 capital resources:

a) Reciprocal cross holdings, arranged either directly or indirectly between financial institutions and that artificially inflate the Tier 2 capital position of the IAIG; and

b) Direct and indirect investments in own Tier 2 capital instruments, not otherwise eliminated.

6.4.3 Treatment of encumbered assets

80. When an IAIG holds encumbered assets in excess of the liabilities and associated risks

for which those assets have been encumbered, an adjustment to Tier 1 capital resources is made.

81. The details of this adjustment are specified in the Level 2 document.

82. The amount of encumbered assets deducted from Tier 1 capital resources is included in Tier 2 capital resources, subject to the limits applicable to Tier 2 (see Section 6.5 on capital composition limits).

6.5　Capital composition limits

83. The Tier 1 Limited and Tier 2 capital resources after adjustments, exclusions and deductions are subject to limits expressed as a percentage of the ICS capital requirement. Those limits, which may differ depending on the IAIG being mutual or non-mutual, are specified in the Level 2 document.

84. The GWS, in consultation with the supervisory college, may apply temporary supervisory forbearance on the limit on Tier 1 Limited capital resources for mutual IAIGs, provided that the IAIG submits a plan to restore its capital position.

85. Tier 1 Limited capital resources that are in excess of the associated limit are eligible for inclusion within Tier 2 capital resources, and become subject to the limit applicable to Tier 2 capital resources.

7　Reference ICS: Capital Requirement-The Standard Method

7.1　ICS Risks and Calculation Methods

86. The categories of risk included in the standard method are: Insurance risk, Market risk, Credit risk and Operational risk. Table 3 lists the risk categories, along with the individual risks in each risk category.

87. The ICS capital requirement is based on the potential adverse changes in qualifying capital resources resulting from unexpected changes, events or other manifestations of the specified risks.

88. Risks are measured using two approaches: a stress approach and a factor-based approach. There is one exception, which is natural catastrophe risk, where a vendor model may be used.

89. The stress approach follows a dynamic approach looking at the balance sheet at two points in time: the IAIG's current balance sheet pre-stress and the IAIG's balance sheet post-stress. The risk charge for each individual risk is determined as the decrease between the amount of capital resources on the pre-stress balance sheet (CR0) and the amount of capital resources on the post-stress balance sheet (CR1). Stresses can be applied individually with individual stressed balance sheets being calculated (CR0 − CR1) to determine the risk charge

四、Level 1 Document: ICS Version 2.0 for the monitoring period

with respect to each individual stress. As a simplification, the change in net asset value is used as a proxy for the changes in qualifying capital resources.

90. The factor-based approach is determined by applying factors to specific exposure measures.

91. The scope of the risks covered by the ICS capital requirement, as well as the applicable measurement method, are outlined in Table 3.

Table 3 Risks, definitions and measurement method

Categories of risk	Risk	Scope/definition: Risk of adverse change in the value of capital resources due to	Measurement Method
Insurance risk	Mortality risk (life)	Unexpected changes① in the level, trend or volatility of mortality rates.	Stress
	Longevity risk (life)	Unexpected changes in the level, trend or volatility of mortality rates.	Stress
	Morbidity/Disability risk (life)	Unexpected changes in the level, trend or volatility of disability, sickness and morbidity rates.	Stress
	Lapse risk (life)	Unexpected changes in the level or volatility of rates of policy lapses, terminations, renewals and surrenders.	Stress
	Expense risk (life)	Unexpected changes in liability cash flows due to the incidence of expenses incurred.	Stress
	Premium risk (non-life)	Unexpected changes in the timing, frequency and severity of future insured events (to the extent not already captured in Morbidity/Disability risk).	Factor
	Claims reserve risk (non-life)	Unexpected changes in the expected future payments for claims or events that have already occurred (whether reported to the IAIG or not) and not yet fully settled (to the extent not already captured in Morbidity/Disability risk).	Factor
	Catastrophe risk	Unexpected changes in the occurrence of low frequency and high severity events.	Stress, except for natural catastrophe, which may use a model.

---

① Expected impacts are assumed to be incorporated in valuation methodologies.

continued

Categories of risk	Risk	Scope/definition: Risk of adverse change in the value of capital resources due to	Measurement Method
Market risk	Interest Rate risk	Unexpected changes in the level or volatility of interest rates.	Stress
	Non-default spread risk	Unexpected changes in the level or volatility of spreads over the risk-free interest rate term structure, excluding the default component.	Stress
	Equity risk	Unexpected changes in the level or volatility of market prices of equities.	Stress
	Real Estate risk	Unexpected changes in the level or volatility of market prices of real estate or from the amount and timing of cash flows from investments in real estate.	Stress
	Currency risk	Unexpected changes in the level or volatility of currency exchange rates.	Stress
	Asset Concentration risk	The lack of diversification in the asset portfolio.	Factor
Credit risk	Credit risk	Unexpected changes in actual defaults, as well as in the deterioration of an obligor's creditworthiness short of default, including migration risk and spread risk due to defaults.	Factor
Operational risk	Operational risk	Operational events including inadequate or failed internal processes, people and systems, or from external events. Operational risk includes legal risk, but excludes strategic and reputational risk.	Factor

92. The individual risk charges are combined in a way that recognises risk diversification, using correlation matrices.

93. The ICS target criteria is a 99.5% Value at Risk (VaR), over a one-year time horizon, of adverse changes in the IAIG's qualifying capital resources.

7.1.1 Risk mitigation techniques

94. In order to promote good risk management and achieve an appropriate level of risk sensitivity, the ICS recognises the effect of risk mitigation techniques, provided certain criteria are met. These criteria are set out in the Level 2 document and are designed to ensure that the risk mitigation techniques are accurately and appropriately reflected within the risk charges.

95. In addition, there are certain conditions that must be met regarding the renewal of risk mitigation arrangements. The conditions vary depending on whether the risk mitigation arrangement applies to a Market risk exposure or non-life Premium risk. These conditions are

四、Level 1 Document: ICS Version 2.0 for the monitoring period

specified in the Level 2 document.

7.1.2 Geographic segmentation

96. For some of the risks, a geographical segmentation is used to calculate the risk charge. The geographical segmentation is set out in the Level 2 document.

7.1.3 Management actions

97. A credit for exercising management actions is taken into account at the level of each risk in the ICS capital requirement, subject to a cap, as described in the Level 2 document.

7.2 Insurance risks

7.2.1 Grouping of policies for life insurance risks

98. For life risks, stress scenarios are applied at the level of homogeneous risk groups, as detailed in the Level 2 document.

7.2.2 Calculation of life insurance risk charge

99. Life risk charges are applicable to life business and similar to life health business (refer to paragraph108).

100. The life insurance risk charge is calculated by aggregating, using the life risks correlation matrix specified in the Level 2 document, the following five sub-risk charges.

- Mortality risk;
- Longevity risk;
- Morbidity/Disability risk;
- Lapse risk; and
- Expense risk.

101. Life insurance risk charges are calculated based on the geographical segmentation specified in the Level 2 document.

102. For each of the five sub-risks, the risk charge is calculated both with and without the impact of management actions.

7.2.2.1 Mortality risk

103. The Mortality risk charge is calculated as the change in net asset value after applying the prescribed stress to the level of mortality rates. The prescribed stresses, based on the geographic segmentation, are specified in the Level 2 document.

104. The Mortality risk charge only applies to those policies that are negatively affected by an increase in mortality rates.

7.2.2.2 Longevity risk

105. The Longevity risk charge is calculated as the change in net asset value after applying the prescribed stress to the level of mortality rates. The prescribed stresses, based on the

geographic segmentation, are specified in the Level 2 document.

106. The Longevity risk charge only applies to those policies that are negatively affected by a decrease in mortality rates.

7.2.2.3 Morbidity and Disability risk

107. The Morbidity/Disability risk charge is calculated as the change in net asset value after applying the prescribed stresses to the four specified mutually exclusive benefit segments. The prescribed stresses, based on the geographic segmentation, benefit segments and contract length, are specified in the Level 2 document.

108. Similar Morbidity/Disability benefits may be classified as life or non-life; however, the Morbidity/Disability risk charge only applies to those policies with benefits classified as similar to life. Examples of policies with benefits similar to life are provided in the Level 2 document. For those classified as similar to non-life, the non-life risk charges (Premium and Claims Reserve risk) apply.

7.2.2.4 Lapse risk

109. The Lapse risk charge is calculated as the maximum of the Lapse risk charge for the level and trend component and the Lapse risk charge for the mass lapse component.

110. The Lapse risk charges for the level and trend component and the mass lapse component are calculated as the change in net asset value after applying the prescribed stresses to the two components. The prescribed stresses, based on the geographic segmentation, are specified in the Level 2 document.

111. The Lapse risk charge takes into account all legal or contractual options that can change the value of future cash flows.

7.2.2.5 Expense risk

112. The Expense risk charge is calculated as the change in net asset value after simultaneously applying the prescribed stresses to the unit expense and expense inflation assumptions. The prescribed stresses, based on the geographic segmentation, are specified in the Level 2 document.

7.2.3 Calculation of Non-Life Risk Charge

113. Non-life risk charges are applicable to non-life business and similar to non-life health business.

114. The non-life risk charge comprises both Premium risk and Claims Reserve risk, which are captured by a factor-based approach with factors applied to ICS segments within defined regions, as specified in the Level 2 document. The Claims Reserve risk factors include the effects of Latent Liability risk.

115. The non-life insurance risk charge is calculated using an aggregation approach that recognises diversification across lines of business and regions. The correlation factors are specified in the Level 2 document. The aggregation approach recognises the following sources of diversification:
- Between Premium risk and Claims Reserve risk;
- Within ICS categories, which is a high-level grouping of the type of business;
- Within a region; and
- Across regions.

116. Premium and Claims Reserve risk charges are calculated based on the geographical segmentation specified in the Level 2 document. The geographical segmentation is further segmented into lines of business based on statutory reporting in certain regions.

7.2.4 Calculation of Catastrophe Risk Charge

117. Catastrophe risk is a risk that affects both life and non-life business. The Catastrophe risk charge covers risks associated with low frequency, high severity events occurring at any point in time in the next 12 months and takes into account all expected in-force business when the event occurs.

118. Risk mitigation arrangements (eg. outwards reinsurance protection purchased) may reduce the overall Catastrophe risk charge.

119. Catastrophe risk is segmented at the risk/peril level. Perils cover both naturally occurring perils (natural catastrophes) and man-made perils/scenarios (other catastrophes) and their consequences.

120. The impact of catastrophe claim events include not only the main peril (eg. windstorm, earthquake) but also the secondary perils associated with the primary peril. Secondary perils can affect all lines of business within the scope of the calculation. Examples of main and secondary perils are provided in the Level 2 document.

121. The perils, scenarios and allowable risk mitigation, along with prudential safeguards for the use of models to calculate the natural catastrophe risk charge, are specified in the Level 2 document.

7.3 Market Risks

7.3.1 Calculation of the market risk charge

122. The market risk charge is calculated by aggregating, using the market risks correlation matrix specified in the Level 2 document, the following six sub-risk charges:
- Interest Rate risk;
- Non-Default Spread risk;

- Equity risk;
- Real Estate risk;
- Currency risk; and
- Asset Concentration risk.

123. When calculating the market risk charges, the following impacts are considered:

- The direct impacts of the prescribed stress scenarios on the value of assets and liabilities; and
- The indirect impacts linked to potential changes in policyholder behaviour following the prescribed stress scenarios.

124. For each of the six sub-risks, the risk charge is calculated both with and without the impact of management actions.

7.3.2 Interest rate risk

125. The calculation of the Interest Rate risk charge is based on a combination of five stresses applied to the entire risk-free yield curve for each relevant currency as identified in paragraph 127:

- A mean-reversion scenario;
- A level up scenario;
- A level down scenario;
- A twist up-to-down scenario; and
- A twist down-to-up scenario.

126. The characteristics of those stresses are specified in the Level 2 document. The stress scenarios are applied only to assets and liabilities that are sensitive to a change in the level of risk-free rates; the identification of assets and liabilities subject to the stresses is specified in the Level 2 document. The impact of those stresses on lapse rates, due to the influence of market conditions on policyholder behaviour, is taken into account as specified in the Level 2 document.

127. The impact of the scenarios listed above is calculated for all currencies in which the IAIG holds interest rate sensitive assets or liabilities. Currencies for which the exposure is non-material may be grouped together. The stress impacts calculated for each currency or group thereof are then combined to derive the overall Interest Rate risk charge.

128. The materiality assessment of a currency exposure, as well as the methodology to aggregate the results across the five stresses and relevant currencies, are specified in the Level 2 document.

7.3.3 Non-Default Spread Risk

129. Non-Default Spread risk is calculated as a bi-directional stress applied to both assets and liabilities. The Non-Default Spread risk charge is calculated as the maximum of an upward and downward stress, subject to a floor of zero.

130. The downward stress is a combination of an absolute and relative stress to the spread levels. This downward stress is specified in a way that prevents positive spreads from becoming negative after applying the stress. The upward stress is designed as an absolute increase of the spread levels.

131. The characteristics of the stresses to apply, as well as the rules governing the identification of those assets and liabilities to which the stress applies, are specified in the Level 2 document.

7.3.4 Equity risk

132. The Equity risk charge is calculated as the change in net asset value following the occurrence of a stress scenario that impacts the level and volatility of the fair value of equities. The stress scenario consists of level scenarios, according to the specified segments of assets, and one volatility scenario measured separately, after management actions. The stress scenario is defined in the Level 2 document.

133. The Equity risk charge applies to direct and indirect exposures to all assets and liabilities with values sensitive to changes in the level or volatility of the fair value of equities as specified in the Level 2 document.

134. The Equity risk charge uses the following segmentation of assets as defined in the Level 2 document:

- Listed equity in developed markets;
- Listed equity in emerging markets;
- Hybrid debt/preference shares; and
- Other equity.

7.3.5 Real estate risk

135. The Real Estate risk charge is calculated as the change in the net asset value, following the occurrence of a prescribed stress scenario, based on a change in the level of real estate prices, after management actions, as specified in the Level 2 document.

136. The Real Estate risk stress scenario is applied to both direct and indirect exposures to real estate prices, without distinguishing between commercial, residential and real estate for own use, as specified in the Level 2 document.

7.3.6 Currency risk

137. The Currency risk charge is equal to the higher of the aggregated losses incurred under two stress scenarios on the exchange rates between the IAIG's reporting currency and those currencies in which the IAIG holds assets or liabilities. The prescribed stresses are applied to the net open position determined for each relevant currency.

138. The net open position in a currency takes into account all direct and indirect exposures to that currency. Where relevant, an amount corresponding to jurisdictional capital requirements in that currency, subject to a cap, may be deducted from the net open position.

139. The two stress scenarios are:

a) Scenario 1: All of the currencies in which the IAIG has a net long position decrease in value against the reporting currency, while all of the currencies in which the IAIG has a net short position remain unchanged; or

b) Scenario 2: All of the currencies in which the IAIG has a net short position increase in value against the reporting currency, while all of the currencies in which the IAIG has a net long position remain unchanged.

140. Within each scenario, the losses by currency are aggregated using a correlation formula, as described in the Level 2 document.

141. The prescribed stresses for each currency pair, the aggregation formula, as well as the rules applicable to the determination of net open positions, are specified in the Level 2 document.

7.3.7 Asset concentration risk

142. The Asset Concentration risk charge is an incremental risk charge above the market and credit risks charges which acknowledges that assets held by IAIGs are not perfectly diversified. Assets in separate accounts or where the investment risks fully flow-through[①] to policyholders are excluded from the calculation of the Asset Concentration risk charge.

143. For real estate, a specified factor is applied to assets in excess of specified threshold. The methodology to calculate the Asset Concentration risk charge is specified in the Level 2 document.

7.4 Credit Risk

7.4.1 Calculation of Credit risk charge

144. The Credit risk charge is the determined by applying prescribed stress factors to

---

① Not considering any guarantee to policyholders that may exist on the value of the overall investment fund (s) such as on variable annuity products.

specified net exposure amounts. Management actions are taken into consideration in the calculation of the Credit risk charge.

145. The prescribed stress factors vary by exposure class, rating category and maturity. The classification of exposures between those categories, as well as the associated stress factors, are specified in the Level 2 document.

7.4.2　Recognition of collateral, guarantees and credit derivatives

146. In determining the net exposure value, collateral and guarantees may be taken into consideration. The Level 2 document specifies the criteria for the recognition of collateral, guarantees and credit derivatives.

7.4.3　Use of external credit ratings

147. External credit ratings may be used for the calculation of the Credit risk charge, provided that the rating agency has published default and transition statistics extending back over a sufficiently long period of time, and satisfying six criteria related to: objectivity, independence, international access/transparency, disclosure, resources and credibility. Those criteria, as well as the required time period for which statistics need to have been published, are specified in the Level 2 document.

148. When external credit ratings are used in accordance with paragraph 147, they are mapped to ICS Rating Categories as described in Section 3.4 and further specified in the Level 2 document.

149. IAIGs may use any ratings by a rating agency currently recognised by their home insurance regulator for local capital determination purposes, subject to clear instructions provided by the home insurance regulator on how to map those credit agency ratings to the ICS Rating Categories and explicit acceptance of the use of those ratings by the IAIS.

7.4.4　Supervisor-owned and controlled credit assessment (SOCCA) processes

150. A SOCCA process is an independent and objective process for assessing Credit risk, owned and controlled by a financial supervisory authority, and that relies upon credit assessment methodologies deemed suitable by the supervisory authority in determining the regulatory capital requirement for Credit risk of supervised entities. An example of a SOCCA is NAIC Designations. The criteria for a SOCCA process to be recognised in the ICS are specified in the Level 2 document.

151. A decision on whether SOCCA processes will be part of the ICS standard method as a

national discretion or included in other methods① will be made by the IAIS by the end of the monitoring period, provided that certain specified criteria are met. The use of SOCCA processes for the purpose of calculating an IAIG's Credit risk charge is recognised in the calculation of ICS coverage ratios.

152. If it is decided that SOCCA processes are to be included in the standard method, then IAIGs would be required to apply the standard method when a rating is available. ② If SOCCA processes are determined to be part of other methods, then IAIGs would be able to use the SOCCA designations, regardless of the availability of other ratings.

7.5 Operational risk

153. The Operational risk charge is determined by applying prescribed stress factors to specified risk exposures.

154. The calculation of the Operational risk charge is based on data items split into geographical segments and the following line of business segments:

- Non-life-insurance products that do not relate to life or similar to life health insurance, often referred to as property and casualty or general insurance;
- Life (risk) -Insurance products that relate to life or similar to life health insurance where the insurer bears investment risk; and
- Life (non-risk) -products where the policyholder bears the investment risk. It includes segmented funds and accumulation annuities.

155. The stress factors, risk exposures and line of business segments for the Operational risk charge are specified in the Level 2 document.

7.6 Aggregation/Diversification of ICS Risk Charges

156. ICS Risk charges are aggregated together using multiple levels:

- A top-level aggregation between major risk categories (Life risk, Non-life risk, Catastrophe risk, Market risk, Credit risk and Operational risk) using a correlation matrix;
- A medium-level aggregation between the sub-risks of Life risk, Catastrophe risk and Market risk, using correlation matrices; and
- An aggregation within individual risk charges (eg. interest rate risk, non-life risk).

---

① Other methods refer to alternative methods of calculating the ICS capital requirement, outside of those under the standard method. Other methods of calculation of the ICS capital requirement will be reviewed and considered for inclusion in the ICS by the end of the monitoring period.

② Under the standard method, if more than one rating is available for the same exposure (which implies different ICS Rating Categories), then the second highest resulting ICS Rating category is used. In order to be comparable, ratings must be based on par value of the instrument and not purchase price. If it is an unrated security, then the designation from the supervisor-owned and controlled credit assessment process is used.

157. The aggregation of risk charges incorporates a degree of diversification between the individual risks, based on a specified dependency between the risks.

158. Correlation matrices are specified for the aggregation of the individual Life Risk charges and the aggregation of individual Market risks charges. A top-level correlation matrix is specified for the aggregation of Life, Non-Life, Catastrophe, Market and Credit risk charges. The Operational risk charge is then added to that aggregate to determine the overall ICS insurance risk charge.

159. The correlation matrices used to aggregate the ICS risk charges are specified in the Level 2 document. The aggregation approach used within individual risk charges is described in the specific risk section in the Level 1 and 2 documents.

8 Reference ICS: Tax

8.1 General principles

160. Deferred taxes, as recognised on the consolidated GAAP or SAP balance sheet, are also recognised on the ICS balance sheet in accordance with Section 5.

161. There are two areas of the ICS that are tax affected:

- Differences in valuation between the jurisdictional consolidated GAAP balance sheet and the ICS balance sheet (ICS Adjustment), made in accordance with Section 5; and
- The ICS insurance capital requirement.

162. The ICS applies a Top-down approach using a group effective tax rate (ETR) to calculate the deferred tax on the ICS Adjustment and the tax effect on the ICS insurance capital requirement.

163. The method to calculate the group ETR is specified in the Level 2 document.

8.2 Deferred tax from the ICS Adjustment

164. The adjustments made to the GAAP/SAP balance sheet in order to derive the ICS balance sheet give rise to corresponding adjustments to deferred tax assets and liabilities. Potential additional DTAs, created as a consequence of those adjustments, are subject to an utilisation assessment. The conditions of recognition and calculation of those tax adjustments, including the utilisation assessment, as well as the conditions in which those adjustments may be offset, are specified in the Level 2 document.

8.3 Tax effect on the ICS insurance capital requirement

165. The mitigating effect of tax is taken into account when determining the ICS capital requirement. That tax effect on the ICS capital requirement is based on the increase in net DTA that would result from an instantaneous operational loss equal to the ICS capital requirement

before tax, post diversification and post management actions. Any increase in net DTA is subject to an utilisation assessment, specified in the Level 2 document.

9 Additional Reporting

166. ICS Version 2.0 also contains additional reporting, at the option of the GWS, of ICS based on GAAP Plus valuation and/or other methods of calculation of the ICS capital requirement.

167. As stated in the KL Agreement, "The reference ICS and additional reporting at the option of the GWS within ICS Version 2.0 are equally important components. Both GAAP Plus and other methods of calculation of the ICS capital requirement are viable options that will be considered for inclusion in the ICS by the end of the monitoring period."

9.1 GAAP Plus

168. GAAP Plus maximises the use of audited, consolidated financial reporting, systems and processes including generally accepted accounting principles as promulgated by the International Accounting Standards Board (IASB) and other jurisdictional standard setters. Adjustments made to the GAAP financials are for prudential purposes and impact the most significant and material items on the balance sheet.

169. GAAP Plus is closely tied to jurisdictional accounting rules, some of which are currently being revised (eg. IFRS and U.S. GAAP). These revisions will promote further convergence in valuation. However, the timing of new rules will require development of GAAP Plus to continue beyond 2020. Additionally, Chinese GAAP Plus is still being developed as it was only included in Field Testing for one year. As such, GAAP Plus (for IFRS, U.S. GAAP and China) will continue development and field testing into the monitoring period. Japanese GAAP will maintain the original five-year monitoring period, along with the reference ICS, beginning in 2020.

170. Further details on the reporting of GAAP Plus are provided in the Level 2 document.

9.2 Other methods of calculation of the ICS capital requirement (other methods)

171. The scope for the additional reporting of other methods during the monitoring period is limited to the capital requirement. That is, the valuation and capital resources elements of the ICS will not change as a result of other methods and are the same as those used for the ICS standard method. Other methods should provide the same level of protection as the standard method, which has a target criteria of 99.5% VaR over a one-year time horizon. In addition, other methods must be able to meet the ICPs and the ICS Principles.

172. Other methods that will be permitted for additional reporting during the monitoring

四、Level 1 Document: ICS Version 2. 0 for the monitoring period

period, at the option of the GWS are:
- Internal models;
- Dynamic hedging; and
- Supervisor-owned and controlled credit assessment processes: the decision on whether SOCCA processes will be part of the ICS standard method as a national discretion or included in other methods will be made by the IAIS by the end of the monitoring period.

173. A decision will be made by the end of the monitoring period whether these other methods will be included in the implementation of ICS as a PCR.

五、Level 2 Document: ICS Version 2.0 for the monitoring period

五、Level 2 Document: ICS Version 2.0 for the monitoring period

About the IAIS

The International Association of Insurance Supervisors (IAIS) is a voluntary membership organisation of insurance supervisors and regulators from more than 200 jurisdictions. The mission of the IAIS is to promote effective and globally consistent supervision of the insurance industry in order to develop and maintain fair, safe and stable insurance markets for the benefit and protection of policyholders and to contribute to global financial stability.

Established in 1994, the IAIS is the international standard setting body responsible for developing principles, standards and other supporting material for the supervision of the insurance sector and assisting in their implementation. The IAIS also provides a forum for Members to share their experiences and understanding of insurance supervision and insurance markets.

The IAIS coordinates its work with other international financial policymakers and associations of supervisors or regulators, and assists in shaping financial systems globally. In particular, the IAIS is a member of the Financial Stability Board (FSB), member of the Standards Advisory Council of the International Accounting Standards Board (IASB), and partner in the Access to Insurance Initiative (A2ii). In recognition of its collective expertise, the IAIS also is routinely called upon by the G20 leaders and other international standard setting bodies for input on insurance issues as well as on issues related to the regulation and supervision of the global financial sector.

International Association of Insurance Supervisors

c/o Bank for International Settlements

CH-4002 Basel

Switzerland

Tel: +41 61 280 8090 Fax: +41 61 280 9151

www.iaisweb.org

This document is available on the IAIS website (www.iaisweb.org).

© International Association of Insurance Supervisors (IAIS), 2020.

All rights reserved. Brief excerpts may be reproduced or translated provided the source is stated.

Contents

1 Introduction 221
2 Components of ICS Version 2.0 for the monitoring period 221
3 General Guiding Principles 221
   3.1 Substance over Form 221
   3.2 Proportionality 221
   3.3 Look-Through 221
   3.4 ICS Rating Categories 221
4 Reference ICS: Perimeter of the ICS Calculation 222
   4.1 Scope for Starting ICS Balance Sheet 222
   4.2 Development of Starting MAV Balance Sheet 224
5 Reference ICS: Market-adjusted valuation 224
   5.1 Valuation Principles 224
   5.2 Calculation of the Current Estimate 225
      5.2.1 Basis for calculation and cash-flow projection 225
      5.2.2 Contract recognition, contract boundaries and time horizon ... 227
      5.2.3 Data quality and setting of assumptions 227
      5.2.4 Management actions 228
      5.2.5 Discounting 228
   5.3 Margin over Current Estimate (MOCE) 237
      5.3.1 Definition and underlying principles 237
      5.3.2 Calculation of the MOCE 238
      5.3.3 Interaction of MOCE with other components 238
   5.4 Obligations replicable by a portfolio of assets 238
6 Reference ICS: Qualifying Capital Resources 238
   6.1 General considerations 238
   6.2 Classification of financial instruments 238
      6.2.1 Tier 1 unlimited financial instruments 238
      6.2.2 Tier 1 limited financial instruments 239
      6.2.3 Tier 2 financial instruments (other than structurally subordinated) ... 241
      6.2.4 Structurally subordinated Tier 2 financial instruments .. 242
      6.2.5 Tier 2 Non-paid-up capital 243

五、Level 2 Document: ICS Version 2.0 for the monitoring period

6.3　Capital elements other than financial instruments ················ 244
　　6.3.1　Tier 1 capital elements ················ 244
　　6.3.2　Tier 2 capital elements ················ 244
6.4　Capital adjustments and deductions ················ 244
　　6.4.1　Deductions from Tier 1 capital resources ················ 244
　　6.4.2　Deductions from Tier 2 capital resources ················ 244
　　6.4.3　Treatment of encumbered assets ················ 244
6.5　Capital composition limits ················ 245
7　Reference ICS: Capital Requirement-The Standard Method ················ 245
　7.1　ICS Risks and Calculation Methods ················ 245
　　7.1.1　Risk mitigation techniques ················ 245
　　7.1.2　Geographical segmentation ················ 248
　　7.1.3　Management actions ················ 248
　7.2　Insurance risks ················ 249
　　7.2.1　Grouping of policies for life insurance risks ················ 249
　　7.2.2　Calculation of life insurance risk charge ················ 249
　　7.2.3　Calculation of Non-Life Risk Charge ················ 254
　　7.2.4　Calculation of Catastrophe Risk Charge ················ 263
　7.3　Market Risks ················ 267
　　7.3.1　Calculation of the market risk charge ················ 267
　　7.3.2　Interest rate risk ················ 267
　　7.3.3　Non-Default Spread risk ················ 270
　　7.3.4　Equity risk ················ 271
　　7.3.5　Real estate risk ················ 273
　　7.3.6　Currency risk ················ 273
　　7.3.7　Asset concentration risk ················ 278
　7.4　Credit Risk ················ 280
　　7.4.1　Calculation of Credit risk charge ················ 280
　　7.4.2　Recognition of collateral, guarantees and credit derivatives ················ 290
　　7.4.3　Use of external credit ratings ················ 298
　　7.4.4　Supervisor-owned and controlled credit assessment (SOCCA) processes ······ 301
　7.5　Operational risk ················ 301
　7.6　Aggregation/Diversification of ICS Risk Charges ················ 302
　7.7　Non-Insurance Risk Charges ················ 303

8	Reference ICS: Tax	304
	8.1 General principles	304
	8.2 Deferred tax from the ICS Adjustments	304
	8.2.1 Utilisation assessment of DTAs recognised from the ICS Adjustments	304
	8.3 Tax effect on the ICS insurance capital requirement	305
	8.3.1 Component a: tax loss carry backs	305
	8.3.2 Component b: post-stress future taxable income projections	305
	8.3.3 Components c and d: Deferred taxes	306
9	Additional Reporting	306
	9.1 GAAP Plus	306
	9.1.1 Overview	306
	9.1.2 Japanese GAAP (J-GAAP) Plus Approach	307
	9.2 Other methods of calculation of the ICS capital requirement ("other methods")	312
	9.2.1 Internal Models	312
	9.2.2 Dynamic Hedging	321
Glossary		322
Annex 1	Treatment of Non-Voting Interest Entities (Asset and Insurance Securitisations)	324
Annex 2	Definition of ICS Non-Life Segments	327
Figures and tables		219

五、Level 2 Document: ICS Version 2.0 for the monitoring period

Figures and tables

Figure 1	Categorisation of non-life risk exposure, showing how Singapore Motor-like ICS Category is aggregated	256
Table 1	Mapping to ICS RC (for instruments not in default)	222
Table 2	List of currencies and associated instruments and LOT	229
Table 3	Eligibility of types of investment	233
Table 4	Geographical segmentation	248
Table 5	Life risks correlation matrix	249
Table 6	Mortality risk stress factors	250
Table 7	Longevity risk stress factors	250
Table 8	Morbidity/Disability risk stress factors-Location of risk Japan	252
Table 9	Morbidity/Disability risk stress factors-All other locations of risk	252
Table 10	Level & Trend Lapse risk stress factors	253
Table 11	Expense risk stress factors	254
Table 12	Within Category Correlation Factors	255
Table 13	ICS Non-Life Segmentation	256
Table 14	Credit stress factors for trade credit	265
Table 15	Market risks correlation matrix	267
Table 16	Stress factors for Non-Default Spread risk	271
Table 17	Stress factors for hybrid debt/preference shares	272
Table 18	Absolute stress factors for implied volatilities	272
Table 19	Equity correlation matrix	273
Table 20	Currency risk stress factors	274
Table 21	Calculation of potential future credit exposure	283
Table 22	Credit risk stress factors for public sector entities	286
Table 23	Credit risk stress factors for corporates and reinsurance	287
Table 24	Credit risk stress factors for securitisations	287
Table 25	Credit risk stress factors for re-securitisations	287
Table 26	Mapping of ICS CM categories, Method 1	288
Table 27	Stress factors for agricultural and commercial mortgages, Method 1	288
Table 28	Stress factors for agricultural and commercial mortgages, Method 2	289
Table 29	Factors for residential mortgages for which repayment depends on income	

	generated by the underlying property	290
Table 30	Factors for residential mortgages for which repayment does not depend on income generated by the underlying property	290
Table 31	Mapping of ratings by other rating agencies	299
Table 32	Operational risk exposures and stress factors	302
Table 33	Aggregation matrix between risks	302

五、Level 2 Document: ICS Version 2.0 for the monitoring period

1 Introduction

No additional information compared to the Level 1 document.

2 Components of ICS Version 2.0 for the monitoring period

No additional information compared to the Level 1 document.

3 General Guiding Principles

3.1 Substance over Form

No additional information compared to the Level 1 document.

3.2 Proportionality

No additional information compared to the Level 1 document.

3.3 Look-Through

1. The look-through approach applies to insurance arrangements and indirect investments (including unleveraged mutual funds, other collective investment vehicles, etc.) in order to identify all underlying exposures embedded in such arrangements and investments, including all indirect holdings that may artificially inflate the qualifying capital resources of an Internationally Active Insurance Group (IAIG).

2. When a full look-through is not possible, a partial look-through may be applied, along the lines provided by the Basel III framework[①].

3. When no look-through is possible, the full investment is considered as unlisted equity for the purpose of calculating the insurance capital standard (ICS) risk charges.

3.4 ICS Rating Categories

4. Whenever the use of an ICS Rating Category (ICS RC) is needed, IAIGs use the agency ratings listed in the table below. Ratings from AM Best can be used only for purposes of calculating the risk charge on reinsurance exposures. Modifiers such as + or - do not affect the ICS RC. Where two ratings are listed in a cell, the first rating represents a long-term rating, and the second rating represents the short-term rating mapped to the same ICS RC. The short-term rating is used only for instruments with a remaining maturity of one year or less.

---

① http://www.bis.org/publ/bcbs266.htm.

Table 1　Mapping to ICS RC (for instruments not in default)

ICS RC	S&P	Moody's	Fitch	JCR	R&I	DBRS	AM Best
1	AAA	Aaa	AAA	AAA	AAA	AAA	
2	AA / A-1	Aa / P-1	AA / F1	AA / J-1	AA / a-1	AA / R-1	A +
3	A / A-2	A / P-2	A / F2	A / J-2	A / a-2	A / R-2	A
4	BBB / A-3	Baa / P-3	BBB / F3	BBB / J-3	BBB / a-3	BBB / R-3	B +
5	BB	Ba	BB	BB	BB	BB	B
6	B / B	B / NP	B / B	B / NJ	B / b	B / R-4	C +
7	CCC / C and lower	Caa and lower	CCC / C and lower	CCC and lower	CCC / c and lower	CCC / R-5 and lower	C and lower

5. Additionally, IAIGs can use ratings issued by a rating agency that the banking regulator in its jurisdiction (or for a subsidiary, in the subsidiary's jurisdiction) has recognised as an External Credit Assessment Institution (ECAI) under the Basel II framework. The ICS RC corresponding to a rating produced by such an agency is the Basel II rating category to which the supervisor has mapped the rating (the combined rating class AAA/AA corresponds to ICS RC 2).

6. ICS RCs 1 to 4 in the table above are considered as investment grade.

7. The use of ICS RCs is further developed in section 7.4.3.

4　Reference ICS: Perimeter of the ICS Calculation

4.1　Scope for Starting ICS Balance Sheet

8. The parameter of the ICS calculation is defined as including all consolidated legal entities within the IAIG.

9. The starting point to derive the balance sheet of the insurance group, prior to application of any Market-Adjusted Valuation (MAV) adjustments, is the consolidated Generally Accepted Accounting Principles (GAAP) balance sheet of the Head of the IAIG, as defined in the Common Framework for the Supervision of IAIGs (ComFrame). For entities that do not have consolidated GAAP financials, see paragraph 15.

10. For purposes of the ICS calculation, balance sheets are segregated into insurance related and non-insurance components. The insurance portion of the balance sheet is comprised of entities that meet the following definitions:

a. Insurer: Insurance legal entity or insurance group.

b. Insurance legal entity: A legal entity, including its branches, that is licensed to conduct insurance, regulated and subject to supervision.

五、Level 2 Document: ICS Version 2.0 for the monitoring period

c. Insurance related entities: Legal entities that mainly exist to support the operations of the insurer.

11. Legal entities that comprise the consolidated GAAP balance sheet are further categorised according to the following definitions in order to apply certain accounting treatment that differs from GAAP as well as to derive a capital requirement for non-insurance components:

a. Insurer and Insurance related entities;

b. Regulated non-insurance financial entity;

c. Non-regulated non-insurance financial entity; and

d. Non-financial entity.

12. The ICS follows GAAP accounting rules for consolidation accounting treatment except for the following:

a. For insurer and insurance related entities that are determined under GAAP to be controlled as joint ventures①, a proportional consolidation method is used unless it is determined through consultation with the group-wide supervisor (GWS) that such treatment is not considered feasible; in which case the entity remains unadjusted and reported as per GAAP as an equity method investment.

b. For insurer and insurance related entities that are determined under GAAP to be controlled as joint operations② and reported by recognising its own assets, liabilities and transactions, including its share of those incurred jointly, the entity may remain unadjusted (ie proportional consolidation on shared assets).

c. For non-insurance financial and non-financial entities that are determined under GAAP to be joint operations and reported by recognizing its own assets, liabilities and transactions, including its share of those incurred jointly, the entity should instead be reported as an equity method investment.

d. For non-insurance financial and non-financial entities that are determined under GAAP to be joint ventures, the entity should be reported as an equity method investment.

13. Adjustments related to non-voting interest entities③:

a. A non-voting interest entity that has been determined under GAAP to be unconsolidated

---

① A joint venture is a joint arrangement whereby the parties that have joint control of the arrangement have rights to the net assets of the arrangement.

② A joint operation is a joint arrangement whereby the parties that have joint control of the arrangement have rights to the assets, and obligations for the liabilities, relating to the arrangement.

③ A non-voting interest entity is an entity where voting or similar rights are not the dominant factor in assessing control. Entities are often thinly capitalised or contain no capital and are designed for a specific purpose (eg, special purpose entities, structured entities, GP/LP structures, trusts and investment partnerships).

is consolidated if either the IAIG or its GWS assesses that it poses a material risk[①] to the group, either individually or in the aggregate.

b. A securitisation originated within the group may not be consolidated provided that it meets all of the conditions outlined in Annex 1;

c. Notwithstanding the materiality assessment or application of additional criteria, a non-voting interest entity is consolidated when the GWS determines that the nature, scale and complexity of the risks cannot be considered insignificant.

14. Other non-GAAP adjustments: Structured settlement agreements with third parties are recorded on a net basis (ie removed from reserves and reinsurance recoverables) when the underlying claim is settled and the risk to the non-life company is contingent upon the life insurer (and the guarantee fund, if applicable) having the ability to pay.

15. Aggregated group balance sheet: IAIGs that do not prepare consolidated or group level financial statements generate a balance sheet on an aggregated basis to reflect group level starting balances.

4.2 Development of Starting MAV Balance Sheet

No additional information compared to the Level 1 document.

5 Reference ICS: Market-adjusted valuation

5.1 Valuation Principles

16. When deriving the adjustments to be made to insurance liabilities, reinsurance balances, financial investments and instruments, and tax, IAIGs apply the following principles:

a. Property for own use is adjusted to fair value using the fair value guidance under the IAIG's GAAP or when the IAIG does not produce a GAAP consolidated balance sheet, the GAAP fair value principles in the IAIG's jurisdiction.

b. Mortgages and loans are adjusted to fair value using the fair value guidance under the IAIG's GAAP or when the IAIG does not produce a GAAP consolidated balance sheet, the GAAP fair value principles in the IAIG's jurisdiction.

c. Reinsurance recoverables are restated on a basis consistent with the determination of insurance liabilities. Recoverables on paid and unpaid balances are reported net of allowances for estimated uncollectable amounts.

---

① Material risk in this case relates to the risks posed to the group. In considering what might significantly contribute to group risks, a firm may assess whether the related entity's gross assets or gross revenue are more than 1% of the group's gross assets or revenue. In addition, an assessment of all immaterial entities exceeding 5% of the group's asset's or revenue, in the aggregate, may indicate that other entities should be consolidated in order to avoid missing material risks.

d. Deferred tax assets (DTA) and liabilities (DTL) are treated according to section 7.7.

e. Deferred acquisition costs and other deferred expenses that are on the balance sheet at the reporting date are adjusted to zero. Future acquisition costs related to future premiums (within contract boundaries – see section 5.2.2) are reflected in the value of insurance liabilities.

f. Premium receivables falling due after the reporting date and related to contracts that are included in the current estimate calculation are reflected in the valuation of insurance liabilities as negative cash flows. Premium receivables for which the due date is prior to the reporting date are not part of the current estimate calculation and remain as assets on the balance sheet.

g. Loans to policyholders are reported separately and are not netted against insurance liabilities.

h. Financial liabilities: upon initial recognition, the valuation of these items is based on the IAIG's reported GAAP, and there is no subsequent adjustment to take account of changes to the IAIG's own credit standing.

5.2 Calculation of the Current Estimate

5.2.1 Basis for calculation and cash-flow projection

5.2.1.1 General considerations

17. The current estimate calculation is based on the probability weighted average of the future cash flows, taking into account the uncertainty relating to:

a. The timing, frequency and severity of claim events;

b. Claim amounts and claim inflation, including where relevant any uncertainty on the value of indices used to determine claim amounts;

c. The time needed to settle claims;

d. The amount of expenses; and

e. Policyholder behaviour.

18. Cash flow projections reflect expected future demographic, legal, medical, technological, social or economic developments, and are based on appropriate inflation assumptions, recognising the different types of inflation to which the entity can be exposed. Premium adjustment clauses are also considered, where relevant.

19. The current estimate is calculated gross of reinsurance and special purpose vehicles (SPV). Recoverables from reinsurance or SPVs are calculated separately and recognised as an asset.

20. The projected cash flows include at a minimum the following items within the contract boundaries:

a. Benefit and claim payments;

b. Direct and indirect expenses incurred;

c. Premiums received;

d. Subrogation payments and recoveries other than from reinsurance and special purpose vehicles; and

e. Other payments made in order to settle the claims.

21. All expenses related to existing contracts and contracts that are recognised at the reporting date, but not yet in force, are included in the current estimate calculation. The expenses estimation assumes that the IAIG will write business in the future. Future expenses relating exclusively to future business are not considered for the current estimate calculation.

22. Where a yield curve is needed as input to assess future returns on assets, IAIGs make use of the relevant IAIS yield curves with specified adjustments.

5.2.1.2 Options and guarantees

23. The expected cash flows relating to options and guarantees embedded in the insurance contract are taken into account for the calculation of the current estimate. All payments connected to the risks insured, and profit participation payments in particular, are taken into consideration for the calculation of the value of options and guarantees.

24. All options and guarantees are valued using arbitrage-free techniques[①] based on the adjusted yield curve as a proxy for the risk-free curve.

5.2.1.3 Policyholder behaviour

25. Where relevant, expected cash flows reflect the contractual right of policyholders to change the amount, timing or nature of their benefits.

26. The likelihood that policyholders will exercise contractual options, including lapses and surrenders, is taken into account with a prospective view, considering in particular:

a. Past and expected behaviour of policyholders, considering also their reaction to management actions;

b. How beneficial the exercise of options would be to policyholders under specific circumstances; and

c. Economic conditions.

27. To the extent that it is deemed representative of future expected behaviour, assumptions on policyholder behaviour are based on appropriate statistical and empirical evidence.

---

① This implies in particular that where relevant, path dependency is taken into account in the valuation of options and guarantees.

28. The assumptions concerning policyholder behaviour are consistent with the assumed investment returns and the yield curves specified by the IAIS.

5.2.1.4 Future discretionary benefits

29. Future discretionary benefits (FDB) are comprised of all non-guaranteed amounts, including those bonuses linked to a legal or contractual obligation to distribute a portion of the IAIG's financial/underwriting profits to policyholders.

30. The current estimate recognises FDB expected to be paid consistently with expected future developments, the economic scenarios on which the liability valuation is based and policyholders' reasonable expectations.

31. The projection of FDB is also consistent with the yield curve applicable to the contract, as well as with the modelling of policyholder behaviour as described in section 5.2.1.3.

5.2.2 Contract recognition, contract boundaries and time horizon

32. A contract is recognised and valued as soon as the IAIG becomes party to that contract, without any possibility to amend or cancel it, even when the insurance coverage has not yet started.

33. A contract is derecognised when all possible claims linked to this contract have been completely settled, and all future cash-flows are nil.

34. Only those contracts recognised at the reporting date are taken into account in the current estimate calculation; in particular, no future business is included in the calculation.

35. All obligations, including future premiums, relating to a recognised contract are taken into account in the current estimate cash flow projection. However, future premiums (and associated claims and expenses) beyond either of the following dates are not considered, unless the IAIG can demonstrate that they are able and willing to compel the policyholder to pay the premiums:

a. The future date where the IAIG has a unilateral right to terminate the contract or reject the premiums payable under the contract;

b. The future date where the IAIG has a unilateral right to amend the premiums or the benefits payable under the contract in such a way that the premiums fully reflect the risks.

36. For group policies, similar rules apply. If premiums can be amended unilaterally for the entire portfolio in a way that fully reflects the risks of the portfolio, the second condition above is considered to be met.

5.2.3 Data quality and setting of assumptions

37. When selecting data for the calculation of the current estimate, IAIGs consider:

a. The quality of data based on the criteria of accuracy, completeness and appropriateness;

b. The use and setting of assumptions made in the collection and processing of data; and

c. The frequency of regular updates and the circumstances that trigger additional updates.

38. When only limited or unreliable data are available from the IAIG's own experience, the IAIG shall supplement its own data with data from other sources. When the characteristics of the portfolio differ from those of the population represented in the external data used, the external data are adjusted in order to ensure consistency with the risk characteristics of the IAIG's portfolio.

39. The assumptions used to calculate the current estimate reflect current expectations based on all information available. This requires an assessment of expected future conditions, in particular as soon as:

a. There is evidence that historical trends will not continue, that new trends will emerge or that economic, demographic and other changes may affect the cash flows that arise from the existing insurance contracts.

b. There have been changes in underwriting procedures and claims management procedures that may affect the relevance of historical data to the portfolio of insurance contracts.

c. Historical data do not capture types of events that may have an impact on the current estimate.

5.2.4 Management actions

40. The management actions recognised for the calculation of the current estimate are confined to decisions by the IAIG that have an impact on future bonuses or other discretionary benefits for participating/profit sharing and adjustable products.

41. Assumed future management actions are consistent with the IAIG's current business practice and business strategy unless the GWS is satisfied that there is sufficient evidence that the IAIG will change its practices or strategy.

42. When calculating the current estimate, future management actions are taken into account only if they can reasonably be expected to be carried out under the specific circumstances to which they apply.

43. The assumptions about future management actions take into account the time needed to implement them, as well as any resulting incremental expenses.

5.2.5 Discounting

5.2.5.1 Determination of yield curves for current estimate discounting

No additional information compared to the Level 1 document.

5.2.5.2 Determination of the risk-free yield curve

44. For all currencies, the start of the third segment as referred to in paragraph 47 of the

五、Level 2 Document: ICS Version 2.0 for the monitoring period

ICS Level 1 document is the later of the following:
- 30 years after the Last Observed Term (LOT); and
- 60 years.

45. The list of currencies for which a risk-free yield curve is calculated and the associated observed instruments and LOT are provided in Table 2.

Table 2 List of currencies and associated instruments and LOT

	Currency	Observed Instrument	LOT (years)	Long-term Forward Rate
AUD	Australian Dollar	Government Bonds	30	3.8%
BRL	Brazilian Real	Government Bonds	10	7.0%
CAD	Canadian Dollar	Government Bonds	30	3.8%
CHF	Swiss Franc	Government Bonds	20	2.8%
CLP	Chilean Peso	Swaps	10	5.0%
CNY	Yuan Renminbi	Government Bonds	10	6.0%
COP	Colombian Peso	Swaps	10	6.0%
CZK	Czech Koruna	Swaps	15	3.8%
DKK	Danish Krone	Swaps	20	3.8%
EUR	Euro	Swaps	20	3.8%
GBP	Pound Sterling	Swaps	50	3.8%
HKD	Hong Kong Dollar	Swaps	15	4.4%
HUF	Forint	Government Bonds	15	6.0%
IDR	Rupiah	Swaps	10	8.0%
ILS	New Israeli Shekel	Swaps	20	4.4%
INR	Indian Rupee	Swaps	10	7.0%
JPY	Yen	Government Bonds	30	3.8%
KRW	Won	Government Bonds	20	4.4%
MXN	Mexican Peso	Government Bonds	20	5.0%
MYR	Malaysian Ringgit	Government Bonds	15	5.0%
NOK	Norwegian Krone	Swaps	10	3.8%
NZD	New Zealand Dollar	Swaps	20	4.8%
PEN	Sol	Swaps	10	6.0%
PHP	Philippine Peso	Swaps	10	7.0%
PLN	Zloty	Government Bonds	10	5.0%
RON	Romanian Leu	Government Bonds	10	5.0%
RUB	Russian Ruble	Swaps	10	7.0%
SAR	Saudi Riyal	Swaps	15	6.0%
SEK	Swedish Krona	Swaps	10	3.8%

continued

	Currency	Observed Instrument	LOT (years)	Long-term Forward Rate
SGD	Singapore Dollar	Government Bonds	20	3.8%
THB	Baht	Government Bonds	10	5.0%
TRY	Turkish Lira	Government Bonds	10	7.0%
TWD	New Taiwan Dollar	Government Bonds	10	4.4%
USD	US Dollar	Government Bonds	30	3.8%
ZAR	Rand	Government Bonds	30	7.0%

46. The Long Term Forward Rate (LTFR) is the sum of the following two components:

a. The expected real interest rate, computed as the simple arithmetic mean of annual real interest rates. Annual real rates r are calculated as:

$$r = \frac{short\ term\ nominal\ rate - inflation\ rate}{1 + inflation\ rate}$$

The expected real interest rate is rounded to the nearest five basis points.

b. The expected inflation target, computed as follows:

• For currencies for which the central bank has announced an inflation target, the expected inflation is based on that inflation target. In this case the expected inflation rate is:

  ○ 1%, where the inflation target is lower than or equal to 1%;

  ○ 2%, where the inflation target is higher than 1% and lower than 3%;

  ○ 3%, where the inflation target is higher or equal to 3% and lower than 4%; and

  ○ 4%, otherwise.

• For currencies for which the central bank has not announced an inflation target, the expected inflation rate is set to 2%. However, where past inflation experience and projection of inflation both clearly indicate that the inflation in a currency area is materially higher or lower than 2%, the expected inflation rate is chosen in accordance with those indicators.

47. In order to determine the expected real interest rate, countries are grouped in the following three geographical areas:

a. Geographical area 1, comprised of the following currency areas: AUD, CAD, CHF, CZK, DKK, EUR, GBP, JPY, NOK, NZD, SEK, SGD, USD;

b. Geographical area 2, comprised of the following currency areas: HKD, ILS, KRW, TWD;

c. Geographical area 3, comprised of all other currency areas.

48. The value of the expected real interest rate component is:

• 1.8% for geographical area 1;

• 2.4% for geographical area 2; and

- 3.0% for geographical area 3.

49. The maximum annual change to the LTFR is limited to 15 bps. The LTFR is changed according to the following formula:

$$LTFR_t = \begin{cases} LTFR_{t-1} + 15bps, & \text{if } LTFR_t^* \geqslant LTFR_{t-1} + 15bps \\ LTFR_{t-1} - 15bps, & \text{if } LTFR_t^* \leqslant LTFR_{t-1} - 15bps \\ LTFR_t^*, & \text{otherwise} \end{cases}$$

where:

- $LTFR_t$ denotes the LTFR of year t, after limitation of the annual change;
- $LTFR_{t-1}$ denotes the LTFR of year $t-1$, after limitation of the annual change; and
- $LTFR_t^*$ denotes the LTFR of year t, before limitation of the annual change.

50. The following spread over the LTFR is added to all LTFR calculated according to paragraphs 46 to 49 above:

- 20 basis points for geographical area 1;
- 25 basis points for geographical area 2; and
- 35 basis points for geographical area 3.

5.2.5.3 Determination of the adjustment to the risk-free yield curve

5.2.5.3.1 Classification criteria

51. Insurance liabilities are eligible for the Top Bucket if they meet all of the following criteria:

a. They belong to the category of life insurance and disability annuities in payment with no cash benefits on withdrawal, taking into account e) below.

b. The portfolio of assets to cover the insurance liabilities is identified and, together with the corresponding liabilities, it is managed separately, without being used to make payments relating to other business of the IAIG. ①

c. The expected cash flows of the identified portfolio of assets replicate the expected cash flows of the portfolio of insurance liabilities in the same currency, up to the LOT of the risk-free yield curve for the relevant currency. Any mismatch, addressed through the carry forward of cash generated from excess of asset cash flows at previous maturities, does not give rise to material risks. Carry forward of cash is limited to 10% of the total undiscounted liability cash flows up to

---

① For both the Top and Middle Buckets, the separate management of assets does not refer to a legal ring fencing but to a portfolio segmentation of clearly identified assets that would support an identified group of insurance liabilities over their lifetime. Should a portfolio be restructured within the entity, this being exceptional, the assets contained therein can only be transferred to another portfolio when done in conjunction with their corresponding liabilities. This does not preclude changes in investments within a portfolio in the normal course of business.

the LOT. Where insurance liabilities are backed with assets denominated in a different currency, those asset cash flows are taken into account in the cash flow testing, provided that the currency mismatch is fully hedged and the cost of hedging is deducted from the asset cash flows.

d. The contracts underlying the insurance liabilities do not include future premiums.

e. The portfolio of insurance liabilities includes either no surrender option for the policyholder or only a surrender option where the surrender value does not exceed the value of the assets identified for this portfolio at the reporting date and at all future points in time.

52. No unbundling is allowed when assessing eligibility for the Top Bucket.

53. Insurance liabilities are eligible for the Middle Bucket if they meet all of the following criteria:

a. The portfolio of assets to cover the insurance liabilities is identified and, together with the corresponding liabilities, is managed separately, without being used to cover losses arising from other business of the IAIG. [1]

b. The portfolio of insurance liabilities include either no surrender option for the policyholder or only a surrender option where the surrender value does not exceed the value of the assets identified for this portfolio at the reporting date.

c. The ICS Lapse risk charge does not represent more than 5% of the current estimate of the liabilities discounted using the risk-free yield curve.

d. The total market value of assets identified for this portfolio is, at the reporting date, greater than the current estimate of the liabilities calculated using the risk-free yield curve. For the calculation of the total market value of assets, all assets identified for this portfolio are taken into account, irrespective of their classification in Table 3.

e. The contracts underlying the liabilities do not include future premiums or include only future premiums that are contractually fixed.

54. No unbundling is allowed when assessing eligibility for the Middle Bucket.

55. All liabilities that are not in the Top or Middle Bucket belong to the General Bucket.

5.2.5.3.2 Adjustments to the yield curve

5.2.5.3.2.1 Eligible investments

56. For the purpose of calculating the Top Bucket and Middle Bucket adjustments, the

---

[1] For both the Top and Middle Buckets, the separate management of assets does not refer to a legal ring fencing but to a portfolio segmentation of clearly identified assets that would support an identified group of insurance liabilities over their lifetime. Should a portfolio be restructured within the entity, this being exceptional, the assets contained therein can only be transferred to another portfolio when done in conjunction with their corresponding liabilities. This does not preclude changes in investments within a portfolio in the normal course of business.

五、Level 2 Document: ICS Version 2.0 for the monitoring period

eligibility of types of investments is specified in the following table:

Table 3　Eligibility of types of investment

Type of investment	Eligible
Cash and other liquid assets not for investment purposes	(Excluded from portfolio)
Investment income receivable/accrued	N
Fixed Interest Government Bonds	Y
Fixed interest Corporate Bonds	Y
Fixed Interest Municipal Bonds	Y
Variable Interest Government Bonds	Y
Variable interest Corporate Bonds	Y
Variable Interest Municipal Bonds	Y
Convertible notes	N
Residential Mortgage Loans	Y
Non-residential Mortgage Loans	Y
Other (non-mortgage) Loans	Y
Loans to policyholders	Y
Residential Mortgage Backed Securities	Y
Commercial Mortgage Backed Securities	Y
Other structured securities	Y
Insurance Linked Securities	N
Equities	N
Hedge Funds	N
Private equity	N
Real estate (for investment purposes)	N
Infrastructure debt	Y
Infrastructure equity	N
Other investment assets	N

57. Assets backing unit-linked or separate account insurance liabilities are not taken into account when those insurance liabilities are valued using the asset replication approach presented in section 5.4 of the ICS Level 1 Document.

58. Government bonds include only debt instruments issued or guaranteed by central governments (excluding exposures to municipal and other public sector entities).

59. Assets featuring call options (used at the discretion of the issuer) are ineligible to back liabilities, unless it can be demonstrated that the exercise of the option does not imply a loss to the IAIG and that the matching of the liability cash flows can be maintained.

5.2.5.3.2.2　Top Bucket

60. The adjustment for the Top Bucket is based on the average spread above the risk-free

yield curve of the eligible assets, as listed in Table 3, identified by the IAIG to back the portfolio of liabilities meeting the Top Bucket criteria.

61. The IAIG may identify different portfolios, which will lead to the calculation of portfoliospecific adjustments.

62. A cap at the level of the ICS RC 4 spread applies for assets with a lower credit quality. The ICS RC 4 cap is based on the spreads earned by the IAIG for ICS RC 4 rated assets denominated in the same currency. Where no such assets exist, the spread defined by the IAIS for the Middle Bucket adjustment calculation is used.

63. The spread is adjusted for credit risk and any other risk, using the same risk correction parameters as specified in paragraph 68.

64. For the Top Bucket, 100% of the spread adjustment is added to the risk-free rate to discount insurance liabilities.

65. IAIGs use the relevant adjusted yield curves according to the currency of the insurance liability cash outflows.

66. Where insurance liabilities are backed with assets denominated in a different currency, the spread adjustment for the currency of the liability includes spreads which may be earned by the IAIG in those assets, provided that the currency mismatch is hedged. The cost of hedging is deducted from the Top Bucket adjustment.

67. The spread adjustment determined according to this methodology is applied as a parallel shift up to the run-off of the liabilities, which may be beyond the relevant LOT.

5.2.5.3.2.3 Middle Bucket

68. For the Middle Bucket, the IAIS provides spreads and risk corrections by credit quality, duration and currency, which serve as a basis for the calculation of the Middle Bucket adjustment.

69. The Middle Bucket spread adjustment is a group-wide adjustment calculated using the Weighted Average of Multiple Portfolios (WAMP) approach based on the eligible assets backing the Middle Bucket liabilities. The Middle Bucket spread adjustment is currency specific but not portfolio-specific; it is applied to all Middle Bucket portfolios in the same currency.

70. Where insurance liabilities are backed with assets denominated in a different currency, the weighted average calculation of the spread adjustment for the currency includes spreads earned by the IAIG in those assets, provided that the currency mismatch is hedged. The cost of hedging is deducted from the adjustment to the spread recognised in the calculation of the Middle Bucket adjustment. In case a rolling hedge strategy is in place, the cost of hedging is deducted from the spread adjustment and an additional haircut of 20% is applied to the spread.

五、Level 2 Document: ICS Version 2.0 for the monitoring period

71. The spread adjustment is calculated according to the WAMP methodology, as specified in the following paragraphs.

72. The $Wamp_{spread}$ for a given currency is calculated as follows:

$$Wamp_{spread} = w_{gov} \times spread_{govafter\ RC}$$
$$+ w_{ICS\ RC1} \times \left(\sum_{durations} w^{ICS\ RC1}_{duration\ band} \times spread^{ICS\ RC1\ after\ RC}_{duration\ band} \right)$$
$$+ w_{ICS\ RC2} \times \left(\sum_{durations} w^{ICS\ RC2}_{duration\ band} \times spread^{ICS\ RC2\ after\ RC}_{duration\ band} \right)$$
$$+ \cdots$$
$$+ w_{Non-eligible} \times 0$$

where:

— w_{gov} is the weight of government bonds;

— $w_{ICS\ RCi}$ is the weight of debt instruments belonging to ICS risk category i;

— $w^{ICS\ RCi}_{duration\ band}$ is the weight of debt instruments that belong to ICS risk category i within the considered duration band;

— $w_{non-eligible}$ is the weight of non-eligible assets in the total portfolio of assets for that currency;

— $spread_{govafter\ RC}$ is the spread after risk correction corresponding to government bonds. When a government bond rate is used for the risk-free yield curve, the applied spread is nil; and

— $spread^{ICS\ RCi\ after\ RC}_{duration\ band}$ is the spread after risk correction corresponding to debt instruments that belong to ICS risk category i within the considered duration band.

73. Debt instruments in ICS RC 4 and lower, as well as unrated debt instruments, are allocated to the ICS RC 4.

74. In the case of currency unions, the sovereign exposure (and the corresponding weight in the WAMP calculation) is split by jurisdiction within the currency union.

75. The Total Observed Matching (TOM) ratio is computed as follows:

$$TOM = \min\left(\frac{M - 1}{\min(LOT, lifetime\ of\ liability)}, 100\% \right)$$

where:

lifetime of liability is the maturity after which the insurance liabilities are not expected to generate any cash flow, and M is the first maturity for which, under the cash flow test described in paragraph 51.c, either the cash carry forward limit of 10% is breached or the remaining cash becomes negative. For the purpose of determining M, asset cash flows in a different currency than liability cash flows can be taken into consideration provided that either:

- the asset cash flows are fully hedged; or

• a rolling hedge is in place and the replacement frequency of the hedge is not less than one month. In this case, a 20% haircut is applied on the asset cash flows.

The cost of hedging is deducted from the expected cash flows.

76. The final spread applied to the yield curve is computed in a way to ensure that the spread adjustment for the Middle Bucket is greater or equal to the spread adjustment for the General Bucket.

$$Spread\ Adj_{MB} = \max[90\% \cdot (TOM \cdot Wamp_{spread} + (1 - TOM) Spread\ Adj_{GB}), 80\% \cdot Spread\ Adj_{GB}]$$

77. The spread adjustment determined according to this methodology is applied as a parallel shift up to year M. After that maturity, the spread adjustment is phased out in such a way that the resulting spot curve remains above the spot curve for the corresponding General Bucket.

5.2.5.3.2.4 General Bucket

78. The spread adjustment for the General Bucket ($Spread\ Adj_{GB}$) is provided by the IAIS, based on a representative portfolio that reflects the assets typically held by IAIGs in a particular currency.

79. The spread adjustment includes a correction for credit risk and any other risk.

80. For corporate bonds, the aforementioned correction is derived from the annualised cumulative default experience for a hypothetical 10-year bond, computed on the basis of transition matrices.

81. For government bonds, the risk correction is determined depending on the data underpinning the risk-free rate. Where risk-free rates are determined based on swap rates, risks other than liquidity risk are assumed to represent 30% of the 10-year average spread. For currencies where risk-free rates are based on government bond rates, no risk correction is applied.

82. 80% of the spread adjustment determined according to this methodology is applied as a parallel shift up to the LOT. For Segments 2 and 3 of the adjusted yield curve, the same extrapolation methodology as used for determining the risk-free yield curve is applied to the adjusted yield curve.

83. IAIGs use the relevant adjusted yield curves according to the currency of the insurance liability cash outflows.

5.2.5.3.3 Alternative adjustments for the General Bucket

84. IAIGs may use two alternative spread adjustments for the calculation of the General Bucket adjustment:

• One specific adjustment for cases where the same currency is shared among different jurisdictions; and

五、Level 2 Document: ICS Version 2.0 for the monitoring period

- One specific adjustment for cases where the IAIG is materially invested in assets denominated in a currency that is different from the liabilities they are backing.

85. Under those two mechanisms, IAIGs may replace the spreads used in the determination of the spread adjustment for a given currency; the weights of the different asset categories remain unchanged.

5.2.5.3.3.1 Shared currency mechanism

86. Where the same currency is shared among different jurisdictions, IAIGs may replace the spreads provided by the IAIS for each Risk Category in that currency ($S_{rc_{crncy}}$) by the spreads (S_{rc}) defined as follows:

If:
$$S_{rc_{adjusted}} - S_{rc_{crncy}} \geq 50bps$$

then:
$$S_{rc} = S_{rc_{adjusted}} - 50bps$$

where:

$S_{rc_{crncy}}$ = spread for currency *crncy* and Risk Category *rc*, as provided by the IAIS

$S_{rc_{adjusted}}$ = modified spread for Risk Category *rc*, using a weighted average of the spreads of the specific jurisdictions (within the common currency) to which the IAIG is actually exposed

5.2.5.3.3.2 Foreign asset mechanism

87. IAIGs may replace the spreads provided by the IAIS for each Risk Category in that currency ($S_{rc_{crncy}}$) by the spreads (S_{rc}) defined as follows:

If:
$$\frac{\text{Hedged eligible foreign currency denominated assets}}{\text{Total investments (excl. cash) converted into the currency of the liability}} \geq 5\%$$

then
$$S_{rc} = S_{rc_{crncy}} + 50\% * (S_{rc_{adjusted}} - S_{rc_{crncy}})$$

where:

$S_{rc_{crncy}}$ = spread for currency *crncy* and Risk Category *rc*, as provided by the IAIS

$S_{rc_{adjusted}}$ = modified spread including the extra spread that can be earned from the hedged assets denominated in foreign currency that exceed the 5% threshold. Where the 5% threshold is exceeded by a combination of exposures in multiple asset categories, the threshold is proportionally allocated to the different asset categories.

5.3 Margin over Current Estimate (MOCE)

5.3.1 Definition and underlying principles

No additional information compared to the Level 1 document.

5.3.2 Calculation of the MOCE

88. The 85th percentile is used to compute the life component of the MOCE and the 65th percentile is used for the non-life component.

5.3.3 Interaction of MOCE with other components

No additional information compared to the Level 1 document.

5.4 Obligations replicable by a portfolio of assets

89. Insurance liabilities are considered to be replicated reliably when their cash flows are in every circumstance precisely matched by cash flows of corresponding assets.

90. The cash flows associated with insurance liabilities are not considered to be reliably replicated when:

a. Policyholders can exercise contractual options, including lapses and surrenders.

b. Obligations depend on mortality, disability, sickness and morbidity rates.

c. Expenses associated with insurance obligations cannot be reliably replicated.

91. Financial instruments used to replicate insurance liabilities must be traded in deep, liquid and transparent markets.

6 Reference ICS: Qualifying Capital Resources

6.1 General considerations

No additional information compared to the Level 1 document.

6.2 Classification of financial instruments

6.2.1 Tier 1 unlimited financial instruments

92. Financial instruments that meet all of the following criteria qualify as ICS Tier 1 unlimited capital resources:

a. The instrument is fully paid-up.

b. The instrument is in the form of issued capital such that it is the first instrument to absorb losses as they occur.

c. The instrument represents the most subordinated claim in a winding-up of the IAIG where the holder has a claim on the residual assets proportional to its share of the issued share capital after all other claims have been repaid, and which is not subject to a fixed or capped amount.

d. The instrument is perpetual (ie it does not have a maturity date).

e. The principal amount of the instrument is not repaid outside winding-up, other than by means of discretionary repurchase permitted under national law.

f. There is not an expectation created by the IAIG at issuance, through the terms of the instrument or otherwise, that the IAIG will repurchase or cancel the instrument.

g. There are no circumstances under which a distribution is obligatory (non-payment of a distribution is, therefore, not an event of default).

h. Distributions are paid out of distributable items, including retained earnings.

i. The instrument is neither undermined nor rendered ineffective by encumbrances. In particular, the priority of claims is not compromised by guarantees or security arrangements given by either the IAIG or a related entity over which the IAIG exercises control or significant influence, for the benefit of investors.

j. Neither the IAIG nor a related entity over which the IAIG exercises control or significant influence has purchased the instrument, nor has the IAIG directly or indirectly funded the purchase of the instrument.

k. The paid-in amount is recognised as equity capital (ie is not recognised as a liability) where a determination that liabilities exceed assets constitutes a test of insolvency.

6.2.2 Tier 1 limited financial instruments

93. Financial instruments that do not qualify as Tier 1 unlimited capital resources, but meet all of the following criteria, qualify as ICS Tier 1 limited capital resources:

a. The instrument is fully paid-up.

b. The instrument is subordinated to policyholders and other non-subordinated creditors and holders of Tier 2 financial instruments but may rank senior to holders of Tier 1 unlimited financial instruments.

c. The instrument is perpetual (ie it does not have a maturity date). For mutual IAIGs①, the requirement for an instrument to be perpetual is considered to be met if redemption at maturity (for a dated instrument) can be deferred subject to supervisory approval or a lock-in② feature, and where an instrument has an initial maturity of at least ten years.

d. The instrument does not contain any incentive to redeem, such as a step-up.

e. The instrument is only callable at the option of the issuer after a minimum of five years from the date of issue and prior supervisory approval is required for any redemption. However, extraordinary calls (defined as tax and regulatory event calls) are permitted at any time after issuance of an instrument, subject to prior supervisory approval, and provided the IAIG was not in a position to anticipate such a call at the time of issuance. Also, an IAIG may not exercise the extraordinary call within the first five years of issuance unless, prior to or concurrent with the

---

① Characteristics of a mutual group typically include the inability to issue substantial amounts of common equity and an ultimate parent within the group that cannot issue common equity.

② A lock-in feature is a requirement for the IAIG to suspend repayment or redemption if it is in breach of its applicable regulatory capital requirement or would breach it if the instrument is repaid or redeemed.

exercise of the call, it replaces the called instrument with capital of the same or better quality, and the replacement of the called instrument is made on terms that are sustainable for the income capacity of the IAIG.

f. The instrument may be repurchased by the issuer at any time with prior supervisory approval.

g. There is not an expectation created by the IAIG, through the terms of the instrument or otherwise, that the IAIG will repurchase the instrument or exercise any right to call the instrument, or that the repurchase or redemption will receive supervisory approval.

h. The IAIG has full discretion at all times to forego or cancel distributions (ie dividends and coupon payments are non-cumulative). The IAIG's obligation to pay missed distributions is forever extinguished and non-payment is not an event of default.

i. Distributions are paid out of distributable items, including retained earnings.

j. The instrument does not have distributions that are linked to the credit standing or financial condition of the IAIG or a related entity, such that those distributions may accelerate winding-up.

k. The instrument is neither undermined nor rendered ineffective by encumbrances. In particular, the priority of claims is not compromised by guarantees or security arrangements given by either the IAIG or a related entity over which the IAIG exercises control or significant influence, for the benefit of investors.

l. Neither the IAIG nor a related entity over which the IAIG exercises control or significant influence has purchased the instrument, nor has the IAIG directly or indirectly funded the purchase of the instrument.

m. The paid-in amount is recognised as equity capital (ie is not recognised as a liability) where a determination that liabilities exceed assets constitutes a test of insolvency.

n. The instrument does not possess features that hinder recapitalisation, such as provisions that require the issuer to compensate investors if a new instrument is issued at a lower price during a specified time frame.

o. If the instrument is not issued out of an operating entity or the holding company of the IAIG (eg it is issued out of an SPV), proceeds are made immediately available, without limitation, to an operating entity or the holding company of the IAIG, through the issuance of an instrument that meets or exceeds all of the other criteria for inclusion in Tier 1 limited capital resources (ie the SPV may only hold assets that are intercompany instruments issued by the IAIG or a related entity with terms and conditions that meet or exceed the criteria for Tier 1 limited capital resources).

6.2.3 Tier 2 financial instruments (other than structurally subordinated)

94. Financial instruments that do not qualify as Tier 1 (unlimited or limited) capital resources, but meet all of the following criteria qualify as Tier 2 capital resources:

a. The instrument is fully paid-up.

b. The instrument is subordinated to policyholders and other non-subordinated creditors of the IAIG.

c. The instrument has an initial maturity of at least five years with its effective maturity date defined to be the earlier of:

   i. The first call date, together with a step-up or other incentive to redeem the instrument; and

   ii. The contractual maturity date fixed in the instrument's terms and conditions.

d. The instrument's availability to absorb losses as it nears its effective maturity is captured by either:

   i. Decreasing the qualifying amount of the instrument from 100% to 0% on a straight-line basis in the final five years prior to maturity; or

   ii. The existence of a lock-in clause.

e. If the instrument is callable within the first five years from the date of issue:

   - Any such call is at the option of the issuer only;
   - Any such call is subject to supervisory approval; and
   - The called instrument must be replaced in full before or at redemption by a new issuance of the same or higher quality instrument.

Other than in cases of replacement outlined above, the instrument is only callable at the option of the issuer after a minimum of five years from the date of issue and prior supervisory approval is required for any redemption prior to contractual maturity. ①

f. The instrument may be repurchased by the issuer at any time with prior supervisory approval.

g. There is not an expectation created by the IAIG, through the terms of the instrument or

---

① In the absence of a requirement for prior supervisory approval, this criterion is considered to be met if the following conditions are met:
- The terms of the financial instrument include a lock-in feature that prevents redemption when a firm does not comply with its regulatory capital requirement (or where redemption would lead to non-compliance);
- Either:
—the supervisor receives prior notification upon redemption, or
—call dates are fixed and known and the supervisor monitors potential redemption; and
- The supervisor has the power to prevent redemption of the instrument.

otherwise, that the IAIG will repurchase the instrument or exercise its right to call the instrument, or that the repurchase or redemption will receive supervisory approval.

h. The instrument does not have distributions that are linked to the credit standing or financial condition of the IAIG or a related entity, such that those distributions may accelerate winding-up.

i. The instrument does not give holders rights to accelerate the repayment of scheduled principal or coupon payments, except in winding-up.

j. The instrument is neither undermined nor rendered ineffective by encumbrances. In particular, the priority of claims is not compromised by guarantees or security arrangements given by either the IAIG or a related entity over which the IAIG exercises control or significant influence, for the benefit of investors.

k. Neither the IAIG nor a related entity over which the IAIG exercises control or significant influence has purchased the instrument, nor has the IAIG directly or indirectly funded the purchase of the instrument.

l. If the instrument is not issued out of an operating entity or the holding company of the IAIG (eg it is issued out of an SPV), proceeds are made immediately available, without limitation, to an operating entity or the holding company of the IAIG, through the issuance of an instrument that meets or exceeds all of the other criteria for inclusion in paid-up Tier 2 capital resources (ie the SPV may only hold assets that are intercompany instruments issued by the IAIG or a related entity with terms and conditions that meet or exceed the criteria for Tier 2 Paid-Up capital resources).

6.2.4 Structurally subordinated Tier 2 financial instruments

95. Structural subordination of debt refers to a situation where a holding company issues a financial instrument directly to third party investors and then down-streams the proceeds into insurance subsidiaries.

96. Structurally subordinated financial instruments that meet the criteria for Tier 2 financial instruments, subject to the clarifications of criteria b), e), and f), and new criteria n), o), and p) below, qualify as Tier 2 capital resources:

b. Subordination to other non-subordinated creditors of the IAIG is not relevant to structurally subordinated instruments that are issued by an IAIG's holding company to senior creditors.

e. The requirement for supervisory approval of such a call within the first five years from the date of issue can be fulfilled through the exercise of supervisory controls and supervisory review, including the ability (direct/indirect) for supervisors to limit, defer and/or disallow the

五、Level 2 Document: ICS Version 2.0 for the monitoring period

issuance or redemption of financial instruments.

The requirement for supervisory approval of redemptions after a minimum of five years can be fulfilledthrough supervisory approval① of dividends prior to their payment from an insurance subsidiary to the holding company.

f. The requirement for supervisory approval of repurchases can be fulfilled through supervisory approval of dividends prior to their payment from an insurance subsidiary to the holding company.

n. The debt instrument has been issued by a clean holding company, which is defined as a holding company that does not have policyholder liabilities on its stand-alone balance sheet.

o. The IAIG and its GWS have determined that the proceeds of the instruments, which have been down-streamed into insurance subsidiaries, are being tracked and reported appropriately.

p. Amounts from the instrument issuance have been down-streamed into an insurance subsidiary of the holding company and the insurance subsidiary is located in a jurisdiction whose regulatory regime proactively enforces structural subordination through appropriate regulatory/supervisory controls over distributions from insurance subsidiaries②.

6.2.4.1 National discretion on acceleration clauses

97. Criterion i) in paragraph 94 is subject to a national discretion. When a GWS elects to apply that national discretion, criterion i) is waived for all IAIGs headquartered in the jurisdiction of that GWS.

98. IAIGs to which the national discretion applies provide a reconciliation of the impact between the reference ICS with and without applying the national discretion.

6.2.5 Tier 2 Non-paid-up capital

99. Non-paid-up capital consists of commitments, received by entities of the IAIG from third parties non-related to the IAIG, to provide capital upon request.

100. Financial items, contracts and arrangements established by mutual IAIGs qualify as Tier 2 Non-paid-up capital resources when they meet all of the following criteria:

---

① For structurally subordinated financial instruments, supervisory approval of ordinary dividends can be met if the supervisor has in place supervisory controls over distributions, including the ability for the supervisor to limit, defer and/or disallow the payment of any distributions should it find that the insurer is presently, or may potentially become, financially distressed.

② Supervisory controls over distributions from insurance subsidiaries refer to the supervisory review and/or prior supervisory approval of all distributions, including the ability for the supervisor to limit, defer and/or disallow the payment of any distributions should it find that the insurer is presently, or may potentially become, financially distressed. As part of its review and/or prior approval of distributions, the relevant supervisor considers surplus adequacy, financial flexibility, the quality of earnings, and other factors deemed to be pertinent as they relate to the financial strength of the insurer and policyholder protection.

a. The item has been approved by the supervisor as satisfying criteria b) to g) below as to its characteristics and amount.

b. The item can be called up on demand by the mutual IAIG and is not subject to any contingencies or conditions that prevent or act as a disincentive to the call being made or satisfied.

c. When called up, the item becomes either a financial instrument that meets in full the criteria for inclusion in Tier 1 or Tier 2 paid-up capital resources or a capital element listed in section 6.3.

d. The item is legally enforceable in each relevant jurisdiction.

e. The counterparty to the contract to provide capital is able and willing to pay the agreed amounts when called upon by the mutual IAIG.

f. The item is neither undermined nor rendered ineffective by encumbrances.

g. The mutual IAIG is required to notify the supervisor of any changes of fact or circumstance that could affect the supervisor's approval of the item.

6.3 Capital elements other than financial instruments

6.3.1 Tier 1 capital elements

No additional information compared to the Level 1 document.

6.3.2 Tier 2 capital elements

101. The Tier 2 basket comprises the following three items, subject to a limit of 15% of the ICS capital requirement:

a. 50% of the value of each net defined benefit pension fund that is an asset on the IAIG's balance sheet, net of any eligible DTL;

b. 100% of the DTA deducted from Tier 1 capital resources; and

c. 10% of the value of computer software intangibles (net of amortisation) deducted from Tier 1 capital resources, net of any eligible DTL.

6.4 Capital adjustments and deductions

6.4.1 Deductions from Tier 1 capital resources

No additional information compared to the Level 1 document.

6.4.2 Deductions from Tier 2 capital resources

No additional information compared to the Level 1 document.

6.4.3 Treatment of encumbered assets

102. The deduction from ICS Tier 1 capital resources is calculated as the total value of encumbered assets in excess of the sum of the value of the IAIG's on-balance sheet liabilities secured by the encumbered assets, plus the value of the IAIG's incremental ICS capital

requirement for encumbered assets and secured liabilities.

103. No ICS Tier 1 deduction is required for encumbered assets relating to off-balance sheet securities financing transactions (ie securities lending and borrowing, repos and reverse repos) that do not result in a liability on the balance sheet.

6.5 Capital composition limits

104. For non-mutual IAIGs, the following limits are applicable:

a. Tier 1 Limited capital resources are limited to 10% of the ICS capital requirement; this limit is increased to 15%, provided that the instruments in excess of the 10% limit possess a Principle Loss Absorbency Mechanism (PLAM);

b. Tier 2 capital resources are limited to 50% of the ICS capital requirement; and

c. There is no allowance for Tier 2 Non-Paid Up capital.

105. For the purpose of paragraph 104, a PLAM is defined as a mechanism providing for either a write-down of the liability (principal and dividend/coupon) or a conversion of the instrument (into a Tier 1 unlimited financial instrument as defined in section 6.2.1) in contractually predefined going-concern conditions.

106. For mutual IAIGs, the following limits are applicable:

a. Tier 1 Limited capital resources are limited to 30% of the ICS capital requirement;

b. Tier 1 Limited + Tier 2 capital resources are limited to 60% of the ICS capital requirement; and

c. Tier 2 Non-Paid Up capital are limited to 10% of the ICS capital requirement.

7 Reference ICS: Capital Requirement-The Standard Method

7.1 ICS Risks and Calculation Methods

7.1.1 Risk mitigation techniques

107. Risk mitigation techniques may be recognised in the ICS risk charges provided they meet all of the following requirements:

a. The risk mitigation technique is effective and legally enforceable in all relevant jurisdictions and results in an effective transfer of risk to a third party.

b. The contractual arrangement ensures that the risk transfer is clearly defined.

c. The calculation of the ICS risk charges allows for the effects of risk mitigation techniques through a reduction of the risk charge commensurate with the extent of risk mitigation. It makes reasonable allowance for any basis risk effects due to changes in risk mitigation assumptions and relationships during a stress scenario and there is appropriate treatment for any corresponding risk embedded in the use of risk mitigation techniques (eg Credit risk). These two effects are treated separately.

d. The calculation is made on the basis of assets and liabilities existing at the reporting date of the ICS calculation.

e. There is no double counting of mitigation effects.

f. The documentation for the arrangement sets out a direct claim on the IAIG's counterparty in the event of its default, insolvency, bankruptcy or other credit event.

g. Providers of risk mitigation are of an adequate credit quality (demonstrable through either adequate rating, capitalisation or collateralisation levels) to ensure with appropriate certainty that the IAIG will receive the protection in the cases specified by the contracting parties. Credit quality is assessed consistently with the definition of credit categories provided in section 7.4.

108. In addition to these requirements, market risk mitigation techniques are based on an explicit reference to specific exposures or a pool of exposures.

109. Where risk mitigation techniques are in force for a period shorter than 12 months and meet the qualitative criteria above, a proportional factor is applied to the risk mitigation effect taken into account in the ICS risk charges. That factor is defined as either:

a. The proportion of the full term of the risk exposure covered by the risk mitigation technique up to a maximum of 100%, where the risk exposure's term is less than 12 months; or

b. The proportion of 12 months covered by the risk mitigation technique up to a maximum of 100%, where the risk exposure term is 12 months or more.

110. However, where the IAIG plans to replace a risk mitigation arrangement relating to a Market risk exposure at the time of its expiry with a similar arrangement, this renewal may be taken into account if the IAIG expects to renew and all of the foreseeable costs of renewal within the time horizon are taken into account. The requirement of an expectation to renew is considered to be met if all of the following conditions are met:

a. The renewal is consistent with previous business practice and documented strategy.

b. The replacement of the risk mitigation instrument does not take place more often than every three months, except for Currency risk or Equity risk where the replacement of the risk mitigation instrument does not take place more often than every month.

c. The risk that the risk mitigation arrangement cannot be replaced due to an absence of liquidity in the market is not material under different market conditions and there is no material basis or operational risks compared to the risk mitigation effect. If the instruments mitigating Currency or Equity risk are replaced more frequently than every three months, then the IAIG justifies to its group wide supervisor that:

i. the market for these instruments is sufficiently liquid at the relevant tenor; and

五、Level 2 Document: ICS Version 2.0 for the monitoring period

ii. these instruments do not pose a materially greater risk than those replaced less frequently than every three months.

d. The replacement of the risk mitigation arrangement is not conditional on any future event that is outside of the control of the IAIG. Where the replacement of the risk mitigation arrangement is conditional on any future event that is within the control of the IAIG, then the conditions are clearly set out in the documented strategy referred to in point a).

e. The renewal is realistic regarding the availability of the arrangement and its cost is deducted from the value attributed to the instrument. This deduction takes into account the risk that the cost may increase during the following 12 months.

f. Any additional risk stemming from the risk mitigation arrangement (eg Credit risk) is taken into account in the ICS risk charges.

g. The IAIG is able to demonstrate to its GWS that the required instruments will be available for renewal from a deep and liquid market under all reasonably foreseeable eventualities over the following 12 months. Where this is not the case, the benefit recognised for the renewal of the risk mitigation arrangement is limited to 80% of the full risk mitigating value of the arrangement at the reporting date.

111. The renewal of risk mitigation arrangements with respect to non-life Premium risk may be taken into account if the IAIG expects to renew and the costs of renewal within the time horizon are taken into account. The requirement of an expectation to renew is considered to be met if all of the following conditions are met:

a. The renewal is consistent with previous business practice and documented strategy;

b. The renewal is realistic with regards to availability of the arrangement and its cost[①]; and

c. Any additional risk stemming from the risk mitigation arrangement (eg Credit risk) is taken into account in the relevant ICS risk charges.

112. When modelling natural catastrophe risk, the renewal of the arrangements may be taken into account if all of the following conditions are met:

a. The renewal is consistent with previous business practice and documented strategy;

b. The renewal is realistic regarding the availability of the arrangement and its cost; and

c. Any additional risk stemming from the risk mitigation arrangement (eg Credit risk) is also taken into account in the natural catastrophe risk modelling.

113. Risk mitigation arrangements are not recognised in the calculation of the ICS Operational risk charge.

---

① Costs may include, but are not limited to, ceded premiums to the reinsurer and commissions.

7.1.2 Geographical segmentation

114. For those risk charges calculated using a geographical segmentation, the following regions are used:

a. European Economic Area (EEA) and Switzerland;

b. US and Canada;

c. China;

d. Japan;

e. Other developed markets; and

f. Other emerging markets.

115. The jurisdictions included in each region are listed in Table 4:

Table 4　Geographical segmentation

Region	Jurisdictions included
EEA and Switzerland	Austria, Belgium, Bulgaria, Croatia, Republic of Cyprus, Czech Republic, Denmark, Estonia, Finland, France, Germany, Greece, Hungary, Ireland, Italy, Latvia, Lithuania, Luxembourg, Malta, Netherlands, Poland, Portugal, Romania, Slovakia, Slovenia, Spain, Sweden, United Kingdom, Iceland, Liechtenstein, Norway and Switzerland
US and Canada	US① and Canada
China	Mainland China and Macao SAR
Japan	Japan
Other developed markets②	Australia, New Zealand, Israel, San Marino, Korea, Singapore, Chinese Taipei and Hong Kong SAR
Other emerging markets	A list of emerging markets is provided in Table E of the Statistical Appendix of the IMF World Economic Outlook April 2016③. For completeness, if a country is not listed in the regions above, it is classified as "Other emerging markets".

7.1.3 Management actions

116. The impact of management actions for each individual risk is calculated consistently with the provisions set out in section 5.2.4. The impact of management actions is based on realistic assumptions and reflects the IAIG's obligations to policyholders as well as legal provisions applicable to the IAIG.

117. A cap on the overall credit for management actions is set at the total amount of

---

① Including American Samoa, Guam, Northern Mariana Island, Puerto Rico and US Virgin Islands.

② 'Other developed' taken from IMF list of advanced economies minus countries mentioned in other regions as of April 2016.

③ See http://www.imf.org/external/pubs/ft/weo/2016/01/pdf/text.pdf (accessed on 12 May 2016).

insurance liabilities for future bonuses or other discretionary benefits. This cap is applied after aggregating the total of management actions post-diversification across the risks.

7.2 Insurance risks

7.2.1 Grouping of policies for life insurance risks

118. The projections of the stressed cash flows are conducted at the same level of granularity as the pre-stress cash flows. Where the pre-stress cash flows have been projected by applying some grouping of policies, the same grouping of policies is applied to the stressed cash flows.

119. From a practicality standpoint, grouping by portfolios of products (or policies) exposed to homogeneous insurance risks within the class can be applied. For this purpose, a homogeneous risk group encompasses a collection of policies with similar risk characteristics.

120. Homogeneous risk groups are reasonably stable over time. Where necessary, for the determination of homogeneous risk groups, IAIGs take into account items such as:

a) Underwriting policy;

b) Claims settlement pattern;

c) Risk profile of policyholders;

d) Product features, in particular guarantees; and

e) Future management actions.

7.2.2 Calculation of life insurance risk charge

121. The correlation matrix used for aggregating the life risk charges is the following:

Table 5 Life risks correlation matrix

	Mortality	Longevity	Morbidity/Disability	Lapse	Expense
Mortality	100%	-25%	25%	0%	25%
Longevity	-25%	100%	0%	25%	25%
Morbidity/Disability	25%	0%	100%	0%	50%
Lapse	0%	25%	0%	100%	50%
Expense	25%	25%	50%	50%	100%

7.2.2.1 Mortality risk

122. The prescribed stress for the calculation of the Mortality risk charge consists of an increase of x% in mortality rates at all ages for all policies where an increase in mortality rates leads to a decrease in the NAV.

123. The stress factors for Mortality risk are given in Table 6:

Table 6 Mortality risk stress factors

Region	x%
EEA and Switzerland	12.5%
US and Canada	12.5%
China	12.5%
Japan	10.0%
Other developed markets	12.5%
Other emerging markets	12.5%

7.2.2.2 Longevity risk

124. The prescribed stress for the calculation of the longevity risk charge consists of a decrease of x% in mortality rates at all ages for all policies where a decrease in mortality rates leads to a decrease in the NAV.

125. The stress factors for Longevity risk are given in Table 7:

Table 7 Longevity risk stress factors

Region	x%
EEA and Switzerland	17.5%
US and Canada	17.5%
China	17.5%
Japan	17.5%
Other developed markets	17.5%
Other emerging markets	17.5%

7.2.2.3 Morbidity and Disability risk

7.2.2.3.1 Segmentation

126. The Morbidity and disability risk is applied to benefits evaluated on a similar to life technical basis. Irrespective of the legal or contractual classification of insurance obligations, the assignment to life or non-life activities is based on the type of techniques used to calculate insurance obligations[①].

7.2.2.3.2 Sub-risks to be covered

127. For the purpose of the calculation of the Morbidity and disability risk charge, similar to life insurance obligations are split in the following four mutually exclusive benefit segments:

a) Category 1: Medical expenses

---

① A technical basis is considered similar to life when it involves the explicit use of biometric variables such as mortality, morbidity and recovery rates by age.

• Products providing any kind of compensation (either fixed or based on real costs) for medical expenses, in-patient or not. The compensation depends directly on the treatment or expenses incurred by the policyholder, and is not directly dependent on the time spent in a given health status.

b) Category 2: Lump sum in case of a health event

• Products providing a single payment at the occurrence of a specified health event or the occurrence of an accident resulting in a certain level of disability.

c) Category 3: Short-term recurring payments

• Products providing a recurring amount of compensation for a period depending on the time spent in a given temporary health status, such as inability to work or hospitalisation.

d) Category 4: Long-term recurring payments

• Products providing a fixed annuity in case of long-term/permanently deteriorated health status.

128. The distinction between Category 3 and Category 4 is made according to the temporary versus permanent characteristics of the recurring benefit. A benefit that is contractually limited to a given period, common to all policyholders, is classified as short-term recurring. A benefit that is to be paid life-long, or for a period depending on individual policyholder circumstances, without any upfront short-term limitations, is considered as long-term recurring.

129. Each benefit category is divided into two segments by original contract term:

a) Short-term: Includes contracts with an original term of up to five years.

b) Long-term: Includes contracts with an original term longer than five years.

130. When a policy includes coverage belonging to several of the above benefit categories, each of the different components of such a policy is subject to the relevant stress. When a policy provides a combination of benefits between medical expenses and short-term recurring payments (Categories 1 and 3), it may either be split into both categories, or considered under Category 3 altogether.

7.2.2.3.3 Calculation

131. The prescribed stresses for the calculation of the Morbidity/Disability risk charge depend on the benefit category:

a) For benefit categories $i = 1, 2$ and 3, the stress is defined as an instantaneous relative increase in inception rates, as specified in Table 8 and Table 9.

The inception rate stress is applied differently depending on the underlying type of benefits:

• For benefits where claim costs are explicitly modelled using inception rates and/or recovery rates, the stress is only applied to inception rates. If only recovery rates are modelled, the stress is applied as a decrease in recovery rates.

• For other benefits in categories 1-3, with no explicit inception rates and/or recovery rates, the stress factors are directly applied to medical claim payment amounts.

b) Forthe benefit category 4, the risk charge is calculated for both contract term segments as the maximum of the Inception Rate risk charge and the Recovery Rate risk charge, where:

• The Inception Rate risk charge is calculated as the change in NAV following the increase in inception rates as specified in Table 8 and Table 9; and

• The Recovery Rate risk charge is calculated as the change in NAV following the decrease in recovery rates of 20% (same stress for both short-term and long-term contracts).

Table 8 Morbidity/Disability risk stress factors-Location of risk Japan

Category (i)	Short-term	Long-term
1	20%	8%
2	25%	8%
3	20%	10%
4	inception rate stress = 25%, recovery rate stress = 20%	inception rate stress = 20%, recovery rate stress = 20%

Table 9 Morbidity/Disability risk stress factors-All other locations of risk

Category (i)	Short-term	Long-term
1	20%	8%
2	25%	20%
3	20%	12%
4	inception rate stress = 25%, recovery rate stress = 20%	inception rate stress = 20%, recovery rate stress = 20%

7.2.2.4 Lapse risk

132. The calculation of the maximum of the level and trend component and mass lapse component, referred to in paragraph 109 of the ICS Level 1 document, is performed at the level of each region listed in section 7.1.2.

133. The Lapse risk charge for the IAIG is then obtained as the sum of Lapse risk charges over all regions.

7.2.2.4.1 Level and Trend component

134. For each region listed in section 7.1.2, the prescribed stress for the calculation of the Level and Trend component is the most adverse of an upward stress and a downward stress.

135. The upward stress consists of an increase of x% in the assumed option take-up rates, subject to a maximum of 100%, in all future years for all homogeneous risk groups adversely

affected by such risk.

136. The downward stress consists of a decrease of x% in the assumed option take-up rates in all future years for all homogeneous risk groups adversely affected by such risk.

137. The stress factors are specified in Table 10:

Table 10 Level & Trend Lapse risk stress factors

Region	x%
EEA and Switzerland	40%
US and Canada	40%
China	40%
Japan	20%
Other developed markets	40%
Other emerging markets	40%

138. All options that can affect the amount of insurance coverage, including options that allow for partial or full termination, or increase in the insurance cover, are affected by the lapse stress factors.

139. For each region listed in section 7.1.2, the Level and Trend component is first determined for each homogeneous risk group before aggregating across all homogeneous risk groups.

140. When the calculation of the current estimate involves the use of a dynamic lapse function[①], the Level and Trend component stress is applied to the base rate of the dynamic lapse function.

7.2.2.4.2 Mass Lapse Component

141. For each region listed in section 7.1.2, the prescribed stress for the calculation of the Mass Lapse component consists of:

- an immediate surrender of 30% of retail policies; and
- an immediate surrender of 50% of non-retail policies.

142. The Mass Lapse component for each homogeneous risk group is subject to a floor of zero.

143. For each region listed in section 7.1.2, the Mass Lapse component is first determined for each homogeneous risk group before aggregating across all homogeneous risk groups.

---

① A dynamic lapse function varies the lapse rate used in the calculation of insurance liabilities depending on the difference between the return the insurer is providing on its policies and the returns provided by competitors.

7.2.2.5 Expense risk

144. The prescribed stresses for the calculation of the expense risk charge consists of a relative increase of x% in unit expense assumptions and an absolute increase of y% per annum in expense inflation, with x and y specified in Table 11.

Table 11 Expense risk stress factors

Region	x% (unit expense)	y% (expense inflation)
EEA and Switzerland	6%	1%
US and Canada	6%	1%
China	8%	Year 1 – 10: 3%; Year 11 – 20: 2%; Year 21 onwards: 1%
Japan	6%	1%
Other developed markets	8%	Year 1 – 10: 2%; Year 11 onwards: 1%
Other emerging markets	8%	Year 1 – 10: 3%; Year 11 – 20: 2%; Year 21 onwards: 1%

145. The stresses to the unit expense and expense inflation assumptions are applied simultaneously.

7.2.3 Calculation of Non-Life Risk Charge

7.2.3.1 Segments/Lines of Business

146. Each exposure for Premium risk and Claims Reserve risk is mapped to a line of business based on the location of risk. Each line of business has a corresponding ICS segment, as specified in Table 13. Any jurisdiction not explicitly listed in Table 13 is allocated to either Other developed markets or Other emerging markets according to Table 4.

7.2.3.2 Definition of ICS Segments and Risk Charges

147. Each ICS segment is assigned:

a. An ICS category: a high level grouping of the type of business (property-like, liability-like, motor-like, other, mortgage and credit); and

b. A risk factor for the purpose of calculating the risk charge.

148. Premium risk factors do not include the impact of catastrophe events since catastrophe risk is a separate risk within the ICS.

149. Some of the Claims Reserve risk factors take into account latent liability risk. The purpose of the latent liability risk charge is to capture risk from liability exposures that is not

五、Level 2 Document: ICS Version 2.0 for the monitoring period

adequately captured by historical claims experience.

150. Table 13 provides the list of ICS segments, the associated ICS category, as well as the risk charges for Premium and Claims Reserve risks. The definitions of ICS segments are provided in Annex 2.

7.2.3.3 Aggregation

151. The calculation of non-life risk charges for each ICS segment takes into account diversification effects.

152. The first step of aggregation combines each ICS segment's Premium risk and Claims Reserve risk charges, applying a 25% correlation factor between the Premium and Claims Reserve risk charges for all segments (with the exception of mortgage and credit as outlined below).

153. Mortgage business and credit business are added across all regions and then aggregated with Real Estate risk and Credit risk, respectively.

154. The second step of aggregation is within ICS categories, where a correlation matrix is applied across segments of a given category. The correlation factors are specified in Table 12 below:

Table 12 Within Category Correlation Factors

ICS Categories	Correlation factor between segments within the category
Liability-like	50%
Motor-like	75%
Property-like	50%
Other	25%

155. The third step of aggregation is within each region listed in section 7.1.2, using a 50% correlation factor between each of the four ICS categories.

156. The fourth step of aggregation is across regions, using a 25% correlation factor between each region's total risk charge.

157. As an example, Figure 1 shows how non-life risk exposures are categorised into regions, geographical segments, ICS categories and ICS segments.

7.2.3.4 Input Data Required

158. The Premium risk charge for each ICS segment is calculated as the relevant risk factor multiplied by the greater of the net premium earned and net premium to be earned.

159. The Claims Reserve risk charge for each ICS segment is calculated as the relevant risk factor multiplied by the net current estimate.

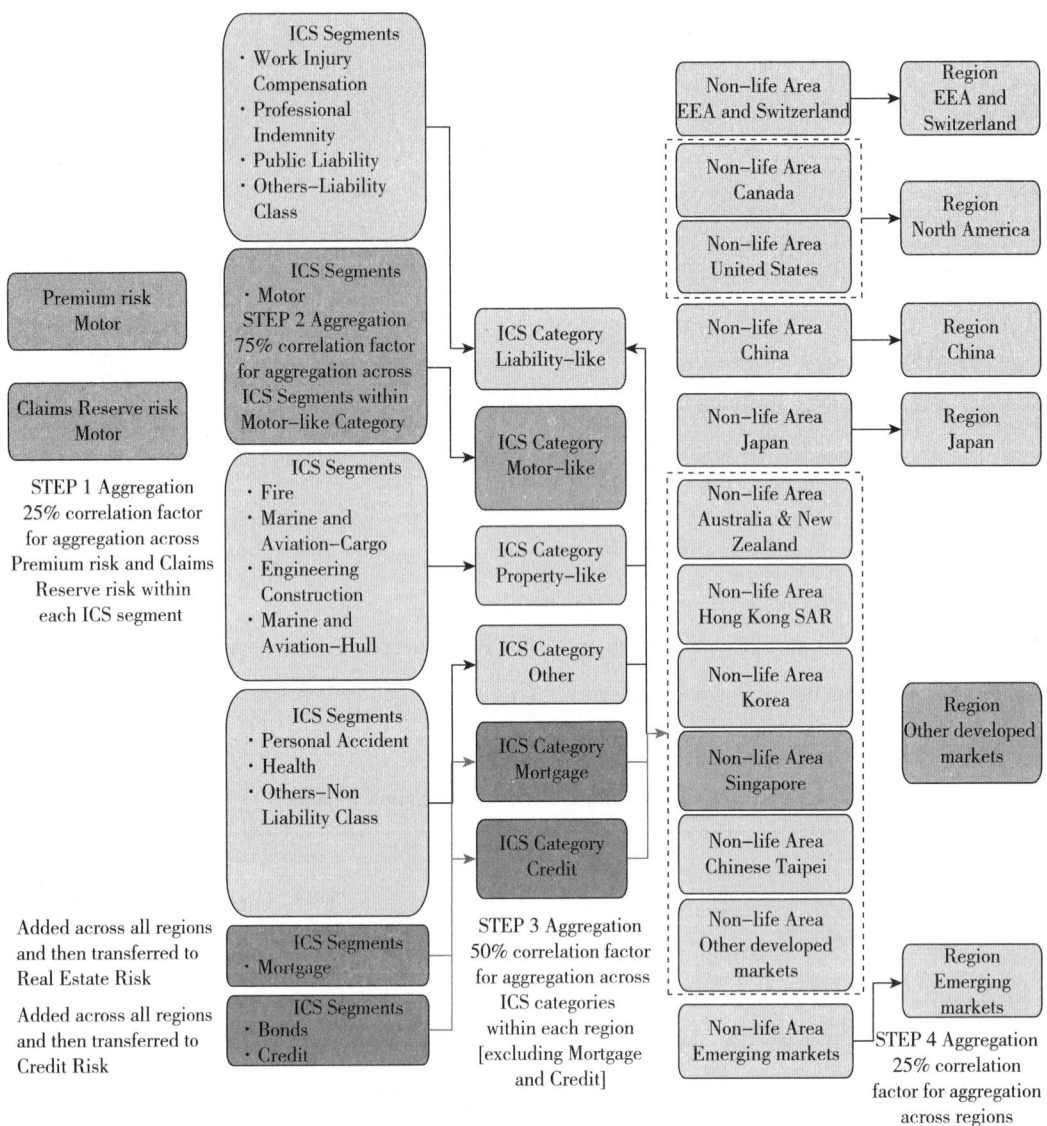

Figure 1 Categorisation of non-life risk exposure, showing how Singapore Motor-like ICS Category is aggregated

Table 13 ICS Non-Life Segmentation

	ICS Segment	ICS Category	Premium risk factor	Claims Reserve risk factor
EEA and Switzerland	Medical expense insurance	Other	15%	10%
	Income protection	Other	25%	35%
	Workers' Compensation	Liability-like	25%	27%
	Motor vehicle liability-Motor third party liability	Motor-like	20%	15%
	Motor, other classes	Motor-like	20%	15%
	Marine, aviation and transport	Property-like	35%	25%

五、Level 2 Document: ICS Version 2.0 for the monitoring period

contined

	ICS Segment	ICS Category	Premium risk factor	Claims Reserve risk factor
EEA and Switzerland	Fire and other damage	Property-like	17.5%	17.5%
	General liability-third party liability	Liability-like	35%	27%
	Credit and suretyship	Credit	35%	50%
	Legal expenses	Other	15%	40%
	Assistance	Other	15%	50%
	Miscellaneous financial loss	Other	30%	35%
	Non-proportional health reinsurance	Other	50%	45%
	Non-proportional Casualty reinsurance	Liability-like	55%	45%
	Non-proportional marine, aviation and transport reinsurance	Property-like	55%	40%
	Non-Proportional property reinsurance	Property-like	45%	40%
Canada	Property-personal	Property-like	35%	25%
	Home Warranty	Property-like	30%	25%
	Product Warranty	Property-like	30%	25%
	Property-commercial	Property-like	30%	30%
	Aircraft	Property-like	45%	35%
	Automobile-liability/personal accident	Motor-like	35%	20%
	Automobile-other	Motor-like	35%	20%
	Boiler and Machinery	Property-like	30%	25%
	Equipment Warranty	Property-like	30%	25%
	Credit Insurance	Credit	45%	30%
	Credit Protection	Credit	45%	30%
	Fidelity	Other	45%	30%
	Hail	Property-like	35%	30%
	Legal Expenses	Other	45%	40%
	Liability	Liability-like	50%	38%
	Mortgage	Mortgage	45%	30%
	Surety	Credit	45%	30%
	Title	Liability-like	35%	30%
	Marine	Property-like	45%	35%
	Accident and Sickness	Other	45%	30%
	Other Approved Products	Other	45%	35%
US	Auto physical damage	Motor-like	12.5%	10%
	Homeowners/ Farm owners	Property-like	30%	15%
	Special property	Property-like	25%	17.5%
	Private passenger auto liability/ medical	Motor-like	15%	15%
	Commercial auto/ truck liability/ medical	Motor-like	15%	15%
	Workers' compensation	Liability-like	15%	16%
	Commercial multi-peril	Liability-like	30%	26%

contined

ICS Segment		ICS Category	Premium risk factor	Claims Reserve risk factor
US	Medical professional liability-Occurrence	Liability-like	40%	45%
	Medical professional liability-Claims-Made	Liability-like	30%	35%
	Other Liability-Occurrence	Liability-like	17.5%	28%
	Other Liability-Claims-Made	Liability-like	15%	20%
	Products liability	Liability-like	45%	47%
	Reinsurance-non-proportional assumed property	Property-like	35%	25%
	Reinsurance-non-proportional assumed liability	Liability-like	45%	39%
	Special liability	Liability-like	30%	25%
	Mortgage insurance	Mortgage	45%	30%
	Fidelity/surety	Credit	35%	40%
	Financial Guaranty	Credit	45%	25%
	Other	Other	25%	35%
	Reinsurance-non-proportional assumed financial lines	Other	45%	20%
China	Motor	Motor-like	10%	20%
	Property, including commercial, personal and engineering	Property-like	30%	45%
	Marine and Special	Property-like	25%	45%
	Liability	Liability-like	10%	36%
	Agriculture	Property-like	25%	35%
	Credit	Credit	45%	35%
	Short-term Accident	Other	10%	10%
	Short-term Health	Other	10%	10%
	Short-term Life	Other	10%	20%
	Others	Other	35%	20%
Japan	Fire	Property-like	20%	35%
	Hull	Property-like	40%	35%
	Cargo	Property-like	35%	40%
	Transit	Property-like	40%	35%
	Personal Accident	Other	10%	15%
	Automobile	Motor-like	7.5%	10%
	Aviation	Property-like	50%	45%
	Guarantee Ins.	Credit	35%	40%
	Machinery	Property-like	35%	40%
	General Liability	Liability-like	17.5%	27%

五、Level 2 Document: ICS Version 2.0 for the monitoring period

contined

	ICS Segment	ICS Category	Premium risk factor	Claims Reserve risk factor
Japan	Contractor's All Risks	Property-like	35%	40%
	Movables All Risks	Property-like	17.5%	25%
	Workers' Compensation	Liability-like	35%	22%
	Misc. Pecuniary Loss	Other	35%	45%
	Nursing Care Ins.	Other	35%	45%
	Others	Other	35%	40%
Australia and New Zealand	Householders	Property-like	30%	20%
	Commercial Motor	Motor-like	25%	20%
	Domestic Motor	Motor-like	25%	20%
	Other type A	Other	25%	20%
	Travel	Other	35%	25%
	Fire and ISR	Property-like	30%	25%
	Marine and Aviation	Property-like	35%	25%
	Consumer Credit	Credit	35%	15%
	Other Accident	Other	35%	25%
	Other type B	Other	35%	35%
	Mortgage	Mortgage	45%	30%
	CTP	Motor-like	45%	35%
	Public and Product Liability	Liability-like	45%	31%
	Professional Indemnity	Liability-like	45%	35%
	Employers' Liability	Liability-like	45%	36%
	Short tail medical expenses	Other	15%	25%
	Other type C	Other	45%	35%
	Householders-non-prop reins	Property-like	45%	30%
	Commercial Motor-non-prop reins	Motor-like	45%	30%
	Domestic Motor-non-prop reins	Motor-like	45%	30%
	Other non-prop reins type A	Other	45%	30%
	Travel-non-prop reins	Other	45%	35%
	Fire and ISR-non-prop reins	Property-like	55%	40%
	Marine and Aviation-non-prop reins	Property-like	55%	40%
	Consumer Credit-non-prop reins	Credit	55%	40%
	Other Accident-non-prop reins	Other	55%	40%
	Other non-prop reins type B	Other	55%	35%
	Mortgage-non-prop reins	Mortgage	50%	35%

contined

	ICS Segment	ICS Category	Premium risk factor	Claims Reserve risk factor
Australia and New Zealand	CTP-non-prop reins	Motor-like	55%	40%
	Public and Product Liability-non-prop reins	Liability-like	55%	43%
	Professional Indemnity-non-prop reins	Liability-like	55%	40%
	Employer's Liability-non-prop reins	Liability-like	55%	43%
	Other non-prop reins type C	Other	55%	40%
Hong Kong SAR	Accident and health	Other	30%	25%
	Motor vehicle, damage and liability	Motor-like	25%	15%
	Aircraft, damage and liability	Property-like	45%	40%
	Ships, damage and liability	Property-like	45%	40%
	Goods in transit	Property-like	45%	50%
	Fire and Property damage	Property-like	35%	20%
	General liability	Liability-like	45%	26%
	Pecuniary loss	Other	45%	35%
	Non-proportional treaty reinsurance	Property-like	45%	25%
	Proportional treaty reinsurance	Property-like	35%	35%
Korea	Fire, technology, overseas	Property-like	25%	30%
	Package	Property-like	35%	50%
	Maritime	Property-like	45%	45%
	Personal injury	Other	35%	50%
	Workers accident, liability	Liability-like	12.5%	31%
	Foreigners	Other	15%	10%
	Advance payment refund guarantee	Credit	50%	50%
	Other Non-life	Other	45%	50%
	Private vehicle (personal injury)	Motor-like	15%	30%
	Private vehicle (property, vehicles damage)	Motor-like	25%	35%
	Vehicle for commercial or business purpose (personal injury)	Motor-like	25%	20%
	Vehicle for commercial or business purpose (property, vehicles)	Motor-like	25%	20%
	Other motor	Motor-like	15%	20%
Singapore	Personal Accident	Other	30%	25%
	Singapore/Health	Other	25%	20%
	Singapore/Fire	Property-like	30%	25%
	Marine and Aviation-Cargo	Property-like	35%	30%

五、Level 2 Document: ICS Version 2.0 for the monitoring period

contined

	ICS Segment	ICS Category	Premium risk factor	Claims Reserve risk factor
Singapore	Motor	Motor-like	30%	25%
	Work Injury Compensation	Liability-like	35%	31%
	Bonds	Credit	35%	30%
	Engineering Construction	Property-like	35%	30%
	Credit	Credit	35%	30%
	Mortgage	Mortgage	35%	30%
	Others- non liability class	Other	35%	30%
	Marine and Aviation-Hull	Property-like	45%	35%
	Professional indemnity	Liability-like	35%	35%
	Public liability	Liability-like	35%	31%
	Others-liability class	Liability-like	35%	31%
Chinese Taipei	Fire-residence	Property-like	25%	40%
	Fire-commercial	Property-like	55%	45%
	Marine-inland cargo	Property-like	30%	25%
	Marine-overseas cargo	Property-like	30%	25%
	Marine-hull	Property-like	55%	45%
	Marine-fish boat	Property-like	45%	45%
	Marine-aircraft	Property-like	55%	45%
	Motor-personal vehicle	Motor-like	25%	25%
	Motor-commercial vehicle	Motor-like	25%	25%
	Motor-personal liability	Motor-like	25%	25%
	Motor-commercial liability	Motor-like	25%	25%
	Liability-public, employer, product, etc.	Liability-like	35%	36%
	Liability-professional	Liability-like	35%	35%
	Engineering	Property-like	55%	45%
	Nuclear power station	Property-like	55%	45%
	Guarantee-surety, fidelity	Credit	55%	45%
	Credit	Credit	55%	45%
	Other property damage	Property-like	35%	40%
	Accident	Other	15%	10%
	Property Damage-commercial earthquake	Property-like	45%	35%
	Comprehensive-personal property and liability	Property-like	45%	45%
	Comprehensive-commercial property and liability	Property-like	45%	45%
	Property damage-typhoon and flood	Property-like	55%	45%
	Property damage-compulsory earthquake	Property-like	55%	45%
	Health	Other	15%	10%

continued

ICS Segment		ICS Category	Premium risk factor	Claims Reserve risk factor
Other Developed	Motor	Motor-like	30%	20%
	Property damage	Property-like	30%	25%
	Accident, protection and health (APH)	Other	35%	30%
	Short tail medical expenses	Other	35%	25%
	Other short tail	Other	35%	30%
	Marine, Air, Transport (MAT)	Property-like	35%	35%
	Workers' compensation	Liability-like	35%	36%
	Public liability	Liability-like	35%	31%
	Product liability	Liability-like	35%	43%
	Professional indemnity	Liability-like	35%	35%
	Other liability and other long tail	Liability-like	35%	36%
	Non-proportional motor, property damage, APH and MAT	Property-like	50%	40%
	Catastrophe reinsurance	Property-like	50%	40%
	Non-proportional liability	Liability-like	50%	44%
	Non-proportional professional indemnity	Liability-like	50%	40%
	Mortgage insurance	Mortgage	45%	35%
	Commercial credit insurance	Credit	45%	35%
	Other medium-term	Other	50%	40%
Other Emerging	Motor	Motor-like	35%	25%
	Property damage	Property-like	35%	30%
	Accident, protection and health (APH)	Other	35%	30%
	Short tail medical expenses	Other	35%	25%
	Other short tail	Other	35%	30%
	Marine, Air, Transport (MAT)	Property-like	35%	35%
	Workers' compensation	Liability-like	45%	36%
	Public liability	Liability-like	45%	36%
	Product liability	Liability-like	45%	47%
	Professional indemnity	Liability-like	45%	35%
	Other liability and other long tail	Liability-like	45%	36%
	Non-proportional motor, property damage, APH and MAT	Property-like	50%	45%
	Catastrophe reinsurance	Property-like	50%	45%
	Non proportional liability	Liability-like	50%	48%
	Non-proportional professional indemnity	Liability-like	50%	45%
	Mortgage insurance	Mortgage	50%	40%
	Commercial credit insurance	Credit	50%	40%
	Other medium-term	Other	55%	40%

7.2.4 Calculation of Catastrophe Risk Charge

7.2.4.1 Scope of Calculation

160. When calculating the Catastrophe risk charge, all lines of business exposed to Catastrophe risk are considered. To avoid double counting with the other ICS risk charges, the following principles are applied:

a. Life and similar to life health business are included only for the pandemic and the terrorism scenarios; and

b. The impact on financial markets and the whole economy (Market and Credit risks) is not included in the calculation of Catastrophe risk.

7.2.4.2 Covered Perils

161. The perils covered by Catastrophe risk are:

a. Natural catastrophe:

　　i. Tropical cyclone, hurricane, typhoon;

　　ii. Extra-tropical windstorm/winter storm;

　　iii. Earthquake; and

　　iv. Other material natural perils, such as:

- Flood;
- Tornado, hail, convective storms;
- Other risks.

b. Other catastrophes (Man-Made Perils/Scenarios):

　　i. Terrorist attack;

　　ii. Pandemic; and

　　iii. Credit and Surety.

162. The impact of catastrophe claim events include both the main peril and any secondary perils associated with the main peril.

7.2.4.3 Natural Catastrophe

163. Stochastic catastrophe models may be used to calculate loss amounts resulting from natural catastrophe events.

164. Loss amounts are calculated considering:

a. The impact of natural catastrophe on all lines of business affected;

b. An allowance for non-modelled exposures including expected new business over the target time horizon of one year that could be affected by the listed perils; and

c. An allowance for non-modelled perils and regions reported as part of the other natural catastrophe losses. This may include perils and regions that are not modelled individually or specifically but for which potential losses are assessed using other approaches.

165. The natural catastrophe risk charge is the difference between the 99.5th percentile and the mean of the total annual aggregate losses, net of protections. The annual aggregate losses are calculated as the aggregation of losses across all regions and perils.

7.2.4.4 Other Catastrophe Scenarios

166. The loss amounts for the following perils are determined according to the scenarios described below.

167. The impact of the scenarios is calculated for all lines of business affected by the respective scenario, unless otherwise specified in the scope of the calculation.

7.2.4.4.1 Terrorist Attack

168. The risk charge is the sum of the losses from the following two components:

a. Total loss of property (including building, content, motor vehicles) from insurance contracts and the impact on other insurance contracts resulting directly from the loss of property; and

b. The losses from life insurance contracts, health coverage and workers' compensation.

169. For both the life and non-life components, the scenario is a five-tonne bomb blast for the largest geographical risk concentration partly or fully located within a radius of 500 metres. To determine this concentration, all buildings (including properties for own use) are considered. The largest concentration is determined separately for the life and non-life components.

170. For property damage, including insured properties and related covers, the following assumptions are made:

- 100% damage ratio within a circular zone of a 200 metre radius;
- 25% damage ratio for the next circular zone up to a 400 metre radius; and
- 10% damage ratio between 400 and 500 metres.

171. For fatalities, the following assumptions are made:

- 15% fatality rate within a circular zone of a 200 metre radius; and
- 1.5% fatality rate between 200 and 500 metres.

172. For disabilities, the following assumptions are made:

- 20% disability rate within a circular zone of a 200 metre radius; and
- 10% fatality rate between 200 and 500 metres.

7.2.4.4.2 Pandemic

173. The scenario is an increase in the number of deaths following a global pandemic. The risk charge is the total loss amount to all individual and group insurance products covering

Mortality risk in any part of the world resulting from the increase of 1.0 in the number of deaths per thousand insureds.

7.2.4.4.3 Credit and Surety

174. The risk charge is the sum of the losses from the following three components:

a. Mortgage insurance;

d. Trade credit; and

c. Surety.

7.2.4.4.3.1 Mortgage insurance

175. The scenario is calculated as an aggregate loss amount resulting from an increase in frequency and severity due to the specified decline in home prices. A 25% decline in home prices is assumed to persist for the entire one-year time period. The total loss amount includes the impact of both an increase in frequency of delinquency and defaults and an increased loss severity that result from the decline in home prices.

7.2.4.4.3.2 Trade Credit

176. The credit stress scenario for trade credit is defined as the total loss amount due to the inability of customers of the policyholder to pay for goods delivered and/or services provided. The trade credit coverage indemnifies the policyholder for bad debt losses incurred due to a customer's inability to pay. A policyholder's customer's inability to pay is indicated by an increase in both the probability of default and the loss given default of that customer. The total loss amount is adjusted for any existing loss mitigation, including reimbursements from policyholder, retention etc.

Table 14 Credit stress factors for trade credit

Rating category	Factor
Investment Grade	80%
Non-Investment Grade	200%

7.2.4.4.3.3 Surety

177. The credit stress scenario for surety is defined as the total net potential loss amount based on the penal sum of the surety bond. A surety bond indemnifies the policyholder from the principal's inability to perform its contractual obligation. The penal sum represents the maximum amount that the IAIG is required to pay to the beneficiary. The IAIG calculates the largest net potential losses for its ten largest exposures to surety counterparties (principals) using the methodology described below. The total net potential loss amount assumes that the two largest net losses have occurred, and is therefore equal to the sum of the two largest net losses.

7.2.4.5 Aggregation of Catastrophe Risks

178. For the purpose of calculating the Catastrophe risk charge, the other catastrophe scenarios are assumed to be mutually independent and independent of the natural catastrophe perils. Consequently, the total ICS catastrophe capital charge will be calculated as follows:

$$ICS_{Cat} = \sqrt{ICS^2_{NatCat} + ICS^2_{Terror} + ICS^2_{Pand} + ICS^2_{Credit\&Surety}}$$

7.2.4.6 Calculation of the Recoverable Amount to be used for the Calculation of Contingent Credit Risk

179. The recoverable amount is calculated as the difference between the risk charge for Catastrophe risk calculated as if the risk mitigation arrangements did not exist, and the risk charge for Catastrophe risk calculated taking into account qualifying risk mitigation arrangements.

180. The recoverable amount is allocated by credit rating categories, using the following steps:

a. For the aggregate of the Natural Catastrophe risk and for each Other catastrophe scenario, calculate the recoveries by rating class and the gross and net losses;

b. Aggregate all gross and net losses using the aggregation approach described above. The difference between aggregated gross and net losses is the total recoverable; and

c. The recoverable by rating class is equal to the total recoverable multiplied by the ratio of the sum over all scenarios of the recoveries in that rating class to the sum over all scenarios of the recoveries for all rating classes.

7.2.4.7 Safeguards for Natural Catastrophe Models

181. In order to assess the appropriateness of stochastic natural catastrophe models, IAIGs provide information on the following safeguards.

• Safeguard 1-Description of the scope of application: IAIGs describe the perimeter of the natural catastrophe model's calculation.

• Safeguard 2-Validation: IAIGs demonstrate that a rigorous process is in place by which they can establish whether their natural catastrophe model framework is sound or whether improvements are needed.

• Safeguard 3-Sign-off by senior management: The senior management of the IAIG has ownership of the natural catastrophe model, and the model complies with the validation process prescribed by the natural catastrophe model governance process.

• Safeguard 4-Statistical quality test: The statistical quality test addresses issues related to the following technical aspects of the natural catastrophe model:

○ methodology and assumptions;

○ coverage of material risks;

　　○ data (including external data) and expert judgment;

　　○ aggregation of risks and diversification effects;

　　○ consistency with the method used for the calculation of technical provisions;

　　○ allowance for risk mitigation techniques and future management actions; and

　　○ financial guarantees and contractual options.

• Safeguard 5-Use test and governance: The use test reflects the IAIG's view of its risks and is used in decision making.

• Safeguard 6-Documentation standards: The documentation of the natural catastrophe model, including its use and other related aspects:

　　○ facilitates the supervisory review of the model;

　　○ facilitates Senior Management's understanding; and

　　○ recognises the weaknesses of the model.

• Safeguard 7-List of catastrophe risk sources that are not modelled: IAIGs recognise the limitations in the scope of their natural catastrophe model. IAIGs make a list of natural catastrophe risks specified in the ICS but not modelled, and explain why those risks are not modelled.

7.3 Market Risks

7.3.1 Calculation of the market risk charge

182. The correlation matrix used for aggregating the market risk charges is the following:

Table 15　Market risks correlation matrix

	Interest rate	NDSR Up	NDSR Down	Equity	Real Estate	Currency	Asset concentration
Interest rate	100%	25%	25%	25%	25%	25%	0%
NDSR Up	25%	100%	100%	75%	50%	25%	0%
NDSR Down	25%	100%	100%	0%	0%	25%	0%
Equity	25%	75%	0%	100%	50%	25%	0%
Real estate	25%	50%	0%	50%	100%	25%	0%
Currency	25%	25%	25%	25%	25%	100%	0%
Asset concentration	0%	0%	0%	0%	0%	0%	100%

7.3.2 Interest rate risk

183. All assets and liabilities sensitive to changes in interest rates are taken into account in the calculation of the Interest Rate risk charge, with the exception of financial instruments issued by the IAIG that qualify as capital resources.

184. For current estimates of insurance liabilities calculated with a dynamic lapse function

that uses the interest rate as an input variable, the base lapse assumptions stay unchanged under the interest rate stresses, but lapse rates react to the interest rate scenarios used to calculate the Interest Rate risk charge.

185. The Interest Rate risk charge is calculated as:

$$\max(0, \sum_i MR_i + \text{VaR}_{99.5}(\sum_i LT_i))$$

where:

- i is an index over all currencies in which the IAIG is exposed to Interest Rate risk;
- MR_i is the result of the mean reversion scenario for currency i, obtained as described in paragraph 188; and
- LT_i is a random variable encompassing the results of the level up, level down, twist up-to-down and twist down-to-up scenarios for currency i, as specified in paragraph 186.

186. For currency i, LT_i is defined as:

$$\frac{1}{N^{-1}(0.995)} \times (LU_i \max(X_i, 0) - LD_i \max(X_i, 0) + TU_i \max(Y_i, 0) - TD_i \min(Y_i, 0))$$

where:

- $N^{-1}(0.995)$ is the 99.5% quantile of the standardised normal distribution;
- LU_i and LD_i are the results of the level up and level down scenarios respectively, obtained as described in paragraph 188;
- TU_i and TD_i are the results of the twist up-to-down and twist down-to-up scenarios respectively, obtained as described in paragraph 188; and
- X_i and Y_i are independent random variables following a standardised normal distribution.

187. In addition, the random variables X_i and Y_i are such that:

- For any $i \neq j$, $\text{corr}(X_i, X_j) = \text{corr}(Y_i, Y_j) = 0.75$; and
- For any i and j, $\text{corr}(X_i, Y_j) = 0$.

188. For currency i, MR_i, LU_i, LD_i, TU_i and TD_i correspond to the change in the IAIG's Net Asset Value when recalculating the value of all relevant assets and liabilities using the mean reversion, level up, level down, twist up-to-down and twist down-to-up stressed yield curves respectively, obtained using the methodology described in paragraphs 189 to 197.

189. For each currency, the stressed yield curve for the mean reversion scenario is obtained by adding the following yield curve to the initial yield curve, up to the LOT:

$$\Delta L.\ Level\ curve + \Delta S.\ Slope\ curve + \Delta C.\ Curvatrue\ curve$$

where:

- *Level curve* is the curve equal to 1 for all maturities;

五、Level 2 Document: ICS Version 2.0 for the monitoring period

- *Slope curve* is the curve equal to $\dfrac{1 - e^{-\lambda\tau}}{\lambda\tau}$ for any maturity τ;

- *Curvature curve* is the curve equal to $\dfrac{1 - e^{-\lambda\tau}}{\lambda\tau} - e^{-\lambda\tau}$ for any maturity τ;

- λ is the exponential decay rate of the Nelson Siegel model[①] for the risk-free yield curve;

- $\begin{pmatrix} \Delta L \\ \Delta S \\ \Delta C \end{pmatrix}$ is the vector defined as $(I - e^{-K})(\mu - V_0)$;

- I is the 3×3 identity matrix;

- $K = \begin{pmatrix} K_1 & & 0 \\ & K_2 & \\ 0 & & K_3 \end{pmatrix}$ and $\mu = \begin{pmatrix} \mu_1 \\ \mu_2 \\ \mu_3 \end{pmatrix}$ are parameters of the process followed by the vector V_t below, described by the equation:

$$dV_t = K(\mu - V_t)dt + \sum dW_t$$

- $V_t = \begin{pmatrix} \beta_{1t} \\ \beta_{2t} \\ \beta_{3t} \end{pmatrix}$, where β_{1t}, β_{2t} and β_{3t} correspond to the Nelson Siegel parameters for the risk-free yield curve at time t; and

- W_t is a 3-dimensional Wiener process and $\sum$ is a lower triangular matrix of real non-negative factors.

190. For the mean reversion scenario, the value of the LTFR remains unchanged.

191. For each currency, the stressed yield curve for the level up scenario is obtained by adding the following yield curve to the initial yield curve, up to the LOT:

s. $N^{-1}(0.995) \cdot [sl_1 \cdot \text{Level curve} + sl_2 \cdot \text{Slope curve} + sl_3 \cdot \text{Curvature curve}]$

where:

- $\begin{pmatrix} sl_1 \\ sl_2 \\ sl_3 \end{pmatrix} = \cos(\theta) M e_1 + \sin(\theta) M e_2$;

- $M = \sqrt{(\sum \sum^T) \odot \left(\dfrac{1 - e^{-(k_i + k_j)}}{k_i + k_j}\right)_{ij}}$, with $\sum$ and K_i denoting the parameters of the

---

① As described in the article Diebold, F. X. and Li, C (2006) Forecasting the Term Structure of Government Bond Yields in Journal of Econometrics, 130, 337 – 364.

equation described in paragraph 189, and $\odot$ the Hadamard product operator;

- e_1 and e_2 are the eigenvectors associated with the highest and second highest eigenvalues, respectively, of the matrix $N^T N$;

- $N = \begin{pmatrix} LOT & & 0 \\ & a & \\ 0 & & b \end{pmatrix} M$;

- $a = \sum_{\tau=1}^{LOT} \dfrac{1 - e^{-\lambda \tau}}{\lambda \tau}$ and $b = \sum_{\tau=1}^{LOT} \left(\dfrac{1 - e^{-\lambda \tau}}{\lambda \tau} - e^{-\lambda \tau} \right)$;

- $\theta = Arctan \dfrac{\sum_{T=1}^{LOT} h_2(\tau)}{\sum_{T=1}^{LOT} h_1(\tau)}$;

- $h_i(\tau) = \left(1, \dfrac{1 - e^{-\lambda \tau}}{\lambda \tau}, \dfrac{1 - e^{-\lambda \tau}}{\lambda \tau} - e^{-\lambda \tau} \right) M e_i$, $i = 1, 2$; and

- $s = \begin{cases} 1 \text{ if } (sl_1. \text{ Level curve}_{LOT} + sl_2. \text{ Slope curve}_{LOT} + sl_3. \text{ Curvature curve}_{LOT}) \geq 0 \\ -1 \text{ otherwise} \end{cases}$

192. For the level up scenario, the LTFR is increased by 10%.

193. For each currency, the stressed yield curve for the level down scenario is obtained by adding the following yield curve to the initial yield curve, up to the LOT:

$- s . N^{-1}(0.995) . [sl_1. \text{ Level curve} + sl_2. \text{ Slope curve} + sl_3. \text{ Curvature curve}]$

194. For the level down scenario, the LTFR is decreased by 10%.

195. For each currency, the stressed yield curve for the twist up-to-down scenario is obtained by adding the following yield curve to the initial yield curve, up to the LOT:

$N^{-1}(0.995) . [st_1. \text{ Level curve} + st_2. \text{ Slope curve} + st_3. \text{ Curvature curve}]$

where:

$$\begin{pmatrix} st_1 \\ st_2 \\ st_3 \end{pmatrix} = \cos(\theta) M e_1 - \sin(\theta) M e_2$$

196. For each currency, the stressed yield curve for the twist down-to-up scenario is obtained by adding the following yield curve to the initial yield curve, up to the LOT:

$- N^{-1}(0.995) . [st_1. \text{ Level curve} + st_2. \text{ Slope curve} + st_3. \text{ Curvature curve}]$

197. For the twist scenarios, the LTFR remains unchanged.

7.3.3 Non-Default Spread risk

198. All liabilities sensitive to changes in spreads are taken into account in the calculation

of the NDSR charge, with the exception of financial instruments issued by the IAIG that qualify as capital resources.

199. All assets that contribute to the calculation of the spread adjustments for valuation purposes (Table 3 in section 5.2.5.3.2.1), are taken into account in the calculation of the NDSR charge, with the exception of sovereign assets.

200. The stresses are applied to spreads after risk correction. For insurance liabilities, the prescribed stresses are applied as parallel shifts to the spreads by risk category used to compute the adjustments specified in section 5.2.5 for valuation purposes.

201. The upward and downward stresses used for the calculation of the NDSR charge are specified in Table 16.

Table 16　Stress factors for Non-Default Spread risk

ICS RC	Up (in bps)	Down (in bps)
1	+50	-50
2	+50	-50
3	+70	-70
4-7	+100	-100
Subject to the following relative limit, calculated based on the absolute value of the spread over the risk-free yield curve:		
Relative limit	No relative limit	50%

7.3.4　Equity risk

202. The following definitions apply to the equity segments listed in the ICS Level 1 document.

203. Listed equity in developed markets includes equities listed on the securities exchanges of equity markets included in the FTSE Developed Index: Australia, Austria, Belgium, Luxembourg, Canada, Denmark, Finland, France, Germany, Hong Kong SAR, Ireland, Israel, Italy, Japan, Netherlands, New Zealand, Norway, Poland, Portugal, Singapore, South Korea, Spain, Sweden, Switzerland, UK, and US.

204. Any equity market not included in the FTSE Developed Index is considered an emerging market.

205. Investments in subordinated debt are included in the equity risk charge within the segment hybrid debt/preference shares.

206. The segment other equity is comprised of all investments not included in the previous equity segments.

207. The four level scenarios (one for each asset segment) and volatility scenario are defined as:

a. An instantaneous decrease by 35% of the market prices of all listed shares in developed markets.

b. An instantaneous decrease by 48% of the market prices of all listed shares in emerging markets.

c. An instantaneous decrease of the market prices of hybrid debt/preference shares by x%, which x based on the ICS rating category (RC) of the asset, as specified in Table 17.

Table 17　Stress factors for hybrid debt/preference shares

ICS RC	x%
1–2	4%
3	6%
4	11%
5	21%
6–7	35%

d. An instantaneous decrease by 49% of the market prices of all assets classified as other equity, as defined in paragraph 206.

e. An instantaneous absolute increase by x% of the implied volatilities of all the asset classes listed above, with x having the values provided in Table 18. For maturities not specified, the increase is interpolated linearly.

Table 18　Absolute stress factors for implied volatilities

Maturity (months)	x%
0–1	42%
3	28%
6	23%
12	20%
24	17%
36	16%
48	15%
60	14%
84	14%
120	12%
144	11%
180	10%
240	7%
300	4%
360 and above	0%

五、Level 2 Document: ICS Version 2.0 for the monitoring period

208. The results of the stresses listed above are aggregated in two steps:

a. Step 1: The total level risk is calculated by aggregating the impact of the stress for each level scenario using the following correlation matrix:

Table 19 Equity correlation matrix

Equity segment	Developed	Emerging	Hybrid/preferred	Other
Developed	100%	75%	100%	75%
Emerging	75%	100%	75%	75%
Hybrid/preferred	100%	75%	100%	75%
Other	75%	75%	75%	100%

b. Step 2: The total Equity risk charge is calculated by summing the total level risk (from Step 1) and the impact of the stress under the volatility scenario.

7.3.5 Real estate risk

209. The stress scenario referred to in the ICS Level 1 document is a decrease of 25% in real estate prices. Assets and liabilities subject to the stress are:

a. Commercial investment real estate;

b. Residential investment real estate;

c. Real estate for own use;

d. Other assets whose value is impacted by a change in real estate prices; and

e. Liabilities, both insurance and other, whose value is impacted by a change in real estate prices.

7.3.6 Currency risk

210. In order to determine the Currency risk charge, IAIGs determine their net open position for all currencies other than the reporting currency. The net open position for each currency is calculated as the sum of the following:

a. The net spot position, defined as all assets less liabilities, including accrued interest and accrued expenses;

b. The net forward position, defined as all net amounts under forward foreign exchange transactions, including currency futures and the interest and principal on currency swaps;

c. The delta equivalent amounts of currency options;

d. Guarantees and similar instruments that are certain to be exercised and are likely to be irrevocable;

e. At the discretion of the IAIG, net future income and expenses not yet accrued but already fully hedged;

f. Any other item representing a profit or loss in the foreign currency;

g. Minus the amount of capital required locally to support the activities in the foreign currency, subject to a cap of 10% of net insurance liabilities in that currency.

211. The deduction referred to in point g) of paragraph210 is applied to long positions only and shall not change any long position to a short position. This deduction applies only if the IAIG has operations in the jurisdiction of the foreign currency.

212. The net open currency position excludes assets that are fully deducted from capital resources, and liabilities that qualify for inclusion in consolidated capital resources.

213. The net insurance liability reported for each currency consists of the current estimate net of any reinsurance assets, plus all deferred tax assets and liabilities associated with the current estimate and reinsurance assets.

214. Forward currency positions are valued at spot market exchange rates as at the reporting date.

215. The Currency risk charge is equal to the higher of the aggregated losses incurred under the following two scenarios:

a. Scenario 1: all currencies in which the IAIG has a net long position decrease in value, while all of the currencies in which the IAIG has a net short position remain unchanged. The amount of the decrease of each foreign currency relative to the reporting currency is found in the currency stress matrix in Table 20 below.

b. Scenario 2: all currencies in which the IAIG has a net short position increase in value, while all of the currencies in which the IAIG has a net long position remain unchanged. The amount of the increase of each foreign currency relative to the reporting currency is found in the currency stress matrix in Table 20 below.

216. For each scenario, the losses by currency are aggregated using a correlation formula for which the assumed correlation of losses between each pair of foreign currencies is 50%.

Table 20 Currency risk stress factors

Ref Curr	Against AUD	BRL	CAD	CHF	CLP	CNY	COP	CZK	DKK	EUR	GBP	HKD
AUD	0%	50%	25%	40%	35%	40%	40%	35%	35%	35%	35%	40%
BRL	50%	0%	50%	65%	50%	55%	55%	60%	60%	60%	55%	55%
CAD	25%	50%	0%	35%	30%	25%	35%	35%	30%	30%	30%	25%
CHF	40%	60%	35%	0%	45%	30%	45%	25%	20%	20%	30%	35%
CLP	35%	50%	30%	45%	0%	30%	40%	40%	40%	40%	35%	30%
CNY	35%	55%	25%	35%	30%	0%	35%	35%	30%	30%	25%	5%
COP	40%	55%	35%	50%	40%	35%	0%	45%	45%	45%	40%	35%
CZK	35%	55%	35%	30%	40%	35%	45%	0%	15%	15%	30%	35%

五、Level 2 Document: ICS Version 2.0 for the monitoring period

contined

Ref Curr	AUD	BRL	CAD	CHF	CLP	CNY	COP	CZK	DKK	EUR	GBP	HKD
DKK	35%	55%	30%	20%	35%	30%	40%	15%	0%	5%	25%	30%
EUR	35%	55%	30%	20%	35%	30%	40%	15%	5%	0%	25%	30%
GBP	35%	55%	30%	30%	35%	25%	40%	30%	25%	25%	0%	25%
HKD	35%	55%	25%	35%	30%	5%	35%	35%	30%	30%	25%	0%
HUF	40%	60%	40%	35%	45%	45%	50%	25%	25%	25%	35%	45%
IDR	45%	60%	40%	50%	45%	35%	45%	50%	45%	45%	45%	35%
ILS	35%	55%	30%	35%	35%	25%	35%	35%	30%	30%	30%	25%
INR	35%	50%	25%	35%	30%	20%	35%	35%	30%	30%	30%	15%
JPY	50%	65%	40%	35%	45%	30%	50%	45%	35%	35%	40%	30%
KRW	30%	50%	25%	40%	30%	25%	35%	35%	35%	35%	30%	25%
MXN	35%	50%	30%	45%	35%	30%	35%	40%	40%	40%	40%	30%
MYR	35%	50%	25%	35%	30%	15%	30%	35%	30%	30%	25%	15%
NOK	35%	55%	30%	30%	40%	35%	40%	25%	20%	20%	30%	35%
NZD	20%	55%	30%	40%	40%	40%	45%	40%	35%	35%	35%	40%
PEN	35%	50%	25%	35%	30%	15%	30%	35%	30%	30%	30%	15%
PHP	35%	50%	25%	35%	30%	15%	35%	35%	30%	30%	30%	15%
PLN	35%	55%	35%	40%	40%	40%	45%	25%	25%	25%	35%	40%
RON	35%	50%	35%	30%	40%	30%	45%	25%	20%	20%	30%	30%
RUB	45%	60%	40%	50%	40%	35%	45%	45%	40%	40%	45%	35%
SAR	40%	55%	25%	35%	30%	5%	35%	35%	30%	30%	25%	5%
SEK	35%	55%	30%	30%	40%	35%	45%	25%	20%	20%	30%	35%
SGD	30%	50%	20%	30%	30%	15%	30%	30%	25%	25%	25%	15%
THB	35%	55%	30%	35%	30%	20%	35%	35%	30%	30%	30%	20%
TRY	70%	75%	70%	75%	70%	70%	75%	70%	70%	70%	70%	70%
TWD	35%	50%	25%	30%	30%	10%	35%	35%	25%	25%	25%	10%
USD	40%	55%	25%	35%	30%	5%	35%	35%	30%	30%	25%	5%
ZAR	45%	60%	45%	55%	50%	55%	55%	50%	50%	50%	50%	55%

Ref Curr	HUF	IDR	ILS	INR	JPY	KRW	MXN	MYR	NOK	NZD	PEN	PHP
AUD	40%	45%	35%	35%	50%	30%	35%	35%	35%	20%	40%	35%
BRL	60%	60%	55%	55%	70%	50%	50%	50%	55%	55%	55%	55%
CAD	40%	40%	30%	25%	40%	25%	30%	25%	30%	30%	25%	25%
CHF	35%	50%	35%	35%	35%	40%	45%	35%	25%	40%	35%	35%
CLP	45%	45%	35%	30%	45%	30%	35%	30%	40%	40%	30%	30%

continued

Ref Curr	Against											
	HUF	IDR	ILS	INR	JPY	KRW	MXN	MYR	NOK	NZD	PEN	PHP
CNY	45%	35%	25%	15%	30%	25%	30%	15%	35%	40%	15%	15%
COP	50%	45%	35%	35%	50%	35%	35%	30%	40%	45%	35%	35%
CZK	25%	50%	35%	35%	45%	35%	40%	35%	25%	40%	35%	35%
DKK	25%	45%	30%	30%	35%	30%	40%	30%	20%	35%	30%	30%
EUR	25%	45%	30%	30%	35%	35%	40%	30%	20%	35%	30%	30%
GBP	35%	45%	30%	30%	40%	30%	35%	25%	30%	35%	30%	30%
HKD	45%	35%	25%	15%	30%	25%	30%	15%	35%	40%	15%	15%
HUF	0%	55%	40%	40%	55%	40%	45%	40%	30%	40%	45%	45%
IDR	55%	0%	40%	35%	50%	40%	45%	35%	45%	50%	35%	35%
ILS	40%	40%	0%	25%	40%	30%	30%	25%	35%	40%	25%	25%
INR	40%	35%	25%	0%	35%	25%	30%	20%	35%	35%	20%	20%
JPY	50%	50%	40%	35%	0%	40%	50%	35%	40%	50%	35%	35%
KRW	40%	40%	30%	25%	40%	0%	30%	25%	35%	35%	25%	25%
MXN	45%	45%	35%	30%	50%	30%	0%	25%	40%	40%	30%	30%
MYR	40%	35%	25%	20%	35%	25%	25%	0%	30%	35%	20%	20%
NOK	30%	45%	35%	35%	40%	35%	40%	30%	0%	35%	35%	35%
NZD	40%	50%	40%	35%	50%	35%	40%	35%	35%	0%	40%	40%
PEN	45%	35%	25%	20%	35%	25%	30%	20%	35%	40%	0%	20%
PHP	40%	35%	25%	20%	35%	25%	30%	20%	35%	35%	20%	0%
PLN	25%	50%	40%	40%	55%	35%	40%	40%	30%	40%	40%	40%
RON	30%	45%	30%	30%	40%	35%	40%	30%	30%	40%	35%	35%
RUB	50%	50%	40%	35%	50%	40%	40%	35%	40%	50%	35%	40%
SAR	45%	35%	25%	15%	30%	25%	30%	15%	35%	40%	15%	15%
SEK	25%	45%	35%	35%	45%	35%	40%	30%	20%	35%	35%	35%
SGD	35%	35%	20%	15%	30%	20%	30%	15%	25%	30%	15%	15%
THB	40%	35%	25%	20%	35%	25%	35%	20%	35%	35%	20%	20%
TRY	70%	75%	70%	70%	75%	70%	70%	70%	70%	70%	70%	70%
TWD	40%	35%	25%	15%	30%	20%	30%	15%	30%	35%	15%	15%
USD	45%	35%	25%	15%	30%	25%	30%	15%	35%	40%	15%	15%
ZAR	50%	60%	50%	50%	65%	45%	50%	45%	45%	50%	50%	50%

五、Level 2 Document: ICS Version 2.0 for the monitoring period

Ref Curr	Against										
	PLN	RON	RUB	SAR	SEK	SGD	THB	TRY	TWD	USD	ZAR
AUD	35%	40%	45%	40%	35%	30%	35%	55%	35%	40%	45%
BRL	55%	50%	60%	55%	55%	50%	55%	70%	55%	55%	65%
CAD	35%	30%	40%	25%	30%	20%	30%	55%	25%	25%	45%
CHF	35%	30%	45%	35%	30%	25%	35%	65%	30%	35%	55%
CLP	40%	40%	40%	30%	40%	30%	35%	60%	30%	30%	50%
CNY	40%	30%	35%	5%	35%	15%	20%	60%	10%	5%	50%
COP	45%	45%	45%	35%	45%	35%	35%	60%	35%	35%	55%
CZK	25%	25%	45%	35%	25%	30%	35%	60%	35%	35%	50%
DKK	25%	20%	40%	30%	20%	25%	30%	60%	25%	30%	50%
EUR	25%	20%	40%	30%	20%	25%	30%	60%	25%	30%	50%
GBP	35%	30%	40%	25%	30%	25%	30%	60%	25%	25%	50%
HKD	40%	30%	35%	5%	35%	15%	20%	60%	10%	5%	55%
HUF	25%	30%	50%	45%	25%	35%	40%	60%	40%	45%	50%
IDR	50%	45%	50%	35%	45%	35%	35%	70%	35%	35%	60%
ILS	35%	30%	40%	25%	35%	20%	25%	55%	25%	25%	50%
INR	40%	30%	35%	15%	35%	15%	20%	55%	15%	15%	50%
JPY	50%	40%	50%	30%	40%	30%	35%	70%	30%	30%	65%
KRW	35%	35%	40%	25%	35%	20%	25%	55%	20%	25%	45%
MXN	40%	40%	40%	30%	40%	30%	35%	60%	30%	30%	50%
MYR	35%	30%	35%	15%	30%	15%	20%	55%	15%	15%	45%
NOK	30%	30%	40%	35%	20%	25%	35%	60%	30%	35%	45%
NZD	40%	40%	50%	40%	35%	30%	35%	60%	35%	40%	50%
PEN	40%	30%	35%	15%	35%	15%	20%	60%	15%	15%	50%
PHP	40%	30%	40%	15%	35%	15%	20%	55%	15%	15%	50%
PLN	0%	30%	45%	40%	30%	35%	40%	55%	40%	40%	50%
RON	30%	0%	40%	30%	25%	25%	35%	60%	30%	30%	50%
RUB	45%	40%	0%	35%	45%	35%	40%	65%	35%	40%	55%
SAR	40%	30%	35%	0%	35%	15%	20%	60%	10%	5%	55%
SEK	30%	25%	45%	35%	0%	30%	35%	60%	30%	35%	50%
SGD	35%	25%	35%	15%	30%	0%	15%	55%	10%	15%	45%
THB	40%	30%	40%	20%	35%	15%	0%	55%	20%	20%	50%
TRY	70%	70%	75%	70%	70%	65%	70%	0%	70%	70%	75%
TWD	35%	30%	35%	10%	30%	10%	20%	55%	0%	10%	50%
USD	40%	30%	35%	5%	35%	15%	20%	60%	10%	0%	55%
ZAR	50%	50%	55%	55%	50%	45%	50%	60%	50%	55%	0%

7.3.7 Asset concentration risk

7.3.7.1 Assets other than real estate

217. For assets other than real estate, the Asset concentration risk charge is calculated as:

$$f \times \left(\frac{\sum_{E_i > T} (E_i - T)(d. K_i^{eq} + K_i^{cr})}{(d. K^{eq} + K^{cr})} + T \right)$$

where:

- $f = 0.71656$;
- $d = 0.95$;
- E_i is the net exposure to group of connected counterparties i;
- T is an exposure threshold determined by the IAIG in such a way that the number of groups of connected counterparties i for which $E_i > T$ is equal to or greater than 10 but does not exceed 100;
- K_i^{eq} is the Equity risk charge associated with counterparty i, before diversification and management actions;
- K_i^{cr} is the Credit risk charge associated with counterparty i, before diversification and management actions;
- K^{eq} is the total Equity risk charge of the IAIG, before diversification and management actions; and
- K^{cr} is the total Credit risk charge of the IAIG, before diversification and management actions.

218. Groups of connected counterparties are determined according to the definition provided by the Basel Committee on Banking Supervision (BCBS)[①]. Specifically, two or more natural or legal persons are considered a group of connected counterparties if at least one of the following criteria is satisfied:

a. Control relationship: one of the counterparties, directly or indirectly, has control over the other (s); or

b. Economic interdependence: if one of the counterparties were to experience financial problems, the other (s), as a result, would also be likely to encounter financial problems.

219. Exposures to national governments are excluded from the Asset concentration risk charge calculation. Public sector exposures, not issued or guaranteed by a national government, such as provincial, state or municipal debt, are included within the Asset Concentration risk

---

[①] As specified in the BCBS publication *Supervisory framework for measuring and controlling large exposures* (April 2014), which also outlines criteria for assessing whether 'control' or 'economic interdependence' exists.

五、Level 2 Document: ICS Version 2.0 for the monitoring period

charge calculation with their corresponding Credit and Equity risk charges.

220. The determination of the gross counterparty exposures includes both on- and off-balance sheet positions, and considers the following:

a. Exposures to reinsurance counterparties are included on a pre-stress basis[①];

b. The determination of OTC derivatives exposures is based on a credit-equivalent basis, as applicable, and exposures to central counterparties are excluded;

c. Exposures are based on a look-through approach for investment funds and structured products;

d. Non-affiliated (external) guarantees, commitments, bank deposits, receivables and any other items subject to the possibility of financial loss due to counterparty default are included; and

e. Gross exposures are calculated based upon the MAV basis described in section 5, except where otherwise specified.

221. The determination of net counterparty exposures considers the following:

a. Exposures from assets held in separate accounts or life insurance contracts where the investment risks fully flow-through to policyholders are excluded. Nevertheless, assets backing any guarantees to policyholders are included;

b. Asset exposures may be netted against liability exposures to the extent that they are subject to a legally enforceable right of offset;

c. For exposures covered by collateral or unconditional and irrevocable guarantees, the substitution approach specified in sections 7.4.2.1.1 and 7.4.2.2.3 may be used for the portion of the exposure covered by the collateral or the guarantees. The exposure to the primary counterparty is then replaced by the exposure to the collateral or guarantor. Where national government exposures are substituted for corporate exposures, the corresponding amounts are excluded from the determination of the Asset Concentration risk charge, in line with the provisions of paragraph 219; and

d. For collateralised non-life reinsurance exposures, the haircut approach specified in section 7.4.2.1.2 is used in lieu of the substitution approach.

7.3.7.2 Real estate

222. In order to calculate the Asset concentration risk charge for real estate, property exposures are determined on the basis of single property, or group of properties within a 250 metres radius, including exposures from both direct and indirect holdings.

[①] The contingent risk associated with catastrophe scenarios is not included in the exposure.

223. The Asset Concentration risk charge for any property exposure as defined above is calculated as 25% of the net property exposure exceeding 3% of the IAIG's total net investment assets relating to insurance activities. The net property exposures are calculated in line with paragraphs 220 and 221.

7.4 Credit Risk

7.4.1 Calculation of Credit risk charge

7.4.1.1 Exposure classes

224. The Credit risk charge applies to all senior debt obligations of specified exposure classes of borrowers. Preferred shares and hybrid obligations, including subordinated debt, are excluded from the calculation of the Credit risk charge, and are instead subject to the Equity risk charge for hybrid debt/preference shares described in section 7.3.3.

225. Credit exposures to national governments, multilateral development banks and supranational organisations are not subject to the Credit risk charge. Regional governments and municipal authorities and other government entities whose debt is not issued or guaranteed by the national government, are classified as public sector entities. Exposures to commercial undertakings owned but not guaranteed by governments or municipal authorities are classified in the corporates category.

226. The corporates category includes exposures to banks and securities dealers, but excludes exposures to reinsurers. Rated commercial mortgages are included in the corporate exposure class.

227. The securitisation category includes all holdings of mortgage-backed securities and other asset-backed securities. It also includes any other assets where the cash flow from an underlying pool of exposures is used to service payments by a SPV to bondholders. If any of the assets in the pool of exposures underlying a securitisation exposure is itself a securitisation, then the exposure belongs to the re-securitisation category.

228. The category short-term obligations of regulated banks includes demand deposits and other obligations that have an original maturity of less than three months, and that are drawn on a bank subject to the solvency requirements of the Basel Framework. All other bank exposures are included in the corporates category.

229. Assets that are held for unit-linked business or in separate accounts and for which all credit risk on the assets fully flows through to policyholders are excluded from the Credit risk charge. However, IAIGs calculate a Credit risk charge for the increase in related liabilities (eg due to decreased future fee income) that would result from a credit risk loss on those assets, calculated as specified in this section.

230. A non-paid-up financial instrument that qualifies for inclusion in capital resources is subject to the same credit risk charge as a direct credit exposure to the contingent capital provider.

231. The Credit risk charge for off-balance sheet exposures is based on credit equivalent amounts calculated as specified in Section 7.4.1.4.

7.4.1.2 Distribution of exposures by maturity

232. For calculating the Credit risk charge, an effective maturity is calculated as follows for each credit exposure:

$$Effective\ Maturity = \frac{\sum_t t * CF_t}{\sum_t CF_t}$$

where CF_t denotes the cash flows (principal, interest payments and fees) contractually payable by the borrower in period t.

233. Where it is not possible to calculate the effective maturity of the contracted payments as noted above, a conservative measure is used, such as the maximum remaining time (in years) that the borrower is permitted to take to fully discharge its contractual obligation (principal, interest, and fees) under the terms of the loan agreement.

234. For OTC derivatives subject to a master netting agreement, the maturity is calculated as the weighted average of the maturities of the transactions subject to netting, with the weights proportional to the transactions' notional amounts.

235. All exposures to a group are aggregated and split by rating category before calculating the effective maturity.

236. When an exposure is redistributed into another rating category due to the presence of an eligible guarantee or collateral, the effective maturity is calculated based on the term of the underlying exposure, not the term of the guarantee or collateral.

7.4.1.3 Reinsurance exposures

237. The use of AM Best credit ratings is restricted to the calculation of the Credit risk charge on reinsurance exposures. The mapping of AM Best insurer financial strength ratings to the ICS ratings categories is provided in section 3.4.

238. Reinsurance exposures include all positive on-balance sheet reinsurance assets and receivables. Negative exposures are not included.

239. Reinsurance exposures are considered net of cessions to mandatory insurance pools that are backed by either a governmental entity or jointly by the insurance market. Cessions to these mandatory pools are subject to a separate calculation.

240. Reinsurance exposures include all credit recognised in the ICS risk charges due to the presence of reinsurance.

241. In the case of catastrophe scenarios and life insurance stresses, the impact of the scenarios and stresses (before management actions) are calculated on a gross and net of reinsurance basis. The difference between the gross and net of reinsurance basis is then allocated to Credit risk categories based on the profile of the reinsurers that have provided cover. This calculation is made at the Catastrophe risk charge and Life insurance risk charge level (ie after diversification of the components of those risk charges).

242. Modified coinsurance and funds withheld arrangements are subject to a risk charge even if there is no on-balance sheet reinsurance asset or the reinsurance asset is fully offset by payables.

243. For funds withheld and similar arrangements, IAIGs may treat payables and other liabilities due to a reinsurer in the same manner as collateral provided that the arrangement meets the all of the following conditions:

a. The IAIG has executed a written, bilateral netting contract or agreement with the reinsurer from which the asset is due that creates a single legal obligation. As a result of such an agreement, the IAIG would have only one obligation for payment or one claim to receive funds based on the net sum of the liabilities and amounts due in the event the reinsurer failed to perform due to any of the following: default, bankruptcy, liquidation or similar circumstances.

b. The IAIG has a written and reasoned legal opinion that, in the event of any legal challenge, the relevant courts or administrative authorities would find the amount owed under the netting agreement to be the net amount under the laws of all relevant jurisdictions. In reaching this conclusion, the legal opinion must address the validity and enforceability of the entire netting agreement under its terms.

i. The laws of all relevant jurisdictions are:

• The law of the jurisdiction where the reinsurer is incorporated and, if the foreign branch of a reinsurer is involved, the laws of the jurisdiction in which the branch is located;

• The law governing the individual insurance transaction; and

• The law governing any contracts or agreements required to effect the netting arrangement.

ii. A legal opinion is recognised as such by the legal community in the IAIG's home jurisdiction or by a memorandum of law that addresses all relevant issues in a reasoned manner.

c. The IAIG has procedures in place to update legal opinions as necessary to ensure continuing enforceability of the netting arrangement in light of possible changes in relevant laws.

五、Level 2 Document: ICS Version 2.0 for the monitoring period

7.4.1.4 Off-balance sheet exposures

7.4.1.4.1 Credit equivalent amount for OTC derivatives

244. The credit equivalent amount for OTC derivatives is calculated using the current exposure method from Annex 4, section VII of the Basel Framework[①]. Under this method, IAIGs calculate the current replacement cost by summing:

a. The total replacement cost (obtained by marking to market) of all its contracts with positive value; and

b. An amount for potential future credit exposure calculated on the basis of the total notional principal amount of its book, split by residual maturity as specified in Table 21.

Table 21 Calculation of potential future credit exposure

Residual Maturity	Interest Rate	Exchange Rate and Gold	Equity	Precious Metals Except Gold	Other Commodities
One year or less	0.0%	1.0%	6.0%	7.0%	10.0%
Over one year to five years	0.5%	5.0%	8.0%	7.0%	12.0%
Over five years	1.5%	7.5%	10.0%	8.0%	15.0%

245. Credit derivatives are not subject to the current exposure method. Credit protection that is received is treated according to the provisions for guarantees and credit derivatives (cf. Section 7.4.2.2), while credit protection that is sold is treated as an off-balance sheet direct credit substitute subject to a 100% credit conversion factor (cf. Section 7.4.1.4.2).

246. For contracts with multiple exchanges of principal, the factors are multiplied by the number of remaining payments in the contract.

247. For contracts that are structured to settle outstanding exposure following specified payment dates and where the terms are reset so that the market value of the contract is zero on these specified dates, the residual maturity is considered to be the time until the next reset date. In the case of interest rate contracts with remaining maturities of more than one year and that meet the above criteria, the add-on factor is subject to a floor of 0.5%.

248. Contracts not covered by any category in Table 21 are treated as other commodities.

249. No potential credit exposure is calculated for single currency floating/floating interest rate swaps; the credit exposure on these contracts is evaluated solely on the basis of their mark-to-market value.

250. The add-ons are based on effective rather than stated notional amounts. Where the stated notional amount is leveraged or enhanced by the structure of the transaction, IAIGs use

---

① Accessible at http://www.bis.org/publ/bcbs128.pdf.

the actual or effective notional amount when determining potential future exposure.

251. Potential credit exposure is calculated for all OTC contracts (with the exception of single currency floating/floating interest rate swaps), regardless of whether the replacement cost is positive or negative.

252. IAIGs may net contracts that are subject to novation① or any other legally valid form of netting provided the following conditions are satisfied.

a. The IAIG has executed a written, bilateral netting contract or agreement with each counterparty that creates a single legal obligation, covering all included bilateral transactions subject to netting. The result of such an arrangement is that the IAIG only has one obligation for payment or one claim to receive funds based on the net sum of the positive and negative mark-to-market values of all the transactions with that counterparty in the event that counterparty fails to perform due to any of the following: default, bankruptcy, liquidation or similar circumstances.

b. The IAIG has a written and reasoned legal opinion that, in the event of any legal challenge, the relevant courts or administrative authorities will find the exposure under the netting agreement to be the net amount under the laws of all relevant jurisdictions. In reaching this conclusion, the legal opinion addresses the validity and enforceability of the entire netting agreement under its terms.

   i. The laws of all relevant jurisdictions are:

   • The law of the jurisdiction where the counterparties are incorporated and, if the foreign branch of a counterparty is involved, the laws of the jurisdiction in which the branch is located;

   • The law governing the individual insurance transactions; and

   • The law governing any contracts or agreements required to effect the netting arrangement.

   ii. A legal opinion is recognised as such by the legal community in the IAIG's home jurisdiction or by a memorandum of law that addresses all relevant issues in a reasoned manner.

c. The IAIG has internal procedures to verify that, prior to recognising a transaction as being subject to netting for capital purposes, the transaction is covered by a legal opinion that meets the above criteria.

d. The IAIG has procedures in place to update legal opinions as necessary to ensure

---

① Novation refers to a written bilateral contract between two counterparties under which any obligation to each other to deliver a given currency on a given date is automatically amalgamated with all other obligations for the same currency and value date, legally substituting one single amount for the previous gross obligations.

continuing enforceability of the netting arrangements in light of possible changes in relevant laws.

e. The IAIG maintains all required documentation in its files.

253. Any contract containing a walkaway clause[①] is not eligible to qualify for netting for the purpose of calculating the Credit risk charge.

254. Credit exposure on bilaterally netted forwards, swaps, purchased options and similar derivatives transactions is calculated as the sum of the net mark-to-market replacement cost, if positive, plus an add-on based on the notional principal of the individual underlying contracts. However, for purposes of calculating potential future credit exposures of contracts subject to legally enforceable netting agreements in which notional principal is equivalent to cash flows, notional principal is defined as the net receipts falling due on each value date in each currency.

255. The calculation of the gross add-ons is based on the legal cash flow obligations in all currencies. This is calculated by netting all receivable and payable amounts in the same currency for each value date. The netted cash flow obligations is converted to the reporting currency using the current forward rates for each value date. Once converted the amounts receivable for the value date are added together and the gross add-on is calculated by multiplying the receivable amount by the appropriate add-on factor.

256. The future credit exposure for netted transactions is the sum of:

a. 40% of the add-on as calculated in paragraph 255; and

b. 60% of the add-on multiplied by the ratio of net current replacement cost to positive current replacement cost (NGR) where:

$$NGR = \frac{level\ of\ net\ replacement\ cost}{level\ of\ positive\ replace\ cost\ for\ transactions\ subect\ to\ legally\ enforceable\ netting\ arrangements}$$

7.4.1.4.2 Credit equivalent amount for other off-balance sheet exposures

257. Off-balance sheet exposures that are not arising from OTC derivatives are converted into credit exposure equivalents through the use of credit conversion factors (CCFs) applied to the item's notional amount:

a. Commitments with an original maturity up to one year and commitments with an original maturity over one year receive a CCF of 20% and 50%, respectively. However, any commitments that are unconditionally cancellable at any time by the IAIG without prior notice, or that effectively provide for automatic cancellation due to deterioration in a borrower's

---

① A walkaway clause is a provision within the contract that permits a non-defaulting counterparty to make only limited payments, or no payments, to the defaulter.

creditworthiness, receive a 0% CCF;

b. Direct credit substitutes receive a CCF of 100%. If an IAIG has guaranteed, sold a credit derivative for, or otherwise assumed the credit risk of a debt security, the risk charge is the same as if the IAIG were directly holding the underlying security;

c. Sale and repurchase agreements and asset sales with recourse, where the credit risk remains with the IAIG, receive a CCF of 100%;

d. Forward asset purchases, forward deposits and partly-paid shares and securities, which represent commitments with certain drawdown, receive a CCF of 100%;

e. Transaction-related contingent items receive a CCF of 50%;

f. Note issuance facilities (NIFs) and revolving underwriting facilities (RUFs) receive a CCF of 50%;

g. Short-term self-liquidating trade letters of credit that an IAIG either issues or confirms arising from the movement of goods receive a 20% CCF;

h. Where there is an undertaking to provide a commitment on an off-balance sheet item, IAIGs apply the lower of the two applicable CCFs;

i. Off-balance sheet securitisation exposures receive a CCF of 100%.

7.4.1.5 Securities financing transactions

258. The rating category for a securities financing transaction is the lower of that of the counterparty to the transaction, or that of the securities lent. Collateral received under securities financing transactions is recognised according to the same criteria as collateral received under regular lending transactions (cf. Section 7.4.2.1).

7.4.1.6 Credit risk stress factors

259. The following tables contain the ICS Credit risk stress factors for the exposure classes by ICS RC and maturity:

Table 22 Credit risk stress factors for public sector entities

ICS RC	Maturity														
	0–1	1–2	2–3	3–4	4–5	5–6	6–7	7–8	8–9	9–10	10–11	11–12	12–13	13–14	14+
1 or 2	0.1%	0.4%	0.5%	0.6%	0.7%	0.8%	0.9%	1.0%	1.0%	1.1%	1.1%	1.2%	1.2%	1.2%	1.3%
3	0.4%	1.0%	1.3%	1.5%	1.8%	2.0%	2.2%	2.4%	2.5%	2.7%	2.8%	2.9%	3.0%	3.0%	3.1%
4	1.0%	2.2%	2.6%	3.0%	3.3%	3.6%	3.9%	4.1%	4.2%	4.4%	4.5%	4.6%	4.7%	4.8%	4.9%
5	2.5%	5.1%	6.0%	6.6%	7.0%	7.3%	7.5%	7.6%	7.6%	7.7%	7.8%	7.8%	7.9%	7.9%	7.9%
6	6.3%	10.8%	11.8%	12.3%	12.5%	12.7%	12.7%	12.7%	12.7%	12.7%	12.7%	12.7%	12.7%	12.7%	12.7%
7	22.0%	24.7%	25.2%	25.3%	25.3%	25.3%	25.3%	25.3%	25.3%	25.3%	25.3%	25.3%	25.3%	25.3%	25.3%
Unrated	2.5%	5.1%	6.0%	6.6%	7.0%	7.3%	7.5%	7.6%	7.6%	7.7%	7.8%	7.8%	7.9%	7.9%	7.9%
In Default	35.0%	35.0%	35.0%	35.0%	35.0%	35.0%	35.0%	35.0%	35.0%	35.0%	35.0%	35.0%	35.0%	35.0%	35.0%

五、Level 2 Document: ICS Version 2.0 for the monitoring period

Table 23 Credit risk stress factors for corporates and reinsurance

ICS RC	Maturity														
	0-1	1-2	2-3	3-4	4-5	5-6	6-7	7-8	8-9	9-10	10-11	11-12	12-13	13-14	14+
1 or 2	0.2%	0.7%	0.9%	1.2%	1.4%	1.6%	1.7%	1.9%	2.0%	2.1%	2.2%	2.3%	2.4%	2.4%	2.5%
3	0.6%	1.3%	1.6%	1.8%	2.1%	2.3%	2.6%	2.8%	3.0%	3.2%	3.3%	3.4%	3.5%	3.6%	3.7%
4	1.4%	3.0%	3.6%	4.1%	4.5%	4.9%	5.1%	5.3%	5.4%	5.6%	5.7%	5.8%	5.9%	6.0%	6.0%
5	3.6%	7.1%	8.3%	9.0%	9.4%	9.7%	9.8%	9.8%	9.8%	9.8%	9.8%	9.8%	9.8%	9.8%	9.8%
6	8.9%	14.4%	15.3%	15.6%	15.6%	15.6%	15.6%	15.6%	15.6%	15.6%	15.6%	15.6%	15.6%	15.6%	15.6%
7	35%	35%	35%	35%	35%	35%	35%	35%	35%	35%	35%	35%	35%	35%	35%
Unrated	6.3%	10.7%	11.8%	12.3%	12.5%	12.6%	12.7%	12.7%	12.7%	12.7%	12.7%	12.7%	12.7%	12.7%	12.7%
In Default	35%	35%	35%	35%	35%	35%	35%	35%	35%	35%	35%	35%	35%	35%	35%

Table 24 Credit risk stress factors for securitisations

ICS RC	Maturity														
	0-1	1-2	2-3	3-4	4-5	5-6	6-7	7-8	8-9	9-10	10-11	11-12	12-13	13-14	14+
1 or 2	0.2%	0.7%	0.9%	1.2%	1.4%	1.6%	1.7%	1.9%	2.0%	2.1%	2.2%	2.3%	2.4%	2.4%	2.5%
3	0.6%	1.3%	1.6%	1.8%	2.1%	2.3%	2.6%	2.8%	3.0%	3.2%	3.3%	3.4%	3.5%	3.6%	3.7%
4	1.4%	3.0%	3.6%	4.1%	4.5%	4.9%	5.1%	5.3%	5.4%	5.6%	5.7%	5.8%	5.9%	6.0%	6.0%
5	10.8%	21.3%	24.9%	27.0%	28.2%	29.1%	29.4%	29.4%	29.4%	29.4%	29.4%	29.4%	29.4%	29.4%	29.4%
6	100%	100%	100%	100%	100%	100%	100%	100%	100%	100%	100%	100%	100%	100%	100%
7	100%	100%	100%	100%	100%	100%	100%	100%	100%	100%	100%	100%	100%	100%	100%
Unrated	100%	100%	100%	100%	100%	100%	100%	100%	100%	100%	100%	100%	100%	100%	100%
In Default	100%	100%	100%	100%	100%	100%	100%	100%	100%	100%	100%	100%	100%	100%	100%

Table 25 Credit risk stress factors for re-securitisations

ICS RC	Maturity														
	0-1	1-2	2-3	3-4	4-5	5-6	6-7	7-8	8-9	9-10	10-11	11-12	12-13	13-14	14+
1 or 2	0.4%	1.4%	1.8%	2.4%	2.8%	3.2%	3.4%	3.8%	4.0%	4.2%	4.4%	4.6%	4.8%	4.8%	5.0%
3	1.2%	2.6%	3.2%	3.6%	4.2%	4.6%	5.2%	5.6%	6.0%	6.4%	6.6%	6.8%	7.0%	7.2%	7.4%
4	2.8%	6.0%	7.2%	8.2%	9.0%	9.8%	10.2%	10.6%	10.8%	11.2%	11.4%	11.6%	11.8%	12.0%	12.0%
5	21.6%	42.6%	49.8%	54.0%	56.4%	58.2%	58.8%	58.8%	58.8%	58.8%	58.8%	58.8%	58.8%	58.8%	58.8%
6	100%	100%	100%	100%	100%	100%	100%	100%	100%	100%	100%	100%	100%	100%	100%
7	100%	100%	100%	100%	100%	100%	100%	100%	100%	100%	100%	100%	100%	100%	100%
Unrated	100%	100%	100%	100%	100%	100%	100%	100%	100%	100%	100%	100%	100%	100%	100%
In Default	100%	100%	100%	100%	100%	100%	100%	100%	100%	100%	100%	100%	100%	100%	100%

260. The Credit risk stress factor for policy loans is 0%. The stress factor for short-term obligations of regulated banks, as defined in paragraph 228, is 0.4%. The stress factor for

receivables from agents and brokers is 6.3%. All other assets receive a stress factor of 8%. IAIGs may exclude outstanding premiums from the exposure if insurance liabilities are recorded for the contracts relating to the outstanding premiums and the outstanding premiums are unrecorded in line with the release of the insurance liabilities when the contracts expire upon the policyholder's default.

7.4.1.7 Mortgage Loans

7.4.1.7.1 Commercial and agricultural mortgages where repayment depends on property income

261. Depending on data availability, the risk charge is calculated using one of the three following methods, in decreasing order of preference:

a. Method 1: risk charge based on the ICS Commercial Mortgage (CM) category as determined by loan-to-value (LTV) and debt service coverage ratio (DSCR);

b. Method 2: risk charge based on the ICS CM category as determined by LTV only; or

c. Method 3: no Credit Quality Differentiator used.

262. For agricultural and commercial Method 1, the mapping of the ICS CM categories 1 to 5 to LTV and DSCR is provided inT able 26. Categories CM6 and CM7 are for delinquent loans and loans in foreclosure, respectively.

Table 26 Mapping of ICS CM categories, Method 1

		LTV					
	CM	<60%	60% to 69.9%	70% to 79.9%	80% to 89.9%	90% to 99.9%	≥100%
DSCR	< 0.6	CM3	CM3	CM3	CM4	CM4	CM5
	0.6 to 0.79	CM3	CM3	CM3	CM4	CM4	CM5
	0.8 to 0.99	CM3	CM3	CM3	CM4	CM4	CM5
	1 to 1.19	CM2	CM2	CM3	CM3	CM4	CM4
	1.2 to 1.39	CM2	CM2	CM3	CM3	CM3	CM3
	1.4 to 1.59	CM1	CM2	CM2	CM2	CM3	CM3
	1.6 to 1.79	CM1	CM1	CM1	CM2	CM3	CM3
	1.8 to 1.99	CM1	CM1	CM1	CM2	CM2	CM2
	≥2	CM1	CM1	CM1	CM2	CM2	CM2

263. For agricultural and commercial Method 1, the following stress factors are used:

Table 27 Stress factors for agricultural and commercial mortgages, Method 1

ICS CM Categories	Stress factors
CM1	4.8%
CM2	6.0%

五、Level 2 Document: ICS Version 2.0 for the monitoring period

contined

ICS CM Categories	Stress factors
CM3	7.8%
CM4	15.8%
CM5	23.5%
CM6	35%
CM7	35%

264. For agricultural and commercial Method 2, where only LTV data is available, the mapping of the ICS CM categories 1 to 4 to LTV and the associated stress factors are provided in Table 28. As for Method 1, categories CM6 and CM7 are for delinquent loans and loans in foreclosure, respectively.

Table 28 Stress factors for agricultural and commercial mortgages, Method 2

ICS CM Categories	Stress factors	LTV Minimum	LTV Maximum
CM1	4.8%	0%	59%
CM2	6.0%	60%	79%
CM3	7.8%	80%	99%
CM4	15.8%	100%	NA
CM5	Not applicable		
CM6	35%		
CM7	35%		

265. For agricultural and commercial Method 3, where LTV and DSCR data are not available, a flat 8% stress factor is used.

7.4.1.7.2 Commercial and agricultural mortgages where repayment does not depend on property income

266. When the LTV ratio of the mortgage is above 60%, the risk factor is that of a regular credit exposure to the borrower. When the LTV ratio of the mortgage is 60% or lower, the risk factor is the lower of 3.6% or the risk factor for a regular credit exposure to the borrower.

7.4.1.7.3 Residential mortgages

267. For performing[①] residential mortgage loans for which repayment depends on income

---

① The distinction between performing and non-performing is consistent with the Basel Committee's definition, which establishes criteria for categorising loans and debt securities that are centred around delinquency status (90 days past due) and the unlikeliness of repayment. As such, non-performing exposures encompass: (1) all exposures defaulted, as defined under the Basel framework; or (2) all exposures impaired (ie exposures that have undergone a downward adjustment to their valuation due to deterioration in their creditworthiness); or (3) material exposures that are more than 90 days past due or where there is evidence that full repayment of principal and interest without realization of collateral is unlikely, regardless of the number of days past due.

generated by the underlying property, the factors applied are based on the mortgage's LTV ratio, as specified in the following table:

Table 29　Factors for residential mortgages for which repayment depends on income generated by the underlying property

LTV	Stress factors
LTV ≤ 60%	4.2%
60% < LTV ≤ 80%	5.4%
LTV > 80%	7.2%

268. For performing residential mortgage loans for which repayment does not depend on income generated by the underlying property, the factors applied are based on the mortgage's LTV ratio, as specified in the following table:

Table 30　Factors for residential mortgages for which repayment does not depend on income generated by the underlying property

LTV	Stress factors
LTV ≤ 40%	1.5%
40% < LTV ≤ 60%	1.8%
60% < LTV ≤ 80%	2.1%
80% < LTV ≤ 90%	2.7%
90% < LTV ≤ 100%	3.3%
LTV > 100%	4.5%

269. For non-performing mortgage loans, the factor applied is 35%.

7.4.2　Recognition of collateral, guarantees and credit derivatives

7.4.2.1　Recognition of collateral

270. A collateralised transaction is one in which:

a. An IAIG has a credit exposure or potential credit exposure; and

b. That credit exposure or potential credit exposure is hedged in whole or in part by collateral posted by a counterparty or by a third party on behalf of the counterparty.

271. Only the following collateral categories are eligible to be recognised:

a. Securities that are either issued by a sovereign entity or have ICS RC 4 or better;

b. Gold;

c. Mutual funds where:

- a price is publicly quoted daily; and
- the mutual fund is limited to investing in the eligible collateral listed above.

d. Letters of credit.

五、Level 2 Document: ICS Version 2.0 for the monitoring period

272. The Credit risk charge calculation takes into account collateral provided all of the following requirements are met:

a. The effects of collateral are not double counted. In particular, collateral on claims for which an issue-specific rating is used that already reflects that collateral is not recognised. All criteria around the use of ratings remain applicable to collateral.

b. All documentation used in collateralised transactions are binding on all parties and legally enforceable in all relevant jurisdictions. The IAIG has conducted sufficient legal review to verify this and have a well-founded legal basis to reach this conclusion, and undertaken such further review as necessary to ensure continuing enforceability.

c. The legal mechanism by which collateral is pledged or transferred ensures that the IAIG has the right to liquidate or take legal possession of the collateral in a timely manner in the event of the default, insolvency or bankruptcy (or one or more otherwise-defined credit events set out in the transaction documentation) of the counterparty (and, where applicable, of the custodian holding the collateral). Furthermore, the IAIG has taken all necessary steps to fulfil those requirements under the law applicable to the IAIG's interest in the collateral for obtaining and maintaining an enforceable security interest, eg by registering it with a registrar, or for exercising a right to net or set off in relation to title transfer collateral.

d. The credit quality of the counterparty and the value of the collateral do not have a material positive correlation. For example, securities issued by the counterparty-or by any related group entity-are not eligible.

e. The IAIG has clear and robust procedures for the timely liquidation of collateral to ensure that any legal conditions required for declaring the default of the counterparty and liquidating the collateral are observed, and that collateral can be liquidated promptly.

f. Where collateral is held by a custodian, the IAIG takes reasonable steps to ensure that the custodian segregates the collateral from its own assets.

g. The collateral is pledged for at least the life of the exposure.

273. Where the collateral is denominated in a currency different from that in which the exposure is denominated, the amount of the exposure deemed to be protected is 80% of the amount of collateral, converted at current exchange rates.

7.4.2.1.1 Default approach to the recognition of collateral: the substitution approach

274. The portion of an exposure that is collateralised by eligible financial collateral valued at market is redistributed into the rating category applicable to the collateral instrument, while the remainder of the exposure is assigned the rating category appropriate to the counterparty.

7.4.2.1.2 Alternative approach for collateralised non-life reinsurance exposures: the haircut approach

275. Under the haircut approach, collateral may be recognised if it satisfies requirements a) to f) of paragraph 272 and is pledged for at least one year.

276. The haircut approach reduces the exposure amount to account for collateral held by the ceding insurer. The adjusted reinsurance exposure is defined by:

Adjusted Reinsurance Exposure = Reinsurance Assets and Receivables + Capital Requirements-Collateral

where Capital Requirements consist of the risk charges for Non-life risk, Catastrophe risk, Market risks and Credit risk on the reinsured business and/or its supporting collateral, aggregated using the correlations specified in section 7.6.

277. The risk charges for Non-life and Catastrophe risks are equal to the reduction in the ICS risk charges attributable to the reinsurance arrangement. This amount is aggregated with the Market risk charge and the Credit risk charges using 25% correlations.

278. The Credit and Market risk charges are specified as follows:

a. The Credit risk charge is calculated for all of the assets held as collateral.

b. The Asset Concentration risk charge is the granularity adjustment for all of the assets held as collateral, calculated on a standalone basis (ie in isolation from the ceding insurer's own asset portfolio).

c. The Currency risk charge is calculated on a standalone basis for the reinsured liabilities in combination with the assets held as collateral. For the purpose of this calculation, the base currency is taken to be the currency in which the ceded liabilities are denominated, and the deduction referred to in pointg of paragraph 210 is not applied.

d. The Interest Rate and Non-Default Spread risk charges are calculated on a standalone basis for the ceded liabilities in combination with the assets held as collateral.

e. The Equity and Real Estate risk charges are calculated for all of the assets held as collateral.

f. The Asset Concentration, Currency, Interest Rate, Non-Default Spread, Equity and Real Estate risk charges are aggregated to obtain the Market risk charge using the correlations specified in section 7.3.1.

279. The resulting Credit risk charge for collateralised non-life reinsurance is equal to the adjusted reinsurance exposure multiplied by the Credit risk factor applicable to the reinsurer.

7.4.2.2 Recognition of guarantees and credit derivatives

280. In order to determine the ICS RC of their counterparties, IAIGs may take into account the credit protection provided by guarantees and credit derivatives, provided that all of the

following conditions are met:

a. The guarantees or credit derivatives are direct, explicit, irrevocable and unconditional.

b. The guarantor or protection provider belongs to a higher rating category than the counterparty covered by the guarantee or protection.

c. The IAIG fulfils certain minimum conditions relating to risk management described in section 7.4.2.2.1.

281. The capital treatment is founded on the substitution approach, whereby the protected portion of a counterparty exposure is assigned the rating category of the guarantor or protection provider, while the uncovered portion retains the rating category of the underlying counterparty.

7.4.2.2.1 Risk management requirements

282. The minimum conditions referred to in paragraph 280, applicable to both guarantees and credit derivatives, are the following:

a. The effects of credit protection are not double counted. In particular, no recognition is given to credit protection on claims for which an issue-specific rating is used that already reflects that protection. All criteria around the use of ratings remain applicable to guarantees and credit derivatives.

b. With the exception of credit protection provided by sovereigns as specified in paragraph 296, a guarantee, counter-guarantee or credit derivative must represent a direct claim on the protection provider and must explicitly refer to a specific exposure or pool of exposures, so that the extent of the cover is clearly defined and incontrovertible.

c. The credit protection contract is irrevocable, except in case of non-payment by the protection purchaser of money due in respect of the credit protection contract.

d. There is no clause in the contract that allows the protection provider to unilaterally cancel the credit cover or to increase the effective cost of cover as a result of deteriorating credit quality in the hedged exposure.

e. The contract is unconditional, ie there is no clause in the protection contract outside the direct control of the IAIG that could prevent the protection provider from being obliged to pay out in a timely manner in the event that the original counterparty fails to make the payment (s) due.

f. All documentation used for documenting guarantees and credit derivatives are binding on all parties and legally enforceable in all relevant jurisdictions. IAIGs have conducted sufficient legal review to verify this and have a well-founded legal basis to reach this conclusion, and undertake such further review as necessary to ensure continuing enforceability.

283. In addition to the requirements set in paragraph 282, the recognition of a guarantee is

subject to all of the following conditions:

a. On the qualifying default/non-payment of the counterparty, the IAIG pursues the guarantor in a timely manner for any monies outstanding under the documentation governing the transaction. The guarantor makes one lump sum payment of all monies under such documentation to the IAIG, or the guarantor assumes the future payment obligations of the counterparty covered by the guarantee. The IAIG has the right to receive any such payments from the guarantor without first having to take legal action in order to pursue the counterparty for payment.

b. The guarantee is an explicitly documented obligation assumed by the guarantor.

c. Except as noted in the following sentence, the guarantee covers all types of payments the underlying obligor is expected to make under the documentation governing the transaction, for example notional amount, margin payments etc. Where a guarantee excludes certain types of payment, the corresponding amounts are treated as unsecured amounts.

284. In addition to the requirements set in paragraph 282, the recognition of a credit derivative contract is subject to all of the following conditions:

a. The credit events specified by the contracting parties cover at a minimum:

i. The failure to pay the amounts due under the terms of the underlying obligation that are in effect at the time of such failure (with a grace period that is in line with the grace period in the underlying obligation);

ii. The bankruptcy, insolvency or inability of the obligor to pay its debts, or its failure or admission in writing of its inability generally to pay its debts as they become due, and analogous events; and

iii. The restructuring of the underlying obligation involving forgiveness or postponement of principal, interest or fees that results in a credit loss event (ie charge-off, specific provision or other similar debit to the profit and loss account).

b. If the credit derivative covers obligations that do not include the underlying obligation, point g) below governs whether the asset mismatch is permissible.

c. The credit derivative does not terminate prior to the expiration of any grace period required for a default on the underlying obligation to occur as a result of a failure to pay.

d. Credit derivatives allowing for cash settlement are recognised for capital purposes insofar as a robust valuation process is in place in order to estimate loss reliably. There is a clearly specified period for obtaining post-credit event valuations of the underlying obligation. If the reference obligation specified in the credit derivative for purposes of cash settlement is different than the underlying obligation, point g) below governs whether the asset mismatch is

五、Level 2 Document: ICS Version 2.0 for the monitoring period

permissible.

e. If the protection purchaser's right/ability to transfer the underlying obligation to the protection provider is required for settlement, the terms of the underlying obligation provide that any required consent to such transfer be not unreasonably withheld.

f. The identity of the parties responsible for determining whether a credit event has occurred is clearly defined. This determination is not the sole responsibility of the protection seller. The protection buyer has the right/ability to inform the protection provider of the occurrence of a credit event.

g. A mismatch between the underlying obligation and the reference obligation under the credit derivative (ie the obligation used for purposes of determining cash settlement value or the deliverable obligation) is permissible if:

i. The reference obligation ranks *pari passu* with or is junior to the underlying obligation; and

ii. The underlying obligation and reference obligation share the same obligor (ie the same legal entity) and legally enforceable cross-default or cross-acceleration clauses are in place.

h. A mismatch between the underlying obligation and the obligation used for purposes of determining whether a credit event has occurred is permissible if:

i. The latter obligation ranks *pari passu* with or is junior to the underlying obligation; and

ii. The underlying obligation and reference obligation share the same obligor (ie the same legal entity) and legally enforceable cross-default or cross-acceleration clauses are in place.

i. Only credit default swaps and total return swaps that provide credit protection equivalent to guarantees are eligible for recognition. Where an IAIG buys credit protection through a total return swap and records the net payments received on the swap as net income, but does not record offsetting deterioration in the value of the asset that is protected (either through reductions in fair value or by increasing provisions), the credit protection is not recognised.

285. When the restructuring of the underlying obligation is not covered by the credit derivative, but the other requirements above are met, partial recognition of the credit derivative is allowed, up to a maximum of 60% of the lower of:

a. The amount of the credit derivative; and

b. The amount of the underlying obligation.

7.4.2.2.2　Eligible guarantors

286. Only the credit protection provided by the following counterparties are eligible for

recognition:

a. Sovereigns;

b. Externally rated public sector entities, banks and securities firms with a higher rating category than that of the counterparty; and

c. Other entities, including parent, subsidiaries and affiliate companies of an obligor, provided they have a higher rating category than that of the obligor.

In addition, a guarantee or credit protection provided by a related party (parent, subsidiary or affiliate) of the IAIG is not eligible for recognition.

7.4.2.2.3 Capital treatment

287. The protected portion of a counterparty exposure is assigned the rating category of the protection provider. The uncovered portion of the exposure is assigned the rating category of the underlying counterparty.

288. Where the amount guaranteed or covered with credit protection is less than the amount of the exposure, and the secured and unsecured portions are of equal seniority (ie the IAIG and the guarantor share losses on a pro-rata basis), the protected portion of the exposure receives the treatment applicable to eligible guarantees and credit derivatives, and the remainder is treated as unsecured.

289. Where an IAIG transfers a portion of the risk of an exposure in one or more tranches to protection sellers and retains some level of risk, and the risk transferred and the risk retained are of different seniority, all tranches are considered as securitisation exposures based on the ratings of the guarantors. If a tranche does not carry a rating, it is considered as an unrated securitisation exposure even if the underlying exposure is rated. Where such treatment leads to a Credit risk charge higher that the risk charge calculated without taking the guarantee into account, IAIGs may ignore the guarantee.

290. Materiality thresholds on amounts due below which no payment is made in the event of loss are considered unrated securitisation exposures.

7.4.2.2.4 Currency mismatches

291. Where the credit protection is denominated in a currency different from that in which the exposure is denominated, the amount of the exposure deemed to be protected is 80% of the nominal amount of the credit protection, converted at current exchange rates.

7.4.2.2.5 Maturity mismatches

292. When the residual maturity of the credit protection is less than that of the underlying exposure (maturity mismatch) and the credit protection has either an original maturity of less than one year or a residual maturity of less than three months, the protection is not recognised.

293. In other cases of maturity mismatch, the following adjustment is applied:

$$P_a = P * \frac{t - 0.25}{T - 0.25}$$

where:

- P_a is the value of the credit protection adjusted for maturity mismatch;

- P is the nominal amount of the credit protection, adjusted for currency mismatch if applicable;

- T is the lower of 5 and the residual maturity of the exposure expressed in years; and

- t is the lower of T and the residual maturity of the credit protection arrangement expressed in years.

294. The residual maturity of the underlying exposure is taken as the longest possible remaining time before the counterparty is scheduled to fulfil its obligation, taking into account any applicable grace period.

295. For the credit protection, embedded options that may reduce the term of the protection are taken into account so that the shortest possible effective maturity is used. In particular:

a. Where a call is at the discretion of the protection seller, the residual maturity corresponds to the remaining time to the first call date.

b. Where a call is at the discretion of the IAIG buying protection but the terms of the arrangement at origination contain a positive incentive for the IAIG to call the transaction before contractual maturity, the residual maturity corresponds to the remaining time to the first call date.

7.4.2.2.6 Sovereign counter-guarantees

296. Claims covered by a guarantee that is indirectly counter-guaranteed by a sovereign may be treated as covered by a sovereign guarantee provided that:

a. The sovereign counter-guarantee covers all credit risk elements of the claim;

b. Both the original guarantee and the counter-guarantee meet all the operational requirements for guarantees, except that the counter-guarantee need not be direct and explicit to the original claim; and

c. The cover is robust, and there is no historical evidence suggesting that the coverage of the counter-guarantee is less than effectively equivalent to that of a direct sovereign guarantee.

7.4.2.2.7 Other items

297. Where an IAIG has multiple types of risk mitigation arrangements covering a single exposure, this exposure is subdivided into portions covered by each type of risk mitigation arrangement and the rating category for each portion is determined separately.

298. When a credit protection provided by a single protection provider has different maturities, it is subdivided into separate protections.

7.4.3 Use of external credit ratings

7.4.3.1 Eligible external credit ratings

299. IAIGs may use ratings produced by rating agencies other than those referred to in paragraph 149 of the ICS Level 1 document, provided that both of the following requirements are met:

a. The rating agency is regulated or recognised by a suitable government authority in all of the jurisdictions in which the agency issues ratings that the IAIG chooses to use.

b. The rating agency publishes at least annually publicly available default and transition statistics extending back at least seven years, and satisfies all of the following six criteria:

i. Objectivity: The rating agency's methodology for assigning credit assessments is rigorous, systematic, and subject to some form of validation based on historical experience. Moreover, assessments are subject to ongoing review and are responsive to changes in financial conditions. The agency has an assessment methodology for each market segment, including rigorous back testing that has been applied for at least one year and, preferably, three years.

ii. Independence: The rating agency is independent and is not subject to political or economic pressures that may influence the rating. The assessment process is free from any constraints that could arise in situations where the composition of the board of directors or the shareholder structure of the assessment institution may be seen as creating a conflict of interest.

iii. International access/Transparency: The individual assessments, the key elements underlining the assessments, and whether the issuer participated in the assessment process are made publicly available on a non-selective basis. In addition, the general procedures, methodologies and assumptions for arriving at assessments used by the rating agency are publicly available.

iv. Disclosure: A rating agency discloses the following information: its code of conduct; the general nature of its compensation arrangements with assessed entities; its assessment methodologies, including the definition of default, the time horizon, and the meaning of each rating; the actual default rates experienced in each assessment category; and the transitions of the assessments, eg the likelihood of AA ratings becoming A over time.

v. Resources: A rating agency has sufficient resources to carry out high quality credit assessments. These resources allow for substantial ongoing contact with senior and operational levels within the entities assessed in order to add value to the credit assessments. Such assessments are based on methodologies that combine qualitative and quantitative approaches.

五、Level 2 Document: ICS Version 2.0 for the monitoring period

vi. Credibility: The rating agency's external credit assessments are widely used by independent parties (investors, insurers, trading partners). In addition, the rating agency has internal procedures to prevent the misuse of confidential information.

7.4.3.2 Definition of rating categories

300. The mapping of the agency's ratings to ICS RCs is based on the average of the three-year Cumulative Default Rates (CDRs) associated with the agency's ratings, as follows:

Table 31 Mapping of ratings by other rating agencies

ICS RC	Average 3-year CDR based on over 20 years of published data	Average 3-year CDR based on between 7 and 20 years of published data
1		
2	$0 \leqslant CDR \leqslant 0.15\%$	
3	$0.15\% < CDR \leqslant 0.35\%$	$0 \leqslant CDR \leqslant 0.15\%$
4	$0.35\% < CDR \leqslant 1.20\%$	$0.15\% < CDR \leqslant 0.35\%$
5	$1.20\% < CDR \leqslant 10.00\%$	$0.35\% < CDR \leqslant 1.20\%$
6	$10.00\% < CDR \leqslant 25.00\%$	$1.20\% < CDR \leqslant 10.00\%$
7	$CDR > 25\%$	$CDR > 10\%$

7.4.3.3 Use of ratings

301. IAIGs choose the rating agencies they intend to rely on and use their ratings consistently for each type of credit exposure.

302. Any rating used to determine an ICS RC is publicly available, ie the rating is published in an accessible form and included in the rating agency's transition matrix.

303. If an IAIG is relying on multiple rating agencies and there is only one rating for a particular security, that assessment is used to determine the ICS RC. If there are two ratings from the rating agencies used by an IAIG, and those two ratings are mapped to different ICS RC, the IAIG uses the ICS RC corresponding to the lower of the two ratings. If there are three or more ratings for a security from an IAIG's chosen rating agencies, one of the ratings that corresponds to the highest ICS RC is excluded, and the rating that corresponds to the highest rating category of those that remain is used to determine the ICS RC of the security.

304. Where a particular security has one or more issue-specific rating, the ICS RC for that security is based on these ratings. Otherwise, the following principles apply:

a. Where the borrower has a specific rating for an issued debt security other than the one in which the IAIG is invested, an ICS RC of 4 or better on the rated security may only be applied to the IAIG's unrated investment if it ranks *pari passu* or senior to the rated security in all respects. If not, the credit rating cannot be used and the IAIG's investment is treated as an unrated obligation.

b. Where the borrower has an issuer rating, only senior securities issued by that issuer will benefit from an investment-grade (ICS RC 4 or better) issuer assessment; other unassessed securities issued by that issuer are treated as unrated. If either the issuer or one of its issues has an ICS RC of 5 or weaker, this rating is used to determine the ICS RC for an unrated claim on the issuer.

c. Short-term assessments for a given security or facility can be used only for that security or securities issued by that rated facility. They can neither be generalised to other short-term securities nor used to support a rating category assignment for an unrated long-term security.

d. Where the rating category for an unrated exposure is based on the rating of an equivalent exposure to the borrower, a foreign currency rating may be used only for exposures denominated in that foreign currency. Domestic currency ratings, if separate, are used to determine the rating category for securities denominated in the domestic currency only.

305. The following additional conditions apply to the use of ratings:

a. External assessments for one entity within a corporate group are not used to determine the rating category for other entities within the same group.

b. No rating based on assets that the entity possesses is inferred for an unrated entity. The use of internal ratings is not allowed.

c. IAIGs do not recognise collateral or guarantees in the Credit risk charge calculation if these credit enhancements have already been reflected in the issue-specific rating.

d. IAIGs do not use a rating that is at least partly based on unfunded support (eg guarantees, credit enhancement or liquidity facilities) provided by the IAIG itself or one of its affiliates.

e. Any assessment used takes into account the entire amount of Credit risk exposure an IAIG has with regard to all payments owed to it. In particular, if an IAIG is owed both principal and interest, the assessment fully takes into account the Credit risk associated with repayment of both principal and interest.

7.4.3.4 Exposures in default

306. Assets for which there is reasonable doubt about the timely collection of the full amount of principal or interest, including those assets that are contractually more than 90 days in arrears, are considered as defaulted exposures for the calculation of the Credit risk charge.

307. The exposure amount for a defaulted asset is taken net of all balance sheet write-downs and specific provisions that have been recorded for the asset.

五、Level 2 Document: ICS Version 2.0 for the monitoring period

7.4.4 Supervisor-owned and controlled credit assessment (SOCCA) processes

308. A SOCCA process may be recognised in the ICS if all of the following criteria are met:

a. Objectivity: The SOCCA's methodology for assigning credit assessments is rigorous, systematic, and subject to some form of validation. Moreover, assessments are subject to ongoing review and responsive to changes in financial condition.

b. Independence: The SOCCA process is aligned with the regulatory objectives of the supervisor, evidenced by the supervisor's approval of the credit assessment process. Any outsourcing arrangement of the credit assessment is held to the same standards of competency and independence as the in-house credit assessment processes.

c. International access/transparency: IAIGs with operations outside the jurisdiction of the SOCCA process can request designations/ratings be assigned to securities they own. Public access to the credit assessment is available through third-party platforms.

d. Disclosure: Default statistics over time are developed for each designation/rating so that three-year cumulative default rates (CDRs) can be derived from published statistics.

e. Resources: Staff has appropriate qualifications and experience to undertake the credit assessment process. The SOCCA process relies on adequate resources to carry out the credit assessments required by the supervisor.

f. Credibility: The SOCCA process relies on internal procedures to prevent the misuse of confidential information. The SOCCA process has at least 10 years of demonstrable business history in assessing the Credit risk of a large number of securities such that statistical performance data can be derived. All designations/ratings are updated at least on a yearly basis; in addition, the designations/ratings are reviewed as soon as a significant event occurs that may affect them.

g. Alignment of interests with the purposes of prudential supervision: The entity performing the credit assessment is fully owned and controlled by a supervisory authority. There are policies approved by the supervisory authority as to how the credit assessment process is applied.

7.5 Operational risk

309. The Operational risk charge is calculated as follows:

$$\begin{aligned} Op\ riskcarge = &\max[non\_life\_premium\_exposure * factor, \\ & non\_life\_liability\_exposure * factor] \\ & + non\_life\_growth\_exposure * factor \\ & + \max[life\_(risk)\_premium\_exposure \\ & * factor, life\_(risk)\_liability\_exposure * factor] \\ & + life\_(risk)\_growth\_exposure * factor \end{aligned}$$

$$+ life\_(non\_risk)\_liability\_exposure * factor$$

310. The Operational risk components are computed as factors multiplied by risk exposures. The same factors are applied across geographical segments as defined in 7.1.2.

311. The exposures and stress factors for Operational risk are set in the following table.

Table 32 Operational risk exposures and stress factors

	Premium	Growth	Liabilities
Risk from Non-life Operations			
Exposure	Gross written premium (GWP) in most recent financial year	GWP in most recent financial year in excess of the growth threshold (20%) compared to the previous year's GWP	Gross current estimate
Factor	2.75%	2.75%	2.75%
Risk from Life Operations			
Exposure	Life (risk): GWP in most recent financial year	Life (risk): GWP in most recent financial year in excess of the growth threshold (20%) compared to the previous year's GWP	Life (risk): Gross current estimate Life (non-risk): Gross current estimate
Factor	Life (risk): 4%	Life (risk): 4%	Life (risk): 0.45% Life (non-risk): 0.40%

312. GWP includes all business (new and renewal) written during the specified financial year before any allowance for reinsurance or other related recoverables. For single premium policies, premiums are included in full as written during the year. For other insurance policies, GWP includes premiums due to the IAIG during the specified time period (financial year) on all business in-force.

313. Gross current estimates are considered before any allowance for reinsurance or other related recoverables.

314. To calculate the growth risk component of Operational risk, the GWP for the two most recent financial years for non-life and life (risk) are used. The figures are considered before the effect of ceded reinsurance and on a consolidated basis.

7.6 Aggregation/Diversification of ICS Risk Charges

315. The top-level aggregation matrix between major risk categories is:

Table 33 Aggregation matrix between risks

	Life	Non-life	Catastrophe	Market	Credit
Life	100%	0%	25%	25%	25%
Non-life	0%	100%	25%	25%	25%

continued

	Life	Non-life	Catastrophe	Market	Credit
Catastrophe	25%	25%	100%	25%	25%
Market	25%	25%	25%	100%	25%
Credit	25%	25%	25%	25%	100%

7.7 Non-Insurance Risk Charges

316. For insurance or insurance-related entities, the capital requirement is calculated as described in sections 7.1 to 7.6.

317. For financial non-insurance entities with a sectoral capital requirement, the capital requirement is as follows:

a. For consolidated banking entities it is the maximum of Basel III risk-weighted assets or leverage ratio.

b. For consolidated non-banking entities it is equal to the maximum of the sectoral capital requirement and 15% of three year average gross income.

c. For banking and non-banking entities reported as an equity method investment it is equal to the proportional sectoral charge.

d. For both banking and non-banking entities reported as a market value investment it is equal to the equity charge on the investment as described in section 7.3.4.

318. For financial non-insurance entities without a sectoral capital requirement, the capital requirement is as follows:

a. For consolidated banking entities it is equal to 4% of the exposure as determined by the leverage ratio.

b. For consolidated non-banking entities it is equal to 15% of three year average gross income.

c. For banking entities reported as an equity method investment it is equal to the proportional sectoral leverage ratio.

d. For non-banking entities reported as an equity method investment it is equal to the proportional 15% of three year average gross income.

e. For both banking and non-banking entities reported as a market value investment it is equal to the equity charge on the investment as described in section 7.3.4.

319. For non-financial entities, the capital requirement is equal to the equity charge on the equity method or market value investment as described in paragraph 207, a) to d).

8 Reference ICS: Tax

8.1 General principles

320. The group effective tax rate (ETR) is calculated as a weighted average statutory effective tax rate, weighted using the previous three-year average of GAAP earnings before tax on a sub-group/entity level basis. The scope of the weighted average calculation is limited to insurance-related activities, and GAAP earnings before tax is floored at zero.

321. Statutory effective tax rates that have been enacted or substantially enacted as of the reporting date are used for the group ETR calculation. ①

8.2 Deferred tax from the ICS Adjustments

322. DTAs and DTLs arising from ICS Adjustments, before the utilisation assessment defined by paragraph 323, may be offset if both of the following criteria are met:

a. The entity has a legally enforceable right to offset current tax assets against current tax liabilities.

b. Deferred taxes relate to income taxes levied by the same taxation authority on either:

• The same taxable entity; or

• Different taxable entities that intend either to settle current tax liabilities and assets on a net basis, or to realise the assets and settle the liabilities simultaneously, in each future period in which significant amounts of deferred taxes are expected to be settled or recovered.

8.2.1 Utilisation assessment of DTAs recognised from the ICS Adjustments

323. The DTA recognised as a result of the ICS Adjustments is capped at any net GAAP DTL plus gross DTL recognised from the ICS Adjustments according to the following calculation:

Add:

a. Gross jurisdictional audited GAAP DTL; and

b. Gross DTL recognised from the ICS Adjustments.

Subtract:

c. Gross jurisdictional audited GAAP DTA; and

d. DTL associated with assets subject to deduction from Tier 1 capital resources (as per section 6.4.1 of the Level 1 Document).

324. If the calculation is negative, the DTA recognised as a result of the ICS Adjustments is zero.

---

① For example, a tax authority announces tax rate changes that would have a material impact for future periods. In such a case, the newly announced statutory effective tax rate is used in the group ETR calculation.

325. The gross jurisdictional audited GAAP DTL and DTA referred to in paragraph 323 are limited to DTL and DTA from insurance-related activities.

8.3 Tax effect on the ICS insurance capital requirement

326. The ICS insurance capital requirement is reduced by the amount of utilisable tax effect.

327. The utilisable tax effect on the ICS insurance capital requirement is calculated using the following formula:

max (0, min (notional tax effect on insurance capital requirement, 20% * ICS insurance capital requirement, a + b + c-d))

where:

- notional tax effect on insurance capital requirement = ICS Insurance capital requirement * group ETR;

- $a = 85\% *$

$$\sum_{Tax\ sub-group/entities} \min\left(\begin{array}{c} Tax\ loss\ carry\ back\ capacity, \\ Allocated\ notional\ tax\ effect\ on\ insurance\ capital\ requirement \end{array}\right)$$

- b = post-stress future taxable income * group ETR;

- c = max (0, DTL for insurance-related activities on ICS balance sheet-DTA for insurance-related activities on ICS balance sheet); and

- d = max [0, min (15% * ICS insurance capital requirement, DTA for insurance-related activities on ICS balance sheet-DTL for insurance-related activities on ICS balance sheet).

8.3.1 Component a: tax loss carry backs

328. A tax loss carry back is defined as a mechanism allowing a sub-group/entity to offset current net operating losses against tax obligations from previous years (the number of years allowed differs between jurisdictions).

329. In order to perform the calculation of componenta in the utilisable tax effect:

- The tax loss carry back capacity for insurance-related activities is evaluated at the legal entity or sub-group level, including any fiscal unity for corporate tax as of the ICS reporting date.

- The notional tax effect on the ICS insurance capital requirement is allocated between tax sub-groups/entities using a weighted average based on GAAP/SAP insurance liabilities.

8.3.2 Component b: post-stress future taxable income projections

330. In order to perform the calculation of component b in the utilisable tax effect:

- When the IAIG projects net losses for the cumulative five-year period, componentb is set to zero.

- Otherwise, component b is approximated by 50% of the total historical five years' GAAP earnings before tax on the consolidated financial statement, adjusted for mergers, acquisitions and dispositions.

8.3.3 Components c and d: Deferred taxes

331. DTA and DTL used in components c and d are net of deferred taxes associated with assets subject to deduction from Tier 1 capital resources (as per section 6.4.1 of the Level 1 Document).

9 Additional Reporting

9.1 GAAP Plus

9.1.1 Overview

332. GAAP Plus begins with the group balance sheet as outlined in Section 4. The following GAAP Plus approaches provide guidelines and specific examples for adjustments under the various jurisdictional GAAPs applicable for IAIGs so that each can arrive at a consolidated GAAP Plus balance sheet following the application of these adjustments. Like the MAV approach under the Reference ICS, GAAP Plus adjustments address only the most significant or material items on the balance sheet, specifically, insurance-related liabilities and invested assets.

333. GAAP Plus consists of four main approaches: US GAAP/SAP, Japanese GAAP, IFRS and Chinese C-ROSS. Japanese GAAP Plus (J-GAAP Plus) is subject to the Monitoring Period as specified in this document. US GAAP/SAP, IFRS and Chinese C-ROSS Plus approaches are excluded from this document as they remain under development and subject to Field Testing.

334. For J-GAAP Plus, the following considerations apply:

a. A liability is recognised and derecognised in accordance with the IAIG's jurisdictional GAAP.

b. The definition of contract boundaries is in accordance with the IAIG's jurisdictional GAAP.

c. GAAP Plus estimates of insurance liabilities (and related reinsurance recoverables) are calculated using discounting yield curves or rates as specified under applicable jurisdictional GAAP rules or as outlined in the applicable specific GAAP Plus approach.

d. The calculation of GAAP Plus adjustments are based on up-to-date information and credible assumptions.

e. Policy loans are reported gross of insurance liabilities.

f. Non insurance liabilities (ie issued debt) are reported in accordance with jurisdictional

GAAP. Balances reported at cost are not adjusted to fair value.

g. Risk margins, conservatism in assumptions and provisions for adverse deviation are removed from the valuation of insurance liabilities where insurance liabilities are not calculated as a whole.

h. MOCE, as defined under the standard method, is added to the balance sheet as a liability.

i. Any adjustments to deferred taxes follow the reference method as outlined in section 7.7.

335. When the insurance liability balances are calculated under more than one set of GAAP rules, the IAIG uses the most appropriate GAAP Plus jurisdictional approach for each component of insurance liabilities in the aggregated balance sheet to adjust balances to a current estimate liability.

336. An AOCI adjustment is included in capital resources in order to exclude any unrealised gains and losses on available for sale debt securities that meet defined criteria provided in section 9.1.2.1.

337. Aside from the AOCI adjustment, all adjustments detailed in section 6 apply equally to J-GAAP Plus as for the Reference ICS.

338. J-GAAP Plus provides specific methodologies for certain risk charges. Unless otherwise specified, the risk charges are calculated consistently with Section 7. These calculations are detailed in sections 9.1.2.2 to 9.1.2.5.

9.1.2 Japanese GAAP (J-GAAP) Plus Approach

339. The following pertains to IAIGs reporting audited consolidated financial statements on the basis of Japanese GAAP.

340. Invested Assets: No adjustment is required. Invested assets are reported consistent with the treatment under J-GAAP. Certain assets backing life liabilities are subject to the AOCI adjustment that reverses unrealised gains and losses reported in AOCI and, in essence, restates asset values from fair value to cost. See the GAAP Plus AOCI adjustment in section 9.1.2.1.

341. Life Insurance Liabilities (excluding group policies): Life insurance liabilities are adjusted to a current estimate by reflecting balances as derived from the Japanese GAAP statutory cash flow test assuming a full time horizon.

a. Under the full time horizon cash flow analysis, life insurers are required to assess whether future cash flows generated from current assets cover the future cash flows (net of cash-inflows and cash-outflows) from insurance liabilities.

b. The net amount in shortage or excess of insurance liabilities at the end of in-force business is discounted and the resulting value is added to (or deducted from) insurance liabilities.

c. The discount rate is the current portfolio investment yield (book yield) plus reinvestment assumption that is consistent with cash flows generated on the asset side defined in paragraph 341 d).

d. For purposes of projecting cash flows, investment returns from reinvestments and new money are defined based on an assumption that an IAIG invests in Japanese Government bonds with an average duration equal to the average duration of Japanese government bonds in which the IAIG invested in the previous financial year.

e. The actual current experience, including mortality, lapse, expense ratio and interest rate, is used in the calculation of the future cash flows for insurance liabilities.

f. New business is not taken into consideration.

g. The current portfolio investment yield (book yield) is used to generate the future cash flows from the current asset portfolio.

h. The future cash flow projection is on a pre-tax basis.

342. Group Life Insurance Liabilities: Group insurance contracts are scoped out from the Japanese GAAP statutory cash flow test. The J-GAAP Plus valuation approach for group contracts is the same as Japanese GAAP and therefore no adjustment is required.

343. Non-life Insurance Liabilities: Non-life insurance liabilities are adjusted to reflect balances as derived from the Japanese GAAP statutory cash flow test assuming a full time horizon.

a. Under the full time horizon cash flow analysis, non-life insurers are required to assess whether reported insurance liabilities (GAAP basis premium provision) is adequate to cover all expected future cash flow.

b. The net amount in shortage or excess of insurance liabilities is discounted and the resulting value is added to (or deducted from) insurance liabilities.

c. The actual experience including claim frequency, lapse, expense ratio and interest rate is used for the calculation of future cash flows in the insurance liability. New business is not taken into consideration.

d. Discounting is based on a government bond yield curve as specified under the future cash flow analysis defined by the article 121 of the Japanese Insurance Act.

344. Liabilities for Options and Guarantees: Options and guarantees are adjusted for J-GAAP Plus using the method described under the MAV approach.

9.1.2.1 Capital Resources: AOCI Adjustment

345. The AOCI adjustment is applicable under J-GAAP Plus where life insurance liabilities

are discounted using an asset book yield and available for sale debt securities backing those liabilities are reported at fair value. The AOCI adjustment is not applicable where liabilities are discounted using a market rate/curve. In order to address the asymmetry in accounting and the resulting volatility in capital resources, an AOCI adjustment has been defined under J-GAAP Plus such that unrealised gains/losses associated with available for sale debt securities are deducted from Tier 1 capital resources if all of the following criteria aremet:

a. IAIGs must meet all operational criteria in order to be eligible to use the AOCI adjustment:

i. The IAIG maintains Asset/Liability Management Policies that provides for specific identification and duration matching of asset/liability portfolios.

ii. The IAIG maintains systems and processes to evaluate the effectiveness of the duration matching including independent verification, regular tests and reporting to the Board of Directors.

iii. Evaluation of the effectiveness of duration matching includes the following test which must be met in order for assets to be included in the AOCI adjustment:

iv. $0.8 \leqslant \dfrac{D(L)}{D(A)} \leqslant 1.25$ where D is duration.

b. The net unrealised gain/loss to be excluded must relate to debt securities that are classified as available for sale and back long-term liabilities.

c. The portfolio is segregated for the purpose of asset/liability matching.

d. The unrealised gain/loss is not likely to be realised.

346. The related asset balances are restated to amortised cost for purposes of calculating the Credit risk charge (Section 7.4) but are not restated on the reported J-GAAP Plus balance sheet. The AOCI adjustment is reported as a direct adjustment to Capital Resources.

347. The AOCI adjustment is calculated beginning with the *Accumulated unrealised gains (losses) on AFS debt securities reported in OCI balance* as reported in the J-GAAP Plus balance sheet. Deductions from this balance are applied for any unrealised gains/losses relating to the following:

a. Debt securities that are backing short-term insurance liabilities. Short-term is defined as having a contract duration of one year or less.

b. Debt securities that are backing liabilities discounted using a market based rate/curve.

c. Debt securities designated as fair value accounting hedges.

d. Debt securities not meeting the operational criteria (eg not specifically identified in a separate portfolio for asset/liability matching or not meeting the operational criteria effectiveness test).

e. Debt securities where, based on management judgment, it is more likely than not that unrealised gains/losses would be realised through sale, conversion, prepayment, etc. For example, this could include certain callable bonds where the call price is lower than the market price or residential mortgage backed securities (RMBS), student loans, consumer or other asset backed securities (ABS) that are likely to be prepaid. A more likely than not assessment in this context is defined as a greater than 50% probability of occurrence based on facts and circumstances known to management as of the reporting date.

f. Debt securities that have experienced significant credit impairment.

348. The AOCI adjustment is calculated net of tax, consistent with how unrealised gains and losses are recorded in AOCI.

9.1.2.2　Capital Requirement: Interest Rate Risk

9.1.2.2.1　Background

349. Under J-GAAP Plus, the valuation of life insurance current estimates utilises a discount rate that is equivalent to the current asset book yield plus a reinvestment assumption equal to a government bond rate. Available for sale debt securities backing those liabilities are essentially reported at amortised cost via an adjustment to capital resources referred to as the AOCI adjustment (see Section 9.1.2.1). Other assets such as loans and held to maturity or held for reserves securities are also reported at cost. For non-life insurance products under J-GAAP Plus, insurance liabilities are discounted using a government bond yield curve, and available for sale debt securities are generally measured at fair value.

350. A shock to a market based curve does not translate to a change in value for assets valued at cost (including assets subject to the AOCI adjustment). In addition, it does not impact the book yield that is applied to discount cash flows used to measure certain life insurance liabilities. The shock only has an impact on any reinvestment assumption portion of the discount rate. For this reason, IAIGs apply the following method to calculate their J-GAAP Plus Interest Rate risk charge.

9.1.2.2.2　Liabilities

351. For those insurance liabilities on the J-GAAP Plus balance sheet that are valued using yield curves/rates based on current market information, the Interest Rate risk charge is calculated using the Reference ICS standard method approach. Thus, the standard method Interest Rate risk approach is applicable for all non-life products under J-GAAP Plus as well as any reported options and guarantees.

352. Where life insurance liabilities on the J-GAAP Plus balance sheet are discounted using

a book yield and a reinvestment assumption, the stressed IAIS yield curve scenarios only apply to the portion of the rate reflecting the reinvestment assumption at each tenor and currency.

9.1.2.2.3 Assets

353. For assets measured at market value on the J-GAAP Plus balance sheet, the stresses are the same as that used in the Reference ICS standard method.

354. For assets measured at amortised cost on the J-GAAP Plus balance sheet (eg loans and bonds classified as held to maturity or held for reserves), interest rate risk stresses are not applied.

355. Where unrealised gains and losses are added back to capital resources via the AOCI adjustment (see Section 9.1.2.1), assets are essentially measured at amortised cost. The interest rate risk stresses, applied through the change in asset value, are offset by the change in the AOCI adjustment. Therefore, the net impact of the stresses are zero, or the same as for assets measured at cost.

9.1.2.3 Capital Requirement: NDSR

9.1.2.3.1 Background

356. Under J-GAAP Plus, the valuation of life insurance current estimates utilises a discount rate that is equivalent to a book yield plus a reinvestment assumption equal to a government bond yield. Assets backing those liabilities are essentially reported at amortised cost via an adjustment to capital resources referred to as the AOCI adjustment (see Section 9.1.2.1). Other assets such as loans and debt securities held to maturity or held for reserves may also be reported at cost. For non-life insurance products under J-GAAP Plus, insurance liabilities are valued using a government bond yield curve, and available for sale securities are generally measured at fair value.

357. The NDSR stress does not translate to a change in value for assets valued at cost (either via the AOCI adjustment or for assets valued at cost on the J-GAAP Plus balance sheet). In addition, it does not impact the discount rate used to measure life liabilities or the government bond yield curve used to discount non-life liabilities. For this reason, IAIGs apply different methodologies to calculate their GAAP Plus NDSR charge, depending on how insurance liabilities and assets are valued.

9.1.2.3.2 Liabilities

358. For non-life insurance liabilities on the J-GAAP Plus balance sheet measured using a government bond yield curve, the NDSR stress is not applicable.

359. For life insurance liabilities on the J-GAAP Plus balance sheet that are discounted using a book yield with a reinvestment rate based on the government bond rate (eg Japanese life

liabilities), a NDSR stress is not applicable.

9.1.2.3.3 Assets

360. For assets measured at fair value on the J-GAAP Plus balance sheet using yield curves based on current market information, the impact of the NDSR stress is calculated by applying the Reference ICS standard method approach.

361. For assets measured at cost on the J-GAAP Plus balance sheet, an NDSR stress is not applicable.

362. Where unrealised gains and losses are added back to capital resources via the AOCI adjustment (see Section 9.1.2.1), assets are essentially being measured at amortised cost. The NDSR stress is applied through the change in asset value, which is offset by the change in the AOCI adjustment. Therefore, the net impact of the stress is zero, or the same as for assets measured at cost.

9.1.2.4 Capital Requirement: Credit Risk

363. Under J-GAAP Plus, available for sale debt securities that are included in the AOCI adjustment to capital resources are reported on an amortised cost basis for purposes of determining the credit risk charge. The credit risk factor is applied to the amortised cost balances in order to remain consistent with the valuation method reflected in capital resources.

9.1.2.5 Capital Requirement: Real Estate Risk

364. Under J-GAAP Plus, the real estate risk charge for owner-occupied property is calculated as the difference, if positive, of the J-GAAP Plus balance sheet value on the reporting date less 75% of the property's fair value on the reporting date. If the fair value of such a property is not available, the risk charge is 25% of the property's book value. The risk charge is determined on a property-by-property basis.

9.2 Other methods of calculation of the ICS capital requirement ("other methods")

9.2.1 Internal Models

365. The main goal of internal models is to calculate capital requirements (at the risk level or at the aggregated level) more tailored to the risks borne by the IAIG. Specificities of an IAIG that cannot be captured in the standard method (eg specific risk mitigation arrangements) can be reflected by an internal model. Internal models can also capture risks that are not included in the standard method if these are material for a specific IAIG. Internal models are particularly relevant in the context of IAIGs, which are large and complex insurance groups operating in multiple jurisdictions.

366. Ten prerequisites, largely based on ICP 17, have been determined for the submission of internal model results for the ICS capital requirement during the monitoring period.

五、Level 2 Document: ICS Version 2.0 for the monitoring period

367. In order to submit internal model results as part of the additional reporting during the monitoring period, IAIGs are required to complete a self-assessment template regarding prerequisites 1 to 10 as outlined in the subsequent sections, within which the IAIG must:

- Briefly describe the scope of application of the internal model (eg partial or full internal model).

- Provide evidence that the internal model to calculate the group capital requirement has been validated independently (Prerequisite 2) (internally or externally) and signed-off by the IAIG's Board of Directors (Prerequisite 3).

- Indicate the degree of compliance of the internal model with prerequisites 4 to 7:
  ○ Statistical quality test;
  ○ Calibration test;
  ○ Use test and governance; and
  ○ Documentation standards.

- In the case of a partial internal model, the IAIG must also complete the self-assessment template regarding Prerequisites 8 to 10, ie they need to:
  ○ Justify the reason for the limited scope of the internal model (ie absence of cherry-picking);
  ○ Provide evidence that the resulting ICS capital requirement more appropriately reflects the risk profile of the IAIG; and
  ○ Explain how the partial internal model's and standard method's results can be integrated.

368. Where the prerequisites are not fully met, but the IAIG would like to submit internal model results during the monitoring period, then the IAIG should discuss this with its GWS. Moreover, the IAIG should indicate the reasons for submitting results, despite not meeting all prerequisites, in its self-assessment template along with details of how the internal model does not meet the prerequisites.

369. Supervisory approval of the internal model for data submission is not a pre-requisite during the monitoring period. Further, a model does not have to be used for regulatory capital purposes to satisfy the pre-requisites for reporting of internal model results during the monitoring period.

370. The specific internal model results to be submitted as part of additional reporting are specified in the Level 3 document.

9.2.1.1 Prerequisite 1-Description of the scope of application of internal models

371. IAIGs must describe the scope of application of their internal model (ie the perimeter

of the internal model's calculation). Two possible approaches are considered for the additional reporting of internal model results during the monitoring period:

a. Partial internal model-which involves the replacement of some parts of the standard method calculation. For example:

   i. One or more risk charges of the ICS standard method capital requirement (eg Market risk);

   ii. One or more sub-risk charges of the ICS standard method capital requirement (eg Equity risk);

   iii. One or more risk charges or sub-risk charges not captured by the the ICS standard method capital requirement; or

   iv. The whole business of the IAIG, or only to one or more major business units or legal entities.

b. Full internal model-which involves the replacement of the entire standard method calculation.

9.2.1.2　Prerequisite 2: Validation

372. Internal model validation requires IAIGs to demonstrate that a rigorous process is in place by which they can establish whether their internal model framework is sound or whether improvements are needed. Validation should enable them to understand the internal model's capabilities and limitations better and confirm that the internal model and the supporting processes are adequate and appropriate for the purpose. Validation should be an iterative process by which an IAIG using an internal model periodically refines validation tools in response to changing market and operating conditions. There is no universal validation method, and the structure of the validation approach depends on the technical specifications of the internal model, its purpose and its intended use.

373. ICP 17.13.6 Guidance states "…the insurer should review its own internal model and validate it so as to satisfy itself of the appropriateness of the model for use as part of its risk and capital management processes". In addition to an internal review, the insurer may consider a regular independent, external review of its internal model by appropriate specialists".

374. ICP 17.18 states, when an insurer uses an internal model to determine regulatory capital requirements, it should:

● "… monitor the performance of its internal model and regularly review and validate the ongoing appropriateness of the model's specifications";

● "… demonstrate that the model remains fit for regulatory capital purposes in changing circumstances against the criteria of the statistical quality test, calibration test and use test";

- "…notify the supervisor of material changes to the internal model made by it…";
- "… properly document internal model changes"; and
- "… report information necessary for supervisory review…".

375. Validation should encompass both quantitative and qualitative elements. While it might be possible to think of validation as a purely technical/mathematical exercise in which outcomes are compared to estimates using statistical techniques, it is insufficient to focus solely on comparing predictions to outcomes. In assessing the overall performance of an internal model, it is important to assess the overall model and each of its building blocks regarding the structure, governance, data and processes.

376. Finally, to achieve an effective validation, an objective challenge is essential. Independent model validation helps IAIGs to evaluate and verify the overall performance of their internal models. Proper independence of the validation function is therefore important, whether the validation is internal or external, and individuals performing the validation must possess the necessary skills, knowledge, expertise and experience.

9.2.1.3 Prerequisite 3: Sign-off of the Board of Directors of the IAIG

377. This prerequisite aims to ensure that the Board of Directors has ownership of the internal model, and that the model complies with the validation process prescribed by the internal model governance process.

378. Moreover, ICP 17 recommends a certain level of engagement by the Board of Directors concerning the internal models as part of the use test, which will be further detailed in the section of prerequisite 6.

9.2.1.4 Prerequisite 4: Statistical quality test

379. Building on ICP 17.14 IAIGs need:
- "… to conduct a 'statistical quality test' which assesses the base quantitative methodology of the internal model, to demonstrate the appropriateness of this methodology, including the choice of model inputs and parameters, and to justify the assumptions underlying the model"; and provide evidence;
- "… that the determination of the regulatory capital requirement using an internal model addresses the overall risk position of the insurer and that the underlying data used in the model is accurate and complete".

380. The statistical quality test addresses issues related technical aspects of the internal model, ie:
- methodology and assumptions;
- coverage of material risks;

- data (including external data) and expert judgment;
- aggregation of risks and diversification effects;
- consistency with the method used for the calculation of technical provisions;
- allowance for risk mitigation techniques and future management actions; and
- financial guarantees and contractual options.

381. The statistical quality test concentrates on the individual building blocks of an internal model. The different elements making up the internal model and the inputs used must pass this test.

382. The statistical quality test set out in ICP 17 allows considerable modelling freedom to insurers. For example, ICP 17.14.1 Guidance states that "A range of approaches could constitute an effective internal model for risk and capital management purposes, and supervisors should encourage the use of a range of different approaches appropriate to the nature, scale and complexity of different insurers and different risk exposures. There are several different techniques to quantify risk which could be used by an insurer to construct its internal model. In broad terms, these could range from basic deterministic scenarios to complex stochastic models. Deterministic scenarios would typically involve the use of stress and scenario testing reflecting an event, or a change in conditions, with a set probability to model the effect of certain events (such as a drop in equity prices) on the insurer's capital position, in which the underlying assumptions would be fixed. In contrast, stochastic modelling often involves simulating very large numbers of scenarios to reflect the likely distributions of the capital required by, and the different risk exposures of, the insurer". IAIGs should be at the high end regarding the nature, scale and complexity of the risks borne and the business models and structure and thus it is expected that the modelling approach is commensurate with such risk and business profile.

383. The statistical quality test also sets the boundaries within which IAIGs should take responsibility for specifying their approach to assess and aggregate risks. In conjunction with internal model validation requirements, the statistical quality test promotes a well-structured, documented and controlled process of model development and refinement which should be consistently applied across the IAIG, including the different modelling areas. For example, ICP 17.14.3 Guidance states that "The IAIS considers that an insurer would generally be expected to decide how best to aggregate and account for the risks to the whole of its business. The determination of overall regulatory capital requirements by the internal model should consider dependencies within, as well as across, risk categories. Where the internal model allows for diversification effects, the insurer should be able to justify its allowance for diversification effects and demonstrate that it has considered how dependencies may increase under stressed

五、Level 2 Document: ICS Version 2.0 for the monitoring period

circumstances".

384. Data used to build the internal model are one of the main drivers of its performance. ICP 17.14.4 Guidance states "Internal models need high-quality data in order to produce sufficiently reliable results. The data used for an internal model should be current and sufficiently credible, accurate, complete and appropriate. Hence, a 'statistical quality test' should examine the appropriateness of the underlying data used in the construction of the internal model". ICP 17.14.6 Guidance deals with the use of external data specifying that "… any data not specific to the insurer would need to be carefully considered before deciding it was appropriate for use as the basis for an insurer's 'statistical quality test'. Even where deemed appropriate, it may still be necessary to adjust the data to allow for differences in features between the data source and the insurer".

385. There is always a certain amount of expert judgement involved when selecting data for an internal model. To this end, ICP 17.14.7 Guidance states that "In assessing suitability of data and of other inputs, eg assumptions, to the internal model, expert judgment should be applied and supported by proper justification, documentation and validation".

386. ICP 17.14.8 Guidance stresses the importance that "The methodology should also be consistent with the methods used to calculate technical provisions".

387. Moreover, ICP 17.14.9 states "statistical quality test should also include a review of the internal model to determine whether the assets and products as represented in the model truly reflect the insurer's actual assets and products. This should include an analysis of whether all reasonably foreseeable and relevant material risks have been incorporated, including any financial guarantees and embedded options. Insurers should also consider whether the algorithms used are able to take into account the action of management and the reasonable expectation of policyholders. Testing should include future projections within the model and to the extent practicable 'back-testing' (the process of comparing the predictions from the model with actual experience)".

9.2.1.5 Prerequisite 5: Calibration test

388. ICP 17.15 states IAIG should "… conduct a 'calibration test' to demonstrate that the regulatory capital requirement determined by the internal model satisfies the specified modelling criteria".

389. The ICP definition of calibration is different from the general definition of calibration used in statistics and actuarial science. For example, model calibration is often defined in statistics as the process of adjustment of the model parameters to obtain a model representation of the processes of interest that satisfies pre-agreed criteria (eg Goodness-of-Fit). ICP 17.15.2

Guidance states "The 'calibration test' should be used by the IAIG to demonstrate that the internal model is calibrated appropriately to allow a fair, unbiased estimate of the capital required for the particular risk measure, level of confidence and time horizon specified by the supervisor". In the case of the ICS standard method, the calibration target is VaR 99.5% over a one-year time horizon.

390. Where an IAIG uses a different confidence interval (eg 99.7% in order to maintain a certain investment grade rating), risk measure (eg TVaR for Cat Risk) or time horizon (eg to ultimate) than the one set out for the ICS standard method capital requirement calculations, it may need to recalibrate its model to the ICS capital requirement target criterion (ie VaR 99.5% over a one year time horizon). Alternatively, the IAIG can provide quantitative evidence on how this outcome compares to the ICS target criterion.

9.2.1.6 Prerequisite 6: Use test and governance

391. According to ICP 17.16, IAIGs need:

- "… to fully embed the internal model, its methodologies and results, into the insurer's risk strategy and operational processes (the 'use test')";

- their "…Board and Senior management to have overall control of and responsibility for the construction and use of the internal model for risk management purposes, and ensure sufficient understanding of the model's construction at appropriate levels within the insurer's organisational structure". In particular, insurers need to provide evidence that their Board and Senior management understand the consequences of the internal model's outputs and limitations for risk and capital management decisions; and

- "… to have adequate governance and internal controls in place with respect to the internal model".

392. The use test is, in effect, the evidence that should support the relationship of trust between the supervisor and the regulated group. This trust is needed for the supervisor to gain assurance that the internal model reflects the IAIG's view of its risks and is used in decision making, and not developed with the purpose of reducing regulatory capital.

393. Consistent with ICP 17.16.1 Guidance, the IAIG should demonstrate that its internal model is widely used and plays an important role in risk management and decision-making, at different levels of management in the organisation, and the assessment of the economic and solvency capital.

394. Moreover, ICP 17.16.5 Guidance states "The 'use test' is a key method by which the insurer can demonstrate that its internal model is integrated within its risk and capital management and system of governance processes and procedures". In other words, the IAIG

must provide evidence that the internal model is fully embedded in its operational and organisational structure and demonstrate that the model remains useful and is applied consistently over time.

395. Furthermore, an IAIG "should demonstrate to the supervisor that an internal model used for regulatory capital purposes remains useful and is applied consistently over time and that it has the full support of and ownership by the Board and Senior management".

396. Another key aspect of the use test is that according to ICP 17.16.6 Guidance the IAIG's Senior management is responsible for the design and implementation of the internal model and for ensuring the ongoing appropriateness of the model.

397. ICP 17.16.7 Guidance also notes that "For a model to pass the 'use test' it would be expected that an insurer would have a framework for the model's application across business units. This framework should define lines of responsibility for the production and use of information derived from the model".

398. ICP 17.16.8 Guidance stresses the importance of the governance, communication, challenge and understanding of the model "An internal model should be subject to appropriate review and challenge so that it is relevant and reliable when used by the insurer. The key elements and results from the internal model should be understood by the key personnel within the insurer, including the Board, and not only by those who have constructed it. This understanding should ensure that the internal model remains a useful decision-making tool. If the internal model is not widely understood, it will not be achieving its purpose and adding value to the business. The 'use test' is key to ensuring the relevance of the internal model to the insurer's business".

9.2.1.7 Prerequisite 7: Documentation standards

399. Building on ICP 17.17 the IAIG should "… document the design, construction and governance of the internal model, including an outline of the rationale and assumptions underlying its methodology". ICP 17.17 states further that "The supervisor requires the documentation to be sufficient to demonstrate compliance with the regulatory validation requirements for internal models, including the statistical quality test, calibration test and use test.

400. The main aims of the documentation are:
- Reducing key person risk;
- facilitating the supervisory review and approval of the model;
- facilitating Senior Management's understanding; and
- recognising the weaknesses of the model.

401. As stated in the ICP 17.17.1 Guidance, documentation should be thorough, detailed and complete enough to be "… sufficient for a knowledgeable professional in the field to be able to understand its design and construction. This documentation should include justifications for and details of the underlying methodology, assumptions and quantitative and financial bases, as well as information on the modelling criteria used to assess the level of capital needed".

402. Moreover, ICP 17.17.2 Guidance states, "The insurer should also document, on an ongoing basis, the development of the model and any major changes, as well as instances where the model is shown to not perform effectively. Where there is reliance on an external vendor/supplier, the reliance should be documented along with an explanation of the appropriateness of the use of the external vendor/supplier".

9.2.1.8 Prerequisite 8: Absence of cherry-picking

403. According to ICP 17.12.4 Guidance, "The IAIS supports the use of internal models where appropriate as they can be a more realistic, risk-responsive method of calculating capital requirements, but discourages any 'cherry-picking' practices by insurers".

404. From a supervisor's perspective, the possibility of mixing and matching internal models for some risks and businesses while using the standard method for the rest of the risks or businesses raises potential concerns about cherry-picking. To help mitigate these concerns, consistent with ICP 17.12.14 Guidance, the IAIG should "… justify why it has chosen to only use internal models for certain risks or business lines". To this end, the IAIG should provide in its self-assessment the rationale for the limited scope of the internal model.

9.2.1.9 Prerequisite 9: The resulting ICS capital requirement more appropriately reflects the risk profile of the insurer

405. According to ICP 17.12.15, "…an insurer should be required to justify the limited scope of the model and why it considers that using partial internal modelling for determining regulatory capital requirements is more consistent with the risk profile of the business than the standardised approach or why it sufficiently matches regulatory capital requirements".

9.2.1.10 Prerequisite 10: Explain how the partial internal model and standard method's results can be integrated

406. It is essential that the integration of the partial internal model and the standard method results is being carried out prudently and consistently to derive the overall ICS capital requirement. To this end, the IAIG should provide evidence that the partial internal model and standard method results can be integrated. This prerequisite is particularly relevant for IAIGs whose internal model construction does not follow a similar design as the standard method (eg risks have not been defined or split along similar lines as in the standard method, the target

criteria are different, etc.).

9.2.2 Dynamic Hedging

407. The reference ICS does not make allowance for the effect of market risk mitigation techniques in the capital requirement beyond the basis of assets and liabilities existing at the reporting date of the ICS calculation. The principles of the ICS standard method ensure that the only risk mitigation arrangements recognised are those that mitigate risk borne by the IAIG as at the reporting date of the calculation.

408. Dynamic hedging arrangements are not recognised for their risk mitigating properties as this would conflict with this principle for the standard method. This is because the risk charges in the standard method are calculated using instantaneous shocks which, by their construction, do not capture any mitigating effects of subsequent hedging adjustments.

409. However, IAIGs are able to provide relevant information on dynamic hedging programmes in order to support a future decision on its inclusion in the ICS. The IAIS is examining whether there are any other methods for valuing these arrangements that could better reflect the risk exposures of IAIGs and be incorporated into the ICS, rather than using the standard method for specific products and risks.

Glossary

Term	Acronym	Definition/Reference
Accumulated Other Comprehensive Income	AOCI	See section 9.1 on "GAAP with Adjustments"
Basel Committee on Banking Supervision	BCBS	https://www.bis.org/bcbs/
Common Framework for the Supervision of IAIGs	ComFrame	https://www.iaisweb.org/page/supervisory-material/insurance-core-principles-and-comframe
Deferred Tax Assets	DTAs	See section 6.3 on "Capital elements other than financial instruments" and section 8 on "Tax Treatment"
Deferred Tax Liabilities	DTLs	See section 6.3 on "Capital elements other than financial instruments" and section 8 on "Tax Treatment"
Financial Stability Board	FSB	http://www.fsb.org/
Future Discretionary Benefits	FDB	See section 5.2.1.4
GAAP with Adjustments	GAAP Plus	See section 9.1 on "GAAP with Adjustments"
Generally Accepted Accounting Principles	GAAP	https://en.wikipedia.org/wiki/Generally_accepted_accounting_principles http://www.accountingfoundation.org/gaap
Insurance Capital Standard	ICS	http://www.iaisweb.org/page/supervisory-material/insurance-capital-standard
ICS Rating Category	ICS RC	See section 3.4
Insurance Core Principles	ICP	https://www.iaisweb.org/page/supervisory-material/insurance-core-principles-and-comframe
International Association of Insurance Supervisors	IAIS	http://www.iaisweb.org/home
International Financial Reporting Standards	IFRS	http://www.ifrs.org/About-us/IASB/Pages/Home.aspx
International Monetary Fund	IMF	http://www.imf.org/external/index.htm
Internationally Active Insurance Group	IAIG	See the ICPs and ComFrame, adopted November 2019 https://www.iaisweb.org/page/supervisory-material/insurance-core-principles-and-comframe

Glossary

continued

Term	Acronym	Definition/Reference
Last Observed Term	LOT	See section 5.2.5 on "Discounting"
Long Term Forward Rate	LTFR	See section 5.2.5 on "Discounting"
Management Actions		See section 7.1.3 on "Management actions"
Margin Over Current Estimate	MOCE	A margin that exceeds the current estimate in valuation of technical provisions to cover the inherent uncertainty of those obligations. http://www.iaisweb.org/page/supervisory-material/glossary See also ICP 14.7
Market-Adjusted Valuation	MAV	See section 5 on "Market-adjusted valuation (MAV) approach"
National Association of Insurance Commissioners	NAIC	http://www.naic.org/
Net Asset Value	NAV	The value of assets minus the value of liabilities
Non-Default Spread Risk	NDSR	See section 7.3.3
Supervisor-owned and controlled credit assessment processes	SOCCA processes	See section 7.4.4
Value at Risk	VaR	An estimate of the worst expected loss over a certain period of time at a given confidence level http://www.iaisweb.org/page/supervisory-material/glossary
Weighted Average of Multiple Representative Portfolios	WAMP	See section 5.2.5.3.2 on "Adjustments to the yield curve"

Annex 1 Treatment of Non-Voting Interest Entities (Asset and Insurance Securitisations)

Asset Securitisations

Insurers must meetall of the following conditions in order to not consolidate a securitisation originated by the group (excerpted from Basel III):

a. Significant credit risk associated with the underlying exposures has been transferred to third parties.

b. The transferor does not maintain effective or indirect control over the transferred exposures. The exposures are legally isolated from the transferor in such a way (eg through the sale of assets or through sub-participation) that the exposures are put beyond the reach of the transferor and its creditors, even in bankruptcy or receivership. Banks should obtain legal opinion that confirms true sale.

c. The transferor is deemed to have maintained effective control over the transferred credit risk exposures if it: (i) is able to repurchase from the transferee the previously transferred exposures in order to realise their benefits; or (ii) is obligated to retain the risk of the transferred exposures. The transferor's retention of servicing rights to the exposures will not necessarily constitute indirect control of the exposures.

d. The securities issued are not obligations of the transferor. Thus, investors who purchase the securities only have claim to the underlying exposures.

e. The transferee is an SPE and the holders of the beneficial interests in that entity have the right to pledge or exchange them without restriction.

f. Clean-up calls must satisfy the following conditions: (i) the exercise of the clean-up call must not be mandatory, in form or in substance, but rather must be at the discretion of the originating bank; (ii) the clean-up call must not be structured to avoid allocating losses to credit enhancements or positions held by investors or otherwise structured to provide credit enhancement; and (iii) the clean-up call must only be exercisable when 10% or less of the original underlying portfolio or securities issued remains, or, for synthetic securitisations, when

Annex 1 Treatment of Non-Voting Interest Entities (Asset and Insurance Securitisations)

10% or less of the original reference portfolio value remains.

g. The securitisation does not contain clauses that (i) require the originating bank to alter the underlying exposures such that the pool's credit quality is improved unless this is achieved by selling exposures to independent and unaffiliated third parties at market prices; (ii) allow for increases in a retained first-loss position or credit enhancement provided by the originating bank after the transaction's inception; or (iii) increase the yield payable to parties other than the originating bank, such as investors and third-party providers of credit enhancements, in response to a deterioration in the credit quality of the underlying pool.

h. There must be no termination options/triggers except eligible clean-up calls, termination for specific changes in tax and regulation or early amortisation provisions.

Asset Securitisations

Insurers must meetall of the following conditions in order to not consolidate a securitisation originated by the group (excerpted from Solvency II):

a. the SPE is any entity other than an insurer or reinsurer, which assumes risks from (re) insurers through reinsurance contracts or similar arrangements, and which funds in full its risk exposures by issuing debt or any other financing arrangement the repayment rights of which are subordinated to the reinsurance obligations of the (re) insurer.

b. where the SPE assumes risks from more than one (re) insurer, the solvency of that SPE is not adversely affected by winding-up proceedings of any one of those (re) insurers.

c. The SPE meets at all time the following conditions:

i. the SPE has at all times assets the market value of which is equal to or exceeds the maximum payments-including expenses-of the SPE, and the SPE is able to pay the amounts it is liable for as they fall due;

ii. the proceeds of the debt issuance or other financing mechanism are fully paid-in.

d. The contractual arrangements relating to the transfer of risk from a (re) insurer to a SPE and from the SPE to the providers of debt or financing meet the following conditions:

i. The transfer of risk is effective in all circumstances;

ii. The extent of risk transfer is clearly defined and incontrovertible;

iii. the claims of the providers of debt or financing mechanisms are at all times subordinated to the reinsurance obligations of the SPE to the (re) insurers of the IAIG;

iv. no payments are made to the providers of debt or financing, if following those payments the SPE would no longer be fully funded;

v. the providers of debt or finance to the SPEs have no rights of recourse to the assets of the (re) insurers;

vi. the providers of debt or finance to the SPEs have no rights to apply for the winding-up of the SPE.

Annex 2　Definition of ICS Non-Life Segments

ICS Segment	Definition
EEA and Switzerland/Medical expense insurance	Insurance obligation that covers the provision or financial compensation for medical treatment or care including preventive or curative medical treatment or care due to illness, accident, disability or infirmity.
EEA and Switzerland/ Income protection	Insurance obligation that covers the financial compensation arising from illness, accident, disability or infirmity (excluding medical expense insurance).
EEA and Switzerland/ Workers' Compensation	Health insurance obligations which relate to accidents at work, industrial injury and occupational diseases and where the underlying business is not pursued on a similar technical basis to that of life insurance.
EEA and Switzerland/Motor vehicle liability-Motor third party liability	Insurance obligations which cover all liabilities arising out of the use of motor vehicles operating on land (including carrier's liability).
EEA and Switzerland/Motor, other classes	Insurance obligations which cover all damage to or loss of land vehicles (including railway rolling stock).
EEA and Switzerland/Marine, aviation and transport	Insurance obligations which cover all damage or loss to sea, lake, river and canal vessels, aircraft, and damage to or loss of goods in transit or baggage irrespective of the form of transport. Insurance obligations which cover liabilities arising out of the use of aircraft, ships, vessels or boats on the sea, lakes, rivers or canals (including carrier's liability).
EEA and Switzerland/Fire and other damage	Insurance obligations which cover all damage to or loss of property (other than those included in motor (other) and marine/aviation/transport) due to fire, explosion, natural forces including storm, hail or frost, nuclear energy, land subsidence and any event such as theft.
EEA and Switzerland/General liability-third party liability	Insurance obligations which cover all liabilities other than those in motor vehicle liability and marine, aviation and transport.
EEA and Switzerland/ Credit and suretyship	Insurance obligations which cover insolvency, export credit, instalment credit, mortgages, agricultural credit and direct and indirect suretyship.
EEA and Switzerland/ Legal expenses	Insurance obligations which cover legal expenses and cost of litigation.
EEA and Switzerland/Assistance	Insurance obligations which cover assistance for persons who get into difficulties while travelling, while away from home or while away from their habitual residence.

continued

ICS Segment	Definition
EEA and Switzerland/Miscellaneous financial loss	Insurance obligations which cover employment risk, insufficiency of income, bad weather, loss of benefit, continuing general expenses, unforeseen trading expenses, loss of market value, loss of rent or revenue, indirect trading losses other than those mentioned above, other financial loss (non-trading) as well as any other risk of non-life insurance not covered by the lines of business above.
EEA and Switzerland/Non-proportional health reinsurance	Reinsurance on a non-proportional basis of health insurance classes.
EEA and Switzerland/Non-Proportional Casualty reinsurance	Reinsurance on a non-proportional basis of casualty classes (motor vehicle liability and general liability).
EEA and Switzerland/Non-proportional marine, aviation and transport reinsurance	Reinsurance on a non-proportional basis of marine, aviation and transport.
EEA and Switzerland/Non-Proportional property reinsurance	Reinsurance on a non-proportional basis of property classes (other motor, fire, credit/suretyship, legal expenses and assistance)
Canada/Property-personal	Insurance against the loss of, or damage to, property, and includes insurance against loss caused by forgery. It includes such classifications as habitational property and multi-peril policies, including residential contents of buildings such as apartments, rooming houses, motels, manufacturing and mercantile buildings and the liability exposure of personal package policies issued with indivisible premiums. This line would include fire policies, householder contents and homeowner personal risks, residential burglary and theft and special residential glass coverage. Casualty coverage such as personal liability for bodily injury would not be included in this category.
Canada/Home Warranty	Refers to a contract of insurance issued by a warranty provider covering defects in the construction of a new home and consequential losses or costs incurred by the owner.
Canada/Product Warranty	Insurance not incidental to any other class of insurance against loss of, or damage to, personal property, other than a motor vehicle, under which an insurer undertakes to pay the costs of repairing or replacing the personal property.
Canada/Property-commercial	Insurance against the loss of, or damage to, property, and includes insurance against loss caused by forgery and all commercial property and multi-peril policies, but excludes all separate classes of insurance as defined by regulators.
Canada/Aircraft	Insurance against: 1. liability arising from bodily injury to, or the death of, a person, or the loss of, or damage to, property, in each case caused by an aircraft or the use of an aircraft; or 2. the loss of, the loss of use of, or damage to, an aircraft.

Annex 2   Definition of ICS Non-Life Segments

continued

ICS Segment	Definition
Canada/Automobile-liability/personal accident	Insurance: 1. against liability arising from bodily injury to, or the death of, a person, or the loss of, or damage to, property, in each case caused by an automobile or the use or operation of an automobile; or 2. that falls within clause (i) or (ii) of the definition of accident and sickness insurance, if the accident is caused by an automobile or the use or operation of an automobile, whether or not liability exists in respect of the accident, and the policy includes insurance against liability arising from bodily injury to, or the death of, a person caused by an automobile or the use or operation of an automobile.
Canada/Automobile-other	Insurance against the loss of, the loss of use of, or damage to, an automobile.
Canada/Boiler and Machinery	Insurance against: 1. liability arising from bodily injury to, or the death of, a person, or the loss of, or damage to, property, or against the loss of, or damage to, property, in each case caused by the explosion or rupture of, or accident to, pressure vessels of any kind or pipes, engines and machinery connected to or operated by those pressure vessels; or 2. liability arising from bodily injury to, or the death of, a person, or the loss of, or damage to, property, or against the loss of, or damage to, property, in each case caused by a breakdown of machinery.
Canada/Equipment Warranty	The sub-class of boiler and machinery insurance that covers loss of or damage to a motor vehicle or to equipment arising from its mechanical failure, but does not include automobile insurance or insurance incidental to automobile insurance.
Canada/Credit Insurance	Insurance against loss to a person who has granted credit if the loss is the result of the insolvency or default of the person to whom the credit was granted.
Canada/Credit Protection	Insurance under which an insurer undertakes to pay off credit balances or debts of an individual, in whole or in part, in the event of an impairment or potential impairment in the individual's income or ability to earn an income.
Canada/Fidelity	Insurance against loss caused by the theft, the abuse of trust or the unfaithful performance of duties by a person in a position of trust; and insurance under which an insurer undertakes to guarantee the proper fulfilment of the duties of an office.
Canada/Hail	Insurance against the loss of, or damage to, crops in the field caused by hail.
Canada/Legal Expenses	Insurance against the costs incurred by a person or persons for legal services specified in the policy, including any retainer and fees incurred for the services, and other costs incurred in respect of the provision of the services.

continued

ICS Segment	Definition
Canada/Liability	Insurance, other than insurance that falls within another class of insurance: 1. against liability arising from bodily injury to a person or the disability or death of a person, including an employee; 2. against liability arising from the loss of, or damage to, property; or 3. if the policy includes the insurance described in sub-clause (i), against expenses arising from bodily injury to a person other than the insured or a member of the insured's family, whether or not liability exists. Includes general liability, cyber liability, directors & liability, excess liability, professional liability, umbrella liability and pollution liability.
Canada/Mortgage	Insurance against loss caused by default on the part of a borrower under a loan secured by a mortgage or charge on, or other security interest in, real property.
Canada/Surety	Insurance under which an insurer undertakes to guarantee the due performance of a contract or undertaking or the payment of a penalty or indemnity for any default.
Canada/Title	Insurance against loss or damage caused by: 1. the existence of a mortgage, charge, lien, encumbrance, servitude or any other restriction on real property; 2. the existence of a mortgage, charge, lien, pledge, encumbrance or any other restriction on personal property; 3. a defect in any document that evidences the creation of any restriction referred to in sub-clause (i) or (ii); 4. a defect in the title to property; or 5. any other matter affecting the title to property or the right to the use and enjoyment of property.
Canada/Marine	Insurance against liability arising from: 1. bodily injury to, or the death of, a person; or 2. the loss of, or damage to, property; or 3. the loss of, or damage to, property, occurred during a voyage or marine adventure at sea or on an inland waterway, or during a delay or a transit other than by water that is incidental to a voyage or marine adventure at sea or on an inland waterway.
Canada/ Accident and Sickness	
Canada/Other Approved Products	Insurance against risks that do not fall within another class of insurance.
US/ Auto physical damage	Any motor vehicle insurance coverage (including collision, vandalism, fire and theft) that insures against material damage to an insured's vehicle.

Annex 2 Definition of ICS Non-Life Segments

continued

ICS Segment	Definition
US/ Homeowners/ Farm owners	Homeowners: coverage for personal property and/or structure with broad personal liability coverage, for dwelling, appurtenant structures, unscheduled personal property and additional living expenses. Farm owners: similar, for farming and ranching risks; property + liability coverages for personal and business losses, on farm dwellings and contents (eg mobile equipment and livestock), barns, stables, other farm structures and farm inland marine.
US/ Special property	Various, including: fire; allied lines; inland marine; earthquake; burglary and theft. Fire insurance includes the loss to real or personal property from damage caused by the peril of fire or lightning, including business interruption, loss of rents, etc. Allied lines are coverages generally written with property insurance, eg, glass; tornado; windstorm and hail; sprinkler and water damage; explosion, riot, and civil commotion; growing crops; flood; rain; and damage from aircraft and vehicle, etc. Inland marine is coverage for property that may be in transit, held by a bailee, at a fixed location, a movable good that is often at different locations (eg, off road construction equipment), or scheduled property (eg, Homeowners Personal Floater) including items such as live animals and property with antique or collector's value. This line also includes instrumentalities of transportation and communication, such as bridges, tunnels piers, wharves, docks, pipelines, power and phone lines, and radio and television towers.
US/ Private passenger auto liability/ medical	Coverage for financial loss resulting from legal liability for motor vehicle related injuries (bodily injury and medical payments) or damage to the property of others caused by accidents arising out of the ownership, maintenance or use of a motor vehicle. Does not include coverage for vehicles used in a commercial business.
US/ Commercial auto/ truck liability/ medical	Similar to private passenger auto liability/medical, except for commercial vehicles.
US/ Workers' compensation	Insurance that covers an employer's liability for injuries, disability or death to persons in their employment, without regard to fault, as prescribed by state or Federal workers' compensation laws and other statutes. Includes employer's liability coverage against the common law liability for injuries to employees (as distinguished from the liability imposed by Workers' Compensation Laws). Excludes excess workers' compensation.
US/ Commercial multi-peril	Two or more insurance coverages for a commercial enterprise, including various property and liability risks, that are included in the same policy. Includes multi-peril policies other than farmowners, homeowners and automobile policies.
US/ Medical professional liability- Occurrence	For a licensed health care provider or health care facility against legal liability resulting from the death or injury of any person due to the insured's misconduct, negligence, or incompetence in rendering professional services. The insurance covers events occurring during the policy coverage period.

continued

ICS Segment	Definition
US/ Medical professional liability-Claims-Made	For a licensed health care provider or health care facility against legal liability resulting from the death or injury of any person due to the insured's misconduct, negligence, or incompetence in rendering professional services. The insurance covers claims presented during the period of coverage.
US/Other Liability - Occurrence	Insurance against legal liability resulting from negligence, carelessness, or a failure to act causing property damage or personal injury to others. Typically, coverage includes liability for the following: construction and alteration; contingent; contractual; elevators and escalators; errors and omissions; environmental pollution; excess stop loss, excess over insured or self-insured amounts and umbrella; liquor; personal injury; premises and operations; completed operations; nonmedical professional, etc. Also includes indemnification coverage provided to self-insured employers on an excess of loss basis (excess workers' compensation). The insurance covers events occurring during the policy coverage period.
US/Other Liability-Claims-Made	Same types of coverages as other liability-occurrence above except that the insurance covers claims presented during the period of coverage. The insurable event does not need to occur during the policy period.
US/Products liability	Products liability-occurrence: covers events occurring during coverage period. Products liability-claims made. -covers claims made during the coverage period. Coverage for the manufacturer, distributor, seller, or lessor of a product against legal liability resulting from a defective condition causing personal injury, or damage, to any individual or entity, associated with the use of the product. Products liability-occurrence: covers events occurring during coverage period. Products liability-claims made. -covers claims made during the coverage period. Coverage for the manufacturer, distributor, seller, or lessor of a product against legal liability resulting from a defective condition causing personal injury, or damage, to any individual or entity, associated with the use of the product. Products liability-occurrence: covers events occurring during coverage period. Products liability-claims made. -covers claims made during the coverage period. Coverage for the manufacturer, distributor, seller, or lessor of a product against legal liability resulting from a defective condition causing personal injury, or damage, to any individual or entity, associated with the use of the product.
US/Reinsurance-non-proportional assumed property	Non-proportional assumed liability reinsurance in fire allied lines, ocean marine, inland marine, earthquake, group accident and health, credit accident and health, other accident and health, auto physical damage, boiler and machinery, glass, burglary and theft and international (of the foregoing).

Annex 2　Definition of ICS Non-Life Segments

continted

ICS Segment	Definition
US/Reinsurance-non-proportional assumed liability	Non-proportional assumed liability reinsurance in farm owners multiple-peril, homeowners' multiple-peril, commercial multiple-peril, medical professional liability, workers' compensation, other liability, products liability, auto liability, aircraft (all perils) and international (of the foregoing).
US/Special liability	Various insurance coverages including ocean marine, aircraft (all perils), and boiler and machinery. Ocean marine is coverage for ocean and inland water transportation exposures; such as goods or cargoes; ships or hulls; earnings; and liability. Aircraft is coverage for aircraft (hull) and their contents; aircraft owner's and aircraft manufacturer's liability to passengers, airports and other third parties. Boiler and machinery is coverage for the failure of boilers, machinery and electrical equipment. Coverage includes the property of the insured, which has been directly damaged by an accident, costs of temporary repairs and expediting expenses and liability for damage to the property of others.
US/Mortgage insurance	Mortgage guaranty is indemnification of a lender from loss if a borrower fails to meet required mortgage payments.
US/Fidelity/surety	Fidelity is a bond covering an employer's loss resulting from an employee's dishonest act (eg, loss of cash, securities, or valuables). Surety is a three-party agreement where the insurer agrees to pay a second party or make complete an obligation in response to the default, acts, or omissions of a third party.
US/Financial Guaranty	Financial guaranty is a surety bond, insurance policy, or when issued by an insurer, an indemnity contract and any guaranty similar to the foregoing types, under which loss is payable upon proof of occurrence of financial loss to an insured claimant, oblige or indemnitee as a result of failure to perform a financial obligation.
US/Other	Coverages not included elsewhere which includes credit coverages, warranty, and, where considered part of property/casualty, accident/health coverages. The Schedule P "International" LOB should be allocated to the region (s) where risk is located, but if this is not possible could be included in this segment.
US/Reinsurance-non-proportional assumed financial lines	Non-proportional assumed reinsurance in the following lines: mortgage guaranty, financial guaranty, fidelity, surety, credit, and international (in the foregoing).
Japan/Fire	This insurance covers property damage for either commercial or household caused by fire, windstorm, hail, water damage and earthquake.
Japan/Hull	This insurance covers damage of vessel.
Japan/Cargo	This insurance covers damage on good and property in transit by vessel.
Japan/Transit	This insurance is called as Inland marine, which covers property being transported by other than vessel or aircraft.

continued

ICS Segment	Definition
Japan/Personal Accident	This insurance covers loss by accidental bodily injury. Under this insurance, policyholder is reimbursed based on actual losses occurred or receives a fixed benefit due to a certain accident event.
Japan/Automobile	This insurance covers personal injury or automobile damage sustained by the insured and liability to third parties for losses caused by the insured. Please note fleet automobile insurance should be included here.
Japan/Aviation	This insurance covers aircraft, goods or property in transit by aircraft and launch to the space, and liability arising from the loss of or damage to the goods or property in transit or bodily injury or property loss or damage to third parties.
Japan/Guarantee Ins.	This insurance covers financial loss caused by the insolvency or payment default of customers to whom credit has been granted.
Japan/Machinery	This insurance protects the insured against loss incurred as a result of machinery breakdown.
Japan/General Liability	This insurance covers any legal obligations to pay compensation and costs for bodily injury, property loss or damage to third parties.
Japan/Contractor's All Risks	This insurance is purchased by contractors to cover damage to property under construction.
Japan/Movables All Risks	This insurance covers loss or damage to property other than motor, aircraft and vessel.
Japan/Workers' Compensation	This insurance covers no-fault basis compensation payments to employees who sustained bodily injury or occupational disease during or which arises out of the course of their employment, and provides employers with protections against claims which their employees make for bodily injury or occupational disease caused by tort.
Japan/Misc. Pecuniary Loss	This insurance provides the insured with tailor-made covers for consequential losses that are not covered by any other classes of business.
Japan/Nursing Care Ins.	This Insurance provides benefit to meet specified conditions requiring the insured to be nursed. Under this insurance, policyholder is reimbursed based on actual cost incurred or receives a fixed benefit for nursing care.
Japan/Others	Includes any other non-life insurance not listed above.
China/Motor	A vehicle insurance that the object of insurance is vehicle itself and related liability to pay compensation.
China/Property, including commercial, personal and engineering	Insurance that the object of insurance is property and related interests.
China/Marine and Special	Insurance that the object of insurance is watercraft and related liability to pay compensation.

Annex 2 Definition of ICS Non-Life Segments

continued

ICS Segment	Definition
China/Liability	Insurance that the object of insurance is assumed liability of the insurant to pay compensation to the third party.
China/Agriculture	Insurance that the object of insurance is the property loss of agriculture caused by disasters.
China/Credit	Insurance that the object of insurance is the economical loss of loaner because of the debtor's incapacity or refusing to pay for the debt.
China/Short-term Accident	A short-term accident insurance, the object of insurance is the death or disability of insurant because of accident. The period of insurance is usually no more than one year.
China/Short-term Health	Health insurance that the period of insurance is no more than one year and without guaranteed renewable terms.
China/Short-term Life	A short-term life insurance, the object of insurance is the lift of insured. The period of insurance is usually no more than one year.
China/Others	Other insurances.
Australia&NZ/ Householders	This class covers the common Householders policies, including the following classes/risks: contents, personal property, arson and burglary. Public liability normally attaching to these products is to be separated. This class also covers proportional reinsurance of householders business.
Australia&NZ/ Commercial Motor	Motor vehicle insurance (including third party property damage) other than insurance covering vehicles defined below under Domestic Motor. It includes long and medium haul trucks, cranes and special vehicles, and policies covering fleets. This class also covers proportional reinsurance of commercial motor.
Australia&NZ/ Domestic Motor	Motor vehicle insurance (including third party property damage) covering private use motor vehicles including utilities and lorries, motor cycles, private caravans, box and boat trailers, and other vehicles not normally covered by business or commercial policies. This class also covers proportional reinsurance of domestic motor.
Australia&NZ/ Other type A	Other classes of business with similar characteristics to householders and motor. This class also covers proportional reinsurance of other type A.
Australia&NZ/ Travel	Insurance against losses associated with travel including loss of baggage and personal effects, losses on flight cancellations and overseas medical costs. This class also covers proportional reinsurance of travel insurance.
Australia&NZ/ Fire and ISR	Includes all policies normally classified as fire (includes sprinkler leakage, subsidence, windstorm, hailstone, crop, arson and loss of profits) and Industrial Special Risk. This class also covers proportional reinsurance of fire and industrial special risk.

contined

ICS Segment	Definition
Australia&NZ/ Marine and Aviation	Includes Marine Hull and Marine Liability (including pleasure craft), and Marine Cargo (including sea and inland transit insurance). Also includes Aviation (including aircraft hull and aircraft liability). This class also covers proportional reinsurance of marine and aviation.
Australia&NZ/ Consumer Credit	Insurance to protect a consumer's ability to meet the loan repayments on personal loans and credit card finance in the event of death or loss of income due to injury, illness or unemployment. This class also covers proportional reinsurance of consumer credit.
Australia&NZ/ Other Accident	Includes miscellaneous accident, all risks (baggage, sporting equipment, guns), engineering when not part of Fire & ISR, plate glass when not package, livestock, pluvius and sickness and accident. This class also covers proportional reinsurance of other accident.
Australia&NZ/ Other type B	Other classes of business with similar characteristics to Fire & ISR, marine, aviation, consumer credit and other accident. This class also covers proportional reinsurance of other type B.
Australia&NZ/ Mortgage	Insurance against losses to a lender in the event of borrower default on a loan secured by a mortgage over residential or other property. This class also covers proportional reinsurance of mortgage.
Australia&NZ/ CTP	Compulsory Third Party business. This class also covers proportional reinsurance of CTP.
Australia&NZ/ Public and Product Liability	Public Liability covers legal liability to the public in respect of bodily injury or property damage arising out of the operation of the insured's business. Product Liability includes policies that provide for compensation for loss and/or injury caused by, or as a result of, the use of goods and environmental clean-up caused by pollution spills where not covered by Fire and ISR policies. Includes builders warranty and public liability attaching to householders policies. This class also covers proportional reinsurance of public and product liability.
Australia&NZ/ Professional Indemnity	PI covers professionals against liability incurred as a result of errors and omissions made in performing professional services that has resulted in economic losses suffered by third parties. Includes Directors' and Officers' Liability insurance plus legal expense insurance. Cover for legal expenses is generally included in this type of policy. This class also covers proportional reinsurance of professional indemnity.
Australia&NZ/ Employers' Liability	Includes workers' compensation, seaman's compensation and domestic workers' compensation. This class also covers proportional reinsurance of employer's liability.

Annex 2 Definition of ICS Non-Life Segments

continued

ICS Segment	Definition
Australia&NZ/ Short tail medical expenses	Insurance obligation that covers the provision or financial compensation for medical treatment or care including preventive or curative medical treatment or care due to illness, accident, disability or infirmity usually made during the term of the policy or shortly (typically, up to 1 year) after the coverage period of the insurance has expired.
Australia&NZ/ Other type C	Other classes of business with similar characteristics to mortgage, CTP, and other liability. This class also covers proportional reinsurance of other type C.
Australia&NZ/ Householders-non-prop reins	Non-Proportional reinsurance of householders business (refer definition).
Australia&NZ/ Commercial Motor-non-prop reins	Non-Proportional reinsurance of commercial motor (refer definition).
Australia&NZ/ Domestic Motor-non-prop reins	Non-Proportional reinsurance of domestic motor business (refer definition).
Australia&NZ/ Other non-prop reins type A	Non-Proportional reinsurance of other type A business (refer definition).
Australia&NZ/ Travel-non-prop reins	Non-Proportional reinsurance of travel business (refer definition).
Australia&NZ/ Fire and ISR-non-prop reins	Non-Proportional reinsurance of Fire & ISR business (refer definition).
Australia&NZ/ Marine and Aviation-non-prop reins	Non-Proportional reinsurance of marine and aviation business (refer definition).
Australia&NZ/ Consumer Credit-non-prop reins	Non-Proportional reinsurance of consumer credit business (refer definition).
Australia&NZ/ Other Accident-non-prop reins	Non-Proportional reinsurance of other accident business (refer definition).
Australia&NZ/ Other non-prop reins type B	Non-Proportional reinsurance of other type B business (refer definition).
Australia&NZ/ Mortgage-non-prop reins	Non-Proportional reinsurance of mortgage business (refer definition).
Australia&NZ/ CTP-non-prop reins	Non-Proportional reinsurance of CTP business (refer definition).
Australia&NZ/ Public and Product Liability-non-prop reins	Non-Proportional reinsurance of public and product liability business (refer definition).
Australia&NZ/ Professional Indemnity-non-prop reins	Non-Proportional reinsurance of professional indemnity business (refer definition).

contined

ICS Segment	Definition
Australia&NZ/ Employer's Liability-non-prop reins	Non-Proportional reinsurance of employer's liability business (refer definition).
Australia&NZ/ Other non-prop reins type C	Non-Proportional reinsurance of other type C business (refer definition).
Hong Kong/ Accident and health	Providing fixed pecuniary benefits or benefits in the nature of indemnity (or a combination of both) against risks of the persons insured 1. Sustaining injury or dying as a result of accident; or 2. Becoming incapacitated in consequence of disease; or 3. Sickness.
Hong Kong/Motor vehicle, damage and liability	This includes 1. Insurance against the risk of the person sustaining injury or dying as a result of travelling as passenger on motor vehicle; 2. Insurance upon loss of or damage to vehicles used on land, including motor vehicles but excluding railway rolling stock; or 3. Insurance against damage arising out of or in connection with the use of motor vehicles on land, including third-party risks and carrier's liability.
Hong Kong/Aircraft, damage and liability	This includes 1. Insurance against the risk of the person sustaining injury or dying as a result of travelling as passenger on aircraft; 2. Insurance upon aircraft or upon the machinery, tackle, furniture or equipment of aircraft; or 3. Insurance against damage arising out of or in connection with the use of aircraft, including third-party risks and carrier's liability.
Hong Kong/Ships, damage and liability	This includes 1. Insurance against the risk of the person sustaining injury or dying as a result of travelling as passenger on marine transport; 2. Insurance upon vessels used on the sea or on inland water, or upon the machinery, tackle, furniture or equipment of such vessels; or 3. Insurance against damage arising out of or in connection with the use of vessels on the sea or on inland water, including third-party risks and carrier's liability.
Hong Kong/Goods in transit	Insurance upon loss of or damage to merchandise, baggage and all other goods in transit, irrespective of the form of transport (ie include goods in transit via motor, aircraft, ships and other transport).
Hong Kong/Fire and Property damage	This includes insurance against loss of or damage to property (other than property to which motor, aircraft, ships or goods in transit relates) due to 1. Fire, explosion, storm, natural forces other than storm, nuclear energy or land subsidence; or 2. hail or frost or to any event (such as theft) other than those mentioned in 1.
Hong Kong/General liability	Insurance against risks of the persons insured incurring liabilities to third parties, the risks in question not being risks to which motor, aircraft or ships relates.

Annex 2 Definition of ICS Non-Life Segments

contined

ICS Segment	Definition
Hong Kong/Pecuniary loss	This includes: 1. Insurance against risks of loss to the persons insured arising from the insolvency or failure of debtors of theirs; 2. Suretyship; 3. Insurance against risks attributable to interruptions of the carrying on of business carried on by them or to reduction of the scope of business so carried on; or 4. Insurance against risks of loss to the persons insured attributable to their incurring legal expenses (including costs of litigation).
Hong Kong/Non-proportional treaty reinsurance	In the event that it is impracticable to allocate the treaty reinsurance business to the respective eight accounting classes of general business above, such business may be shown under 2 broad classes, namely, Non-proportional Treaty Reinsurance and Proportional Treaty Reinsurance
Hong Kong/Proportional treaty reinsurance	In the event that it is impracticable to allocate the treaty reinsurance business to the respective eight accounting classes of general business above, such business may be shown under 2 broad classes, namely, Non-proportional Treaty Reinsurance and Proportional Treaty Reinsurance
Korea/ Fire, technology, overseas	This includes fire insurance, technology insurance, original overseas insurance, reinsurance assumed from overseas. —fire insurance: insurance for residential fire, factory fire, general fire (insurance for fire in any ordinary building and movable property therein, excluding residential houses and factories) and other fire. —technology insurance: insurance for construction, assembling, machinery, electronic devices and others. The definitions for each are set out below. 1) construction: protection against damage and liability for damage to a building under construction. 2) assembly: protection against damage and liability for damage to a structure in assembling progress. 3) machinery: insurance for damage to machinery. 4) electronic devices: insurance for damage to electronic devices and costs and expenses for restoration of data. —original overseas insurance: insurance for property damage, bodily injury, or liability for damages in connection with any goods located in a foreign country. —reinsurance assumed from overseas: assuming other insurer's risk as a reinsurer from overseas.
Korea/Package	This includes package insurance for household and for business. —for household: insurance for two or more types of damage among insurance for an individual person's property damage, bodily injury, and liability for damages. —for business: insurance for two or more types of damage among an enterprise's property damage, liability for damages, and insurance for bodily injury of its members.

continued

ICS Segment	Definition
Korea/Maritime	This includes Marine, Transportation and aviation. More specifically this includes cargo, ship, general maritime, marine liability, transportation, aviation, space, and other maritime. 1) cargo: insurance for risks in marine transportation of cargoes. 2) ship: insurance for damage to a ship. 3) general maritime: insurance for risks in marine activities, such as risks in marine construction. 4) marine liability: protection against liability for damage on the seas, such as insurance of liability for marine contamination (excluding ship and general marine). 5) transportation: insurance for risks in cargoes in inland transportation. 6) aviation: insurance for damage to aircraft, such as operation and navigation of aircraft (property) and protection against liability for damages related to accidents of aircraft (liability for damages). 7) space: insurance for risks in successful launching and performance of missions of artificial satellites (property) and protection against liability for damages related to accidents of artificial satellites (liability for damages). 8) other maritime: marine insurance products other than those classified above.
Korea/Personal injury	This includes injury, travel and others (excluding those for foreigners). 1) injury: insurance for an insured person's bodily injury caused by a sudden and unexpected accident. 2) travel: insurance for injuries inflicted while travelling within the Republic of Korea (domestic travel), insurance for injuries inflicted while travelling abroad (overseas travel) and insurance for injuries inflicted on persons staying abroad for a long time, such as students studying abroad and personnel stationed abroad (long stay abroad). 3) others: injury insurance products not listed above.
Korea/Workers accident, liability	This includes insurance for workers' compensation for accidents and insurance for liability. —Workers' compensation for accidents includes: 1) domestic: indemnity for accidents and employer's liability. 2) overseas: indemnity for accidents and employer's liability. 3) seafarers: indemnity for accidents and employer's liability. 4) occupational trainee: indemnity for accidents and employer's liability. —Insurance for liability includes: 1) general liability: personal liability, business liability, ship owner's liability, excursion and ferry ship business, road transportation business, gas accident, sports facilities, local government and others. 2) product liability: product liability, product recall and product guarantee. 3) professional liability: malpractice and errors and omissions (E&O).

Annex 2 Definition of ICS Non-Life Segments

contined

ICS Segment	Definition
Korea/Foreigners	This includes insurance for injury, travel and others provided for foreigners.
Korea/Advance payment refund guarantee	Insurance purchased by a builder for damage that a buyer may sustain due to non-performance of repayment of advance payment in connection of building of a ship or construction of marine facilities.
Korea/Other Non-life	General insurance products other than those specified above.
Korea/Private vehicle (personal injury)	Insurance that indemnifies the policyholder from the liability for damages incurred to a victim by killing or injuring another person as a consequence of an accident incurred while the insured owns or manages a vehicle, among covers provided under an automobile insurance policy for a private motor vehicle, which shall include the liability insurance under Article 5 (1) of the Guarantee of Automobile Accident Compensation Act.
Korea/Private vehicle (property, vehicles damage)	Insurance that indemnifies the policyholder from the liability for damages incurred to another vehicle or the policyholder's own vehicle as a consequence of an accident incurred while the policyholder owns or manages a vehicle, among covers provided under an automobile insurance policy for a private motor vehicle.
Korea/Vehicle for commercial or business purpose (personal injury)	Insurance that indemnifies the policyholder from the liability for damages incurred to a victim by killing or injuring another person as a consequence of an accident incurred while the policyholder owns or manages a motor vehicle, among covers provided under an automobile insurance policy for a motor vehicle for commercial or business purpose, which shall include the liability insurance under Article 5 (1) of the Guarantee of Automobile Accident Compensation Act.
Korea/Vehicle for commercial or business purpose (property, vehicles)	Insurance that indemnifies the policyholder from the liability for damages incurred to another vehicle or the policyholder's own vehicle as a consequence of an accident incurred while the policyholder owns or manages a vehicle, among covers provided under an automobile insurance policy for a motor vehicle for commercial or business purpose.
Korea/Other motor	Automobile insurance other than insurance products specified above.
Singapore/Personal Accident	Refers to the insurance business of writing personal accident policy.
Singapore/Health	Refers to the insurance business of writing health policy.
Singapore/Fire	This insurance covers property damage for either commercial or household caused by fire, windstorm, hail, water damage and earthquake.
Singapore/Marine and Aviation-Cargo	Includes insurance against risk of loss or damage of any cargo in transit, and any liability arising from such cargo in transit arising from the use of a vessel or ship or aircraft.
Singapore/Motor	Includes insurance against risk of loss, damage or liability arising out of or in connection with the use of motor vehicles.
Singapore/Work Injury Compensation	This insurance covers compensation payments to employees who sustained bodily injury or occupational disease during or which arises out of the course of their employment.

continued

ICS Segment	Definition
Singapore/Bonds	Includes maid insurance and insurance under which an insurer undertakes to guarantee (other than guarantees to which "Credit/ Credit related" relates to) the due performance of a contract or undertaking, or the payment of a penalty or indemnity for any default.
Singapore/Engineering Construction	Includes insurance against construction, erection, or engineering risks such as the loss or damage involved in a construction project, and installation and erection of ready built-engineering projects. It also includes boiler and pressure vessel insurance, construction all risk insurance, engineering all risk insurance, erection all risk insurance, machinery all risk insurance and insurance on any other specialised equipment or machinery that are excluded from the standard property insurance.
Singapore/Credit	Insurance protecting against the risk of non-payment of goods and services by buyers and importers.
Singapore/Mortgage	Insurance protecting against losses on mortgage loans arising from default by borrowers.
Singapore/Others- non liability class	Other non-liability classes not covered elsewhere.
Singapore/Marine and Aviation-Hull	Includes insurance against risk of physical loss or damage of vessel or ship used on sea or inland water or aircraft, any liability arising from such vessel or ship or aircraft, and damage of vessel or ship or aircraft while under construction. It also includes marine terminal operator insurance and airport operator insurance and insurance against aerospace risks.
Singapore/ Professional indemnity	Includes insurance for professionals against risk of their liability to their principals, clients, principal's clients, or any third parties arising out of neglect, omission or error in the discharge of their professional duties. It also includes directors and officers liability insurance, and errors and omission insurance.
Singapore /Public liability	Includes insurance against risk of the insured's liability to third party in respect of bodily injury, property damage or any monetary losses arising out of negligence (other than liability to which business classes "Cargo", "Marine Hull", "Aviation Hull" and "Motor" relate to).
Singapore /Others- liability class	Other liability classes not covered elsewhere.
Chinese Taipei / Fire-residence	Fire insurance for personal residence.
Chinese Taipei / Fire-commercial	Fire insurance for commercial building.
Chinese Taipei / Marine-inland cargo	Marine insurance for inland cargo.
Chinese Taipei / Marine-overseas cargo	Marine insurance for overseas cargo.
Chinese Taipei / Marine-hull	Marine insurance for hull.
Chinese Taipei / Marine-fish boat	Marine insurance for fish boat/vessel.

Annex 2 Definition of ICS Non-Life Segments

contined

ICS Segment	Definition
Chinese Taipei / Marine-aircraft	Aviation insurance for aircraft.
Chinese Taipei / Motor-personal vehicle	Motor insurance for personal vehicle.
Chinese Taipei / Motor-commercial vehicle	Motor insurance for commercial vehicle.
Chinese Taipei / Motor-personal liability	Motor insurance for personal liabilities.
Chinese Taipei / Motor-commercial liability	Motor insurance for commercial liabilities.
Chinese Taipei / Liability-public, employer, product, etc.	Public liability insurance, employer liability insurance, product liability insurance, etc.
Chinese Taipei / Liability-professional	Professional liability insurance.
Chinese Taipei/ Engineering	Engineering insurance.
Chinese Taipei / Nuclear power station	Insurance for nuclear power station.
Chinese Taipei / Guarantee-surety, fidelity	Surety insurance, fidelity insurance, mortgage insurance, etc.
Chinese Taipei / Credit	Trade credit insurance, credit card insurance, small-amount loan credit insurance, etc.
Chinese Taipei /Other property damage	Property damage insurances not included in other LOBs, eg cash insurance, theft insurance, glass insurance, etc.
Chinese Taipei / Accident	Accident insurance for personal injuries or death.
Chinese Taipei / Property Damage-commercial earthquake	Earthquake insurance (other than compulsory earthquake insurance).
Chinese Taipei / Comprehensive-personal property and liability	Comprehensive insurance for personal property and liabilities.
Chinese Taipei / Comprehensive-commercial property and liability	Comprehensive insurance for commercial property and liabilities.
Chinese Taipei / Property damage-typhoon and flood	Typhoon and flood insurance.
Chinese Taipei / Property damage-compulsory earthquake	Compulsory earthquake insurance (compulsory for personal residence).
Chinese Taipei / Health	Health insurance.

continued

ICS Segment	Definition
OTHER/Motor	This includes: Motor property damage: Damage to own and third-party motor vehicles (and related property damage) through accident, theft, fire and weather events, excluding liability for personal injury; and Motor bodily insurances: Insurances relating to the injury or death of third parties due to or related to motor vehicles and accidents involving them. This may also extend to include the driver involved.
OTHER/ Property damage	This includes, but is not limited to: 1. Property: Insurance of house or other property (including house contents) against loss through fire, windstorm etc., insurance of contents against losses due to theft, fire, windstorm, earthquake, impact, damages, water damage, and other natural and man-made perils. Contents insurances may extend to loss or damage to property outside the home or its usual location. 2. Fire and industrial: Loss or damage and loss of earnings due to damage to commercial buildings and other physical infrastructure due to fire, windstorm and other perils. 3. Consequential losses: Products covering consequential losses (such as 'loss of profits' or 'business interruption') is also included in this segment; 4. Construction: This includes 'construction all risks and erection all risks' (CAR/EAR) or similar written in connection with construction projects. This includes the construction and erection of infrastructure projects and buildings.
OTHER/ Accident, protection and health (APH)	This includes, but is not limited to: 1. Accident and sickness: Accident cover provides benefits if an accident result in bodily injury or death. Benefits are lump sum or periodic (typically for at most 2 years). Sickness cover is often an extension of accident insurance; 2. Other consumer accident: Property damage other than householders or motor vehicle. For example, travel insurance. 3. Other commercial accident: Commercial property insurance other than Fire and Industrial risk and MAT, and other than commercial long-term liability; 4. Consumer credit: Guarantee of repayments on consumer credit contracts due to involuntary loss of employment; 5. Consumer liability: Private individual's liability for personal injury through personal actions or property.
OTHER/ Short tail medical expenses	Insurance obligation that covers the provision or financial compensation for medical treatment or care including preventive or curative medical treatment or care due to illness, accident, disability or infirmity usually made during the term of the policy or shortly (typically, up to 1 year) after the coverage period of the insurance has expired.
OTHER/ Other short tail	Any non-Life products which do not fit into the segments above, do not fit the definition of non-life medium-term business and where claims are usually made during the term of the policy or shortly (typically, up to 1 year) up to after the coverage period of the insurance has expired.

Annex 2 Definition of ICS Non-Life Segments

contined

ICS Segment	Definition
OTHER/ Marine, Air, Transport (MAT)	This includes: 1. All damage or loss of river, canal, lake and sea vessels, aircraft, goods in transit, liabilities from use of aircraft, ships and boats. ; 2. Loss or damage to property, consequential third party liability for damages to the property of others, and consequential third party liability for personal injury to operators, passengers and other.
OTHER/ Workers' compensation	This insurance covers compensation payments to employees who sustained bodily injury or occupational disease during or which arises out of the course of their employment.
OTHER/ Public liability	Public liability insurance for bodily injury or damage to property.
OTHER/ Product liability	Product liability insurance for bodily injury or damage to property for claims attributed to the use of products.
OTHER/ Professional indemnity	Professional indemnity for a professional person or organisation for claims for losses legal and other) attributed to professional negligence (and related) in the services provided. For example, medical malpractice and directors and officers insurance products.
OTHER/ Other liability and other long tail	Any non-life products which do not fit into the defined segments above, do not fit the definition of non-life medium-term business and where claims may be made many years (typically 1 or more years) after the coverage period of the insurance has expired. All other liability classes not covered elsewhere.
OTHER/ Non-proportional motor, property damage, APH and MAT	Non-Proportional reinsurance of motor, property damage and accident/protection/health business, marine, aviation and transport (refer definition).
OTHER/ Catastrophe reinsurance	Catastrophe Reinsurance is an inwards reinsurance line of business providing excess of loss protection or proportional protection in respect of aggregate losses arising from a single event or a combination of events. Typically, such business is covering damages to property and is sold with an 'hours' clause and provides protection against natural catastrophe perils such as windstorms, earthquakes and man-made catastrophe such as acts of terrorism.
OTHER/ Non proportional liability	Non-Proportional reinsurance of public liability, product liability and other liability (refer definition).
OTHER/ Non-proportional professional indemnity	Non-Proportional reinsurance of professional indemnity (refer definition).
OTHER/ Mortgage insurance	Indemnity to credit providers for losses due to the failure of a borrower to repay a loan secured by a mortgage over property.
OTHER/ Commercial credit insurance	Indemnity for financial losses due to the failure of a commercial entity to repay outstanding credit contracts or failure to perform contracted services or deliver contracted products other than short-term trade credit and suretyship insurance.

continued

ICS Segment	Definition
OTHER/ Other medium-term	Any other non-life medium-term insurance products other than the above and not included in non-life insurance segments above. This includes, but is not limited to: Financing or monetising Insurance-linked securities (ILS, for example catastrophe bonds). For example, embedded Value/Present Value of Future Profit securitisations, ILS with financial risk as material trigger condition.

后 记

《以风险为基础的全球保险资本标准》（ICS）是国际保险监督官协会（IAIS）全球偿付能力监管改革的一项重要阶段性成果。为便于各方全面认识理解ICS，我们对ICS进行了研究，形成了本书4篇述评文章。经IAIS授权，组织翻译了ICS，形成了中文译文，并附上ICS英文文本（其版权属于IAIS）供读者参考。

译者及相应篇目如下：

任笛："1 介绍""2 ICS2.0 监测期""3 一般指导原则""8 基准ICS：税的计量"；

董杨："4 基准ICS：评估范围"；

王瀚："5 基准ICS：MAV方法"；

马文杰："6 基准ICS：实际资本"；

李岗："7.1 风险分类和基本计量方法""7.5 操作风险""7.6 最低资本聚合"；

崔雯昕："7.2.1 寿险保险风险保单分组""7.2.2 寿险保险风险最低资本计算"；

张翔、孙晓筱："7.2.3 非寿险保险风险最低资本计算""7.2.4 巨灾风险最低资本计算"；

余贵芳："7.3 市场风险"；

王浩："7.4 信用风险"；

魏洪涛："9 附加报告"。

郭菁、朱丽、张佳、刘梦泽、翟潇、于洋等对中文译文进行了审校。中国银保监会偿付能力监管部赵宇龙主任对全书进行了审定。

世界银行贷款中国经济改革促进与能力加强技术援助项目（TCC6）对本书出版提供了资金支持。中国金融出版社对本书出版给予了大力支持。在此，对所有支持和参与本书编辑出版的相关单位和人员一并表示感谢！

由于ICS专业性强，加之编写时间紧迫，虽经反复讨论、核校，本书仍难免存在疏漏，恳请读者批评指正。本书中文译文如与英文文本存在出入，请以英文文本为准。

编委会

2021年10月